"The most interesting and inventive business book on the market today . . . a publishing phenomenon." —*TRAINING* MAGAZINE

"Better than money: Praise and personal gestures motivate workers. Things that don't cost money are ironically the most effective." —*THE WALL STREET JOURNAL*

"Welcome to Bob's World: A place of above-average managers and workers, all committed to personal excellence, good will and, of course, company profits. [This book] details how a little praise goes a long way." —*THE PHILADELPHIA INQUIRER*

"There's a difference between having someone show up for work and bringing out the best thinking and initiative in each person. To do that requires treating employees more as partners, not as subordinates. Being nice isn't just the right thing to do, it's also the economical thing to do." —*SEATTLE POST-INTELLIGENCER*

"[Helps managers] take certain rewards and mold them into new management styles at their companies." —*THE NEW YORK TIMES*

"Crammed with tips on how to motivate all types of workers, through both formal and informal incentive and recognition programs. If you don't have a budget for recognition, here are lots of low-cost incentives." —*INCENTIVE* MAGAZINE

"This blockbuster guide does wonders for morale! . . . Use of its ideas is changing the face of rewards and recognition in the workplace." —*SUCCESS* MAGAZINE

"A must read for anyone in business." —SMALL BUSINESS FORUM

OTHER BOOKS BY BOB NELSON

1501 WAYS

Low-Cost and No-Cost Ideas. Best Practices.

TO REWARD

Latest Trends. Proven Strategies.

EMPLOYEES

Ways to Motivate the Millennial Generation.

BOB NELSON, Ph.D.

WORKMAN PUBLISHING • NEW YORK

Library of Congress Cataloging-in-Publication Data is available.

ISBN 978-0-7611-6878-2

Interior design by Ariana Abud
Cover and interior illustrations by Stephen Schudlich

Special thanks to KellyOCG for permission to draw from their
white paper entitled "Seven Seismic Shifts: Trends Shaking the
HR Profession and Reshaping Strategic HR Value."

Workman books are available at special discounts when purchased in
bulk for premiums and sales promotions as well as for fund-raising or
educational use. Special editions or book excerpts can also be created
to specification. For details, contact the Special Sales Director at
the address below, or send an email to specialmarkets@workman.com.

Workman Publishing Company, Inc.
225 Varick Street
New York, NY 10014-4381
workman.com

WORKMAN is a registered trademark of Workman Publishing Co., Inc.

Printed in the United States
First printing February 2012

10 9 8 7 6 5

"At Zappos, we believe that if we get the culture right, most of the other stuff, including great customer service, will fall into place on its own. Long term, we want the Zappos brand to be about the very best customer service and the very best customer experience. This book gives readers ideas on how to inspire their employees to deliver the best performance every day— for little or no cost."

—TONY HSIEH, *NEW YORK TIMES* BESTSELLING AUTHOR OF *DELIVERING HAPPINESS* AND CEO OF ZAPPOS.COM, INC.

CONTENTS

PART II: *Using Recognition & Rewards*

PART I

The *New Realities*

THE RECOGNITION REVOLUTION

"There are two things people want more than sex and money: recognition and praise."
—Mary Kay Ash, *Founder, Mary Kay, Inc.*

There's a revolution going on in today's workplaces. Workers want respect, and they want it now. They want to be trusted to do a good job; they want autonomy to decide how best to do it; they want to be asked their opinion and involved with decisions—especially as those decisions affect them and their work; and they want to be supported, even if they make a mistake. Most important, they want to be appreciated when they do a good job.

These considerations are more important for today's employees than they were in previous eras—or even five to ten years ago, for that matter. Providing workers with recognition and respect can make a world of difference in getting the best efforts out of them, keeping them, and helping you develop a reputation for treating employees in a way that helps attract talent to work for you and your organization.

What Is Recognition?

R ecognition is a positive consequence provided to a person for a desired behavior or result. Recognition can take the form of acknowledgment, approval, or the expression of gratitude. It means appreciating someone for something he or she has done for you, your group, or your organization. It also can come in the form of asking someone's opinion, involving them in a decision, or encouraging them in their career. Recognition can be given while an employee is striving to achieve a certain goal or behavior, or once he or she has completed it.

Employee recognition can be broken down into the following:

1. FORMAL RECOGNITION: *A structured or planned program of recognition for desired performance. Examples include President's Award, Years of Service awards, and Employee of the Month awards. This recognition can be significant and symbolic, given the public forum in which it is typically presented.*

2. INFORMAL RECOGNITION: *A spontaneous gesture of sincere thanks for desired behavior or performance. Examples include: Creating a "pass around" trophy to acknowledge exceptional customer service; bringing in donuts or a pizza to celebrate a department success. These forms of recognition are increasingly more important to today's employees than formal recognition.*

3. DAY-TO-DAY RECOGNITION: *Daily feedback about positive employee performance. Examples include: Dropping by to tell someone "good job" on an assignment; a simple thank you in person or in front of others for a job well done. This is the ultimate form of recognition—it's where the rubber meets the road in creating a results-oriented culture of recognition for your organization.*

What Is a Reward?

It's an item or experience with monetary value (but not necessarily money) that is provided for desired behavior or performance, often with accompanying recognition. Harvard Business School professor and management consultant Rosabeth Moss Kanter defines a reward as "something special—a special gain for special achievements, a treat for doing something above-and-beyond."

Why Isn't Money Enough?

When it comes to rewards, most managers think money is the top motivator for employees. While money is important to almost everybody, it is certainly not the only motivator. Today's employees value many other things where they work, and surprisingly, some of the top motivators, such as praise, involvement, and support, have the least financial cost. Monetary rewards such as salary, merit increases, bonuses, and the like are important, but seldom are they today's employees' only motivators for making their best efforts on the job.

In a 2008 study by Maritz Research, the following anomalies about cash rewards were revealed:

- Rewards that are strictly monetary are not as effective as non-cash-based items. Because they tend to be less personal, the opportunity to develop and grow interpersonal relationships is hindered.
- Monetary rewards do little to establish a link between the behavior and the incentive. Instead of furthering company values, they diminish them and promote a culture of unnecessary spending.

Cash rewards have one more problem. In most organizations, performance reviews—and corresponding salary increases— occur only once a year (even less if salaries are frozen), whereas the things that cause someone to be motivated today are typically activities that have happened recently within the immediate work group. To motivate today's employees, managers need to recognize and reward achievements and progress toward goals on a more frequent, even daily basis, especially thanking them when they do good work.

There is a common misconception about the use of rewards and recognition to motivate employees: that it costs a company too much money—or more money than is readily available—but rewards, recognition, and praise do not need to be lavish or expensive to be effective. Most motivating and meaningful forms of recognition, as reported by today's employees, typically cost little or nothing at all.

A Simple "Thanks" Will Do

It all starts with a thank you. And sometimes that's all it takes. Most employees don't just need to be thanked, they *expect* to be thanked for something they've done. And they expect it to be said immediately or soon after their good performance. Waiting too long shows indifference and that it was really more of an afterthought or something you've put off. Even affirmation from coworkers can change employees' attitudes and give them a greater sense of contentment.

Employees need to feel as though their efforts are well spent, even if the results can realistically be classified as baby steps. Focusing on accomplishments gives your employees the encouragement they might need to keep moving forward in a difficult time. If they feel as though they're consistently giving their all, only to hear it's not enough, the time will come when they'll simply throw in the towel.

While recognition of success is important to include in regular meetings, impromptu celebrations added at the last minute to an agenda are almost more effective. Overcoming the cloud of negative energy that befalls an organization during downtimes can be gradually chipped away by taking the time to point out your employees' strengths. For the time being, forget about shortcomings; save those for reviews or specific feedback. So many small successes go unnoticed because they are merely a part of a large accomplishment, leaving many key contributors in the shadow of others who ultimately receive praise and recognition.

Employee Recognition Starts with Knowing Your Employees

1. FIND OUT WHAT YOUR EMPLOYEES WANT—DON'T ASSUME YOU KNOW. *By unilaterally deciding what to do or what to give employees who perform well, you run the risk of missing the motivational mark. Instead, involve employees in determining what would best reward or recognize them for doing good work—avoid surprises!*

2. LEAD BY EXAMPLE—MODEL THE BEHAVIOR YOU EXPECT OTHERS TO FOLLOW. *Having top managers practice employee recognition sets the tone for all managers and sends the message, "If I can make time to do this, no one else in the organization has an excuse not to." The publisher of* The Washington Post *is said to give handwritten notes to reporters he feels have written excellent* *articles. Similarly, one bank president gold plates quarters a roll at a time to pass out to individual employees as their performance merits special acknowledgment.*

3. REALIZE THAT ONE TYPE OF RECOGNITION NO LONGER FITS ALL. *Paying even above-market rates or having a few traditional (and predictable) recognition activities or a single great formal recognition program is no longer enough. Update formal recognition programs to make them exciting and relevant. Johnson & Johnson surveyed employees and found that some of the organization's traditional awards were not considered recognition by over half the employees. Accordingly, the organization made adjustments that were most meaningful to their employee population. In short, you've got to be experimenting, learning, and discussing recognition ideas and activities on an ongoing basis.*

The Business Case for Recognition

"I have yet to find the man, however exalted his station, who did not do better work and put forth greater effort under a spirit of approval, than under a spirit of criticism."—Charles Schwab

Is Recognition Really All That Important?

The link between effective strategies for sales, public relations, and marketing and increased sales is not only well established and taught in all business schools, it is also common sense. Executives know that the results from such strategies are easy to track, benchmark, and adjust. Not surprisingly, when evaluating a company's profits, executives tend to focus almost exclusively on these areas. With this focus on spreadsheets, what is too often lost is the fact that *people* are behind the strategies management institutes. It is easy to create business plans that directly attack an organization's goals, but today's most profitable and successful organizations know that actually achieving them requires indirect and creative action—and that that indirect and creative action comes from their employees.

Take the case of Circuit City and Best Buy. In 2007 Circuit City laid off 3,400 of what it called its "highest paid employees" and replaced them with employees who were paid much less. While these 3,400 employees might indeed have been highly paid, they were also the most seasoned and productive salespeople Circuit City had. Looking only at numbers, the executives at Circuit City figured they could get the same results from their new batch of employees that they had received from their previous employees. The result? Investors promptly rewarded Circuit City with a 4 percent drop in its stock price, and the retail chain, which was by no means doing well, experienced nearly exponential drops in the quarters following and ultimately went bankrupt in 2009 with no buyer. At the same time Circuit City was letting go of its top talent, Best Buy, its largest competitor, was nurturing its talent. In 2007 management at Best Buy instituted a new program entitled "ROWE" (Results Only Work Environment), in which employees at its headquarters could come to work whenever they liked, set their own hours, and even work from home just as long as their goals were met or exceeded each quarter. The result? A big boost in morale, a significant drop in turnover, a healthy jump in productivity, and best of all, increased sales.

As proven business practices that were once a sort of "secret sauce" to a select few have filtered their way through organizations worldwide because of the explosion of the information age, the result has been a standardization in which price- and cost-cutting become the only means for revenue increases, which, in turn, leads to the loss of the all-important competitive edge. As such, today's top executives understand that their employees, far more than any strategy they learned at business school, are truly their competitive edge and that more than anything, they must protect and nurture this. As business guru Peter F. Drucker wrote, ". . . developing talent is business's most important task—the sine qua non of competition in a knowledge economy." Circuit City, which didn't understand this, saw its employees as an expense; Best Buy, which did, saw its employees as an investment.

The Benefits of Recognition

Since people are, and will increasingly be, the competitive edge of organizations, treating employees right has never been more important. Jeffrey Pfeffer, a Stanford Business School professor, recently concluded, "Companies that manage people right will outperform companies that don't by 30 percent to 40 percent."

One of the strongest tools in a business's arsenal for increasing motivation is recognition. According to my doctoral research, 99.4 percent of today's employees expect to be recognized when they do good work, while research by Maritz has found that only 12 percent of employees strongly agree that they are consistently recognized in ways that are important to them and nearly three times as many (34 percent) disagree or strongly disagree that they are recognized in ways that are meaningful to them. In addition, Maritz has found that employees who do receive recognition where they work are:

- 5 times more likely to feel valued
- 7 times more likely to stay with the company
- 6 times more likely to invest in the company
- 11 times more likely to feel completely committed to the company

And, according to research conducted by Towers Perrin, committed employees have been shown to deliver 57 percent more effort than uncommitted ones. Add to that the true cost of employee turnover (which recent studies from the Society for Human Resource Management place at 1.5 times an employee's annual salary) and the numbers quickly become significant to the organization in terms of the actual cost of replacing employees, as well as lost opportunity when experienced employees leave.

Recognition is a significant driver of employee engagement, and having engaged, satisfied employees leads to increased customer satisfaction, greater customer loyalty, and profitability, thus enhanced bottom-line success for the organization. Indeed, Watson Wyatt's 2009 "WorkUSA Report" found that organizations with highly engaged employees enjoy 25 percent higher employee productivity and a lower turnover risk, and attract top talent more easily than those without engaged employees. Furthermore, a study by the Office of the Auditor General of British Columbia concluded that "recognition has been shown to motivate staff, increase morale, productivity, and employee retention, and decrease stress and absenteeism." Towers Perrin, in 2008, found that ". . . companies with high employee engagement had a 19% increase in operating income and a 28% increase in earnings per share. In contrast, companies with poor employee engagement scores had declining operating incomes and an 11% drop in earnings per share." And the Corporate Executive Board, in its study "Driving Employee Performance and Retention Through Engagement," found that recognition was one of the top methods for increasing employee retention.

Why are effective recognition and rewards important? Because they constitute one of the most significant strategies for driving performance that matters to the success of the organization. People do not commit 40 or 50 or 60 hours a week or more out of their lives to just show up at work. They want to make a difference in their work—and to be appreciated for doing so. Further evidence points to the power of recognition:

- In recent surveys of American workers, 63 percent of the respondents agreed that most people would like more recognition for their work and the same percentage ranked "a pat on the back" as a meaningful incentive.
- Robert Half International, the nationwide staffing firm, recently conducted a survey of why people leave their jobs and found the number one reason to be a lack of praise and recognition.
- According to the "People, Pay, and Performance" study by the American Productivity and Quality Center in Houston, TX, it generally takes 5 to 8 percent of an employee's salary to change behavior if the reward is cash, as compared to approximately 4 percent of the employee's salary if the reward is not cash.

The Recognition–Performance Link

Recognition improves job performance, and improved job performance compels managers to provide additional recognition.

In my doctoral study I found evidence to support the recognition–performance link in at least three ways.

First, several performance-related variables were found to have broad support by all managers in the study, the majority of whom agreed or strongly agreed with the following items (listed with percent of agreement):

- Recognizing employees helps me better motivate them. (90.5 percent)
- Providing nonmonetary recognition to my employees when they do good work helps to increase their performance. (84.4 percent)
- Recognizing employees provides them with practical feedback. (84.4 percent)
- Recognizing my employees for good work makes it easier to get the work done. (80.3 percent)
- Recognizing employees helps them to be more productive. (77.7 percent)
- Providing nonmonetary recognition helps me to achieve my personal goals. (69.3 percent)
- Providing nonmonetary recognition helps me to achieve my job goals. (60.3 percent)

Second, 72.9 percent of managers reported that they received the results they expected when they used nonmonetary recognition either immediately or soon after the employee's action, and 98.8 percent said they felt they would eventually obtain the desired results.

Third, of the 598 employees who reported to the managers in this study, 77.6 percent said that it was very or extremely important to be recognized by their manager when they do good work. Employees expected recognition to occur: immediately (20 percent), soon thereafter (52.9 percent), or sometime later (18.8 percent).

Principles of Recognition

All performance starts with clear goals and expectations, but even more significant than setting expectations at work is following up to see what was achieved and noting that success. Recognition can have a powerful impact on the management and motivation of any employee, group, or organization. In fact, I find that one of the great challenges of the topic is to get people to take recognition seriously. Because recognition sounds so easy to do, people often feel that they must already be doing it! Unfortunately, more times than not, that is not the case. I often find myself telling managers, "Yes, I *know* you *can* do recognition. My bigger concern is *will* you do so?"

You Get What You Reward

The most proven principle of management and motivation known to mankind (we're talking about evidence from hundreds of studies) is the simple and commonsense notion that "you get what you reward." That is, the behaviors and performance that you notice, inspect, recognize, appreciate, reward, incentivize, or acknowledge will be repeated by those you acknowledged and perhaps others as well who noticed or heard what happened. In fact, it could even be said that *all* behavior is driven by its consequences. If there is a positive consequence, the behavior will tend to be repeated; if there is a negative consequence, the behavior will tend to stop. Here are a few of the other core principles of effective recognition:

The Best Recognition Is Contingent

Many managers mistakenly think that recognition is just "being nice to people." This view misses the point. Recognition is most effective when it is in response to something significant that someone did. You should avoid using recognition "just to be nice," for example, or "because you want your people to like you" or "because you feel guilty." Instead link recognition to the performance objectives, values, and behaviors that will have the greatest impact on your continued success. In this way, recognition becomes a self-fulfilling prophecy in reinforcing those things you most wanted to happen so that they occur again over and over.

The Best Recognition Is Timely, Specific & Meaningful

The sooner you recognize desired behavior and performance when it occurs and the stronger the reinforcement, the sooner the behavior or performance will be repeated. Generalities should be replaced with a more exact focus when using recognition. If you are specific in stating exactly what the recognition is for when you give it to someone, the interaction will serve a practical purpose of making clear to the individual exactly what you appreciated that he or she did, which in turn will help increase the chances of the behavior or results being repeated. Good recognition also has to be meaningful to the recipient. If it is something they don't value or want (for example, giving a plaque or certificate to someone who already has dozens), giving them yet another is likely to do more to demotivate the individual than to make them feel valued and important.

The Best Recognition Is Free

One of the most amazing and delightful ironies about the topic of recognition is that the most powerful forms of it cost little or nothing. While money is, of course, a top motivator for all of us (and it is nice to receive gifts and merchandise, especially in response to having done a good job), simple, sincere words and actions can and do have the most significant impact on how people feel about what they do, whom they work for, and where they work. Asking someone for their opinion, involving them in a decision, granting them permission to pursue an idea, or supporting them when a mistake is made can resonate the deepest in terms of showing the trust and respect you have for the person in your working relationship. In fact, probably the very best form of recognition is a simple thanks for having done a good job.

Four Types of Praise

In my research I've found that simple praise represents four of the top ten categories of motivators when employees do good work. I identified four types of praise:

Personal praise: *face-to-face thanks and acknowledgment for a job well done*

Written praise: *written note or formal letter of thanks*

Electronic praise: *personal thanks and acknowledgment via e-mail or voice mail*

Public praise: *recognition in front of one or more other people, in a public forum such as a meeting or a broad form of communication such as a newsletter or newspaper*

At first glance these forms of praise might all seem the same, but I've learned that this is not the case. Each of these dimensions is mutually exclusive and provides a different value and meaning to an employee. Being praised to one's face is different from receiving an e-mail or note or being praised in front of others.

At meetings, allocate some time for recognition of outstanding effort or the sharing of success stories. End meetings on a high note, especially those whose agendas are laden with less-than-happy line items; it's a great way to remind employees that even in downtimes there are still good things happening.

Elements of a Good Praising

"Many know how to flatter, few understand how to give praise."—Greek proverb

In the workplace, praise is priceless, yet it costs nothing. In one survey of 65 workplace incentives, the incentive ranked number one by workers was a personal praising from their manager for doing a good job, yet 58 percent of employees say they seldom if ever receive such a praising. Although giving effective praise may seem like common sense, a lot of people have never learned how to do it. I suggest an acronym—ASAP-cubed—to remember the essential elements of a good praising. Praise should be as soon, as sincere, as specific, as personal, as positive, and as proactive as possible.

AS SOON

Timing is critical. To be most effective, the thank you should come soon after the achievement or desired activity has occurred. If you wait too long to thank a person, the gesture loses its significance: Your employee assumes that other things were more important to you than taking a few minutes with him or her.

AS SINCERE

Words can seem hollow if you are not sincere. Your praise should be based on a true appreciation of and excitement about the other person's successes; otherwise your thanks may come across as a manipulative tactic—for instance, a ploy used only when you want an employee to work late. As the saying goes, "People don't care how much you know, until they know how much you care."

AS SPECIFIC

Avoid generalities in favor of details of the achievement. Compliments that are too broad tend to seem insincere. Specifics give credibility to your praise. Say what the employee did and why her effort was of value. For instance, "Thanks for staying late to finish those calculations I needed. It was critical for my meeting this morning."

AS PERSONAL

The most effective forms of recognition are the most personal ones. They show that recognition is important enough for you to put aside everything else you have to do and focus on the other person. Since we all have limited time, the things you do yourself indicate that they have a high value to you. Recognition by way of a quick e-mail or voice-mail message is certainly appreciated, but praise in person means much more.

AS POSITIVE

When you say something like "You did a great job on this report, but there were quite a few typos," the "but" erases all that came before. Save the corrective feedback for the next similar assignment. Separate even constructive criticism from your acts of praise.

AS PROACTIVE

Praise progress toward desired goals. Don't wait for perfect performance; praise improvements and behavior that are approximately right. You will get the results you want sooner.

High-quality praise simply communicates (1) I saw what you did, (2) I appreciate it, (3) here's why it's important, and (4) here's how it makes me feel. You can praise an employee one-on-one, directly or in front of others, or you can even praise someone who is not around, knowing that your remarks will more than likely make their way back to the person.

The Role of the Manager in Recognizing Employees

"Continuous, supportive communication from managers, supervisors and associates is too often underemphasized. It is a major, major motivator."—Jim Moultrup, *Management Perspectives Group*

The Impact of the Manager on Employees

It's difficult to overstate the impact a manager has on his or her employees. For most people, if you have a good manager, you have a good job. Likewise, "People leave managers, not companies" pretty much sums up what study after study has proved: The number one reason why employees leave an organization is over a bad relationship with their immediate manager.

Over the course of 20 years, and interviews with literally millions of employees, the Gallup Organization, the most authoritative expert on this topic, has come to the conclusion that "the single most important variable in employee productivity and loyalty turns out to be not pay or perks or benefits or workplace environment . . . it's the quality of the relationship between employees and their direct supervisors."

> Simple techniques, such as including employees who directly report to you on your weekly "to-do" list and checking the names off when they have met or exceeded their job responsibilities, can go a long way toward making employee recognition behavior simple and doable.

Employees expect to be recognized by their managers when they do good work. This is a truism supported by dozens of studies and surveys, and it is easily confirmed by asking almost any employee. Thanking employees for doing good work increases the likelihood that they will want to continue to work for your organization, and it serves as a catalyst for attracting talented new recruits.

The Most Effective Recognition Comes from One's Manager

One of the most common misconceptions managers have about recognition is that it's the responsibility of the human resources department, that managers simply have too much to do to worry about making staff feel good. The belief isn't entirely unfounded, as far too many organizations actually mandate this.

Let's turn this belief on its head for a moment. Suppose you are approaching your five-year anniversary and you walk in to work and find a plaque on your desk from HR in commemoration of this milestone. Ask yourself: How important would it be to me that someone in HR knew it was my five-year anniversary? Now, suppose your immediate supervisor threw a party for you during lunch for the same five-year anniversary and presented the same plaque to you. My guess is that you would almost certainly prefer that your manager, rather than human resources, recognize you for this milestone. Why? The best and

> Every time you communicate, you are offered a chance to recognize employees. Exchanging praise and recognition in newsletters, posting an "applause" bulletin board on the company's intranet, and commenting in meetings are just a few possibilities for formalizing communication about employee recognition.

most effective recognition comes from those we hold in high esteem. They are the ones we want recognition from. Research shows that the best forms of recognition are contingent in nature, and yet the bulk of recognition dollars are still spent on programs that reinforce presence over performance.

This is not meant to disparage the role of human resources, as the best recognition programs are often managed from HR and implemented by managers. Recognition consists of formal, informal, and day-to-day components. HR is usually best at managing formal recognition (with managerial involvement), but managers alone are responsible for the informal and day-to-day recognition components, which have the greater impact.

Overcoming Obstacles & Barriers to the Use of Recognition

"If success were determined by good intentions alone, everyone would be successful."—Dean Spitzer, *Senior Managing Consultant, IBM*

Six Excuses Why Managers Do Not Use Recognition

Organizations must confront the beliefs of managers who prefer not to use recognition (low-use managers) if they are going to make recognition a personal, practical, and positive experience. Misperceptions and constraints must be overcome, objections and obstacles removed, excuses fronted. Here are the six leading "excuses" for not using recognition that I learned from my doctoral research, as reported by low-use managers themselves, and examples of how to deal with each excuse:

1. "I DON'T KNOW HOW BEST TO RECOGNIZE MY EMPLOYEES."

Most low-use managers consider giving recognition to be a difficult task. They need to become aware of the importance of recognition, be trained in the skills of recognition, be provided with individual feedback, and be shown positive examples and techniques that they can actually use, no matter their time and resource constraints. To get buy-in, managers should discuss potential recognition strategies with their staff and seek feedback on their own recognition behaviors.

> **At the Boston-area branches of Bank of America, managers give employees a blank index card on their first day of work and ask them to make a list of the things that motivate them. The manager ends up with an individualized checklist for every employee.**

2. "I DON'T FEEL THAT PROVIDING RECOGNITION IS AN IMPORTANT PART OF MY JOB."

As has been previously asserted, the evidence for the positive impact of recognition is simply too compelling to ignore. Moreover, organizations need to set up the expectation that providing recognition is not an optional activity, but rather an integral part of the organization's strategy, specifically linked to achieving the company's goals. Managers should be evaluated on their frequent and meaningful efforts at providing recognition. Recognition should be an important part of the planning of organizational, team, and individual goal setting, and not "management by announcement," where an initiative is announced once and then never heard of again.

> **A vice president of AAA of Southern California personally writes thanks to individuals in field offices, demonstrating to all managers under him that if he can find time to acknowledge employees, they need to do so as well.**

3. "I DON'T HAVE THE TIME TO RECOGNIZE MY EMPLOYEES."

Who does have time to do something they don't feel is important to do? High recognition–use managers view time as a facilitator of recognition because some of the best forms of recognition (personal or written praise, public recognition, positive voice-mail or e-mail messages, and so on) require very little time to accomplish. Thus, the reaction by low-recognition users of not having enough time is often no more than an excuse for not doing it.

> **All managers and supervisors at Busch Gardens in Tampa, Florida, are provided tokens inscribed with the words *Thank you* to use as an on-the-spot form of recognition, which takes only a moment to do, for any employee caught demonstrating one of the organization's core values.**

4. "I AM AFRAID I MIGHT LEAVE SOMEBODY OUT."

Low-use managers take this concern and interpret it as an excuse for not recognizing employees at all, but high-use managers translate this concern into a greater commitment to be sure that no one is left out. This might, for example, mean checking with a team leader to see if you have all the names of the people who assisted with a successful project before commending the team in public. If at any time someone deserving is left out, it is perfectly acceptable to acknowledge the oversight, apologize for it, and still provide the recognition. Managers who learn from such an experience get better at it.

> **I recently attended an awards presentation at Florida Hospital, in Orlando, Florida, in which the presenter and top manager personally checked in advance to see that everyone who was receiving an award that evening was present so that no one's name would be called who was absent (the individuals who were not present were acknowledged separately in person by the leader).**

5. "EMPLOYEES DO NOT VALUE THE RECOGNITION I HAVE GIVEN IN THE PAST." *Instead of being put off by what might not have worked in the past, low recognition–use managers should seek to find out what forms of recognition their employees would most value and make an ongoing commitment to do those things. Managers can talk with employees one-on-one or have a group discussion about potential rewards and incentives; or they can ask each of them to bring two suggested motivators to the next staff meeting to share with the group. By involving employees in decisions that affect their own motivation, managers increase the employees' commitment and buy-in, as well as the likelihood that what is done will be successful.*

> **A manager at the Hyatt Corporation asked her employees at a staff meeting what ideas they had for increasing recognition. One of the employees suggested that the department rotate the responsibility for recognition throughout the group so that each week one person would be responsible for finding an individual or group achievement and then recognizing it in some way of their own choosing. Creativity flourished; recognition skyrocketed as employees were empowered to be an integral part of the process.**

6. "MY ORGANIZATION DOES NOT HELP FACILITATE OR SUPPORT RECOGNITION EFFORTS." *Although recognition efforts can flourish even in the absence of formal organizational support, such support, if made available, can help managers maintain their commitment. Information, training, recognition tools, budget, and recognition programs that reinforce desired behavior and performance should be made available on an ongoing basis—even if all managers do not use these resources—to support recognition efforts and the organization's expectation that every manager take the responsibility of providing recognition seriously.*

At each morning's plantwide meeting at Honeywell's industrial fibers plant in Moncure, NC, employees are allowed to publicly exchange thanks and acknowledgments with other employees. Upon hearing of an achievement from one of his managers, the plant manager suggests possible recognition awards or activities for that manager to consider doing for his people. Looking for and facilitating opportunities for recognition to occur within the organization helps to increase the activity and make it an integral part of the organization's people philosophy, culture, and daily practices.

Common Obstacles to Implementing Recognition

An employee's motivation is directly affected by the work environment. Oftentimes there can be factors in an environment that get in people's way and keep them from doing their best job. Sometimes the best thing a manager can do to motivate employees is to remove those obstacles. Following are some ways to remove such obstacles in your organization.

SIMPLIFY POLICIES.

If your organization is rule-bound with policies and procedures, chances are that employees' productivity is stymied. Many organizations today are replacing their volumes of policies and procedures with simpler, less restrictive versions that trust employees and allow them to take responsibility for their actions. For example, a few years ago, Houston, TX–based Continental Airlines symbolically burned its legalistic several-hundred-page policies and procedures manual and replaced it with a relatively short document titled "Working Together Guidelines." The new guidelines rely on "the judgment of the people who really run this airline," that is, line employees. Similarly, GM, after its 2009 federal bailout, began greatly reducing its bureaucracy.

DON'T BLOCK EMPLOYEES FROM TAKING RISKS.

Most managers want employees to take initiative, but if an employee happens to make a mistake while taking initiative, they are usually punished severely—sometimes to the point of losing their jobs. So on the one hand, management bemoans the fact that employees don't take initiative, but on the other hand they are quick to punish employees for making mistakes when they take risks. Managers need to recognize and accept the fact that mistakes might happen—but greater good is attained by allowing employees to take initiative.

At Hershey Foods in Hershey, Pennsylvania, chairman and CEO Richard Zimmerman wanted to encourage employees to exercise initiative in their jobs and to take risks without fear of retribution. To encourage such risks, The Exalted Order of the Extended Neck was created. According to Zimmerman, "I wanted to reward people who were willing to buck the system, practice a little entrepreneurship, who were willing to stand the heat for an idea they really believe in." The award has been given out on numerous occasions, including to a maintenance worker who devised a way to perform midweek cleaning on a piece of machinery without losing running time. Similarly, Google attributes much of its incredible success to failure. Like Zimmerman, Eric Schmidt, Larry Page, and Sergey Brin have explicitly stated the importance of "failing forward."

DON'T HINDER COMMUNICATION.

There are many aspects to good communication, but one of the most important aspects is to provide employees access to it when they most need it, not when management happens to have time for it. For example, many companies have an "open-door" policy, but employees frequently find managers are not available—so employees stop using it. By contrast, there are numerous ways to ensure good communication when it is needed. For example, in many companies, such as Dell Computers in India, managers conduct regularly scheduled "one-on-one" meetings with their employees.

O r you might try opening the doors to improved communication with more high-tech solutions. Hal Rosenbluth, former CEO of Rosenbluth International, was accessible to all his employees through an 800-number "voice-mail box." Employees were encouraged to call in with suggestions, problems, or praise, and, on average, about seven employees did so every day.

It is important to periodically assess what obstacles are keeping employees from doing their best work and what elements are helping employees do a better job. Clearing employee obstacles can be an important first step to enhancing employee performance in most organizations.

Implementing & Leveraging Recognition for Greatest Impact

The Individual Level

The most powerful type of recognition occurs at the individual level, one-on-one. All managers need to take personal responsibility to see that they recognize their employees, and they need to keep at it on a daily basis. The best way to do this is to plan for it.

When planning individual recognition, a good (and simple) approach is to use the what, who, when, where, and how format. This planning format doesn't even need to be written down, but systematically thinking it through will help you.

1. *What do I want to recognize?* As mentioned, the best recognition is contingent; that is, in response to a specific behavior or performance.

2. *Who do I want to recognize?* Identify the person or people most responsible for the desired behavior or performance.

3. *When should the recognition be done?* The best recognition takes place soon after the desired behavior or performance.

4. *Where should the recognition be done?* The best recognition is personal; that is, delivered directly to the individual being acknowledged—ideally, in person.

5. *How should the recognition be done?* The best recognition is done in a way that enhances its motivational value to the recipient. Who performs the recognition? Is it done in public or private? Asking yourself these questions will help make sure that the recognition activity has the greatest impact.

Recognition Techniques for Immediate Application

➤ Take a few moments at the end of the day to reflect on whose performance you've noticed. Write those individuals thank-you notes and leave the notes by their workstations as you leave.

➤ Manage by wandering around! Get out of your office to see, meet, and speak with employees about work they are doing. Take different routes in and out of the premises.

When you read your mail, look for positive items to share with others or at all-department meetings.

➤ Greet individual employees by name and with eye contact. Take a few minutes to see how they are doing. Be sincere.

Make an effort to meet with employees you don't see or speak with very often. Take a break together, have coffee or an off-site lunch.

➤ Act on good news! Catch people doing something right and thank them for it.

➤ Take time to listen when employees need to talk. Be responsive to people, not just to problems.

Take time at the beginning or end of meetings to share positive news such as letters from customers or ask if there are any praisings from one team member to another.

➤ Remember the 4:1 rule! Every time you criticize or correct someone, plan to praise or thank that same person at least four times.

➤ Think of mistakes as opportunities for learning. Help employees learn from their mistakes; don't criticize employees for making mistakes—especially not in front of others.

➤ Be quick to thank and compliment others and slow to criticize and judge them.

➤ Spread positive gossip! Tell others what you are pleased about and who is responsible.

Praise publicly; reprimand privately.

Take time to celebrate individual or group milestones, desired behavior, and achievements!

Other Low-Cost Recognition Strategies

Here's a list of low-cost ideas that I have collected from companies over the years:

Personal thanks

Thank-you notes

E-mail praise

Voice-mail praise

Public praise

Pass-around trophy

Time with manager, president

Car wash by manager or executive of choice

Employee parking space

Read positive letters from customers at staff meetings

Referenced in company newsletters

Featured in community newspaper

Name days in employee's honor

Wall of fame—photos of achievers

Team projects scrapbook in company lobby

Certificate of appreciation

Balloons and computer banners

Pack lunch for employee

Loan your car to employee

Create an award (Golden Banana, Spirit of Fred, Order of the Extended Neck, etc.)

Time off (extra break, long lunch, 3-day weekend, etc.)

Do a least-favored or menial task for someone else ("Dump a Dog" program)

Victory celebration

Performance passes to use a lending library for books & audios

Coupons to bring employee's pet to work

Feature in company ads

Confetti committee for spontaneous celebrations

Baking cookies, distributing candy, making ice-cream floats

Cook and serve meal (barbecue, breakfast, etc.)

Management challenge (if goal is met, manager shaves head, dresses in crazy outfit, etc.)

Additional Guidelines for Rewarding Individuals

A few other considerations can help your recognition be even more on the mark:

MATCH THE REWARD TO THE PERSON.

Have one-on-one conversations with each of your employees to find out the type of praise they prefer, and to determine how to deliver it in a way that would not provoke jealousy in your department. This is about personal, daily awareness—the annual service awards banquet is beyond the scope of this discussion.

Does the employee prefer recognition in private, public, or either? Will a thank you do? Does he enjoy the times when his peers are aware of good performance? How about occasional on-the-spot candy, free lunch, certificate for ice cream, small gift, etc.? Find out what works for individual employees. Establish an action plan that fits the needs of individual employees rather than trying to fit all employees into one big category.

MATCH THE REWARD TO THE ACHIEVEMENT.

Tap into your leaders to recognize deserving employees, for example awarding lunch with the director. Do larger forms of recognition for greater achievements, but remember to do the fun, simple things as well. For example, every couple of months have some members of your leadership staff wheel around a cart of treats to each employee in your office. Ideas include a variety of ice-cream bars/popsicles; granola bars/candy bars; doughnuts/pastries; and so on. Make it fun by doing something goofy (if you serve ice-cream bars, cut out the pictures of them on the box and tape them to your back so employees know what varieties they have to choose from). This is sure to get some laughs and feelings of recognition/togetherness in your department, not to mention the interaction they are getting with leadership.

MATCH THE REWARD TO YOUR BUDGET.

Realize that you can do a *lot* of recognition with little or no budget, such as public recognition in a format like Energizers; having thank-you cards on hand for employees to use to recognize one another; a monthly recognition program, such as employee of the month (have your staff vote on who they feel is most deserving).

Using Recognition for Its Greatest Impact

E ffective recognition programs, even at the individual and team levels, require a substantial investment of time and money. Even though the best recognition is free, the time and effort involved still cost money. Let's consider, for example, an organization in which 100 supervisors are spending, as a realistic average, two hours and $25 a week each on recognition. If the fully burdened cost (hourly wage plus the cost of benefits) of each supervisor is $50 an hour, the time that the supervisors devote to their recognition efforts alone costs the company approximately $650,000 per year.

And that's just the beginning. Say that ten teams (with ten employees on each team) are spending one hour per person (at a fully burdened rate of $25 per hour) and $30 a week per team on recognition-related activities. That works out to an additional $140,000 per year in real cost to the company. The grand total of this very simple approach to individual and team recognition is close to $800,000! And this is before we even think about adding in the costs of an organizational recognition program.

If you were the CEO of this company, wouldn't you want to know what benefits the organization was getting for this significant investment of company resources?

A smart CEO, of course, would have no problem with the $800,000 expenditure, provided she was confident that the program was an investment that would produce in excess of the cost. Unfortunately, poor recognition can easily turn a huge investment into a huge expense with low return and major morale consequences for the organization. However, when recognition is executed properly, the benefits far exceed the time and money put into it.

Recognition to Improve Performance

Recognition geared at improving performance is goal-oriented. It is targeted at helping an organization achieve a desired outcome.

People do things largely for the positive consequences they anticipate. Recognition in the form of contingent promises (incentives) and after-the-fact recognition (positive reinforcers) for desired behaviors or results are major motivators of both individual and group performance of all types.

In one of the most frequently cited applications of work performance recognition, Emery Air Freight, now a part of Consolidated Freightways, used positive reinforcement to dramatically reduce its costs of doing business. Emery was losing a lot of money because its containers were not fully loaded when shipped. Workers knew that they were supposed to ship fully loaded containers; the performance expectations had been communicated to them many times. However, while workers reported that their containers were fully loaded 90 percent of the time, a review found that the containers were actually fully loaded only 45 percent of the time. Through the use of positive reinforcement and feedback on performance (primarily just praise from management!), the percentage of full containers increased from 45 percent to 95 percent, saving the company millions of dollars.

———

In a similar type of praise-for-performance program, Weyerhaeuser Paper Company increased their logging trucks' productivity, going from 60 percent to more than 90 percent.

———

Recognition Tied to the Company's Goals & Values

Although recognizing employees is certainly a nice thing to do, for maximum impact it must be tied to an organization's goals and values. If your organization has taken the time and effort to clearly establish a core mission, values, and strategies, which it almost certainly has, then your reward and recognition systems should clearly and systematically reward the behaviors and outputs that reinforce those elements.

However, before recognition can help move an organization toward achieving its goals, employees should be thoroughly aware of those goals. And once they are, managers should recognize employees for the actions and behaviors that contribute to successfully achieving those company goals, telling them what goal of the organization they helped achieve and how they helped do so. Before long, employees will start to understand that "this is what it takes to get recognized around here" and begin moving the organization toward its objectives.

Recognition Tied to Employees' Goals

Managers should meet regularly with employees to map goals and to seek ideas on how they can work together to meet these goals. In addition, management should identify the kinds of rewards and recognition that motivate employees to try to attain these goals. Having the end in sight and empowering employees to be creative and to develop their own skills and abilities can tap into a tremendous reserve of energy, ideas, and initiative.

Keeping employees focused on goals is best accomplished by providing feedback on their progress in achieving the goals so that they clearly know how they are doing. Use regular performance review meetings as a time to discuss corporate and individual goals with employees. Encourage employees to think outside the box to find new and innovative ways to participate in the company's success. For example, managers can help employees establish goals that are linked to finding new cost-savings measures or to better ways of conducting an existing practice or procedure.

Traditionally, performance reviews occur once, maybe twice, a year. Consider for a moment the content of most performance reviews: a list of discussion items related to completed projects or tasks throughout the year. More frequent reviews of employees' performance and efforts to achieve set goals lets employees know where they stand before the work is completed. With proper guidance during the course of the year, many unintentional mistakes or behaviors can be averted. Performance reviews should be given quarterly, rather than annually, to ensure that managers and employees are on the same page regarding their goals and performance. More frequent review discussions should concentrate on goals—of the employee and of the organization—and should always include discussions about the future and about development opportunities for employees.

Creating a Culture of Recognition

There's a big difference between getting people to come to work and getting them to do their best work.

While money or other forms of compensation are important to employees, what tends to motivate them to perform at higher levels is the thoughtful, timely, personal kind of recognition that signifies true appreciation for a job well done. Yet, most organizations, I have found, are woefully inept at building an organizational culture that fosters recognition.

A recognition culture is one in which individuals (regardless of rank, title, expertise, or tenure) freely and readily recognize one another's contributions. Individuals are trusted, respected, and excited about their own successes and the successes of others in the organization.

THE ZAPPOS CULTURE

Zappos.com's CEO Tony Hsieh has revolutionized selling shoes online by creating a culture built on the strategy of making people happy. He's succeeded on multiple levels, including reaching $1 billion in sales. Customers rave about the company's superior service, and *The Zappos Culture Book* is filled with comments from employees "enthused" about working for the online retailer. Every year management invites staff to submit 100 to 500 words describing what the Zappos Culture means to them. The text is published—unedited—and used as a manual to show prospective employees and to orient new ones. "At Zappos, our belief is that if you get the culture right, most of the other stuff—like great customer service or building a great long-term brand, or passionate employees and customers—will happen naturally on its own," wrote Hsieh in a recent blog post.

Sustaining a Culture of Recognition

In most organizations, the executive management team sets the tone for how people are treated. Are employees frequently valued for what they do on an individual basis or are they treated in aggregate as a line item in the budget? Increasingly, executives in today's most successful and innovative organizations are initiating actions that demonstrate their commitment to valuing their employees in a very hands-on manner.

Simply put, there is no greater strategy for the sustained practice of recognition in an organization than for that company's leadership to practice recognition and to be seen practicing it. Executives must model the behavior they expect others to follow. Having top managers practice employee recognition sets the tone for the behavior of all managers in the organization and symbolically says, "If I can make time to do this, no one else in the organization has an excuse not to."

Strategies to Keep Recognition Going

On an individual level, what keeps people from acting on their best intentions to recognize employees more frequently? Usually, you can raise managers' levels of awareness about the importance of recognizing employees, and you can have them practice their interpersonal skills so they can increase their ability and comfort level, but you can't force them to keep up the desired behavior once they get back on the job. I'm convinced that the ratio of success increases when we help people develop an individualized strategy and support plan to stay committed.

Following are several tactics I've seen work in a variety of organizations. Try them, adapt them, and combine them.

LINK THE ACTIVITY TO YOUR DAY PLANNER.

For many people, the key to changing their routine is to make the new behavior part of their current planning and organizing system. I've been successful at getting analytical, task-oriented managers to start praising employees more by getting them to think of their people as "things to do."

ELICIT THE HELP OF OTHERS.

Managers are likely to have significantly better results when they involve others and discuss what they are trying to do. They could have people work with a partner for recognition activities; this could be a colleague they met in a training session or someone from a different area of the company with whom they want to keep in touch. They could exchange action plans with specific times for follow-up and discussion of progress. In this "buddy system," the partner acts as a designated monitor, counselor, and enforcer all in one—essentially, a soul mate to encourage and act on the new behaviors.

Alternatively, at the next staff meeting, a manager can say, "I'm going to be trying some new tactics and would appreciate your feedback on it. Specifically, I'm going to be acknowledging people when I see them doing a good job. I'm trying to do this in a timely, specific way. Let me know how it feels to you and give me feedback as to how I can do it better."

HOLD ONE-ON-ONE MEETINGS.

One systematic approach for making more time for your employees is to start holding one-on-one meetings. Set a minimum acceptable standard for "face time" with each employee. One employee might want feedback on a project she recently completed, another may want to get advice on how he can improve a working relationship with another employee (they may try to figure it out through role-playing), and another person might want to discuss career options and skills she would like to learn on the job.

SCHEDULE TIME FOR RECOGNITION.

You can also provide structures or systems in your work environment that will encourage praise. Some managers save time at the end of every staff meeting to ask if anyone has any praise they'd like to share. Typically, people do. Other companies schedule "bragging sessions" with upper management in which they update (and celebrate) the progress of major projects.

One of the biggest challenges in recognizing others is doing it in the midst of the daily operations of your business, when you— and your employees—are the busiest. The Walt Disney World Dolphin Resort in Orlando, Florida, offers an excellent example of how to provide recognition under pressure. Instead of viewing "being busy" as an executive excuse for why they didn't recognize employees, they focus their energies on new and creative ways to do more recognition. For example:

- When surveyed, Dolphin employees reported that managers weren't around much when things were busiest. As a result, management initiated "Five-Minute Chats" where all managers were assigned ten employees who didn't report to them. Their assignment: to check in with each employee for five minutes over the next 30 days.
- During busy days—when employees simultaneously checked more than 1,000 customers in and out—supervisors set up

refreshments and balloons in the employee area behind the hotel check-in counter. Supervisors were there to cheer employees on and to jump in during employee breaks.

- Dolphin management started using "Wow!" cards, trifolded wallet cards made from different colored construction paper in which employees and managers could provide a quick written thank you to others who "wowed" a customer or another employee. "Captain Wow," their very own superhero, dropped by regularly to thank them and acknowledge their work.

No matter what your business, look for the times when you and your employees are most under pressure and develop ways to thank, acknowledge, and recognize employees during those times. Doing so can be the best pressure-relief valve you'll ever have.

Strategies to Keep Recognition Fresh and Meaningful

Even the best recognition program doesn't last forever. To keep your program fresh and the energy for it high, you need to periodically review what's working well (and what's broken) with the program and then revitalize it.

At Johnson & Johnson, employees were asked what items and activities they valued most. It turned out that more than half of them didn't consider the organization's traditional years-of-service awards to be meaningful recognition. What they wanted was recognition that involved their families, such as receiving a basket of goodies or movie passes for the whole family. The company made the necessary adjustments. Through this experience, Johnson & Johnson learned a very important lesson:

One of the keys to recognition success is consistently surveying employees, not assuming that management knows best. It may very well be that years-of-service awards are important to your employees. The point is: Find out.

———

One of the best ways to revitalize a recognition program is through the use of motivators. Here are just a few of the possibilities:

VARIETY
Sometimes simply adding a new celebratory activity can do wonders to revitalize recognition. Brainstorm the ways in which variety can be added, without necessarily changing any of the core aspects of the program. For example, during a one-month period, you might recognize all employees who praise or nominate another employee for an award.

NEW RECOGNITION OPPORTUNITIES
Establish new opportunities for recognition and celebration. Even within a well-defined area of recognition, you should be able to identify many new recognition opportunities. For instance, if you have individual safety awards, establish a new category for team safety awards.

NEW RECOGNITION LEVELS
Choose new triggers for recognition. To make sure employees do not feel you are constantly changing the rules for recognition in your organization, be consistent in what you recognize, but add new levels for greater forms of employee achievement.

ENHANCING THE SCOREKEEPING PROCESS

Make use of this powerful measurement and feedback mechanism. Providing new scorekeeping methods can have a significant revitalizing impact on recognition programs. For example, one organization posted huge scoreboards throughout the company to call attention to its revitalized recognition program; another created a giant recognition "utilization thermometer" for the lobby to track the number of employees who participated in the company's recognition program.

More important, top managers need to use the program daily to show that they really believe in it. They need to point out recognition opportunities for other managers to consider and encourage those managers to use available recognition programs.

The Importance of Measuring Recognition

One of the best strategies to sustain recognition is to measure its impact. Once its benefits become clear through data, recognition often becomes institutionalized.

An old management maxim says, "If you can't measure it, you can't manage it." Recognition is no exception. Justifying the time, effort, and expense of any recognition program means demonstrating its impact, which requires that you be able to determine a baseline and any change—ideally, improvement—in that baseline.

Using Donald Kirkpatrick's model for evaluating the impact of training (a "soft" behavioral discipline), we can identify four levels of measurement for recognition:

LEVEL I: REACTION

The first level of measurement is often obtained at the end of a training seminar or resource simply by asking employees, "How did the training feel to you?" using a scale of 1 (didn't like it) to 5 (thought it was excellent). With recognition, this measure often surfaces in employee attitude surveys. When morale is low, employees typically rank one or more of the following items very low:

- My manager recognizes me when I do good work.
- My manager makes time for me when I need to talk.
- My manager has discussed my future career aspirations with me.
- I feel appreciated for the work I do.
- I feel I'm a valuable member of the team/department.

Surveying attitudes can be a useful way to determine whether employee perceptions of the company are improving and a way to quantify the level of individual, group, and organizational morale.

LEVEL 2: LEARNING

The second level of evaluation deals with what participants actually learned during the training session. Kirkpatrick defines learning as the "extent to which participants change attitudes, improve knowledge, and/or increase skill as a result of attending the program." It is typically easier to determine what new knowledge or skills participants acquired than it is to determine the ways in which the training changed their opinions, values, and beliefs. Tests are the most frequent method of evaluating learning.

As it applies to recognition, we can measure if certain skill or awareness levels have changed based on recognition training or the rollout of one or more recognition programs. Managers can be asked (before and after recognition training) how important it is to recognize employees, how often they should do so, in what types of situations, and in what ways. In a seminar they can be taught guidelines for effective praising and be allowed to practice the skill with feedback from others. Other measurable recognition skills include knowing how to praise publicly, how to write a persuasive nomination for an employee award, and what forms of recognition work well for different types of performance.

Managers need more than an academic understanding of the importance of recognition. They must have specific skills associated with effective recognition techniques and be comfortable using those skills. Tracking progress as managers acquire these skills can thus be a significant measurement for any organization.

LEVEL 3: BEHAVIOR

The third level of measurement involves the impact of the training back on the job. Trainees can learn and demonstrate new skills and then never use those skills after they return to work. This form of evaluation can be time-consuming and costly, involving direct observation, follow-up interviews, and surveys—of participants as well as those with whom they work. It is somewhat easier if the measurement is established as part of the program (for example, a tracking report), not as a separate activity to be done later.

For recognition, we can measure how frequently a manager recognizes his or her employees, perhaps by the increase in use of available recognition tools and programs. We can also track the number of employees who receive a written praising from managers, peers, or customers; the number of employees nominated for awards; the number of managers who make nominations; the number of formal awards given; and so on.

This data can be useful in examining variations over time by manager or department, by level in the organization, or by facility. Comparisons can be done of corporate offices versus field operations and among different regions, and so on.

LEVEL 4: RESULTS

If the recognition isn't getting desired results, it doesn't matter how people feel about recognition or how good they are at using it—something must change. Even when the intent of a program is simply to increase employee morale, indirect measures exist (or can be built) to examine the results of the program's effectiveness beyond morale.

Here are some examples of questions you can ask about results:

How much are sales incentive programs helping to increase sales revenue?

What is the impact of employee suggestion programs on improving the business?

How much do attendance programs reduce absenteeism?

Are customer service awards improving customer retention?

Are team awards enhancing inter- and intradepartmental cooperation?

Are safety recognition programs increasing safe behavior and reducing on-the-job injuries?

Are quality awards programs increasing product quality?

Usually results are defined as the bottom-line outcomes of the organization (such as profits, sales, and so on), but the tendency to reduce everything to financial terms is dangerous because it trivializes many nonfinancial organizational effectiveness measures. (Kaplan and Norton's "balanced scorecard," which is currently revolutionizing management thinking about organizational evaluation, is a response to this "bean-counting," quantifying mentality.)

In addition to the traditional bottom-line results, there are countless intermediate results called "organizational effectiveness" indicators. These hundreds, even thousands, of operational measures exist in every organization and include manufacturing efficiency, inventory levels, lost-time accidents, order entry accuracy, abandoned calls, defects produced, equipment utilization, cycle time, and so on. These indicators are also Level 4 measures. Conveniently, organizational effectiveness indicators already exist and can be used without any additional investment.

Begin with the end in mind. One of the added benefits of good measurement, especially at Level 4, is that the more recognition activities and programs drive significant organizational performance and strategic results, the easier it is to justify the effort and funds to support them. We all want to have recognition programs that are rewarding for employees, easy to use, and readily applicable on the job—and that improve the organization's performance in meaningful ways. To do this, you must reverse the evaluation strategy and begin with the end in mind. First, clearly understand your employees' needs and wants. Then define the results you desire to ensure that the program can achieve them. Starting with a clear idea of your audience and the goals and performance you want from them will strengthen the link of recognition to results now and in the long term.

The profound implications of these four levels escape most people. But remember: What you measure is what you are likely to get. The level where you focus most of your attention is where you are most likely to see results. Obviously, measuring at all four levels is most likely to achieve the most complete results, but you should measure other levels only if you feel it is necessary to obtain feedback from them.

New Trends in Recognition & Rewards

Recognition has been around for eons, but trends in recognition and rewards change from year to year. Following are some of the most significant new trends in recognition and rewards in recent years.

Peer-to-Peer Recognition

Increasingly, recognition can come from anyone at work, not just from one's manager. Following are some examples of peer-to-peer recognition, which should make up the basic foundation of interpersonal interaction for any strong recognition culture.

Some agencies of QSource, the Memphis-based nonprofit health care management expert, erect an "Angels Among Us" table in the office. When someone nominates a peer for doing something exceptional, they decorate the table as a tribute, including a copy of the nomination, an explanation of why the person is being honored, photos of the staff member, and flowers.

———

At Montana's Cookhouse, the large restaurant chain based in Mississauga, Ontario, employees praise their peers' work in external and internal customer service, health, and safety. Feedback is entered on the company's intranet site and sent to the person's manager, who reads the note to staff; notes are posted on the website. About 1,500 comments were filed in the first nine months of the program.

———

Employees at S. C. Johnson & Son, Inc., the global manufacturer of household cleaning supplies based in Racine, WI, nominate and give standing ovations to their peers for remarkable performance.

———

At La Posada at Park Centre in Green Valley, AZ, employees give each other "You're a Star" cards, which can be redeemed for money or days off.

———

Julie Blind, administrative director of business services for Sierra View District Hospital in Porterville, CA, designates a "Pal of the Week" in which she asks everyone in the department to do or say something nice to the person in the course of the week. The designation rolls over to another member of the department and the previous designee is responsible for reminding everyone to do something nice for the new Pal the following week. The honor continues until everyone has served as a Pal and then the process repeats. Members of Julie's department also use "Kindness Coins"—simple medallions—to

PEER-TO-PEER TIPS

➡ Let employees vote on employee awards.

➡ Have a vote for the company's top performers/all-star team.

➡ Let employees recognize others' performance on individual/group projects.

➡ Encourage a group/department to recognize another group's/department's accomplishment.

thank others for their help and actions. The coins represent an emotional currency of personal appreciation that has a real payoff to those that receive them.

———

At KFC restaurants in Australia, workers rewarded colleagues with "Champs" cards, for cleanliness, hospitality, and accuracy. Recipients were entered in drawings for prizes, such as movie tickets, car washes, or babysitting. Yum Brands Inc., the Louisville, KY, parent of restaurant chains KFC, Taco Bell, and Pizza Hut, believes peer recognition helped lower turnover, which measured 181 percent for its hourly restaurant workers in 1997.

———

Anyone at Spectrum Chemicals & Laboratory Products in Gardena, CA, can give anyone else a written note of thanks that includes a $25 gift certificate for Trader Joe's or a restaurant of their choice. Most often, the person offering the thanks personally presents the note and certificate to the honoree in front of the sales department. Individuals are also allowed to give themselves a Thumbs Up award for those times when they are the only person who knows the specifics of their achievement.

———

Human resources employees at software maker Symantec Corporation, based in Cupertino, CA, give each other "Serendipity" awards. At the end of the quarter, the HR VP randomly selects names among the recipients for prizes worth $40 to $50.

———

"We call it our Recognition Fish Line," says Nikki Sturgeon, employee services coordinator in Human

Resources for Royal Victoria Hospital in Barrie, Ontario. The fish line is a voice mailbox used to leave anonymous appreciative messages for anyone who has been caught doing something right. The messages are recorded on notes, attached to a special "fish" ribbon, and sent to their managers who then get to recognize the individual personally. Because of the ease and simplicity of leaving a message, it is widely used by all levels in the organization.

——

At aircraft manufacturer Boeing, based in Chicago, employees complete an online form and the program automatically sends e-mails to the giver's and the recipient's managers. The company publicizes the program by sending fliers to employees' homes and through monthly e-mail reminders. Employees receive electronic cards or points that can be redeemed for merchandise.

——

ComDoc in Uniontown, OH, encourages employees (they refer to themselves as "partners") to recognize each other as "Passionate Partners." "One partner sends an e-mail or letter recognizing a 'Passionate Partner' to me," says Judi Adam, manager of corporate administration, "and I, in turn, send out a 'Passionate Partner' e-mail to all ComDoc partners, recognizing that person for their accomplishments, good deeds, acts of kindness, or whatever it is for which they are being recognized." Often this prompts other partners to send appreciative e-mails to the Passionate Partner. It further reminds everyone to think about others who need recognition.

——

LaPorte Medical Group in LaPorte, IN (part of Memorial Hospital and Health System of South Bend), has a program called Secret Pals. Denice Boyce, RN and clinical supervisor, created the Secret Pal concept. In November of each year, employees are invited to participate in the program and are given a sign-up form and helpful hints. The sign-up form asks for information such as birthday, wedding anniversary, employment anniversary, and favorite restaurants, foods, movies, hobbies, and so on. The Secret Pals committee knows who is assigned to whom and monitors special recognition opportunities, keeping people informed so they can give additional recognition. At a get-together in December of the following year, people find out who their secret pal was for the previous year. Then they draw a name for the upcoming year. Says Denice, "I have been here at LaPorte Medical Group for thirty-two years. It's like family and it's because we respect and recognize each other."

Toronto-based Scotiabank, one of North America's premier financial institutions and Canada's most international bank, is well known for its award-winning Scotia Applause program. Multidimensional and web-based, it was designed to help strengthen employees' focus on Scotiabank's corporate values and on delivering exceptional customer service. It includes formal recognition of top performers, online training, and Peer Recognition certificates, which allow employees to recognize each other for "living" the corporate core values. Employees earn rewards points that are redeemed for items in an online merchandise catalog. The need for greater employee engagement was heavily marketed in 2006, resulting in a record 500,000+ peer recognition certificates sent by employees recognizing each other.

The Sterling Group, a property management firm based in Mishawaka, IN, has a Silver Star program, an example of how a little effort—and minimal cash outlay—can create positive results. The program encourages employees to recognize each other with a special note that contains a personalized message of appreciation. They also have informal events such as summer barbecues, Cinco de Mayo celebrations, and chili cook-offs.

Wells Fargo has an electronic peer-to-peer praise program called E-wards that allows any employee to recognize any other employee for doing a great job. It's made up of three parts:

- E-cards are online thank-you cards that anyone can send to anyone else with a copy going to a recognition mailbox for tracking purposes. Those being thanked are entered into a quarterly drawing for prizes. In their first year alone, Wells Fargo employees used 1,600 e-cards.
- E-wards are used to praise consistent performance over time based on five values of the organization (leadership, "e-novation," teams, entrepreneurship, and customer service). The electronic award goes to the nominee's manager for approval. The awardee then gets a certificate with the details of the achievement and a scratch-off ticket for a gift worth $50 to $250. In its first year, 900 e-wards were distributed in the organization.
- Ride the Wave is a once-a-year celebration for select recipients of the E-card or E-wards recognition. Senior managers review nominations, select the 70 most impressive achievements, and invite the winners to attend a three-day, off-site special event with a guest of their choice. The event

combines professional development with fun and includes even more recognition.

———

Bank of America has a similar program that uses electronic thank-you cards. They also provide electronic tool kits to managers that show them how to make recognition more meaningful to employees.

———

Colin Service Systems in White Plains, NY, has recognized employees with awards such as Most Helpful Employee and Nicest Employee. Coworkers vote for the employees they think should win the titles, and executives make the presentations.

———

Walmart.com has a recognition program called "Tell me something good!" in which associates can report on good work that is done by coworkers.

———

The Cleveland, OH, office of accounting firm KPMG gave each employee a box of thank-you notes to use and send to fellow coworkers.

———

Employees at Oregon-based Flying Pie Pizzeria restaurants complete a "This Paycheck Brought to You in Part By" or "TPBTYIPB" form after seeing a team member create a remarkable result—one that will help increase revenue, and help employee paychecks clear the bank. Employees fill out two to ten forms every night and post them on a bulletin board for the week, and the Store Leader chooses two or three from the week that seem especially valuable, types them up, and writes comments on why they are exceptionally good for the restaurant; for example, "This act helped us sell more of product X than ever before." Then the forms go to the restaurant owner, who comments again; for example, "This act was great because it can be repeated by any employee." The resulting document is stapled to paychecks with about ten other TPB stories to inform and inspire others. The TPB is given as a monetary award, too. Every quarter of the year, the restaurant has a random drawing, and each published TPB from the 13 weeks gets two names dropped into the hat: those of the person who did the great action and the person who captured and shared the action. A total of $500 is awarded ($50 each to ten people). Another one: This $100 cash award is given for an action that will save or earn the restaurant more than $100 in the next two years. The story is published and posted for everyone to see, and a copy of the story is kept in a binder so that crewmembers can be inspired and see how simple it is to win the award.

Experiential Incentives

In the past, rewards that were primarily used in the incentive industry were formal merchandise, such as etched crystal and logoed jewelry, used in formal recognition programs. Then lifestyle and family incentives became more the vogue. Now one of the cutting edges of new employee incentives is found in experiential rewards.

Dimension Data Canada Inc., the network-related technology company, appointed a

EXPERIENCE TIPS

➡ Provide a free makeover.

➡ Give a full-day pass to a spa.

➡ Give passes for bungee jumping, skydiving, hot-air balloon ride, whitewater rafting.

➡ Provide lessons: golf, scuba, flying, rafting, tennis, horseback riding, cooking, painting.

Chief Fun Officer in its Toronto office, a title given to an employee who's willing to create fun. CFOs get a budget to organize monthly activities, such as paintball or bowling.

———

Chicago-based Radio Flyer, Inc., a toy products company, hosts a Heritage Celebration that includes an all-staff party and the Radio Flyer Olympics, where employees compete in tricycle races and doughnut eating.

———

Brainstorm Marketing in Des Moines, IA, rewards employees with a trip to Kansas City in appreciation for completing a project.

———

Circles, a Boston marketing company, gave CFO Hugh Merryweather a choice of an experience as part of his anniversary reward with the company. He opted for a Red Sox baseball game with special perks and took his young son with him.

———

San Diego–based Quantum Design rewards employees for extra effort by booking time for them at a senior executive's ski condo. The rent is being paid anyway, and employees feel refreshed after being away from the city for the weekend.

———

Dominy & Associates, a top San Diego architectural firm, takes all of its 25 employees and a guest of his or her choice on an all-expenses-paid, week-long skiing trip to Mammoth, CA. Company founder Lou Dominy says, "We like to create memories." The company always plans a stop along the way to tour one of the buildings the firm had built or renovated, adding to the sense of pride and team building the trip creates.

———

Marsh, Inc., the insurance brokerage subsidiary of New York City–based Marsh & McLennan, hosted top performers and their partners to a trip to a Phoenix dude ranch.

———

Flying High Pizzeria restaurants, which are headquartered in Portland, OR, offer annual raft trips. One trip of note: The company took 64 people to Costa Rica for a week, an event mentioned in AP wire stories around the globe.

———

Texas Roadhouse, the Louisville, KY, restaurant chain, held its 12th annual "managing partners" conference in New York City. Over 1,000 employees and vendors were treated to a stay at the Waldorf Astoria Hotel, an evening at Radio City Music Hall, and a Charlie Daniels Band concert.

———

Restaurant Equipment World (REW) of Orlando, FL, hosts million-dollar parties for everyone in the company when a department reaches $1 million in sales. REW treats employees to ventures outside the office to avoid workday interruptions, as well as to give employees a greater opportunity to bond. Trips include group cooking lessons, pottery classes, bowling, laser tag, zip-lining, and visits to a factory to make chocolate. Behind-the-scenes employees are included and recognized, too. REW spends

EXPERIENCE TIPS

➡ Give a dinner cruise, a boat or bus tour.

➡ Hire a professional chef to prepare a gourmet meal at employee's home.

➡ Arrange for employee to throw out first pitch at a baseball game.

➡ Arrange for employee to be a guest announcer at a ball game.

➡ Send employee on an Outward Bound trip.

just under $50 per person for its recognition events, about $500 to $1,000 per party.

_____

Wellness/Work-Life Balance

Another trend in incentives is the increased use of wellness and work-life balance incentives for employees.

Yvon Chouinard, founder of Patagonia, the outdoor-clothing maker based in Ventura, CA, told employees in a speech, "You can take time off, whether it's two hours or two weeks, as long as your work gets done and you don't keep others from doing their work."

_____

A Boston-based economic consulting firm, Analysis Group, focuses on maintaining an ideal work-life balance for every employee. Female executives account for about 30 percent of the principals and 40 percent of directors. Staff members are eligible for 12 weeks of paid maternity leave, with options for extensions. Several female employees work either less than full-time or part-time from home. The firm limits the number of business trips workers must take.

_____

FTEN, the New York City-based financial technology firm, offers its employees a holistic approach to wellness, including nutrition, exercise, and stress-reduction workshops. Workers also receive a healthy, free daily breakfast and bimonthly in-house massages. New hires work at ergonomically designed computer desks. With more employees adhering to a diet and exercise regimen, FTEN anticipates that its medical costs will drop.

———

New York City–based Rand Engineering & Architecture provides free yoga classes and an on-site gym. They also let working mothers regularly bring their babies to the office or take a leave of absence without jeopardizing their position or tenure.

———

Protective Life, a financial services and insurance company based in Birmingham, AL, uses the Virgin HealthMiles incentive platform to help employees become healthier. The company also offers an on-site health clinic, massage services, a nutritionist, and health education programs. Just over 60 percent of Protective's employees are enrolled in the Virgin HealthMiles program. Desktop kiosks are available for employees to take biometric readings such as blood pressure, weight, and body fat measurements. Employees get credit for using the kiosks each month, and points accrue for walking, running, or doing aerobics. They are rewarded with gift cards and cash. In a 12-month period, employees can earn up to $400 in cash or choices of gift cards, which are also available via the Virgin HealthMiles platform.

———

To encourage a more balanced work life, employees at Eddie Bauer, the clothing store chain based in Bellevue, WA, are allowed to "call in well" and take time off.

———

HEALTH & WELLNESS TIPS

➡ Pay for gym/health club membership.

➡ Pay a medical bill.

➡ Pay a dental/ orthodontic bill for employee/dependent.

➡ Pay for Lasik eye surgery.

Accounting giant Ernst & Young uses a program that focuses on pre- and postmaternity counseling and support. The firm provides a coach to work with the mother before she leaves to have her baby and talk about what life will be like when the baby comes and how she can manage work and life when she is ready to return. She is also paired with a mentor internally who has been a successful working mother.

———

At Sprint, the telecommunications firm based in Overland Park, KS, sales representatives are eligible for "lifestyle awards." Through the program, a sales representative can submit receipts for personal expenses, and the company can elect to reimburse them.

———

"No one person is more important than anyone else on the team," said co-owner Steve Coombs of Downtown (Spokane, WA) Honda. So, to promote teamwork and build a healthy work culture, he "let go" some of the car dealership's top salespeople. "There are no prima donnas here." The Washington State Psychological Association named Downtown Honda one of the most psychologically healthy workplaces in the state.

———

HR NETworks' annual planning meeting one year was held at a spa. The meeting room was reserved for six hours, with massages scheduled afterward for all eight employees.

———

Since Western Virginia Water Authority started offering wellness programs and financial planning seminars, they report that their voluntary turnover rate has dropped from 8.93 percent in fiscal 2007–2008 to 2.28 percent in fiscal 2009–2010.

At its headquarters in Sugar Land, TX, all employees of Heavy Construction Systems Specialists (HCSS), a Houston, TX–area software developer, are eligible to receive $100 annually for each good result from an annual health screening. "The wellness initiative seems to be a win for both employees and the company," says founder and chief executive Mike Rydin. The company-paid annual health insurance premiums fell to $2,318 per employee in 2008, from $2,950 in 2004. The company credits this to its wellness program and to its introduction of a high-deductible health plan coupled with health-reimbursement accounts—to which the company contributes $1,000 to $3,000 annually for employee and dependent out-of-pocket health expenses.

Censeo Consulting Group, a strategy and operations firm based in Washington, DC, takes an unconventional approach to client work. Most consultants work from home and spend minimal time at client sites. Some even work outside Washington, DC, though many clients are based there. The emphasis on work–life balance has helped the firm recruit many experienced consultants from other firms and top business schools. It also saves clients money, since they traditionally pay for consultants' travel costs.

NetApp, the data storage and software company based in Sunnyvale, CA, treats its employees like family. When marketing director J. P. Gallagher was diagnosed with cancer and took several months off, the company heavily supported him and his family. His wife was pregnant, and employees set up a night nanny and the delivery of dinners to their home for six months. The company held his job and raised $30,000 in his name for the American Cancer Society. NetApp has helped him build a database of gastric-cancer patients around the country and made a significant contribution of equipment to his foundation. "I get a little choked up when I think about it. It just shows you what an amazing place this is," said Gallagher.

> **HEALTH & WELLNESS TIPS**
>
> ➡ Give exercise equipment, resource tools. Pay for massages.
>
> ➡ Arrange a day at the beach (or closest body of water).
>
> ➡ Treat to a day at a spa.
>
> ➡ Pay for pilates/yoga classes.

At Wegmans, the food market chain based in Rochester, NY, employees are regarded as "family members" and encouraged to talk with everyone else in the company, no matter the level or title. Nugget Market, the supermarket chain based in Woodland, CA, also encourages its employees to get to know each other. There are no televisions in break rooms, helping to develop deeper interpersonal relationships. Because socially invested employees earn more at IBM, the technology and consulting firm based in Armonk, NY, started a program to foster interpersonal relationships.

Bruce Power, based in Tiverton, Ontario, offers incentives for employees to use its extensive wellness program, and for exhibiting healthier and personal growth behaviors.

One of the world's largest providers of employee incentives, Maritz, Inc., headquartered near St. Louis, MO, offers a wellness program called Healthy Frontiers for its employees in conjunction with their health care provider, Great-West Healthcare, based in Denver. The program supports two major strategies for the organization: wellness/prevention and education/consumer awareness. The program provides participants with comprehensive information, support tools and tests, and activities via a Web portal. Participants earn points for completing activities, and the points are seamlessly integrated with Maritz's Exclusively Yours points system, to be reimbursed for upscale merchandise and experiences from their 2,000-item catalog. Participants can choose from a variety of six-week programs, each designed to help adopt healthy habits. They can easily track progress on goals via a Web portal, get assistance from a health coach or medical expert, and get online access to registered nurses 24/7. Lab results are sent directly to employees without employer access, helping to ensure privacy and confidentiality for every participant.

Going Green

Companies and employees are also becoming more politically correct and environmentally aware in their use of incentives, as well.

Chicago-based toy products company Radio Flyer, Inc., has an employee-run environmental-issues committee that has held a presentation on global warming and launched a campaign to get employees to reduce their carbon footprints both at home and at work. They also introduced a new benefit where employees get paid 55 cents a mile to ride bikes to work. The workplace efforts extend to Radio Flyer's office in China.

———

GREEN TIPS

➡ Purchase a plant in honor of employee.

➡ Go with employee to a nursery and let them pick out whatever they want (within a predetermined amount).

Genentech, Intuit, Cisco Systems, Dow Chemical, and others offer healthier foods and programs that can also slash environmental waste. As companies expect low-fat or low-calorie menu items to help reduce health care costs, they also are adopting greener policies such as turning cafeteria waste into compost. For example, Cox Enterprises in Atlanta has gone green: Food-service packaging is produced using sustainable, renewable sources. Plates and bowls are made from sugarcane, and cups and salad plates are made from corn—both degrade within 60 days. San Diego State University only uses trans-fat-free oil for cooking—which they recycle to produce biofuel for campus vehicles. They have a food-composting program, and leftover biodegradable food scraps are used for campus landscaping. In one year alone, 50 tons of waste were converted to compost. "Some of the changes were initiated by students and faculty," says Paul Melchior, director of dining services.

———

Dow Chemical, based in Midland, MI, which has a goal of reducing health risks to its employee population by 10 percent by the year 2014, provides healthy foods in cafeterias and vending machines. Dow has about 43,000 employees globally. "This needs to be a company-driven effort," says Karen Tully, global health-promotion leader with Dow. Food choices include fresh fruit, yogurt, baked chips, peanuts, and granola bars in vending areas.

———

SAS in Cary, NC, a provider of business intelligence and software, offers heart-healthy entrees and vegetarian items at each of its three on-site cafés. Break room options are also heart-healthy: free fresh fruit, reduced-fat whole-grain crackers, and nuts. The on-site health care center offers full-time nutritionists who can create personalized eating plans for employees. "It's a growing initiative," says Julie Steward, SAS food-service manager. "We got more comments on the healthy food initiative than we've gotten on any other initiative we've done."

———

Businesses that provide food services to employers also say there is a significant demand for sustainable foods and healthier options. Bon Appetite Management in Palo Alto, CA, provides food services for such companies as eBay, Yahoo, Best Buy, and Oracle. They use organic, local, and sustainable food, with programs that include direct purchasing from small local farmers and a healthy options program with vegan and whole-grain items.

———

Charity/Giving/Community Service

The final category of the latest incentive trends is the increased use of charity incentives and the support of employees for community service. Following are examples of this category.

At McCormick & Company, Inc., a manufacturer of seasonings, spices, and frozen foods based in Baltimore, MD, employees are encouraged to work on one "Charity Day" Saturday every year. Employees donate their pay for the day at time and a half to a charity. More than 90 percent of employees participate!

———

Ford Motor Company in Dearborn, MI, encourages employees to participate in various activities held locally during National Breast Cancer Awareness Month and Race for the Cure runs/walks. Employees sign up their own sponsors, who write checks directly to the charities involved.

———

At Decision Analyst of Arlington, TX, the 200 employees choose a family to adopt for Thanksgiving and bring food to be delivered to the family for the holiday.

———

Robert W. Baird, a financial services company based in Milwaukee, recently introduced a new program that allows associates to take one paid day per year to perform volunteer service. In addition, many of its departments and branches organize food drives and holiday gift-giving events and support fund-raising walks for local charitable organizations.

———

Kaiser Permanente's corporate offices in Oakland, CA, join together for a team-building activity every December. This type of fun activity pulls people together and the final product is auctioned off for charity.

———

Texas Utilities Company encourages its 13,000 employees to participate in charitable activities and gives time off for employees to volunteer for charities of their choice.

———

Tom Thumb, the supermarket chain based in Houston, TX, encourages each store to select a local family in need of assistance and matches whatever funds employees raise.

———

For $5, employees of participating divisions of Lee Company, apparel makers headquartered in Merriam, KS, can "buy" the right to wear jeans to work; all proceeds go to the Komen Foundation.

———

D.D.B. Needham Worldwide, a New York–based advertising agency, gives all employees a day or an afternoon off the job to work with a charity or homeless shelter of their choice or to clean up a local park. This activity is often combined with an open house at the company for the supported charities to share what they do for the community with all employees.

———

At The Thomson Corporation, publisher of the *Canadian HR Reporter*, employees are nominated and the winning employees choose a cause to which the company donates cash.

———

When employees of Heartland Dental Care in Effingham, IL, bring in 10 percent over its sales goal, if the entire dental office agrees, earned proceeds from the office can be donated to a charity of the employees' choice.

———

CHARITY & SERVICE TIPS

➜ Schedule a charity activity with any off-site meeting.

➜ Hold a Habitat-for-Humanity Day or Week.

➜ Sponsor/Participate in a charity event.

➜ Have a food/toy drive for a charity of the employee's choice.

➜ Start an "Emergency Time-Off Bank" pool for employees.

Four Seasons Flower Shop in Poway, CA, uses a "Good Neighbor Day" in which on a given day the store distributes a dozen free roses to anyone who comes into the shop, on the condition that the person keep one of the roses and pass the rest of the bunch on to someone else, instructing the next person to do the same. Barbara Bertran, the store's owner, obtained the support of several other local businesses to sponsor this event, in which they distributed some 10,000 medium-stemmed roses.

———

The Austin (MN) Medical Center changed its employee rewards program to "Chamber Bucks," a move that put thousands of dollars back into the community. The rewards program issues monetary amounts for workers who are recognized for several things, including years of service, birthdays, outstanding service, and going above and beyond. Chamber Bucks are used the same way regular money is used, but they can only be used at one of the 350+ businesses that are members of Austin's chamber of commerce. "The changes reflect our commitment to the community and to providing better value to staff receiving recognition," says Rod Nordeng, vice president of organizational support. "The feedback has been positive, which is a good thing for staff and patients alike."

___

First Commonwealth Corp., based in Indiana, PA, operates branches in several western Pennsylvania counties and prides itself on being a community bank. When Jeanine Fallon, senior vice president, received the company's prestigious Golden Tower Award, she was cited for her service to the community, including the Dress for Success program, which helps disadvantaged women in the region gain and retain meaningful jobs. "I was so honored. It says a lot about the company that they are concerned about the community," says Fallon. "We are a community bank, and we're really showing our true colors."

___

Traditional awards and awards programs can also be effective—with or without added perks. At Atlantic Richfield Company (ARCO), annual community service awards are given to employees who have made outstanding contributions in the community, plus the company matches on a two-for-one basis any employee or retiree donation to a social service organization or college.

___

When Texas Roadhouse held its 12th annual "managing partners" conference in New York, attendees also spent time stuffing 10,000 gift bags with cookies and iTunes cards for soldiers abroad, served meals to the homeless at a local church, and painted ceiling tiles for children's hospitals across the U.S.

___

The soft drink company PepsiCo, based in Purchase, NY, encourages associates to get outside by offering them plots of land to start organic gardens and luring them on head-clearing walks with lush outdoor grounds. Patagonia, the outdoor apparel store headquartered in Ventura, CA, sent a manager to Patagonia, a vast area spanning Chile and Argentina, to work for three weeks as part of its efforts to help set up a 173,000-acre national park.

_____

Intuit Inc., a Mountain View, CA, tax and financial software provider, lets employees use their recognition awards to make charitable donations to organizations such as the International Red Cross. Graham Co., an insurance broker in Philadelphia, PA, allows employees to take time off to volunteer. Bellevue, WA, accounting firm Clark Nuber launched "Caring, Serving and Giving," a program that lets employees apply for grants of up to $500 to fund community service projects.

_____

Bath and body products company Thymes, based in Minneapolis, helps employees lead enriching lives by offering them volunteer opportunities. The organization has an employee volunteer committee—who are paid for up to eight hours a year—that helps nonprofits such as Art Buddies and the United Way. At Coles Salon, also in the Minneapolis area, employees walk for breast cancer or give proceeds from haircuts to support the Ronald McDonald House. Employees of Securian Financial, the financial services firm based in St. Paul, MN, spent a day packing supplies and delivering backpacks to a school full of disadvantaged kids.

_____

SEVEN IMPORTANT LESSONS IN MOTIVATING EMPLOYEES

1. YOU GET WHAT YOU REWARD. *Be sure you have clearly defined what you want to get, then use rewards and recognition to move toward those goals.*

2. WHAT MOTIVATES PEOPLE, MOTIVATES PEOPLE. *What is motivating to individuals varies from person to person. To be on target, ask employees what they want.*

3. THE MOST MOTIVATING REWARDS TAKE LITTLE OR NO MONEY. *Try a sincere thank you, providing information, involvement in decision making—especially as it affects your employees.*

4. EVERYONE WANTS TO BE APPRECIATED. *Competent people, quiet people, even managers want to know that what they are doing is important and meaningful.*

5. ALL BEHAVIOR IS CONTROLLED BY ITS CONSEQUENCES. *Positive consequences will most quickly lead to desired behavior and enhanced performance.*

6. MANAGEMENT IS WHAT YOU DO WITH PEOPLE, NOT TO THEM. *Tell employees what you want to do and why. By involving them, you'll more easily gain their commitment and support.*

7. COMMON SENSE IS OFTEN NOT COMMON PRACTICE. *It's not what you believe or say—it's what you do. Practice recognizing people and their achievements on a daily basis.*

Employees of Pfizer, the pharmaceutical giant based in New York, convinced company leadership to make Pfizer medications free to all former U.S. employees who had been laid off. The program, MAINTAIN, had a big morale-boosting effect within the organization. Employees donated their own money to the program, with the Pfizer Foundation matching all employee donations.

Summary

What is the best way to motivate employees in challenging times? Surveys, studies, and discussions with employees from all walks of life in all industries have revealed a very simple formula for successfully rewarding employees: Treat your employees with respect, pay them fairly, and recognize and reward them when they do good work.

Although money is a motivator, it is not the only one, and it does have its limitations. Often, simple, creative, no-cost ways to show your appreciation in a timely way can have a greater impact on your employees in making them feel special and motivating them to rise to the occasion in difficult times. *If you don't recognize performance when it happens, you won't get the results you most want.*

Praise is important to today's employees and comes in several forms: personal, written, electronic, and public. You should recognize employees for small accomplishments, as well as the big ones when those occur. You should also recognize both individual and group accomplishments.

Once you've applied the principles and ideas discussed in this overview, you will be well on your way to shaping a more motivating workplace. If you keep at it, you will soon have employees who are dedicated to your (and their) success, and a work environment in which people are excited about their jobs, enjoy their coworkers, and want to do the best work possible each and every day. Not only will this give your organization a competitive advantage, it will also make you proud to be a leader in a culture of recognition. You will have created the kind of work environment we all dream of—an environment that puts people first, and rewards and recognizes their contributions to their customers, coworkers, and organizations. Your job, however, will not be done. To sustain the results you obtain, you will need to keep at the changes and challenges over time. Motivation is a moving target and requires an ongoing community.

FIVE TRENDS AFFECTING TODAY'S WORKFORCE

Every business will increasingly be confronted by a daunting array of challenges when it comes to attracting, motivating, and retaining its workers. In the aftermath of historical highs in unemployment, there is supposed to be an abundance of talent—yet attracting the best people has become more difficult than ever. Additionally, some 84 percent of current employees report that they plan to change jobs in the upcoming year, according to a recent *CNN Money* report.

A proliferation of new social networking and database technologies is transforming the way people look for work. As important, technology has changed the way companies look for, hire, and manage its workers, as well. And a new generation of independent, transient, and globalized workers in the burgeoning knowledge economy is creating new rules around hiring and the engagement of workers.

Although most every company claims that "people are

its most important asset," there is increasing pressure to live up to that slogan and better align workers with key strategic drivers of business performance. Measurement of performance in organizations is shifting and becoming more demanding, requiring all employees to demonstrate their contribution to corporate goals, not just their functional output.

This section examines the metatrends that are shaping the new workforce, and provides insight into how managing employees is being severely stressed to meet the needs of business and commerce in the 21st century. These key work trends are imperatives management must address worldwide. This is not simply a short-term cycle but part of a longer-term trend that is shaping the fundamental way that people think about work and interact with their employers and each other.

Trend #1: Attracting & Retaining Talent: The Growing Shortage of Skilled Workers

Recent events have brought national economies shuddering to a halt, and, with that, a sudden shift in the critical labor shortages that had plagued developed economies for more than a decade. With millions of workers having lost their jobs in recent years, the basic rule of numbers would suggest that the labor supply should be plentiful. And while it is true that unemployment levels in many countries remain historically high, the issue facing most businesses is an increasingly critical shortage of talent—individuals who bring to an organization education and occupational skills that can make an immediate and lasting impact.

As economic growth gathers pace, shortages in certain industries appear almost as acute as before the recent economic collapse. In some areas of health care, science, and IT, the talent shortage never actually disappeared, and those remain highly challenging environments for hiring, motivating, and retaining key talent.

We are entering a phase in the demographic cycle that will be characterized by chronic talent shortages in certain sectors over the long term, as part of a longer-term trend dictated by population cycles. Population growth in major economies is below replacement rates, meaning there will be increasingly fewer people of traditional working age, relative to the older population. The total fertility rate (TFR) is a measure of the number of births per woman in the population and serves as a proxy for population growth. A rate of 2.3 children per woman is generally considered the replacement rate in developing countries, while 2.1 is the rate in developed economies. Above this rate, population is increasing, and below, it is generally falling.

Fertility rates are in sharp decline in the vast majority of industrialized countries, while they are growing significantly in many underdeveloped countries. Unfortunately, many of the countries with fast-growing populations do not have the educational infrastructure to develop a level of skilled labor that can be readily substituted for the shortfall in industrialized countries. This results in a paradox: Economies may see record unemployment while at the same time recognizing a global shortage of talent. This paradox may be more or less pronounced depending on the specific employment sector, but it is an inevitable emerging trend.

The trend is marked and becoming more acute at a time when workplaces are demanding higher levels of skill and knowledge. So while economic conditions may ease the unemployment rate, that will not provide a reprieve to the long-run trend of a diminishing supply of skilled labor.

This is the new operation reality for businesses of all types and sizes. The best-educated and skilled technical and professional employees will be in greater demand, harder to find, and harder to keep, and will command a premium to switch or relocate to new jobs.

Just as entire countries modify their national immigration policies to counter this trend, companies seeking highly skilled talent will need to consider strategies that will enable them to circumvent this demand-supply impasse. Of all the forces that are converging on business, few will be as daunting as this demographic shift, simply because it is virtually locked in for at least the next 30 years.

Implications for Managing and Motivating Workers

To meet this shortage of skilled workers, companies will need to get more creative in hiring and motivating workers. For example, a greater percentage of part-time employees will be used to tap into the new demographics of hiring more single-parent workers, retirees, and students. Tata Motors in India, for example, makes a targeted recruitment focus on ex-military employees and single-parent mothers—both of whom they have found to be reliable workers who possess skills they need in their organization. The company also has built relationships with technical education institutions, recruiting students as interns or in work/study programs in which the students alternate attending school and working in successive quarters, which typically leads to permanent hiring upon graduation.

More than 18 million people choose to work part-time, according to the U.S. Bureau of Labor Statistics. About 61 percent of these part-timers have some college education. Women represent two thirds of the part-time workforce, which they increasingly seek in their prime earning years to balance work and family responsibilities. "Professional moms would be thrilled to lower their hours to spend more time with their children, and they don't mind giving up benefits to achieve that work/life balance," reports Alison Doyle, an About.com job search and employment subject matter expert. "Other part-time labor sources include near-retirees and older workers who don't want to retire or are unable to retire but don't want to commit to full-time positions." And in a study by Corporate Voices for Working Families, a Washington, DC–based research firm, researchers found that engagement was 55 percent higher for hourly workers with flexibility than for those without, while turnover was half.

Likewise, companies and each of their managers must become better skilled at keeping employees—especially those with prerequisite skills and experience. Changes will need to be made to prevent treating nontraditional workers (for example, part-timers, Millennials, and contingent workers) as second-class citizens, and rather to embrace their alternative perspectives on motivation and work.

In another example, the use of volunteers in the organization can be better harnessed as well. Vern Lake, a volunteer services consultant with the Minnesota Department of Public Welfare, shares ways they have helped volunteers enjoy what they do even more—and more often:

- Provide them with the best possible preservice training.

- See volunteers as working partners with paid staff.
- Invite them to attend staff meetings.
- Offer them advocacy roles.
- Utilize them as consultants.
- Be familiar with their assignments.
- Arrange for them to get discounts on the organization's products and services.
- Put up a suggestion box for volunteers only.
- Send newsworthy information (include their accomplishments) to the media.
- Commend people to supervisory staff.
- Tell the volunteers' friends about their accomplishments.
- Recommend them to prospective employers.
- Invite them to quarterly social mixers attended by top management.
- Add them to your holiday card list.

Trend #2: They're Special!
The Millennials Are Changing the Rules at Work

Millennials, the youngest generation of workers, born roughly between the mid-1970s and 2000, are entering the workforce in droves. An estimated 44 million are already working, and 46 million more are to become a part of the workforce in the upcoming years ahead. This generation will come to dominate the workforce in both number and attitude, and in the process reshape the work experience that all employees will come to have. What is important to this generation, and how can employers best tap into the potential they have to offer at work? Given that 75 percent of this generation say they plan to find a new job as the economy improves, it is worth taking a closer look at how you can best attract, motivate, and retain them in your organization today.

The influx of the Millennials into the workforce is changing many of the ground rules that prevailed for the previous generations. They have entered the workforce with different attitudes, expectations, and ambitions. There are identifiable traits and attitudes that range across issues of job selection, tenure, work–life balance, remuneration, promotion, and not least, the use of technology. The Millennials are the first truly globalized generation of workers. They have grown up with technologies that have shrunk the workplace, expanded their horizons, and made them feel comfortable operating in a borderless world. For them, the digital workplace means dealing with colleagues from different cultures in different time zones.

Whereas the previous generations have the greatest direct experience in the global business environment, the Millennials are becoming the driving force for change. They see global experience as a positive differentiator in job selection and promotion.

For the Millennials, the lines between work and personal life are blurred. They are the first generation that's been raised in a 24/7 environment. The communications revolution has made that possible, and the Millennials don't view it as a burden.

Issues around work–life balance become important because in an environment where work and social life are ill-defined, there needs to be some level of compromise. The workplace itself is evolving to meet some of these requirements. For the Millennials, the workplace is not solely about work—it is a place for social interaction and shared learning and meaning and purpose in their lives. Workplace culture, relationship building, and ongoing learning are thus critical to these individuals.

The Millennials are also bringing new approaches to the issue of ethics, the environment, and social responsibility in the workplace. They are more likely to want to work for firms that have a good reputation for ethical and environmental performance, and they are ready to tell others when their employer is doing well or doing poorly. They are acutely sensitive to the changing fortunes of brands and the way in which social, ethical, and cultural influences can enhance or destroy corporate reputation.

The issues of career paths, responsibility, and promotion frequently arise in regard to Millennials. Some people say they are overly ambitious, even impatient. What is apparent is a significant focus on making the most of opportunities and advancing one's career. This can affect decisions concerning job stability and tenure.

The task of recruiting and managing these latest entrants to the workplace can seem bewildering, especially for those whose approaches are based on old notions of command and control. The benefits of diversity in the workplace are well documented, and the Millennials bring a rich opportunity to challenge established notions, refresh practices, and tap into new thinking, technologies, and attitudes.

Understanding the varying needs of the different generations—everything from communication style to management techniques to organizational structures—becomes important if everyone's needs are to be met. When generational differences are better understood, there is a better chance of creating a high-performing workplace in which everyone works better together to achieve common objectives.

Employers worldwide are adapting to these behaviors and striving to get the best out of this diversity that characterizes the modern workplace. Critical to recruiting and motivating this generation is an understanding of their social and cultural drivers, something that is beyond many organizations today. Additionally, once employees are hired, a renewed focus on employee engagement must be put in place.

Profile of the Millennials

Known by a variety of names (Gen Y, the Nintendo Generation, the Microwave Generation, Generation Next, the Net Generation, Generation Why, the Echo Boomers, and the Trophy Generation), the young people of this generation are well educated, and they have high aspirations for themselves and their careers and a lofty sense that who they are and what they do matters. They love all things high-tech, have and expect instant connections, and are highly optimistic and socially responsible. The Millennials bring some tremendous skills and attributes to the workplace, which can at times be offset by perceived negatives of their generation.

UPSIDES

Millennials are techno wizards, not only at complete ease with today's technology, but avid users more so than any generation to come before them. They are quick learners and very resourceful—quick to look for answers from whomever and wherever those can be found. They are optimistic, hardworking, and high achieving, systematically setting and then achieving goals in rapid sequence. While these characteristics can be found in high achievers of any age or in any generation, they are common elements found in the majority of Millennials,

HIGH-TECH TIPS

➡ Join and use the social networks they use.

➡ Find ways for them to use the latest technologies.

➡ Ask them to teach you to use the technologies.

not just a select few, and, better yet, these attributes all happen to be ideal characteristics that most every employer needs from its employees in order to be competitive today.

DOWNSIDES

The challenges of working with Millennials are: They tend to have an inflated opinion of themselves and are overconfident, especially given their limited work experience. They expect to have meaning and purpose in their jobs from the very first day of work and look to be challenged—some might say entertained—constantly. They want to earn more sooner and to have both job status and respect, even before either has been earned. They need and demand instant feedback and praise on an ongoing, daily basis. Other generations tend to react negatively to these attributes, feeling that Millennials are a generation of spoiled youth that need to wake up to the realities of work in which everything does not revolve around them. They need to "pay their dues" and earn the respect of their colleagues and management before they are trusted with greater responsibility. However, if managers can look past Millennials' limitations and shortcomings, they will have an easier time tapping into the vast potential this generation has to offer.

Reframing Expectations

This generation feels very entitled and expects more from its employers. Again, Millennials have been raised to believe they are very special; a generation that has been told they can achieve anything. They have big dreams and plans and are in a hurry to achieve those. These are positive attributes, but they need to be channeled—and that's the job of their managers (like it or not).

I'm not talking about abdicating your role as a manager. Or about letting them do whatever they want. I'm talking about connecting their values and skill set to the work that you need them to do.

Everybody wants everyone else to be just like them: to value what they value, to act like they act, and to conform to their norms. Just as easy to accept is the notion that we can allow people to be who they are, i.e., different from one another, but still keep a clear focus on the performance that is needed to get the work done. As is the case for the perceived differences in this generation's work ethic, if you give younger employees a reason to get excited, they will and do show an extraordinary work ethic and passion to get the work done—and to have fun in the process. Keep the focus on the work and not on things that may not matter anyway, e.g., dress, informality, working hours, communication preferences, and so on.

In my research, work's most motivating aspects to employees in general—and especially for this generation—are things that don't cost much, if any, money. Taking time to get to know them, asking their opinions, involving them in decisions (especially those that affect them and their work), creating socializing opportunities at work, focusing on learning and development opportunities—these are the motivational opportunities that any manager can deploy.

Young Employees: An Invaluable Resource

Scott Cook, founder of Intuit, lives by the notion that the newest and youngest employees are often the most valuable when it comes time to make changes and inject fresh ideas. He makes an effort to spend time with them, and believes that he can learn from them, whereas the common perception is that it is senior management who usually ought to serve as mentors for more junior employees. His approach, Cook has found, ignites the creative process and makes employees feel more valued.

This practice at Intuit has been so successful because Cook doesn't just solicit ideas from younger employees. For example, rather than take accepted proposals and assign them to more senior managers, Cook lets the employees who introduced the concept take the project and run with it. Not only does this put less-visible employees at the head of very visible projects, it encourages innovative thinking and shows that the company truly values input from all employees, no matter their rank.

Motivating the Millennials

The keys to motivating this generation can be found in harnessing these aspects of the work relationship: Managerial Time, Work Direction, Personal Development, Social Interaction, Feedback and Praise, and Meaningful Rewards.

MANAGERIAL TIME

In studies of the younger generation, one of the consistently most motivating variables was "time with one's manager." Managers need to make special efforts both to be available and to actually connect with younger employees on a more frequent basis at work. For example:

In some organizations, managers are expected to have one-on-one discussions with their direct reports at least once every two weeks, in which employees set the agenda of questions they need answered, items they want to discuss, or advice they need from their manager.

- Larry Meadows of the Asheville Mall Chick-fil-A restaurant in Asheville, NC, makes a special point to call individuals into his office on a regular basis to discuss how things are going and hear their concerns.
- At Genentech, the San Francisco–based founder of the biotechnology industry, scientists have access to top managers.
- New hires at ViaSat, the satellite communications company based in Carlsbad, CA, are free to approach upper management with questions or to contribute new ideas. The door to executive leaders is always open.

WORK DIRECTION

Millennials want and expect to be constantly excited about how they are spending their time at work. They are consummate multitaskers, very capable of managing a multitude of activities at once. Easily bored, they want and need to be challenged, which is a blessing for managers who want to take advantage of their energy, skills, and resourcefulness.

Provide clear work expectations, but allow Millennials to bring their own imprint to their jobs. Show them the "big picture" as to how their jobs relate to the mission, strategic objectives, and core values of the organization. Ask for and use their ideas as much as possible, or encourage them to pursue their own ideas when those have merit. This generation is very socially conscious, so linking them as directly as possible to the mission of your nonprofit organization would have a strong impact; likewise for volunteering. For example, if the

MULTITASKING TIPS

➡ Give them more than one assignment/project at a time.

➡ Challenge them to find a better way.

➡ Give them many opportunities to play at work.

organization is Meals on Wheels, let the Millennial go on home visits to see directly who the organization is helping and hear their appreciation, or task them with helping to increase the organization's online presence to expand the reach of its mission.

PERSONAL DEVELOPMENT

Millennials expect constant learning and personal development and growth, and their manager can easily serve as a coach and mentor to them. Talk in terms of "development opportunities" and in long-term time frames that exceed any given task or assignment. If you shape the context for your relationship with Millennials as extending years into the future in regard to how you will help them grow and gain experience, they will be more likely not to look to change jobs at the first sign of frustration or disappointment.

Millennials' managers need to take the time to help coach Millennial employees and in the process show them how they can make a positive, meaningful impact at work. Redefine the time frame for this generation's focus and show them how the things they are doing now can lead to things they want to be doing later. Talk with them about their interests and the ways they can apply their skills; talk about career paths and needs of the organization; discuss opportunities that they can pursue, and help them prepare to meet future opportunities.

SOCIAL INTERACTION

Millennials are very social and perhaps more peer group–oriented than previous generations. Most of their upbringing and educational experiences were in groups, as was the bulk of their social experience, be it playing interactive video games, group sports, or connecting on Facebook with their friends.

Use these generational preferences to your advantage by allowing them to work together on projects and assignments, and set up frequent nonwork social situations such as team-building activities and celebrations. If they tend to work best with others, and the way they get into a project is to talk it through with coworkers—great, let them do that. Make clear what you need the end result to be, but let them bring the imprint of who they are to the task so they can be excited about the work and even have fun getting it done. You may not need your job to be fun to get it done, but don't fault them if that's their preference.

FEEDBACK & PRAISE

One of the most defining characteristics of this generation is its significant need for constant praise at work. This can be frustrating for other generations to understand (as in "I just told him last week that he was doing a good job, do I really have to tell him again?") and easy to dismiss as being a symptom of a generation whose parents spoiled them, showering them with constant praise and protecting them from any of the harsh realities of life. Instead, consider this perspective:

The Millennials have learned that in times of change one needs a constant source of feedback (think "video game") to be on the mark and to adjust their performance accordingly. Since job requirements and expectations are constantly in flux, yesterday's feedback may no longer be relevant today. Constant feedback, thus, is not to pump up a frail ego as much as to assure employees that they are on track to continue to do good work day after day for their employer. Feedback and praise serve as reinforcement as well as a corrective mechanism for this generation.

By this I don't mean "micromanaging," a negative term that is almost always associated with an ongoing stream of negative feedback and corrections that a manager makes in working with employees. No one feels micromanaged when the boss tells them in explicit detail what he or she most liked about a great job the employee did. As such, I'd recommend making it a high priority to provide greater and more frequent praise and recognition in a greater variety of forms. Equally important, but far less often (quarterly?), would be having "developmental discussions" in which you can focus on ways the employee can improve. When you build on a strong foundation of ongoing positive feedback, employees are more likely to trust that you are on their side and thus be willing to accept constructive criticism from you when it is offered.

FREQUENT FEEDBACK TIPS

➡ Frequently catch them doing things right.

➡ Praise them early and often for their contribution and repeat how valuable it is.

➡ When necessary, redirect them in a supportive manner, without reprimanding.

➡ Ask them questions and listen to their answers.

Provide frequent feedback based on the performance of Millennials, which might be a new perspective for many of them who grew up getting trophies even when their team lost or all *A*s as a result of rampant grade inflation in schools. Provide a context for how their contributions relate to team and organizational goals, to the organization's customers, and even to society. This systematic framing of feedback and praise takes it from being unearned hype to a practical information stream that can help shape desired behaviors and results you need from them.

Finally, be authentic, providing direct and honest feedback and evaluations that can best help the Millennial to excel—and to trust you, his or her manager, all the more in the process.

MEANINGFUL REWARDS

Millennials want rewards that are meaningful and exciting to them when they have done good work or an outstanding job. This includes financial incentives, and, of course, EVERYONE wants to make more money, not just the Millennials. Millennials, however, may have the least realistic expectations as to what is needed to earn more money (especially if their role model is P. Diddy, Lindsay Lohan, or A-Rod), and that's where you can help them out. Show them the skills they need to learn and the contribution they need to make in order to make more money, and show them the path that will get them there working for you in your organization.

This translates into discussions in which a manager needs to state things like: "I can't just pay you more because you want to make more. I can pay you more when you have increased your contribution to the organization to a level that warrants earning more. Let's talk specifically about what that would look like." Then you can channel the person's energy into things he or she can directly impact, such as implementing a cost-savings idea, or delighting an important customer, or helping to streamline a process, or helping to bring in a new account, and so on. Of course, there will probably be limits as to what they could ever be paid by your organization, in which case you can focus on skills you are helping them develop that they can use over their entire career or to one day run their own business.

When this generation is acknowledged for doing good work, they have expectations that the reward experience will be fun and exciting, not the same old boring thing the company has done for years. They increasingly expect rewards that are creative, varied, and personalized. *Creative* in that the rewards are fun and unique—not the same certificate, plaque, or trophy that has been passed out to employees for years. *Varied* in that the employee has a choice and a say in what they can get when they are rewarded for doing a good job. The days of one size fitting all are long gone when it comes to employee motivation. What thrills and delights one employee may be boring and insulting to another. Avoid this problem by allowing employees to choose what best motivates them—be it the latest electronic merchandise, an experience, or a charity donation—when they have the opportunity to be thanked for having done a great job. *Personalized* in that the reward needs to be tailored to their unique interests, which can be a hobby, travel, or a life experience.

Millennials Examples

Junior employees at Hitachi in Portland, OR, get 300 hours of training a year on average.

———

The law firm of Kelley, Kronenberg, Gilmartin, Fichtel, Wander, Bamdas, Eskalyo and Dunbrack in Miami, FL, values collaboration and promotes an open-door policy for younger associates to chat with more seasoned attorneys.

———

SAS, the world's largest privately held software business, based in Raleigh, NC, allows employees to come to work at any time in the morning as long as they get their work done. The typical week is 35 hours and many employees set their own schedules. "What we don't do is treat our employees like they're all, you know, criminals," says Jenn Mann, vice president of Human Resources.

At the Microsoft office in Portland, OR, employees can work in their pajamas.

———

Social networking giant Facebook, based in Palo Alto, CA, is known for its open culture and lack of enclosed work spaces, walls, or cubicles. Neither the COO nor the CEO has an office.

———

At Zubi Advertising, headquartered in Miami, manager Michelle Zubizarreta gives younger staffers a seat at the table. She asks them how they would talk to young consumers for a business pitch. Another initiative is the creation of innovation groups, setting up teams to develop ad-related iPhone apps and other original ideas.

———

Chicago-based insurance company Assurance Agency has many initiatives to motivate Millennial employees. Since many of these employees have no insurance background, 75 percent participate in continuing education. Employees get $100 when they pass a class. Fun programs include the Assurance Casino: Employees get a chip when they meet goals, increasing their chances for winning cash prizes. There is also an Employee Appreciation Day and an Assurance 5K run. Instead of using a suggestion box, the agency created Ivan Idea, a mascot shaped like a lightbulb, to collect ideas from employees. Employees get $5 for every business improvement idea they submit. The best idea wins a $250 gift card.

———

PROVIDE JOB-SHADOWING OPPORTUNITIES

Job shadowing, essentially, is offering employees experiential, hands-on learning opportunities. Shadowing affords a current or prospective employee the chance to be immersed in the actual job environment, making it possible to see an experienced worker apply the skills and traits needed to accomplish the work. An insightful observer can glean information about the personal characteristics that contribute to success in the position.

Some employers prefer to orient new employees before involving them in job shadowing to build on the new employee's existing knowledge of the company. Post-orientation job shadowing can reinforce loyalty, strengthen the orientation or "onboarding" process and subsequent training processes, and shorten the time it takes a new hire to get up to speed. Pamela Genske, Human Resources director for Blue Cross & Blue Shield of Rhode Island, says her firm's employees learn about shadowing opportunities in orientation and can ask for a shadowing assignment any time after joining the company. "People remember what happens in situations they've been placed in much more effectively than they recall a theory they've been taught in a classroom," says Genske. The Indiana Department of Corrections and the YMCA are other organizations that offer job shadowing.

O regon Cascade Plumbing and Heating, based in Salem, OR, regularly hosts contests, and awards a Kermit the Frog statue to whomever has the best-decorated office or the ugliest shirt.

———

D efense contractor Lockheed Martin in Fort Worth, TX, reached thousands of students and potential new hires during National Engineers Week in February through various

hands-on projects and presentations that showed how
engineering impacts everyday life.

———

Chicago-based Total Attorneys, a process-improvement firm
that helps small law offices and solo practitioners streamline
their practices, does its best to give Millennial employees a sense
of ownership and belonging. CEO Edmund Scanlan has lunch
with every new employee, where he tells them they have freedom
to do what they want—for example, decorating their office in
unique ways or checking their Facebook pages. Employees enjoy
an on-site gym, a TV room, and beer-and-wine Fridays. They can
also attend corporate events that the company hosts.

———

The Peace Corps and the U.S. State Department offer
opportunities to learn a foreign language and live and work
overseas.

———

Google, based in Mountain View, CA, has a policy that
requires each new office to have a tenured Googler as one
of its first ten employees in order to ensure that the culture is
passed along from veterans to rookies. The company has also
developed "Culture Clubs," made up of volunteers who help
maintain the culture. And in an attempt to attract top human
resource professionals to Google, the company introduced
the HR Rotational Associate Development program for recent
college graduates. Every year, 10 to 15 undergraduates, many of
whom were Google interns, complete three 9-month rotations
in a distinct area of People Operations: Analyst, Generalist, and

Specialist. Career development is another component of the program meant to help associates advance in the company.

Investment firm Morningstar, based in Chicago, sends its entry-level employees through a two-year rotational process called the Morningstar Development Program. The new employees learn the business and where they fit into it. They stay in one role for one year and can then move to different roles to learn skills in other areas. The firm also gives its Millennial employees relatively high levels of responsibility.

At travel company Orbitz Worldwide, free time is valued just as much as work time. Within the first four years in the company, employees get 12 vacation days, 5 floating holidays, 10 regular holidays, and numerous sick hours. They also get two volunteer days, a free flight, and a free hotel night.

Euro RSCG, the Chicago-based marketing and advertising agency, offers outreach and community programs, extensive training, lunch-and-learn sessions and art-making events, and a Ping-Pong table to its workforce. Millennial employees have access to senior employees, and the CEO regularly sends e-mails and letters to keep them abreast of the agency's operations.

According to Jeff Ellman, Homescout Realty cofounder and managing broker, the Chicago-based agency was built around Millennials. "I care more about culture than anything," says Ellman. "We won't hire someone if they don't fit. We have a culture-based interview based on the 5 Fs: Fit, Family, Fun,

Fortune, and Freedom. If you don't fit in our culture, this won't be the right fit for you."

———

FactSet, a software company based in Connecticut, sends new hires who are college seniors a gift basket and a "good luck" note before they take their final exams.

———

Marriott Hotels offers a "Teamwork-Innovations" program for employees to improve efficiency by working together and scheduling their own hours.

———

Kimley-Horn and Associates, an engineering firm in North Carolina, holds regular lunchtime forums for employees to network, share advice, and plan social get-togethers.

—

 Scottrade, a firm based in St. Louis, MO, has implemented a peer recognition program, Above and Beyond, that provides rewards such as jewelry and iPods.

———

Umpqua Bank in Oregon has outfitted its branches with cafés and couches and often provides recreational activities in the office for its employees.

———

Intuit has a Rotational Development Program for new hires to switch between finance, marketing, and product development every 6 to 12 months.

———

Accounting firm Deloitte and Touche makes new recruits immediately eligible for its "Future Leaders Apprentice Program."

———

L'Oreal USA created the "L'Oreal Brandstorm Competition" for college students to play the role of a L'Oreal brand manager; they helped develop marketing and advertising campaigns. Winners received a trip to Paris to interact with top L'Oreal managers.

———

Trend #3: Everyone's His/Her Own Boss: The Rise of the Contingent Worker

One of the most important workforce trends of the past two decades has been the rise of a new breed of contingent workers—consultants, freelancers, contractors, "micropreneurs," and temporary, "permanent" temporary, and part-time employees. Many of them are professionals who have been dislodged from salaried careers as a consequence of business restructuring and economic upheaval. Instead of waiting for new opportunities to come to them, they have started up their own businesses, providing services to clients on a project-by-project basis.

According to the 2010 U.S. Department of Labor, Bureau of Labor Statistics, contingent workers comprise four categories of workers:

1. Independent contractors, who make up the largest of the four alternative work arrangements with 10.3 million workers, 36 percent of whom have at least a bachelor's degree, and were more than likely to be in management, business, and financial operations; sales and related occupations; and construction and extraction occupations.

2. On-call workers make up the second largest group of workers employed in alternative arrangements with 2.5 million workers; they tend to be younger employees with less than a high school diploma, working primarily in construction, education, and health services. About 44 percent of on-call workers work part-time, a much higher proportion than either traditional workers or workers in other alternative arrangements.

3. Temporary help agency workers represent about 1.2 million workers who are likely to be women, young, and black, Hispanic, or Latino. These workers are more likely to hold office and administrative support and production, transportation, and material moving jobs, and are often employed in the manufacturing and professional and business services industries.

4. Workers provided by contract companies make up the fourth and smallest category of contingent workers; 70 percent are men working at the customer's worksite in professional, service, and construction and extraction occupations, most frequently employed in the construction industry and public administration.

In the United States alone, there are over 10 million self-employed individuals, and almost 22 million nonemployer firms, or businesses with no payroll. Christopher Dwyer, an analyst for Aberdeen Group, says contingent workers make up 20 percent of the labor force and will likely increase to 25 percent shortly. It is now estimated that 57 percent of all work being done in organizations is by nonemployees. These workers are operating across a vast range of industries, with the greatest numbers in the services sector. Traditionally, staffing firms found jobs for office, clerical, and industrial workers, but today engineers, lawyers, drug researchers, and even senior executives make up the contingent labor force.

Those who describe themselves as self-employed are a rising share of the workforce in many industrialized economies. They have redefined the orthodoxy of lifelong employment to one of lifelong employability. "Contract or freelance work can bolster job security by severing workers' ties to the fortunes of one company," says Steve Armstrong, general manager of U.S. operations for staffing firm Kelly Services.

There are relatively few people in today's labor market who can honestly say that they have job security or, in some cases, employer loyalty—certainly not in the same sense as applied in earlier eras. Now the emphasis is on attaining the skills that will allow for lifelong learning as a pathway to long-term employability.

As more people go solo, they need to become more flexible, entrepreneurial, and responsive to the needs of the market. They take on personal responsibility for updating their skills and staying relevant. They do not operate under the security of permanent employment and thus need to think afresh about the skill sets that will sustain them for the long haul. They need to always have an eye on the next project and the next employer, even as they are immersed in a current project; networking becomes a lifeline,

INDEPENDENT CONTRACTOR TIPS

➡ Treat them like employees. Keep them informed.

➡ Include them at all company events.

➡ Give them company products and some company perks that employees get.

➡ Make referrals to other projects/opportunities within your organization.

➡ Write a testimonial letter.

➡ Meet with them frequently throughout the project.

not just a social endeavor; and marketing their services needs to become second nature. They also need to worry about things traditional employees often take for granted: employee benefits, vacation time, and finances for retirement, for example.

The rise of the contingent workforce is also shaping new patterns of business behavior. The recruitment of staff needs to account for the shifting needs of the business, and the availability of a pool of skilled workers with specific expertise suited to particular projects. Assignments can be for a period of weeks or months. The needs of the contingent workers become very different from the needs of a permanent workforce, and businesses need new skill sets to understand and manage a contingent workforce that may be spread across various states, countries, and time zones. The organization's ability to attract needed talent, maximize the motivation of such talent, and be able to access that talent over uneven periods of work becomes paramount.

It's been described as the age of the "disposable worker" or the "permanent temporary" workforce. As organizations have looked to cut back on fixed costs, they have progressively cut a wide range of employment and pension benefits, and now have turned the cuts to the work itself, seeking to find ways to have lower-cost and more-flexible work arrangements with a wider variety of workers.

Implications for Managing and Motivating

For employers, hiring contingent workers ushers in a new era of flexibility, with all the benefits that brings. Ken Lancaster, owner of Lancaster Advertising, who began using freelancers to cut costs after the 2001 terrorist attacks pummeled the economy and his business, found graphic artists, Web designers, and illustrators for as little as one tenth the cost of traditional employees on Elance, an online freelance marketplace. He says, "You never have to fire anybody, and if they don't live up to expectations, you just don't use them again."

But utilizing contingent workers also heralds a much more complex way of managing organizational talent. If key people can jump from one assignment to the next, how do organizations retain the critical talent and competence that provide the organization's competitive advantage? How do they protect the knowledge and intellectual property that can slip out the door? How do they go about accessing the talent they need across the globe, juggling myriad legal, financial, and regulatory issues across jurisdictions? How can organizations find, let alone manage and motivate, such talent?

The strategies to attract, motivate, and retain contingent workers can be as varied as the workers themselves. You can offer them:

- Orientation that allows them to understand the mission of the organization and how the work they will be doing ties to that mission
- Ongoing communication from periodic meetings and inclusion in communications that all full-time employees receive
- Flexible work schedules that allow them the hours they most want to work
- Training that can benefit the workers by developing their skills as well as provide the skills your organization needs
- Varied work assignments that allow their work to have interest and interactions with others in the organization, as

opposed to just the boring, rote tasks that no one else in the office wants to do

- Business services such as MBO Partners, www.mboco.com (formerly MyBizOffice) or concierge services that can provide useful time-saving services for the contingent employee
- Invitations to join staff for department or companywide meetings, team-building activities, and celebrations

Most important, perhaps, is taking time to get to know them: their names, abilities and aspirations, what motivates them, and praising them when they do good work for you and the company.

Remember, you will never receive first-class performance from a contingent employee who feels that he or she is treated as a second-class citizen!

Other Approaches for Motivating Contingent Workers

Since 60 percent of temporary workers say they'd prefer to have full-time work, many companies have created "temp to hire" programs that look first to hire full-time employees from the pool of temporary workers who are known to the company, rather than on the open market. Other employers have moved to creating their own pool of contingency workers that provides a stability of repeat work for those who have established themselves with the employer as being good workers.

For employees, contingent work entails a new approach to upgrading, deploying, and marketing their skills. They need to be alert to changes in the market that can open up new business opportunities, as well as ones that can make them redundant. They need to be open to exploring new strategies for obtaining work and often many new strategies at once because they can never be certain which strategy will work. They have to be wary of longer-term projects with larger employers, for while such projects provide needed and often well-deserved financial rewards, they also can provide a false security that takes them away from the pulse of the market and its ever-changing needs and priorities. Thus, contingent workers need to constantly be flexible and to avoid becoming too comfortable in working for any one employer or on any one given assignment.

These factors greatly impact the types of assignments they select. Assignments that enhance their skills, increase their visibility, or solidify their reputation can offer a win–win for both parties. For employers, such projects can help attract the most talented workers who are eager to be on the cutting edge of market needs; for employees, it keeps them at the forefront of relevant skills—often defining such skills and competencies for everyone in the market.

The task of grappling with a shifting contingent labor force while safeguarding critical knowledge and maintaining morale in the permanent workforce will be one of the key challenges of the coming decade.

Contingent Worker Examples

San Francisco–based Bank of America offers the My Work program, which encourages people to work from home 60 percent of the time.

———

New York–based CitiGroup has more than 11,500 employees enrolled in flexible/alternative work programs globally, which enables the company to offer alternatives to employees affected by site closures. Across town at American Express, one satisfied employee says working from home gives her more fulfillment because she has more time to volunteer.

———

Capital One, the financial institution based in McLean, VA, provides flex programs, including four-day workweeks and job sharing. The company makes prospective employees aware of these benefits when recruiting.

———

Midland Memorial Hospital in Midland, TX, is experimenting with allowing employees to take the summer off and continue their benefits during that period.

———

CONTINGENT WORKER TIPS

➡ Include interns, volunteers, and retirees at all company events.

➡ Give them company products and some company perks that employees get.

➡ Help set up job interviews for interns and volunteers.

➡ Write letters of recommendation.

➡ Meet with them frequently throughout the term.

➡ Ask for their opinions.

Island One Resorts, an Orlando, FL, time-share company, offers flexible work schedules, tuition reimbursement, and telecommuting options to its workers.

———

At pharmaceutical manufacturer Merck Frosst Canada & Company in Kirkland, Quebec, several employees take advantage of flexible work plans involving either telecommuting or job sharing.

———

Claims adjusters with Farmer's Insurance in San Diego work from home, connected online with the district office in Orange County. Adjusters receive case details via phone or e-mail, investigate property damage, and return to their home offices to file the reports.

———

At Reader's Digest in Pleasantville, NY, employees work 35-hour weeks and may choose a flextime schedule.

———

At TRW, now part of the Mission Systems and Space Technology sectors of Northrop-Grumman and many other defense contractors, employees can work a "9/80" work schedule in which they work nine hours a day and receive every other Friday off. In a recent survey, employees ranked this benefit as being more important to them than their health care coverage provided by the company.

———

At Deloitte Touche Tohmatsu's West Palm Beach, FL, office, employees have the freedom to move between part-time and full-time schedules to raise their young children.

———

Robert W. Baird, a financial services company located in Milwaukee, offers flexible summer schedules and time off on Friday afternoons. Many associates enjoy "flexible work arrangements," which include job sharing, telecommuting, flexible hours, compressed work schedules, and part-time working arrangements to accommodate family needs. More than 20 percent of the company's associates take advantage of flextime opportunities.

———

Pharmaceutical giant GlaxoSmithKline provides most benefits for a new type of worker—sales representatives who are limited to a three-year employment period.

REI, the recreational equipment company based in Kent, WA, offers some form of health coverage to all employees, including temporary and seasonal workers. The best plans are available when employees work 20 or more hours a week. Other perks include an employee product discount, retirement and profit sharing plans, and discounted travel through the REI Adventures program. Similarly, every part-time employee who works at least 20 hours a week at Seattle-based Starbucks Coffee can get full benefits including health, retirement, stock options, plus a free pound of coffee every week.

After employees put in 400 hours of work, Whole Foods Market, headquartered in Austin, TX, provides health, dental, and vision plans, retirement plans, paid time off, and a 20 percent store discount.

Upscale Nordstom department store, based in Portland, OR, offers its part-timers health insurance, a 401(k) retirement plan, and paid time off. They also get disability and accidental death insurance and adoption assistance.

Shipping giant UPS, based in Atlanta, GA, offers what it promotes as a "world class" benefits package to part-time workers, including medical, dental, and vision coverage, and life and long-term care insurance.

Trend #4: We're All Connected: The Evolving Role of Virtual Employees

K arla Herzog had a problem. As the president of Total Personnel Service in San Diego, she knew it was important to stay in touch with the employees she hired and placed with clients, but since she hardly ever saw them once they were hired, the task was daunting. How could she connect with employees who were always with clients at locations other than her own? How could she make them feel special when she never saw them and knew nothing of their needs, frustrations, and successes in their jobs?

With the changing nature of work today, more managers are in Herzog's spot. They have to adapt to new circumstances for recognizing employee performance. Increasingly, empowered employees are working more independently in their jobs, with the authority and autonomy to act in the best interests of the company. Many organizations are also moving to decentralized operations, so an employee's manager may physically be located at a different facility or even in a different state. And global companies increasingly expect executives to oversee staff in remote, and often overseas, locations.

> **VIRTUAL EMPLOYEE TIPS**
>
> ➡ Keep them informed. Ask for their opinions.
>
> ➡ Frequently ask how they are doing and what they need.
>
> ➡ Use technology to share important events, meetings, celebrations.

Make the Most of Virtual Technology

Times have changed drastically over the decades, due in part to continual technological advances. As such, the way in which business is conducted has changed as well. Operating on a global scale has become much easier, and more streamlined, thanks

SCAN HEALTH PLAN ENCOURAGES WORK FROM HOME

SCAN Health Plan encourages employees to stay home and work by offering free high-speed Internet access and free office furniture. The health care industry is continuing to expand, in spite of the current economic state, but companies in the industry are struggling to find ways to grow without spending more money. SCAN found a way around this by allowing employees to work from home, and making it comfortable and convenient for them to do so. Allowing employees to work from home eliminates the need to find larger office buildings and reduces the overhead of offices that are already up and running.

to new methods of communication that have aided in decision making, smoother operations, and ease of expansion. Fortunately, this has also opened up new possibilities for how employees work.

Gone are the days of communication limited to fax and phone lines or face-to-face meetings. These days, some businesses operate entirely on a virtual platform, with employees scattered throughout the country or the world. While not every company is able to operate this way, a large percentage of jobs can be done outside the typical 9 to 5 or in the office. As a result, in recent years, many companies have experimented with flexible schedules or telecommuting options.

While it's tough for some managers or business owners to welcome the option of employees working remotely, it's important to remember that employees are adults and should be treated as though they are responsible people. Most employees will perform better if they feel empowered and trusted. Consider some of these statistics:

- 86 percent of employees today report that they wish they had more time to spend with their families.
- Nearly 30 percent of workers in the last five years have voluntarily made career changes that resulted in a salary reduction in an effort to lead a more balanced life.
- Almost 50 percent of employees value the option of flexible or work-from-home hours.
- 54 percent of employees appreciate the option to leave work early to tend to family or child matters.
- A large percentage of workers would reduce hours or pay if it allowed them to have more time for personal interests or to spend with family.
- More than 60 percent of workers feel that their jobs are part of their identity, rather than simply a paycheck.

A sense of work–life balance tops the list of most employees when asked what they need in order to feel good about their work. Not to be mistaken with just a desire to "work from home," the definition of balance to employees translates, for the most part, to the ability to retain their sense of identity. Even though a large percentage of employees feel as though their jobs constitute their identity, that's not necessarily the way they would like it to be. Encouraging employees to explore interests outside of their daily roles, or expressing interest in their lives outside the office, can convey a dedication to ensuring a good balance.

Manager Accessibility and Support

The workplace itself is being redefined to include such arrangements as telecommuting, flexible working hours, and job sharing. "Futurework: Trends and Challenges for Work in the 21st

Century," a report by the Department of Labor, found that roughly one in ten workers fits into an alternative work arrangement, with nearly 80 percent of employers offering some form of nontraditional staffing arrangements. And some 47 percent of employees today now do some amount of telecommuting.

So how can managers best recognize performance when employees may not even have physical contact with their managers for weeks or months at a time? In a virtual environment, recognition needs to be more of a conscious and planned act because there are not as many spontaneous opportunities to acknowledge an employee's hard work and accomplishments. Making sure a virtual employee stays motivated, happy, and productive is the key to ensuring the success of a virtual workplace.

Karla Herzog understood that, and found new ways to manage, communicate with, and recognize her employees. That means delivering recognition awards to the employees at the client site, or sending them to the client to present to her employees. She uses every type of communication with

ENCOURAGING EMPLOYEES TO TAKE PERSONAL TIME

At one Silicon Valley employer a horn blows at 5 P.M. on Friday, signaling everyone to go home.

Encourage employees to refrain from checking e-mail on the weekends. One firm went so far as to enable an automatic note that pops up when employees access their e-mail, reminding them that it's the weekend.

Closely monitor vacation days and encourage employees to use them, especially if they haven't taken a day off in a while.

her employees as an opportunity to recognize and better communicate. Herzog has the payroll department include fax-back forms with all employee paychecks to see how things are going, and she asks her employees to tell her of any questions or concerns. She then takes those issues seriously—and gets back to the employees quickly to resolve them.

Make Time for People

There's no substitute for face time when it comes to building trusting relationships. At The Ken Blanchard Companies in Escondido, CA, the company expects all managers to hold one-on-one meetings with each direct report at least once every two weeks for at least 20 minutes. Sometimes those meetings are on the phone, but the employee always sets the agenda. If your employees are in the office less, coordinate your schedules so that you are at work when your employees are there. This could be a set time each week or during "core hours" when everyone is present (if your company operates that way). Talk about issues of real importance to employees, to the work, or to the company in general. A robust employee training and orientation program is another priority for building a strong foundation with every employee.

Employees are motivated by managers who take the time to get to know them. A recent survey of 500 professional employees by MasteryWorks in Annandale, VA, found that the primary factor affecting a respondent's decision to leave an organization was whether or not the manager developed a trusting relationship with them. Says Caela Farren, CEO of MasteryWorks, "Managers who get to know their people, respect and trust the competency of their employees, and listen continually for how employees are doing relative to their aspirations, quality of work life, and sense of career advancement, will have a far greater chance of developing and retaining their employees."

Edward Jones makes every effort to make its employees feel valued, and the results are evident in the longevity and positive attitude of nearly every employee. A survey of Edward Jones employees conducted by *Fortune* revealed that 96 percent of employees considered the company a friendly place to work, and more than 89 percent felt that managers followed through on what they said or promised. But the most telling statistic is

24 HOUR FITNESS FOCUSES ON EMPLOYEES' HEALTH, TOO

The founder of 24 Hour Fitness, Mark Mastrov, believes in showing an interest in employees' personal lives and thus encourages managers to have conversations with their staff regarding their goals and how the company can help achieve them. He also wants them to talk about things that are outside of work: family, school, personal interests. Doing so shows employees that they're more than just a part of the company's workforce, they're individuals as well, and the company cares just as much about that.

The approach of 24 Hour Fitness has resulted in not just a successful global business, but one that can pride itself on having happy, productive, and dedicated employees. Motivation among the company's employees starts with a sense of knowing that managers genuinely care about them as individuals and want them to succeed. Moreover, employees feel noticed and that their contributions, no matter how small, do not get overlooked. Employees who are reminded that they are appreciated tend to show higher levels of productivity, motivation, and desire to do what they can for the good of their employer.

that 83 percent of employees have every intention of working at Edward Jones until they retire.

The vast majority of employees cited their reason for holding the company in such high regard as a sense of truly being cared for. And even though the company has grown rapidly over the years, the culture has remained the same. Employees who have been with the company for decades feel as though principles and values have remained intact throughout all the growing pains. The company encourages employees to move around within the organization, a practice that has resulted in low attrition rates, infrequent boredom among employees, and a broader, more fulfilled group of employees.

The personal and professional growth of their employees is of utmost importance to managers at Edward Jones. Employees are encouraged to explore new opportunities within the company, which combats the threat of their becoming bored and looking for new experiences outside the company. Some employees are asked directly to lead or participate in new ventures ranging from moving around within the office in which they are based to traveling overseas to launch new departments, projects, or offices. The philosophy behind this practice is centered on Edward Jones's culture, which strives to develop initiative and drive in all employees. The company encourages employees to seek out new opportunities, and if the fit is right, employees are given the autonomy to forge ahead with the role or project. If the employee is lacking in a few key areas, the company provides the training necessary to effectively move into the desired role.

———

Make Every Employee Feel Valued

Here are some guidelines for building rapport with and providing support for your employees:

TAKE TIME WITH EMPLOYEES.

It all comes back to communication. Getting out and talking to employees, spending time with frontline staff, and making an effort to truly listen to employees can open your eyes to seemingly small accomplishments that would otherwise go unnoticed. No matter how small, the roles and responsibilities of every employee are a critical factor in the overall success of an organization.

BE AVAILABLE FOR QUESTIONS FROM EMPLOYEES.

Best, Best and Krieger, a large law firm in Southern California, promotes an open door policy wherein anyone who has questions or concerns regarding their personal or professional security is free to discuss their worries with the firm's managing partner. Employees are facing some very real fears, and ignoring these can only make them worse.

SHOW UNDERSTANDING AND EMPATHY.

It's important for all employees to feel that their managers are on their side, rooting for their success and seeking to help them succeed in any way possible. When employees are faced with life changes, tragedies, or circumstances demanding more of their time than usual, it is important that they feel comfortable discussing these scenarios with their managers or employers. If they are met with understanding and a willingness to help, they won't ever forget it. And the happier and more stable your employees, the better your business will fare.

SUPPORT EMPLOYEES WHEN THEY MAKE MISTAKES.
To sustain employees' trust and respect, it's especially important for their manager to support them when they make a mistake. It's easy to find fault and openly criticize an employee, perhaps even in front of their peers. But if you take that approach, you may never again get back what you lose in terms of an employee's self-esteem and willingness to act independently and use their best judgment.

Keeping the Sense of Teamwork

One of the cornerstones of the virtual office is making sure that virtual employees feel that they are an important part of the team. Working as a virtual team may mean that employees are working on the same project, but limited face-to-face contact can make virtual employees feel isolated from other team members and they may be unable to see how their efforts contribute to the results.

Managers must take a proactive role in fostering a sense of teamwork by involving virtual workers in all team meetings through any available means—telephone conferencing, e-mail, chat rooms, etc. Be sure to include some form of recognition in all team meetings. Verbal ways include:

- Acknowledging a good comment
- Recognizing small accomplishments
- Rewarding the honoring of commitments
- Thanking a "lurker" (someone who doesn't often post comments to e-mail discussions or chat rooms) for giving input to the discussion
- Praising someone for bringing up a not-so-popular opinion or idea
- Recognizing and praising group dynamics

Increase Communication as You Increase Distance

We know from electronics that the farther the source, the weaker and more distorted the signal. Likewise, the greater the distance from one's manager, the greater the effort both parties have to make to keep in touch. This can be done through updates and/ or more frequently scheduled meetings and visits. When Intel Corp. founder and chairman Andy Grove visits his company's workplaces, he has an open-comment session in the cafeteria and invites employees to bend his ear. Another executive I know keeps office hours when he visits his company's plants, so that any employee can sign up for an individual meeting. Consider using other means to stay connected: newsletters, Web chats, electronic message boards, and conference calls. Provide the same types of communication, recognition, and rewards that you provide for the employees who are located closer to you.

Use Technology, Don't Let It Use You

Too often, managers use technology like voice mail or e-mail as another means to dump work on their employees. It may seem faster and more efficient to do so, but employees are denied even a chance to ask questions about projects that are assigned when work is delegated via such one-way communication vehicles.

So use technology as a communication tool, not just as a way to off-load a new project. As more employees work off-site on either a full- or part-time basis, managers will need to incorporate the Internet and company intranets into their reward and recognition programs. These vehicles also can be used to promote the exchange of information and encourage questions. Managers can create problem discussion boards, host "chats," or create an "applause" bulletin board to capture the exchange of group praising. That's the approach at Hughes Network Systems, a high-tech company I've worked with in San Diego. Whenever anyone in the company logs on to the company's intranet, a bulletin board pops up labeled Applause and anyone can add a comment of praise for someone else in the organization to this message board, which after a few days scroll off the screen. AG Edwards, the financial services firm, hosts weekly audio conference calls of all employees—nationwide. Employees at Home Depot love the weekly satellite feeds to every store, which are dubbed "Breakfast with Bernie and Arthur," their chairman and CEO. These examples show the ability companies have today to use technology to personally connect in real time with dispersed employees.

Creating a Virtual Reward and Recognition Program

Realize that employees at other locations or who telecommute from their homes already feel they are second-class citizens. They imagine they are the last to hear about changes and news in the organization. Be empathetic with employees who do not work full-time at the main office: Duplicate any form of communication, recognition, or celebration that is done at the central office. I know of one employee in a field office who reported receiving a check from corporate for $1.18 on his birthday—the cost equivalent to two movie tickets bought in bulk and distributed to employees at the home office.

With any reward and recognition program, managers must be sure to reward the behavior they desire with recognition that is valued by and meaningful to their employees—not themselves. This is especially true when designing the virtual reward and recognition program, because the state of being virtual brings a whole new set of issues to bear that need to be identified and addressed in the plan.

So in creating a recognition program, managers should start with the motivational needs of their employees and build from there. Ask virtual employees what they want! This can be done in one-on-one discussions or by other techniques, such as sending an employee an index card to list items they find motivating, as they do at BankBoston. One financial analyst there told me that he listed "time off," "lunch with his manager," and "Starbucks coffee" on his index card, returned it to his manager, and forgot about it. He was elated, however, a month or so later, when he finished a project and was given a coupon for a Starbucks coffee with a personal note of thanks from his manager. The fact that a manager took the time to find out what would be meaningful and then used that information in a timely way left quite an impression.

You can use simple survey techniques to find out what is important to your employees. Or you can ask everyone to share two items they find motivating at an upcoming meeting—in person or online. As you involve the people you are trying to motivate, not only are you likely to be more on the mark, but others will more likely take ownership of the recognition program or activities. Discuss whether people would like more recognition and, if so, what form it should take. Ask who in the group would like to help get some new forms of recognition going. Involvement equals commitment. Today, the best management is what you do with others, not to them.

Managers have to work hard to help all employees feel integral to their jobs. Keeping virtual employees motivated to do their best is a very achievable task if done with the right focus at the right time. Take the time and the effort to recognize all your employees and you will reap the rewards of a more excited, energized, and productive staff.

Other Examples of Virtual & Long-Distance Employee Recognition

The Executive Committee of the Society for Human Resources Management (SHRM) recognizes associates in other regions by calling to thank them for a particular job well done.

Barbara Green, office manager for Buckingham, Doolittle and Burroughs in Canton, OH, shares this example of "virtual applause": "We sent an e-mail to our entire staff asking everyone to applaud the great efforts of our office services department at 4 P.M. at their desks. Members of that department work throughout the building and are rarely in one place at the same time, so this was a terrific way for each staff member to receive the benefit of the praising at exactly the same time and in the same way."

Noticing that most client letters of appreciation were never shared with home-based employees, Cruise.com, headquartered in Ft. Lauderdale, FL, created the Friday Fan Mail eBulletin, which recognizes excellence in service. Every week, agents forward e-mails or letters to Human Resources, where they are compiled and sent out in an e-bulletin to all employees. Once a month, the agents who have submitted customer e-mails participate in a drawing for a $25 gift certificate.

During the hot summer months when staffers put in a lot of driving time, agencies of QSource, the Memphis-based nonprofit health care management expert, leave bottles of ice water in the staff workrooms. They replace the bottle labels with ones that read "Stay hydrated! We care about YOU!" Says Barbara Meadows, MSN, RN, a home care quality improvement specialist for the organization's Nashville office, "We've got a creative bunch of folks with big hearts and little budgets."

Based in Wayzata, MN, Hammer Residences, a service provider for people with disabilities, offers remote working arrangements for employees who must move out of the area.

Trend #5: The World Is Getting Smaller: The Impact of Globalization

The march of globalization has spread across a range of markets as diverse as motor vehicles, natural resources, energy, and food. Labor is the latest "market" to be engulfed by the tide of globalization, as human talent becomes a fluid and exchangeable asset across international borders.

The concept of globalization often attracts bad press. The image of hooded protesters hurling objects through the plate glass of McDonald's at a G20 summit is the ugly fact of the trend. But globalization, as a phenomenon, has been advancing at a hectic pace in recent decades, fueled by greater international mobility, prosperity in the developed world, and a communications revolution that has transformed the exchange of information.

Distance is no longer the obstacle it used to be in the predigital era. In many industries, a trained professional in, for example, Guangzhou, China, can easily supplant a similar professional in New York or Dubai. In certain industries where skills are highly transferrable, there is little to stop workers from being recruited for assignments in any location around the world.

This is truly revolutionizing the way that we search for, locate, and deploy talent. There are still clearly many jobs that require a central locality. But there are an increasing array of jobs, and elements of jobs, that can be tasked to individuals in any part of the globe.

E-health means that diagnostic tools can be accessed by patients and health care professionals remotely; scientific research is becoming highly internationalized; in construction and manufacturing, use of standardized CAD techniques mean the design elements can be outsourced to wherever they can be implemented competitively. In the growing knowledge economy, there is virtually no limit to the breadth and scale of functions that are open to globalization.

All this presents a unique challenge for any business. In a relatively short time, it has moved from a comfortable position in which the boundaries of its work were defined by its physical location, to one where the talent pool is literally global and may be sourced from anywhere.

This issue raises a new hurdle for the businesses: workforce virtualization. With the growing use of new technologies, companies are faced with a decision of whether to move the work or the worker. In many cases, the work can be performed anywhere that skilled talent exists rather than the worker having to be on-site. Workforce virtualization allows an organization to source talent globally, but tasks their Information Technology with having an efficient, cost-effective, and workable solution that may not yet be ready to address the challenges of the global shift in worker availability.

Companies realize the potential of tapping into a vast global labor pool, especially at times of talent shortage. They are heading in this direction and will need help in doing so. Companies will be expected to become proficient with a range of technologies and platforms that support an ever-broadening set of functions. They will also need knowledge of labor markets, cultural differences, key recruiting methods, and laborer laws in a variety of jurisdictions, requiring a level of expertise that may not exist today.

The globalization challenge will require practitioners who are able to exploit networks and resources across multiple locations, and who can apply the best of their knowledge to the benefit of a local enterprise. It may also require the organization to be willing to explore outsourcing certain functions to providers with the global reach to enable their business strategies.

Motivating and Rewarding a Globally Diverse Workforce

U.S. companies continue to expand their operations globally at breakneck speed. In the process of going global, one of the most significant challenges organizations face is learning how to motivate, recognize, and reward people of all cultures.

The key to success lies in understanding the cultural attitudes and business practices of other countries. Companies that foster cultural sensitivity and help workers from varying backgrounds feel comfortable can increase employee productivity and job satisfaction.

Since the beginning of the decade, U.S. corporations have invested $400 billion abroad and employed more than 60 million overseas workers; also, more than 100,000 U.S. firms have engaged in global ventures valued at more than $1 trillion. In the International Relocation Trends Survey report by Windham

International and the National Foreign Trade Council, 61 percent of surveyed companies increased their expatriate population over the last five years and 85 percent expect continued or increased expatriate activity.

Cultural Sensitivity Is Essential for Global Success

Over the next decade, almost all real economic growth will occur outside the United States and Europe. As ethnically diverse workforces continue to become a significant part of our new business reality, sensitivity to the cultural and business practices of other nations will be critical. To successfully motivate a global workforce, it is essential that U.S. corporations put aside their assumptions about the superiority of American business practices.

"One of the stepping stones to a world-class operation is to tap into the creative and intellectual power of each and every employee," says Harold A. Poling, former chairman and CEO, Ford Motor Company. The best way to do this is to energize employees by using rewards and forms of recognition that are meaningful and motivating to the individual regardless of that person's nationality.

In America, most companies use individual public recognition, rewards, ceremonies, and bonuses. Employee of the Month awards, gift certificates, time off, and other incentives are also used to motivate and reward employees. As organizations cross borders, however, they are learning that what motivates their American employees might not work for their counterparts in Latin America, Asia, Europe, and Africa. Worse, an action that is favored in the U.S. might be inappropriate and result in the opposite effect on an offended employee elsewhere.

In Germany, for example, business is serious and workers are conservative and very private. Rather than an energizing force, public ceremony and recognition of accomplishments would tend to embarrass the German worker. Other cultures look at the American focus on praise and recognition as a weakness. "Why are Americans so insecure about themselves?" an Asian businessman might ask. "Why do they have to be reassured about everyday activities they were hired to do?"

Companies Must Move Toward a Multicultural Mindset

Some recognition practices can be standardized across many countries—they just need to be managed locally. For example, the New York–based Colgate-Palmolive Company conducted a global review of its performance-evaluation systems to ensure that all tied in with the company's underlying premise of respect. While parts of the performance-evaluation system easily transferred abroad, the company made revisions to reflect the cultural differences of various countries. In another example, the company ran a pilot survey in Brazil, sent out in translation. One of the questions, "Do you feel you receive equal opportunity in the organization?" presented difficulty because the term "equal opportunity" was unknown. In response, Colgate rewrote the question: "Do you feel you're treated fairly?"

Instead of exporting the American approach, Colgate-Palmolive attempts to blend cultures. Ron Martin, director of global employee relations, says, "We want people to understand the Western piece, but we have to maintain objectivity and say just because we do something a certain way doesn't mean that it's the only way it can be done, nor that it's the right way to do it. It's taking a look at all people and everything that makes them different from each other, as well as the things that make them similar."

While some recognition practices are manageable across multiple cultures, this is not usually the case. U.S. corporations must overcome the assumption that American views and business practices are universally held. "In the United States we've made a mistake thinking that because we're U.S.–based, what's good for us is good for everybody around the world," says Carol Kaplan, manager of global compensation and benefits at Applied Materials, Inc. "What happens then is that we export programs that aren't culturally sound and then end up creating animosities toward corporate headquarters."

In fact, from one country to the next, the list of differences is significant: our perception of time; our future orientation; our strong business focus on profit; and our view of relationships. In the U.S., for example, change is often viewed positively and is seen as progress and strongly linked to future success. In contrast, the cultures of Europe and Asia are steeped in history and tradition, and great pride is taken in doing things the same way previous generations did. Countries such as France and India value stability, continuity, and tradition—factors that are not as strongly valued in typical U.S. businesses.

In more traditional cultures, change is considered a disruptive and destructive force to be avoided if possible. To effectively recognize employee contributions in these countries, employees would likely prefer recognition for upholding the values and traditions of the organization. Praising them for enhancing the reputation of the company or for their loyalty and years of service will show these workers that you value their culture—and will recognize them in a way that is meaningful and motivating.

Adjusting Rewards and Recognition for Local Cultures

Sensitivity to local attitudes and customs, cultural expectations, economics, political situations, and the history of the countries in which businesses are operating is critical to creating a successful global rewards and recognition program. U.S. companies cannot transfer American customs and business practices into the global market and expect them to be successful. There are many cross-cultural issues that need to be addressed, including different styles of managing, communicating, giving feedback, and negotiating.

Understanding the way a particular culture drives behavior will indicate how companies should energize and reward a diverse workforce. Some areas with significant differences across borders include:

TIME

Attitudes toward time vary significantly from one country to the next. In the U.S., time is a major driving force, a precious resource not to be wasted. Americans are always in a hurry. Foreign visitors sense that Americans are more concerned with getting things done on time than with developing meaningful relationships. As a result, Americans are much more abrupt in their business dealings. They conduct meetings, review agendas, and make snap decisions with an eye on the clock. Most of Northern Europe is also time-sensitive.

In contrast, much of Latin America, Africa, and the Middle East has a more casual view of time. In these countries, greater emphasis is placed on developing relationships. In Mexico, for example, it may take several breakfast or lunch meetings before people feel comfortable with you as an individual and are ready to begin conducting business.

U.S. companies operating in countries where time is not a controlling factor and relationships are greatly valued will need to consider these differences when determining how to reward and recognize employees. For example, company policies that reward employees for meeting timeliness standards might be modified, placing more emphasis on the desired results, not on how they were obtained.

COMMUNICATION

Americans typically prefer an open and direct communication style—considering anything other than that to be dishonest and insincere. In Sweden, a direct approach is also valued as a sign of efficiency, but unlike the U.S., heated debates and confrontations are very unusual. The Swedish business culture strongly favors compromise, and individuals will not risk the feeling of consensus and agreement. In Germany, Sweden, and Switzerland, business is serious and humor is not generally a part of business. In Asia, company leaders are expected to be sensitive to the feelings of subordinates and understanding of others' needs.

Eye contact is another important aspect of communication—and one that is important to look at by culture. For example, in France, direct eye contact is a frequent and intense part of communication, as it is in Latin America, much more so than in the U.S. Direct eye contact in other cultures would be considered challenging and aggressive. For example, in Japan, direct communication and eye contact is considered a sign of disrespect.

By understanding the cultural differences in how people communicate, companies can more effectively recognize and reward their global workforce for their contributions. For example: Finnish and German employees tend to prefer written communication to face-to-face interaction. In these cases, a letter recognizing employee accomplishment would be most effective. Japanese employees usually prefer quiet recognition. Open praise at a staff meeting will generally not be effective, nor would singling out individuals for praise in public. In Mexico and Latin American countries, communication is open and personal, with a strong emphasis on developing relationships. Recognition of employees' contributions, particularly relationship-building successes, will be well received.

ACTION/WORK ORIENTATION

While companies in the U.S. have taken some steps toward creating a "family friendly" work environment, the prevailing attitude is still that Americans live to work, and a significant part of most Americans' identity is determined by "what they do for a living." Americans typically believe that leisure activities should assume a relatively small part of a person's total life.

Respect for the individual's family life is generally greater outside the U.S. In Latin America, the Middle East, and Africa, there is a clearer division between work and family. In Mexico, the family is of vital importance, and issues affecting the family take priority over work. In many Asian and European cultures, the family is viewed as an essential institution and treated with high regard. For example, in Singapore sustaining traditional values and family strength are seen as intangible factors in the success of East Asian economies. In these cultures, economic and social progress are viewed as being inextricably linked. However, in Asia work is often viewed as an extension of the family, that is, the division between work time and private time is blurred. A Japanese company often expects employees to work late or on weekends, entertain business guests on weekends, or send employees on business that involves personal time.

There are a variety of ways to recognize employees that will underscore strongly held family values:

FLEXTIME TIPS

➜ Discuss with them what the boundaries are and why.

➜ Trust them to achieve what they say they will.

➜ Be patient with them.

➜ Monitor their results.

➜ Treat them as peers.

- Write a letter acknowledging an employee's accomplishment and send it to the employee's family.
- Allow time off, or at least a flexible work schedule, so employees can attend to family matters.
- Send birthday cards, get-well cards, and flowers, when appropriate, to family members.
- Hold "open houses" at work and invite family members to company celebrations.
- Grant employee time off to volunteer in a child's classroom or to attend school field trips or sporting events.

COMPETITION VS. COOPERATION

Americans tend to believe that competition brings out the best in individuals. As such, contests and public sharing of work progress are often the norm. Americans conduct business at rapid speed with intense focus on results, and are often compelled to make decisions quickly without soliciting input from other employees, clients, or vendors. And although many U.S. companies are striving to be more participative, many still tend to hold most power and authority in top executive levels.

Many cultures outside the U.S. promote cooperation and teamwork over competition. For example, in Sweden and Japan a good manager is seen as a coach who leads his employees through cooperation and agreement, not through his power and position. In many European and Asian companies employee input is sought on nearly every business matter, often starting with the workers' opinions. And in Japan participative management in decision making within business is well-documented.

To be successful in many countries overseas, U.S. companies need to shift the focus from valuing individual contributions to recognizing the value of teamwork and cooperation for obtaining desired results. Recognizing employees with these values for their ability to work together—to make group decisions, to offer team suggestions, to manage themselves—will show that you understand their culture and will motivate them with recognition that is meaningful and powerful. For example, Japanese employees will be pleased to be valued as a team player, but not for individual successes that put the employee above the group. Compliments within the workplace would be much more indirect. For example, a manager wishing to compliment a subordinate could ask an employee's opinion or he could invite him to a meeting he would not normally be invited to. So, to effectively reward employees for their successes, it's important to understand the cultural differences that influence employee contributions.

The Payoff: An Energized, Diverse Workforce

Many companies already understand the importance of a reward system that recognizes the contributions of all employees. As U.S. companies become increasingly more global, differences between

American-style business practices and those of other cultures will become magnified. To be successful, organizations need to be flexible and willing to adapt their way of thinking. This means putting aside our vision of the world as we know it and working to understand the dynamics of the culture we are operating in. That's the challenge U.S. companies face.

Regardless of our differences, unleashing the power of a workforce that feels motivated, challenged, and supported is the only true way for a company to attain success in today's competitive, global environment. Hal Rosenbluth, former CEO of Rosenbluth International (now a part of American Express Travel) says, "The highest achievable level of service comes from the heart, so the company that reaches its people's hearts will provide the very best service." With almost all real economic growth over the next decade expected to take place outside the U.S., learning how to inspire, recognize, and reward a multicultural workforce can mean the difference between success or failure for any global company. Companies that find ways to build on common denominators among cultures will be better able to motivate their employees and will reap the benefits of an energized workforce.

Additional Examples of Organizational Diversity

The e-mail marketing firm e-Dialog, based in Burlington, MA, launched a program for newly promoted employees, with a focus on women mentoring women. Through participation in particular projects or committees, women work with real business problems and are exposed to decision makers. They learn how to navigate the corporate world and find new opportunities. Future plans include starting a working-moms group, connecting them to options for child care and financial planning.

MOTIVATING EMPLOYEES AROUND THE WORLD

Michael Losey, president and CEO of SHRM, has pointed out that the lack of global experience among HR executives could have profound implications as U.S. companies head into the new global business era. As he stated it: "HR policies will be influenced more and more by conditions in other countries and cultures. HR managers will need to sensitize themselves and their organizations to the cultural and business practices of other nations."

Understanding what motivates employees in different cultures is essential to the success of U.S. corporations doing business globally. The following are some of the issues companies should look at when considering ways to motivate, recognize, and reward employees in different cultures.

JAPAN

Individual recognition programs have not worked well because Japan has a collectivist culture and workers do not want to be conspicuous. Individual pay for performance is considered potentially disruptive to pleasant working relationships and is not used. Instead, year-end bonuses are given based on loyalty, years of service, and one's family situation. Team awards have been effective—some include salary increases and an allowance system as incentives for outstanding performance.

KOREA

The Korean government has a long tradition of prize and discipline incentive systems to enhance productivity. Few group incentives are used. Employees with service of over 20 years can receive a special award of 10 days' paid leave.

ASIA AND THE MIDDLE EAST

Teaching is considered the most important thing a person can do. The manager's role is seen as that of a teacher and facilitator—someone who helps those around him learn. For instance, in Asian corporations, particularly in Japan, the manager is always present when a subordinate is being trained. This indicates that the manager believes the learning is important. In these cultures, it is important for an employee to be seen as a whole person—with needs beyond professional and technical ones. This is also true for Africa.

SCANDINAVIA

Employees have a voice in management decisions, particularly those that relate to compensation, safety, and capital expenditures. Training begins when employees start new jobs. It is also important to incorporate new employees into the corporate culture.

SWEDEN

Management is based on the premise that the individual is willing and able to do a good job. A Swedish manager is generally thought of as a coach who motivates staff, leads employees through principles of cooperation and agreement, and is a good listener. Getting emotional when discussing a problem is considered inappropriate. All employees have the freedom to make decisions and solve

unexpected problems without asking permission from superiors. Sweden has a high rate of employed women and a reputation for having a high ratio of family-friendly men who are seeking a better integration of work and family. Therefore, there is a broad acceptance of home-based telework.

AUSTRALIA, AUSTRIA, GERMANY, FRANCE, AND BRAZIL

Employees with one year of service are automatically given 30 days' paid vacation.

LATIN AMERICA

Companies are very concerned about the family and family values. When companies hire a person, it's as if they are hiring the entire family.

RUSSIA

Money is the most important factor in determining whether a Russian will take and keep a job—but it is not the only one. Russians want benefits such as pension plans, health care, regular performance reviews— and lunch. In Soviet times, most offices had a cafeteria, which offered a modest midday meal for a pittance.

At Leominster Credit Union of Leominster, MA, the company's "Respectful Workplace Charter" presents core values for the organization, including "valuing each other's uniqueness and contributions and ethnic and cultural diversity." All employees sign the charter, which is reviewed annually.

———

Root Learning Inc., a management consulting firm based in Sylvania, OH, honors individuality at work. The company displays caricature drawings of every employee in the lobby. The drawings integrate images of each person's individual interests or talents—such as writing children's books, riding bikes, or solving puzzles.

———

International company Alcoa, Inc., with several thousand employees in more than 25 countries, tailors its service awards and recognition programs to follow local customs. Likewise, Kennametal, which operates facilities in about a dozen countries, has a global service award program that varies by location and is tailored to each culture and region as appropriate.

———

Conclusion

The worker trends discussed in this section affect organizations everywhere and increase the challenges of connecting workers to the strategic business objectives of the organization. The transformation will have a significant impact on management, essentially requiring managers to look at their human resources as they affect the strategic issues of the business, and to consider how different parts of the business link together and what role people play from top to bottom.

These trends mean thinking out how the "people element" adds value at every stage of the organization, and the factors that both enhance and dilute value—focusing on the broader business outcomes that the organization is trying to attain. This strategic shift comes at a price: Management will need to better value their people and become better skilled in hiring, motivating, and keeping them in more competitive times.

DIVERSITY TIPS

➡ Find areas of commonality.

➡ Acknowledge the value of their opinions, ways, customs.

➡ Share information about the global economy and what your company's opportunity is. Ask for their opinions.

SIX STRATEGIES FOR ENGAGING EMPLOYEES IN CHALLENGING TIMES

Management in any company can make a marked difference in its ability to better engage its employees in ways that allow the organization to compete more effectively. Managers can do this by motivating their employees to achieve focused, revised goals that touch all aspects of the business from innovation and cost-cutting ideas, to process improvement and enhanced customer service, to strategies for enhancing sales, referrals, and follow-on services.

While this focus may seem like good management practice that companies should already be doing, not doing these things can make the difference between success and failure for many organizations. For example, Quantum Workplace, a company that tracks employee engagement scores of over 1.5 million employees within 5,000 companies nationwide, has found that 66 percent of the firms they studied saw a decrease in employee engagement in recent years that seemed to be in direct response to the negative circumstances of the recessionary economy. A comparison of those employers who had higher engagement scores with those whose scores had dropped revealed a number of key differentiators, each of which will be addressed in this section.

Today's employees want to work for organizations that (1) create a clear, compelling direction; (2) have direct, open, and honest communication; (3) involve employees and encourage initiative; (4) grant employees autonomy, flexibility, and support; (5) provide a continued focus on career growth and development; and (6) recognize and reward high performance. "Employers can significantly influence, if not control, how motivated and satisfied their employees are," says Greg Harris, president of the firm. "A more engaged workforce can act as insulation, a buffer if you will, from the effects of the economic downturn," concludes Mark D. Hirschfeld, principal of Goldenrod Consulting, Inc.

Strategy #1: A Clear and Compelling Direction

The starting point of any organizational effort is having a clear and compelling vision for the organization. If employees don't know, or are not inspired by, what the organization is trying to do, it will be more difficult for them to have the motivation to succeed—especially in tough times. Frances Hesselbein, president of the Leader-to-Leader Foundation, once put it this way: "No matter what business you're in, everyone in the organization needs to know why."

Do a reality check and ask employees what the mission and purpose of the organization are. If you get a different answer from each person you ask, it's a good indication that things have drifted or perhaps have not been clear for some time. Use this opportunity to revisit the purpose of your business group or function. Management guru Peter Drucker used to advocate that management ask three questions: (1) What is our business? (2) Who is our customer? (3) What does our customer consider value? In this way, Drucker helped connect what organizations were trying to achieve with their customers in the marketplace.

Clarifying one's vision is a useful starting point for deciding what is most important for the organization (or department or team) to focus on to be successful. And the result needs to be a compelling purpose that can inspire everyone. "A vision is not just a picture of what could be, it is an appeal to our better selves, a call to become something more," says Harvard professor Rosabeth Moss Kanter. From that vision you can shape your "unique competitive advantages," that is, those aspects that you have to offer your customers that your competition does not. These advantages represent your strengths in the marketplace that you most need to capitalize on to be successful. In changing times, the unique advantages you have to offer and the needs of your customers can shift drastically, so it makes sense to look at this frequently.

Internet retailer Zappos has become famous in part because it has a unique vision of "Creating Happiness" and a simple mission statement that inspires all employees to "deliver WOW." The core values, derived from a list generated by all employees, focus more on individual attributes to inspire each employee

DIRECTION TIPS

➡ Tell them what results the company expects, and how it benefits customers, them, and society.

➡ Share what you expect from them and why, how their role is valuable and meaningful.

➡ Define the overall boundaries of what the organization does and what it doesn't do.

➡ Explain and give examples of core and operational values.

than on the traditional business elements of revenue, profit, and market share:

1. Deliver WOW Through Service

2. Embrace and Drive Change

3. Create Fun and a Little Weirdness

4. Be Adventurous, Creative, and Open-Minded

5. Pursue Growth and Learning

6. Build Open and Honest Relationships with Communication

7. Build a Positive Team and Family Spirit

8. Do More with Less

9. Be Passionate and Determined

10. Be Humble

At the end of their training, to make sure new hires fit into the Zappos culture and truly want the job, each person is offered $3,000 to quit. That's right, $3,000 if they agree not to come back. The new hires talk about the offer with their friends and significant others, and most decide they would rather have the job and opportunity than the extra money.

Ken Jones, CEO, believes in connecting with employees to set goals for individuals and for the company. He hosts an annual meeting with a leadership team to analyze company goals, discuss what the competition is doing, and look at the company performance both past and future. The head of each department also gets the opportunity to present ideas based on predetermined common themes. The themes are the company's goals for the year and serve as a template for senior staff meetings. The company has found that by including all employees—from managers down—implementing new processes and revised goals is much easier. At Zappos, goals are based on employee input, rather than being solely created by top management and relayed to employees from the top. One very important thing that Jones has realized in this process is that employees know the ins and outs of their department better than he does. He values their experience and expertise to help set attainable and substantial goals, which in turn sparks a drive in employees to deliver and meet those goals.

———

Visual Marketing, based in Chicago, makes decals for various commercial purposes and decided to focus just on the basics when it came to revising their goals. The company shifted its focus to innovation with increased employee involvement and empowerment. So, rather than focusing solely on output, employees were the ones considered to make the difference, and because of this, each employee went through teamwork training and was regularly surveyed for suggestions on process improvements. The company also revised its mission statement and then had each employee sign it. Doing so signified an understanding of and commitment to the company's goals, which served to increase employee focus and motivation.

———

Excelon, one of the nation's largest power generation and distribution companies, makes an extra effort to develop organizational culture and positive attitudes. First, the company created a vision document that outlines goals and values. Then, it created a strategic direction document that exists to protect company values and to grow long-term value. These two documents are the foundation of everything Excelon does. From goal setting to business decisions, the company relies upon the contents of these documents for guidance. This is also how its employees' performance, potential, and forward thinking are measured.

———

The CEO of Huron Consulting Group, a health care consulting firm based in Chicago, has developed a program by which all 3,000 employees participate in a goal-setting meeting with their manager each year. At the end of the year, it is easy to identify the top performers. Those who have achieved their goals are rewarded, and those who have failed to do so not only miss out on rewards but are also moved to the front of the line if and when layoffs become necessary. Huron's CEO makes it very clear to all employees that not following through on the goals they have helped set for themselves does not serve them well. The company prides itself on having employees who give 110 percent, for themselves and for the business, so the process of setting and achieving goals is extremely important to their overall success. The response from employees has been largely positive: Because Huron offers a positive work environment, and generously rewards employees who perform well, all the company's employees know that working hard will pay off in the long run.

———

Robert Polet, CEO of Gucci, has helped develop a performance review process that is based on previously established behaviors he most values in employees. This has helped managers at Gucci better identify individuals who show leadership promise, and identify employees who can be handpicked for strategic tasks or roles when revisions to the business or mission become necessary. As a result, Polet has found that during downtimes, it's much easier to quickly choose employees who are needed to step in to help work through a particular challenge or serve on a special project group. The benefits are twofold: The employee is given an opportunity to further develop his or her skills and experience new levels of responsibility, while the company is assured of having the best people involved in a crucial task.

Strategy #2: Direct, Open & Honest Communication

The need to know what is going on is pervasive throughout one's job. People want to know not just the information needed to do the work they are assigned, but what others are doing and how the organization is doing, as well. It is important to communicate to employees information about the organization's mission and purpose, its products and services, strategies for success in the marketplace, and even what's going on with the competition. I was intrigued to learn while working with FedEx Corporation, for example, that the most popular column in the company's internal employee newsletter was information about the latest developments at UPS and what that company was doing in the marketplace.

In my research, the highest-ranking variable that 65 percent of employees most want from their managers is to be provided with information they need to do a good job at work, which has a degree of significance that places it in a category of its own. These research findings correlate with recent research from Accountemps that found communication to be the leading variable that 48 percent of executives reported could best affect low morale in their organization.

One of the most common errors many organizations and managers make in challenging times is not sharing adequate information with employees. Sometimes this is the case because management itself is uncertain about the constantly changing competitive landscape. In other instances, management tries to "protect" employees from fears regarding the potential of losing their jobs or the ability of senior management to effectively handle a crisis. More often, these well-intended actions to "protect" employees backfire. Closed-door meetings and hushed hallway conversations create a sense of unease among employees and lead to speculation, heightened fear, and worst-case-scenario rumors.

Employees want and need to know what is going on within an organization, even if the information is not always positive. There's nothing wrong with being honest with employees when a firm is struggling. Doing so will almost always lead to an increase in teamwork and dedication, especially if delivery of the bad news is also used as an opportunity to brainstorm and communicate with employees about ideas and plans for turning things around. Bringing employees into the loop during the downtimes can instill a greater sense of involvement and responsibility that ultimately increases feelings of value and trust.

MANAGER AVAILABILITY TIPS

➡ Periodically meet with employees to make sure they are making progress on their desired path.

➡ Have the CEO hold a monthly breakfast or lunch with one person from each department, cycling through until everyone has a chance to go.

➡ Arrange a lunch or dinner with the president/CEO.

➡ Arrange a visit from the company president.

➡ Hold a town hall meeting for employees to have their issues addressed.

➡ Set up office hours where employees can talk directly to company executives.

Direct, Two-Way Communication Is Most Effective

When discussing major issues, such as organizational changes, communication should come in the form of a dialogue, rather than a lecture, and questions should always be encouraged. Employees must be made to feel as though they have the freedom to express their fears and concerns, and that they will receive honest and informative responses. Feedback sessions, departmental meetings, or companywide gatherings should ideally serve two purposes. First, to gather feedback, and second, to provide information.

When Best Buy began experiencing financial strains, CEO Brian Dunn decided to take a look at the employee discount program. After careful consideration, a change was made that would save the company close to $15 million. A small change was centered on store-brand products and wasn't well accepted by employees primarily because it was introduced out of the blue and caught everyone by surprise. Best Buy's social networking site became the primary forum for employees to vent their frustrations. Dunn set aside time to review the site and read the feedback from his employees, and eventually reversed his decision. Dunn's major error? Not discussing the idea with employees before making the change.

———

Allied Steel faced communication challenges because its employees were located in five separate office buildings. President and cofounder Mike Lassner got together with employees and developed the following systems for accurately communicating information across the organization:

- Continually repeated information to reinforce their messages
- Frequently hosted events or meetings where employees from all offices were in attendance, creating a sense of community
- Developed newsletters with feature stories or clips from each office
- Didn't isolate great ideas to one office, which promotes competition rather than teamwork
- Prepared, planned, and strategized
- Didn't mistake daily casual conversations for effective communication, and instead had an agenda and schedule
- Remained flexible and open to change, and didn't lose sight of their goal

Have a Plan for Ongoing Communication

Communication cannot be successful if it is approached piecemeal. Preferably, develop a communication plan that takes a longer-term view of the activity. Thinking through possible challenges and developing systems to communicate effectively can better prepare both management and employees when miscommunication does arise, which it will.

Engineering firm MWH takes informal polls of its employees to determine which colleagues they rely upon most for help and support. In an effort to reveal communication gaps and strongholds, executives use this information to develop a roadmap of connections among employees. Often a very-little-known bit of information within companies, this understanding of employees' communication connections has helped MWH develop a more solid and complete communication strategy and improve productivity. Some organizations have adopted similar practices, known as a social network analysis, with much success.

In addition to fostering collaboration, the technique has helped companies such as Computer Sciences Corporation improve customer service and support and aided a lobbying group in pinpointing weaknesses in its networking. When MWH began using social network analysis, the primary goal was to reduce costs by improving communication among its technology centers. For example, the center in Denver and the center in Pasadena each created programs that would track address changes among employees. Yet neither location communicated the effort, resulting in a duplicate expenditure of time and resources.

Techniques for Communicating

In today's dynamic, fast-paced workforce, enlightened companies recognize that employees want an environment that encourages a constant dialogue between employer and employee. Today employees want and need continuous performance feedback. They want to be recognized and rewarded for their accomplishments, and at the same time, most employees want feedback if their performance is missing the mark so they can make changes as appropriate. "Men and women want to do a good job, a creative job, and if they are provided the proper environment they will do so," says Bill Hewlett, cofounder of Hewlett-Packard.

Employees want to know how they're performing and they want—and need—to know more frequently than annually. Continuous, supportive communication from managers, supervisors, and associates is too often underemphasized—yet it is a major motivator. After all, a motivated workforce, willing to take initiative when they see the opportunity, is a powerful advantage for a company.

Communicating with employees varies depending upon the situation. Group settings require different interaction than does one-on-one communication. Following are some suggestions for best handling individuals and groups:

INDIVIDUALS

- Periodic "one-on-one" meetings with each employee
- Personal support and reassurances, especially for your most valued employees
- "Open door" accessibility to management
- Inviting employees to write anonymous letters to top management about concerns and other matters

GROUPS

- Town hall meetings
- CEO breakfasts
- Brown-bag lunches
- 24-hour "news desk" on the company intranet
- Periodic "state of the union" updates on the business
- Being open and honest in explaining the current situation and upcoming challenges
- Taking questions and providing answers

MEETINGS

- Taking questions in advance of the meeting or allowing them to be written anonymously on index cards
- Recording staff meetings and distributing to those who couldn't attend the meeting

- Creating a question-and-answer section in your internal newsletter or company website

———

Joe Zimmerman, CEO of KB Homes, carves time out of his day to spend time with his employees. Except he doesn't just take the time to be a physical presence, he actually listens to what they have to say. His open door policy applies even when his door isn't open. Every member of his organization is encouraged to drop in and share their ideas, no matter how premature they might be. When employees present concepts in the early stages of development, Zimmerman has still managed to find nuggets of value. He even walks the hallways soliciting ideas and exchanging information. In his eyes, an idea coming from the rank and file does not diminish its potential for being a good idea.

———

Winchester (MA) Hospital, a 178-bed facility recently named by *The Boston Globe* as a top place to work in the state, gives employees the same personal attention that patients receive. Executive leaders continually communicate with employees to understand how they like to be recognized for good work. They make regular "rounds" during day and night shifts to get patient and staff feedback, and keep index cards listing employee preferences. Managers frequently give "spot awards," small gifts worth up to $25.

———

At Subaru's Illinois manufacturing plant, employees requested information about new models the company was planning to market, which helped them serve as ambassadors for the products.

———

O regon-based Flying Pie Pizzeria restaurants formed a committee called The C-Team that plans parties and special events. It meets weekly, alternating between two restaurant locations, and is run by managers and long-time employees. However, all employees are invited to sit in, participate, and give their own ideas. Rewards conceived at C-Team meetings have included improving stereos for restaurants and attending concerts together. The company also created an Odd Duck form. When employees see an "odd" problem, they fill out the form to let management know that attention is needed to prevent something from falling through the "quacks."

W hen Nancy Quasarano, supervisor in training for Best Buy in Kalamazoo, MI, led her department meeting on improving performance, she used the *Dumbo* movie as an analogy to improve her coworkers' attitudes. Dumbo was an elephant that was born to fly, but didn't have enough faith in himself to try. It was only after he was given a magic feather that he started to fly. When he lost the feather, he realized that he'd had the power in him all along. Nancy gave each person a feather and made a poster that read "Today I made a choice. Today I chose my attitude. Every day is another chance to turn it all around and make the most of the time I have." She encouraged her employees and told them that once they knew they didn't need the feather, they could tape the feather to the poster board. By the end of the week, all feathers were attached to the board and department performance started to improve.

J im Dixon, building services director at Keepsake Village assisted living center near Syracuse, NY, makes a point to tell every new employee, "There's no task that I'd ask you to do that I wouldn't do myself."

———

In just one year, Rare Method Interactive Corp., an interactive marketing firm based in Calgary, Alberta, cut its staff from about 100 to 50 employees. Realizing that some of his best employees were choosing to leave, President Tom Short held one-on-one chats with top performers, reiterating his vision for the business and how their contributions tied to overall company goals. He sought their input about their jobs, decision making, management, and the company itself. They became more engaged and contributed great ideas for changing and streamlining processes. "It's about re-earning trust," Mr. Short says. "You want to retain your good people, because they are the ones who can always get a job anywhere." The payoff: The company is more optimistic, seeing increased excitement from employees.

———

When company sales dropped, instead of jeopardizing respect and trust by firing staff or reducing pay, Robert Meggy, president of Great Little Box Co. of Richmond, British Columbia, found other ways to cut expenses. When employees retired or took maternity leave, for example, the firm chose not to replace them. The firm cut back on social events and held several brainstorming sessions with employees to get money-saving ideas. Sharing corporate and financial information with employees created a sense of trust and transparency; everyone knew where the company stood and why decisions were made. "If employees trust that you have their best interests at heart," Meggy says, "they'll stay committed to the organization."

———

At Johnson Inc., a St. John's, Newfoundland, insurance broker with over 50 offices and several hundred employees across Canada, CEO Ken Bennett, hosts frequent employee lunches and "up close and personal" sessions, giving staff company news and updates and fielding questions ranging from issues about the company's growth to his vacation plans. Bennett says, "Our people drive our business. So, we have an absolute passion in doing the right thing so they feel proud to work here."

———

Pioneer/Eclipse, a manufacturer in Sparta, NC, takes customers to meet line workers who have had a part in developing their products. Workers love to tell customers about their ideas and listen to what is needed.

———

At Ivanhoe Cambridge Inc., a shopping center company based in Quebec province, managers hold "10 plus 10" meetings: They have ten minutes to give staff a business update, and employees have ten minutes to ask questions and give feedback, which is relayed to senior management. Sessions are held at least quarterly.

———

Cargill, Inc., the U.S.'s largest private corporation and agribusiness giant based in Wayzata, MN, received a 2007 Best Practice Award from Recognition Professionals International (RPI) for its outstanding employee recognition strategy, management ownership, and events and celebrations. "Cargill management is very involved in making their recognition program a success," said Christi Gibson, executive director of RPI. "Getting management onboard early and continually [involved] is a key factor in every highly functioning recognition program."

Strategy #3: Involve Employees & Encourage Initiative

Communicating better with employees is the first step in empowering them to act in the best interests of the organization. But that's just the beginning. Once employees are armed with more frequent and relevant information, they'll be more likely to act on that information in ways that can best help the organization. The act of honest and open communication shows both trust and respect that management has for its employees. Adding to that the explicit request and encouragement for employees to get involved in helping the company can lead to profound results.

According to a survey I conducted of employees in a variety of industries, 50 percent of employees want their managers to ask for their opinion and ideas at work, and more than 50 percent want their managers to involve them in decisions that are made at work. The average American worker makes 1.1 suggestions per year where they work today—one of the lowest rates of any industrialized nation. Contrast that average with 116 per employee made each year by the average Japanese worker and you can see the potential that exists if only you can find a way to tap into it.

Managers and workers are entering into a new kind of partnership that is forming the basis of a new joint focus in the workplace. Today's managers are discovering that they have to create an environment that encourages employees to *contribute* their best ideas and work, to help seek out new opportunities, such as new sources of revenue, and to overcome obstacles facing the company, such as cutting costs, wherever possible. Workers are discovering that, if they expect to survive the constant waves of change sweeping across the global business marketplace—as well as hold on to their current job—they have to join together with other employees to contribute to their organizations in ways that they have never before been called upon to do.

Although I've yet to see an organization that didn't have an open door policy in which employees were encouraged to speak to their manager about any concerns, ideas, or suggestions they had, in practice this policy often doesn't work very well. Solicitation of ideas needs to extend beyond the traditional scope of employee involvement. Anonymous surveys and casual questions at the tail end of a meeting are not enough to accomplish the task ahead during a recession. After initial cost-savings measures are put into place, it's time to talk seriously about how best to move forward in an economical yet productive manner to make the changes stick. Policies and procedures need to be revised to reinforce the company's effort to do things smarter, cheaper, and better.

In order to maximize buy-in as well as motivation, employees need to be challenged for identifying ways to improve. Employees need to understand that you need their efforts now more than ever before. Once this has been communicated, it's time to create new mechanisms that inspire employee involvement. Would you like to get more ideas from your

INVOLVEMENT TIPS

➡ Invite employees' spouses to attend company orientations and open houses.

➡ Set up a "Take the New Hire Out to Lunch" sheet and have employees take turns treating the new hire to lunch during first two weeks.

➡ Create a podcast about company news or updates, industry news, and personal announcements (e.g., employee accomplishments, birthdays, etc.).

➡ Share company financial reports and post highlights of corporate meetings.

➡ Encourage employees to submit questions to be answered at corporate meetings.

employees? Ideas for saving money, improving customer service, streamlining processes, and so forth? What business manager or owner wouldn't?

Although they will vary from organization to organization, here are some typical areas of employee focus that can yield benefits to the organization:

Revenue-Generating Ideas: *How can the company generate additional income? Whether it's new fees, cross-selling, or up-selling, what new ideas could be tried?*

Cost-Saving Suggestions: *How can costs be trimmed, delayed, or eliminated? What are critical expenses, versus optional ones that could at least temporarily be cut?*

Process Improvements: *What steps in the organization's processes can be streamlined, saving time, resources, and money along the way?*

Customer Needs & Requests: *How can employees help others in the company who are focused on customer needs and requests? How can customer needs be further explored?*

New Products or Services: *What ideas exist for new products or services? How could those ideas be better developed and implemented?*

Morale & Teambuilding: *Who would be interested in helping to improve employee teamwork and morale? In what ways could this be done at little cost?*

I'm convinced that every employee has at least one $50,000 idea on the tip of his or her tongue. The trick is to find a way to let it out. Yet I find most companies do little if anything to get ideas from their employees. Or if they do decide to take action, it's in the form of a "suggestion box" that is placed in the lunchroom with (for some reason) a lock on it. The first dozen or so employees who submit suggestions, if they hear back at all, often receive a form letter months later that more or less states, "Here's why we're not using your silly idea . . ." The result? The suggestion program grinds to a halt. In fact, I recently heard of one company that ended their dead suggestion program because, they announced, *the company had gotten all the ideas*. Right. How convenient.

They don't feel that's the case at AT&T Universal Card Services in Jacksonville, FL, where they get some 1,200 ideas *per month* from employees, month after month. They don't feel that way at Valeo, a French automaker that in a recent year received 250,000 ideas for improvement from employees.

———

Pelican Products, a Los Angeles–based designer and manufacturer of advanced lighting systems and cases, encourages idea sharing through a group called the "Blue Sky Committee," in which representatives from each department provide suggestions on how to enhance business. Anyone in the company can bring ideas to them, whether as a sketch, a sample, or simply a concept.

———

At Café Natura in the Sault Ste. Marie (Ontario) Elgin Integral Health Centre, the best source to tap to save money is the employees' suggestions. Once a week after lunch, they discuss how to reduce costs. "They have come up with many good ideas," says owner Kelly Burton, who provides them with free lunch every day and trains them for all roles from food preparation to handling cash.

———

Analytical Graphics Inc., an aerospace and defense company based in Exton, PA, solicits employee ideas through annual surveys and quarterly town hall meetings. Every Friday, the company hosts "Storytime," when employees talk about their projects and work. Likewise, the staff at Bailard, Inc., a private investment firm based in Foster City, CA, meets every Monday shortly after 9:00 A.M. to discuss company news, investment markets, and internal projects and to introduce new employees.

———

Dorchester Hotel in London, UK, uses a graffiti board to collect employee suggestions. Ideas employees have recommended and that have been implemented include uniting with other organizations to raise money for charity, replacing showers in staff changing rooms, and producing an annual employee yearbook—detailing staff parties and grand openings, photos of newborn babies, and annual financial data.

———

Shell Oil sought the advice of its "pride builders," otherwise known as the top supervisors, on how to improve the performance of one of its plants in Texas. Believing that these individuals were the most in tune with the other employees, the company turned to them to learn how to best motivate employees and instill in them the drive to help improve plant operations. The result of Shell's program was a vast improvement in overall morale, a better idea of what it takes to develop more top supervisors, and a 30 percent reduction in avoidable maintenance.

———

Texas Commerce Bank holds focus groups with employees to determine what procedures most frustrate employees and customers. Acting on the feedback, the bank nearly doubled its $50 million cost-savings goal.

———

American Strap in Diamond City, AK, found that employees became more and more creative after their suggestion system was launched. Just finding that their suggestions were being taken seriously changed the workers' attitudes, and they became even more willing to find ways to help the company improve.

———

Hospira Inc., a global pharmaceutical company based in Lake Forest, IL, uses an employee engagement survey to find out what employees think and need. They also encourage employees to "just come forward with ideas." In response to recent surveys, the company now provides female employees with more opportunities for networking, mentoring, leadership development, and charitable work. They also created the Ignite program, which allows employees to submit grant applications for ideas to help improve employee effectiveness. To make the point that employees are being heard, managers use a stamp, "Your Ideas in Action," when they announce changes as a result of employee feedback. All employees are highly engaged in achieving the firm's goals on a daily basis. They do this through "huddles," the initial 10 to 15 minutes each work group shares *every morning* in which all employee-owners describe their number one priority for the day and any barriers to achieving that priority. They all vote on the top priority, and then their manager passes their collective number one on to a second-level huddle that is held immediately following the first one. At the second huddle, the same process is repeated, along with a review of the previous day's metrics. The manager groups can choose to resolve any or all of the barriers that arise, and then they, too, vote on the number one priority, which is passed on to the executive team for that group's meeting, which is up next.

O n Fridays, The SCOOTER Store breaks its "meeting rhythm," as they call it, for "IQs," that is, "Ideas or Questions" that every employee has for achieving that quarter's overarching goals, which they refer to as "Rocks."

Soliciting Ideas from Employees

Only 41 percent of surveyed employees believe the typical company listens to employees' ideas. One of the best ways to involve employees in an organization and to energize them in the process is soliciting their ideas and opinions. Real motivation comes from within. People have to be given the freedom to voice their opinions and make suggestions. Various systems and programs—known by a wide variety of names, including total quality management, continuous improvement, or simply the good old suggestion box—seek employees' opinions and encourage them to make suggestions. It is important for employees to know that their suggestions are taken seriously and that they can make a big difference. By carefully reviewing employee suggestions and quickly implementing those that have merit, management sends a message to employees that they are valued.

When implementing employee suggestion programs, it is important to keep in mind a few key points:

- Encourage employees to make suggestions for improving either the workplace or service to your customers.
- Encourage any idea, no matter how small. Sometimes you have to get through simple suggestions before employees begin offering more significant ones.
- Publicly acknowledge the individuals who make suggestions and the improvements that result.

Numerous companies have found innovative ways to make employee suggestions programs work. For example, an oil refinery in Texas City, TX, uses a program that has saved millions of dollars in two years. The plant awards gift certificates to suggesters in front of their fellow workers during lunch breaks, publicizing them on the refinery's internal TV system and in local newspapers, and entering them in contests for Employee of the Month or Year. Winners garner gifts like pen-and-pencil sets and weeklong vacations, which are presented by the plant manager at plantwide dinners.

———

TAKING INITIATIVE
AT BOARDROOM, INC.

Boardroom, Inc., a newsletter and book publisher based in Greenwich, CT, expects every employee—from receptionist to chairman—to submit at least two ideas every week for improvements. Initially established to encourage cost savings, the Boardroom, Inc., program is called "I Power," and they credit the suggestion program with a fivefold increase in revenues, as well as untold benefit to the morale, energy, and retention of their employees. All the suggestions are evaluated the same week by an employee volunteer. For many of the suggestions, the evaluator says "What a great idea!" and then returns the idea to the person who suggested it with the implicit permission to proceed to implement the idea.

As Martin Edelston, chairman and CEO of Boardroom, says, "Sometimes the best idea can come from the newest, least experienced person on your staff." Like the hourly paid shipping clerk who suggested that the company consider trimming the paper size of one of its books in order to get under the four-pound postal rate and save money on postage. The company made the change and did indeed save some postage: half a million dollars the first year and several years since. Explains Marty: "I had been working in mail-order for over 20 years and never realized there was a four-pound shipping rate. But the person who was doing the job knew it, as do most employees know how their jobs can be improved."

During the first year of the program, suggestions were

Everyone Counts is a program at Black & Decker, headquartered in Towson, MD, that has used teams to brainstorm and develop ideas about training, communication, administration, and rewards. People from different departments were grouped into 39 teams, and two evaluation committees for managerial personnel were named to receive ideas and judge limited to one's own job, until employees got the idea that the intention was less to complain about things than it was to try to think of how they could improve things. The company even now has group meetings just to brainstorm and share ideas about specific issues or functions in the company.

And the benefits of the suggestions are not limited to saving money. Says Antoinette Baugh, director of personnel, "People love working here because they know they can be a part of a system where they can make a contribution." Adds Lisa Castonguay, renewals and billing manager: "My first couple of weeks I was kind of taken aback because everyone was smiling and everyone was open." She recalls her first day of work, in which she was pulled into a group meeting and within 30 minutes of walking in the front door was asked,

"What do you think we should do about this problem?"

Lisa almost fell on the floor. Why? Because she had just come from a company where she had worked for eight years and no one had ever asked her opinion about anything. Once she got over the initial shock, it felt pretty good to have her opinions and ideas sought after and valued by those she worked with. As a result it was easy for her to want to think of additional ways to help the company.

The impact is both positive and contagious. "People became agents of their own change," says Marty. "There's so much inside of all of us and we don't even know it's there until someone asks about it. And in the process it just builds and builds." Adds Brian Kurtz, vice president of marketing: "It's a constant flow of communication. People are not sitting in a cubicle, totally insulated from one another."

their merit. The evaluation teams also noted leadership potential in some employees when they made their presentations. A total of 200 ideas were submitted and 59 approved. The first 12 ideas to be implemented dealt mostly with improved operations that resulted in cost savings. One $700,000 idea concerned the substitution of new material in one of the company's product lines. The program also improved upward lines of communication in the company.

———

At Eastman Kodak in Rochester, NY, an employee whose suggestion is implemented receives 15 percent of the out-of-pocket savings achieved in the first two years of use. If a suggestion results in a new product, the award is equal to 3 percent of the sales achieved in the first year. Kodak has given awards—averaging $3 million annually—to more than 30,000 people.

———

Employees at Levi Strauss, based in San Francisco, nominate one another for the firm's Koshland Award for showing initiative, taking risks, generating cost-saving measures, coming up with creative ideas for promoting products at the retail level—anything that puts the company at a competitive advantage. Winners receive a plaque at an annual awards ceremony and a cash prize.

Give Employees the Chance to Take Initiative

One of the most significant organizational strategy activities that energizes employees is encouraging the freedom to take initiative. Taking initiative at work is a key ingredient in making improvements, solving problems, dealing with change, and providing customers with service that far exceeds their expectations. And it's the employees doing the jobs who are in the best position to do their job better, to resolve problems as they arise, and to benefit the most from their actions. A poll of executives asked: "What do you feel is the single best way for employees to earn a promotion and/or raise?" Topping the list for 82 percent of respondents was "Ask for more work and responsibility."

Too often, however, employees are reluctant to take the initiative they need to excel, in part because they don't feel it's what the manager really wants. According to a Gallup survey of 1,200 U.S. workers, for example, 66 percent of respondents say their managers have asked them to get involved in decision making, but only 14 percent feel they have been empowered to make those decisions; that is, they are not given the authority, resources, and support necessary to be successful.

The more supportive and encouraging the environment, the more willing employees will be to take initiative that organizations need to compete and excel. "How a company deals with mistakes suggests how well it will ring out the best ideas and talents of its people, and how effectively it will respond to change," says Bill Gates, chairman and former CEO of Microsoft Corporation. "When employees know that mistakes won't lead to retribution, it creates an atmosphere in which people are willing to come up with ideas and suggest changes. This is important to a company's long-term success."

There are a variety of ways organizations can produce a work environment in which employees feel charged—almost compelled—to be creative. For example, at 3M in St. Paul, MN, employees are encouraged to develop and create new products. Professional staff members whose ideas are given the nod by management can receive funding to build their own businesses within the company. Those who are successful in their efforts are given promotions and pay raises. There is no penalty for those who are not successful. Employees are motivated by the opportunity to see their ideas come to fruition, and a significant portion of the company's revenue now comes from products introduced through this program.

TOP TEN WAYS TO TAKE INITIATIVE AT WORK

In today's fast-moving, constantly changing business environment, the need for employees to take initiative and do what needs to be done without waiting to be told is greater than ever. In addition to helping your organization save money, improve processes, or delight customers, taking initiative makes your job more exciting—you are able to make things happen and get a reputation for doing so. Here, then, are top ways you can take initiative and make a difference at work.

1. THINK HOW THINGS COULD BE IMPROVED. *It's the person who does a job that knows best how it can be done better. Ask silly questions such as "Why do we do it this way?" A secretary at Johnsonville foods asked why the company didn't sell directly to customers and was soon put in charge of what became a multimillion-dollar direct-sales division.*

2. THINK LIKE A CUSTOMER. *Look at the business from your customers' perspective, asking what would make it easier to do business with your company. An employee at Kacey's Fine Furniture in Denver suggested changing the store's operating hours to times that were more convenient for working customers, and sales instantly rose by 15 percent.*

3. TRACK YOUR OWN PERFORMANCE. *Track activity in your own job to build a case for possible improvements. An assembler for United Electric Controls who tracked his numbers was able to devise a simpler way to inventory parts that saved the company much money.*

4. TAKE ACTION ON YOUR IDEAS. *Having ideas is good, but don't just plop them on the table and expect others to run with* *them. Be an advocate for your ideas. An employee at Starbucks pushed a frosty new coffee drink she believed in, and with time the Frappuccino became a $100 million product for the company.*

5. DO YOUR HOMEWORK. *Think your ideas through. Decide what steps need to be taken, what the costs and benefits are, and collect supporting data. A part-time employee of the State of Massachusetts independently researched the state's Medicaid rules on her own time and was able to uncover an accounting glitch. As a result, the state was able to obtain higher reimbursements. She received a cash award and special thanks from the governor.*

6. BUILD CONSENSUS. *Start with those who will most likely be interested in your idea to get them involved in supporting it. In the early days of the Internet, an IBM employee sent an internal memo to employees urging them to "get connected" and a list of actions they could take. He immediately got support for his initiative from others about the vision he saw for the future. He was later named chief technology officer.*

7. SPEAK UP AT MEETINGS. *We've all been in meetings that have gotten sidetracked or bogged down. Be the person who speaks up to say, "It may just be me, but have we been over this ground before? Perhaps we should summarize the choices and take a vote for how we want to proceed." Others will appreciate your intervention, and you will help move the group closer to its goals.*

8. VOLUNTEER FOR NEW ASSIGNMENTS. *Whether it is a pressing problem, a special task force, or someone else in the department that needs help, be the person to step forward to help out. A new employee at the Gap in Toronto, who noticed that the company's policy manual didn't cover half the issues that came* *up in the store, drafted a concise training manual that is now used throughout the country.*

9. MANAGE YOUR MANAGER. *Try to understand your manager's priorities and fit your ideas into those. Tell your manager what you need in order to do the best job for him or her. An employee at a company in San Jose told her manager that she wanted to meet once a month to review her work and get feedback about her progress. These short meetings kept her manager informed of her needs and successes—and reenergized her.*

10. STICK WITH YOUR IDEAS; PERSEVERE. *It's very infrequent that ideas are met with open arms. Stay the course with the ideas you most believe in that will help the business. When management nixed one employee's idea for a flextime work schedule, she simply waited until a new manager came on board to propose the idea again, which was then accepted.*

To spur their creativity, researchers at electronics manufacturer Hewlett-Packard, headquartered in Palo Alto, CA, are given access to 24-hour laboratories and are urged to devote 10 percent of their time to personal pet projects.

Involve Employees in Decision Making

Most business decisions in organizations come from the top down, but is that always the best direction? No one knows jobs or departments better than the people who live and breathe them every day—doesn't it make more sense to start there? If you're looking for a way to cut back on office supplies, talk to the person responsible for ordering them or managing inventory. If a reporting process is ineffective or costly, talk to the individual responsible for managing the process. A perfect example of this can be found in a receptionist at Champion Solutions Group in Florida who received expense reports from field sales representatives via overnight delivery. When her suggestion that the reports be faxed instead of shipped was implemented, the company saw a 40 percent reduction in postage costs. This led to company leaders seeking the advice of employees for other ways in which cost savings could be realized.

When employees believe they have a say in a decision, companywide buy-in and participation is much easier to obtain. If the general consensus among staff is that decisions will be made with or without their input, the likelihood of anyone providing open and honest feedback is quite small. In fact, in one survey conducted by Gallup, 66 percent of respondents say their managers have asked them to get involved in decision making, but only 14 percent feel they have been empowered to make those decisions. Asking employees for their input on decisions shows that you have respect for and trust in them, and this will likely increase the quality of the decisions being made. Ultimately, however, the responsibility still remains with the manager.

Employees who offer solutions that result in cost savings should not go unrecognized. Incentives, such as bonuses, trips, or gift cards will not only reward the employee but inspire others to develop cost-saving ideas of their own. Make the process fun and rewarding. Hold contests, departmental competitions, or other organized events to increase involvement and interaction. Managers need to ensure that employees are given the opportunity to be involved in the decision-making process.

Strategy #4: Increase Employee Autonomy & Flexibility

"**I**f you ride a horse, sit close and tight. If you ride a man, sit easy and light."

This sage advice from *Poor Richard's Almanac* is relevant today for managers trying to get the most from their employees.

Ranked as one of the top motivators for employees in their jobs today is the notion of autonomy and authority: having a say in how they do their work and the ability, power, and support to do what is necessary to get the job done. In my research employees ranked the following items as very or extremely important: "being allowed to decide how best to do one's work" (89 percent), "being given increased job autonomy" (87 percent), and "being given increased authority in the job" (85 percent).

Autonomy and authority create the foundation of trust and respect that today's employees so highly value. It provides them with a sense of independence and a freedom to bring their own imprint to their work. This freedom is important for fostering employee creativity, resourcefulness, and best efforts, which in turn lead to higher performance and increased employee satisfaction and fulfillment at work. With autonomy and authority, employees feel more confident in taking initiative with their work and more competent that the initiative they take will pay off, leading to better results and an enhanced ability to take on greater assignments and responsibilities.

No one likes to work for a micromanager, although in the book *My Way or the Highway*, by Harry Chambers, it's reported that four out of five workers say they have done just that—and one out of three workers has even changed jobs because of it. To tap into the wellspring of potential every employee has to offer, you need to give them more room and encourage them to take responsibility—and recognize them when they do.

Every employee needs to have a say in how they do their work to make it more meaningful. When employees find their work to be meaningful, they become more engaged and effective. In tough times the need for employees to become engaged in their jobs is amplified. It is critical that they go beyond their job descriptions to do whatever they can to make a difference in their jobs, as well as for the greater good of the company.

AUTONOMY TIPS

→ Give them a special assignment.

→ Have them train others.

→ Let them lead a weekly meeting.

→ Give them first choice of a work schedule.

→ Let them choose a project to work on.

Once employees have been enlisted to get involved and make suggestions and improvements, they need to be encouraged to run with their ideas, take responsibility, and champion those ideas through to closure and completion. Managers can encourage this increase in autonomy by the way they delegate assignments and provide flexibility to employees—including whom employees can approach for help, and authority to use resources and take necessary actions to get the work done. To the extent that managers or the organization is able to provide those motivators for employees, it can greatly impact their morale and performance in having them do their best work possible.

The vast majority of employees prefer to be assigned a task and allowed the freedom to develop a work plan that suits them. No one likes to be micromanaged. Roles and responsibilities may be previously defined, but they are customized based on the individual who occupies the position. Here is where truly knowing your employees becomes important: Understanding their strengths and weaknesses allows a manager to properly assign projects and tasks. Take it a step further by allowing employees to pick and choose the projects and responsibilities they can work on.

Companies today cannot afford to stifle themselves in a culture of entitlement. To be able to respond quickly and effectively to advances in technology, competitive threats, and the changing workplace in general, employees must be committed and devoted to making a difference in their organizations. They must want to make a contribution . . . and thrive because of it.

———

Chip Conley, owner of Joie de Vivre Hospitality, a chain of 20 eclectic "boutique hotels" in California, used the work of psychologist Abraham Maslow to help his company survive the recent economic recession. Conley sought a systematic way to satisfy people's higher needs. First, he convinced salaried employees to accept a two-year salary freeze so he could avoid layoffs among his 800 hourly employees. Then he upgraded the company's recognition programs, handing out prizes to employees who went above and beyond, and making sure executive meetings ended with each member nominating an employee who deserved special recognition. Conley created meaning for all employees by giving them more freedom to choose how they do their jobs, including them in annual strategy retreats, devising a two-word mantra, "create joy," describing their shared purpose, and involving them in JdV's philanthropic activities. He designed similar needs frameworks for customers and investors. Between

2001 and 2005, JdV tripled in size and has since doubled its number of properties.

———

Anthony Wilder Design/Build, a home-remodeling firm based in Cabin John, MD, teaches financial management to its employees. Employees are expected to understand how their work and their department's work affect the bottom line and to seek efficiencies on the job. The company also altered its bonus system so employees get a set portion of net quarterly profits, rather than bonuses based on individual performance. In monthly companywide breakfast meetings, all employees discuss company finances. Employees are asked to speak up about what types of issues they're facing on the job and brainstorm ways to save or generate more revenue. Ideas enacted have ranged from cutting text-messaging service on company cell phones to taking on smaller-scale remodeling projects. When the economy got really bad, senior managers asked employees to take pay cuts. Most took cuts of 20 to 30 percent, while the owners took 50 percent. "Having employees fully understand the financial situation—and seeing the founders make a bigger sacrifice—helped garner support for the cuts," Elizabeth Wilder said. As the economy recovered, the company gave out back pay.

———

Management at Phelps County Bank in Rolla, MO, formed the Problem Busters committee to give employees the authority to make decisions and encourage them to solve their own problems.

———

Employees at Microsoft in Redmond, WA, are given great latitude in deciding how to do their jobs.

———

Reference International Software in San Francisco allows customer service representatives one day a week to work on any project they choose. Some results have been better systems and salable products—and really great employee morale.

———

When the supervisor of the membership development department of the Girl Scouts of Santa Clara County, CA, left the organization, chief executive Nancy Fox declined to fill the vacancy and, instead, handed over responsibility of all department duties to its staff. Department employees set their own work schedules and determine how they will do their jobs. Says Fox, "Individuals on the team tell me they feel more responsible and connected to what they do."

———

Carolina Safety Associates, a fire protection company in Gastonia, NC, shared financial results with employees and gave them freedom to make changes that had a positive impact on the bottom line. Employees reported increased job satisfaction and formed several off-line, problem-solving task forces on their own.

———

At Genentech, the San Francisco–based founder of the biotechnology industry, employees pursue their own projects, and hierarchy is kept to a minimum in an atmosphere of "casual intensity."

———

At Hitachi's Tokyo, Japan, headquarters, the appliance manufacturer has removed formal titles, somber suits, and morning calisthenics. The goal is to promote individuality and innovation. Company spokeswoman Emi Takase says employees are being urged to wear polo shirts and slacks, hoping that more casual clothing will bring out people's personalities and stimulate creativity, which will in turn lead to new ideas on how to improve the company. Workers are no longer required to address supervisors by formal titles and may use personal names.

Allow Flexible Work Schedules

One significant motivation for today's employees is increased flexibility in their work schedules. Depending upon the type of work, flexibility could increase the efficiency of getting the work done. Companies that have enacted policies regarding working from home or flexible schedules have reported the following results:

- 34 percent reduction in absenteeism
- One-third fewer sick days used
- Overall decrease in cholesterol and blood pressure among employees
- 93 percent of employees feel as though the company cares about the work they do
- 91 percent of employees care about the company, not just their jobs

For example, at one point I managed a work group that experimented with having employees work from home on certain projects. Everyone logged their hours and was available as needed to discuss work issues, etc. Not counting the commute time that was saved, we found employees to be twice as efficient in what work they could accomplish. There was less socializing and there were fewer interruptions, so employees could better focus on the work at hand.

Many employees struggle with how to effectively maintain a work–life balance without compromising their success as employees, parents, or spouses. Research has shown that involvement in activities outside work can serve as a stress reducer and creates a better, well-rounded employee. Companies can help employees achieve a better balance in their lives by implementing policies that promote a life outside the workplace. There are many options for increasing flexibility, including alternate hours (arrive early and leave early or vice versa), four-day work weeks in which longer hours are worked on fewer days, telecommuting, job sharing, or even just the ability to allow an employee to leave work early, when necessary, or time off to compensate for extra hours they had worked.

Many companies have found that by giving employees the option of a flexible schedule, or telecommuting, morale and productivity are increased. For some, the attractions are a reduction in the amount of time spent each week in a car and saving money on gas or mileage. Others may find it beneficial to

FLEXIBLE HOURS TIPS

➡ Start work an hour later; extend a lunch break; give an extra break during the day; allow one hour off from work; end work one hour early.

➡ During summer, allow employees to leave early on Friday afternoons.

➡ Give a paid half/full day off; half day off before holiday weekend.

➡ Give a 3-day weekend; an extra vacation day.

➡ Give a paid day off on birthday; a paid "Day Off Coupon."

➡ Give a week off with pay (have employee's work done for him or her).

➡ Let employee work from home for a period of time.

limit child care expenses, or simply to have the opportunity to spend more time with their children. Whatever the motivation, employees appreciate the option of being able to have some control over their own schedules and, as a result, feel as though the company has their best interest in mind.

Employees are looking for ways to better integrate the demands of their personal lives with their roles at work. Technology has helped create a work environment where communication is more streamlined, companies are better integrated, and most work can be completed from virtually anywhere. Tapping into some of these resources and finding the ways they best work within a company can do wonders for alleviating stress, which makes for much happier, more productive employees.

Employco USA, based in Westmont, IL, offers flexible work hours and time off to take care of children and aging parents. At Holmes Corp., a company based in Eagan, MN, that designs, markets, and distributes educational materials for professional associations, employees can leave work early to watch their children's sports games or work from home to assist elderly parents. Boston Consulting Group, the Boston-based management consulting firm, gives employees the flexibility to work from home and to modify how their work is scheduled—as long as they get the work done.

———

At Railroad Associates Corp., a Hershey, PA, railroad engineering and contracting firm, employees have flexible schedules. A few years ago, the young daughter of Brian Hiltz, a truck driver for the company, needed back surgery in Philadelphia. Rather than dock his vacation or sick time, company president Michael Kennedy told him to take off all the time he needed. "He covered for me that entire week while I was off," Hiltz says. "How often is the president of the company going to jump in and run a tractor trailer for a week?" The exemplary employee relations, empowerment, and accountability seem to work. Kennedy estimates that the company saves $500,000 annually in salaries and other overhead costs.

———

Hi-Tech Hose, a flexible hose and ducting products maker in Newburyport, MA, lumps all vacation time, holidays, and sick days into a single account. Employees can take time off whenever they need it and for whatever personal reasons. ZocDoc, an online doctor-locating service recently listed in *Crain's New York Business* as the "best place to work in New York City," lets its employees take as much vacation time as they need. It's part of its flexible-rules culture. "Some people wear suits to work, others don't even wear shoes," says chief executive Cyrus Massoumi. "They're just happy that they're a part of something growing, rather than thinking their company is not in its best year or worrying about their job."

———

Cygna Group, an engineering and consulting group based in Oakland, CA, uses a "Take the Rest of the Day Off and Do" reward when employees finish a big project.

———

JS Communications gives its employees two free "I Don't Want to Get Out of Bed" days. "You don't have to worry about seeing your boss later in the day," says Alissa Pinck, general manager and vice president of the New York office. "The day is yours, and you can do whatever you want with it." Employees can use the gift on any day when they do not have a meeting or conference call scheduled.

———

Brigate Trading, a New York trading firm, works hard from 9:30 A.M. to 4 P.M., but the rest of the day is spent having fun: going to the movies, playing tennis, and visiting their kids.

———

Minneapolis-based advertising agency Carmichael Lynch offered "Summer Time Off," an additional seven paid days to enjoy the outdoors. Deland, Gibson Insurance Associates, Inc., of Wellesley Hills, MA, rewards employees with summer hours from Memorial Day to Labor Day. Everyone takes 15 fewer minutes at lunch four days a week and leaves an hour early on Fridays. Employees say they appreciate it.

———

Brainstorm Marketing in Des Moines, IA, gives employees a paid day off on their birthdays. Marlene Herman, owner of two Aamco Transmission & Complete Car Care franchises in the Cleveland, OH, area, gives her ten employees a half day off with pay.

———

Hedy Ratner, copresident of the Women's Business Development Center, a nonprofit organization that assists women with business development and expansion, walks the walk. The center, based in Chicago, has 24 full-time staff members who have the choice of flexible hours for personal and educational purposes and generous time off. The result,

Ratner says, is "happy and productive employees." Many former employees have started their own businesses and have returned to the center to provide consulting services.

———

Sun Microsystems allows employees to telecommute as their work permits it. Result: Those employees who averaged 2.5 days at home each week saved $1,700 a year in gas and vehicle wear-and-tear.

———

The core of Home Shopping Network's (HSN) operations are their call centers. At a time when the trend in call centers leans toward outsourcing, often overseas, HSN decided to try something different: They sent their reps home. While competitors, and other companies, field complaints about the quality of their customer service experience with overseas call centers, HSN put a stop to some of their outsourced work in the Philippines and stepped up staffing efforts in the U.S.

HSN currently employs close to 1,500 part-time and full-time workers and of those, close to 900 are equipped to work from home. Whereas most call centers fail at their attempts to allow employees to work from home, HSN has seen a tremendous success on many levels. Many applicants placed working from home above earning a higher salary on their list of desirable traits in a new job that broadened HSN's network of potential employees quite drastically. Currently the majority of HSN's reps are drawn from infrequently tapped markets such as retirees or disabled customers. Not only were these candidates given an opportunity to have a schedule that accommodated their needs, they were given an opportunity, period.

HSN reports that employing people who work from home

is more costly than some of the alternatives, but that the cost is more than made up for in the improving attrition rates: Once at a whopping 120 percent a year, employee turnover is now down to around 35 percent. The popularity of their flexible scheduling has been a huge attraction for job candidates.

What has this done for customer satisfaction ratings? They've improved quite a bit. As has sales performance.

The most difficult part of implementing a work-from-home program at any company is trusting that employees will keep up with their responsibilities and not become too isolated. HSN takes the following precautions that have aided in their success:

- Take the time to carefully screen new applicants.
- Develop a training program that can closely monitor employees' comfort level and determine their readiness to be independent.
- Establish a "home base" where work-from-home employees can go to reconnect with their team and other coworkers.
- Ensure that employees have regular, face-to-face meetings with supervisors.
- Host frequent events on-site to maintain employees' connection to the corporate culture.
- Encourage social networking among work-from-home employees to foster a sense of camaraderie and support.

Strategy #5: Continued Focus on Career Growth & Development

E mployee development pays important dividends for both organizations and employees. Many organizations have created comprehensive training programs to ensure that their employees have the chance to improve their work skills and to prepare them for advancement within the organization. While some of the programs are highly structured, others allow employees to identify their own training opportunities. In a recent study of workforce practices, it was found that companies that invest in their employees find it well worth it. According to the study, firms that invest in employee development have significantly higher market values than those that don't, and firms that actively encourage employee development and offer opportunities for employee involvement make much larger gains in productivity than those that didn't.

Most employee development occurs on the job, with existing opportunities to take on new challenges and assignments and, in the process, learn new skills. Managers need to support their employees in the learning of new skills and allow them to participate in special assignments, problem-oriented initiatives, and various other learning activities. They should develop learning goals with each employee, for the year and even for specific projects, and discuss what was learned in the debriefing of any completed project. Periodically, managers should also hold career development discussions with each employee, perhaps as part of his or her annual performance review, to go over career options and potential career paths.

Instead of laying off employees when markets for certain products decline, Motorola in Schaumburg, IL, has a policy of retraining them. This commitment has led to the development of one of the most extensive and successful training efforts of any corporation. It's Motorola's policy that every worker has the right to retraining and, if the worker fails the retraining, he still has a right to a job at Motorola. Eventually, a fit will be found for the employee.

―――――

At Lowe's Companies, the second-largest U.S. building supply retailer, headquartered in North Wilkesboro, NC, all vice presidents and managers are required to work in one of the retail stores for a week. Not only does this give managers a better appreciation for what life is like on the front line of the business, but it also gives headquarters staff the chance to get to know regular employees—making the organization a better place to work for managers and workers alike.

―――――

Jim Baka, president of CERAC, a specialty chemical maker in Milwaukee, cross-trains employees to ensure that they understand how their work fits into the overall operation. According to Baka, the results speak for themselves: "Thanks to cross-training, we've been able to push sales up 15 to 20 percent per year, while maintaining a high-quality product, delivering performance, and providing technical customer service."

Take Stock of Your Employees

Before assigning new responsibilities, managers must first take stock of their employees to determine who has the interest, capacity, and ability to take on new responsibilities and assignments. If you haven't already done so, take time to meet with all your employees to discuss their job interests and ambitions and create an "inventory of readiness" for your staff. Who has skills that aren't currently being utilized in the department? Who is interested in learning more about other areas of the business, its clients, processes, products, or services? Who wants to get into a management position someday? What does everyone want to be doing five years from now? With this initial baseline of information about your team, you will be able to evaluate who might fit emerging needs. Navigating through a recession is an ideal time to tap the hidden talents of all employees and expand traditional roles to help move the organization forward.

While development opportunities are traditional motivators to most employees, during crunch times such opportunities take on a new sense of urgency. A needed position is frozen or another position is terminated: How can that work best get completed? A new project emerges: Who in the group is ready to help out? New leaders need to come forward in all levels of the organization: Who has the interest and ability to step up to the plate?

As organizational needs arise ask, "Who can best benefit from that opportunity?" and approach that individual. American Express developed a teaching concept called "Label and Link" that they trained all managers to use. As a development opportunity arose, a manager would label the task as an opportunity and link it to something that was important to the employee. For example, instead of dumping a work assignment on an already overloaded employee, a manager might say, "Gary, we are forming a new client task force to deal with a new market opportunity and I immediately thought of you for the team since I know from our past conversations how interested you are in working more directly with our clients. I also know that you've got a lot on your plate right now, so if you feel you are too busy to take this on I won't hold it against you—there will be other opportunities in the future. But if you are interested, let me know, because I'll take whatever time is necessary to help you with the assignment. In fact, it might even take more of my time than if I just joined the task force myself, but I'm willing to make that investment in you because of what I've seen in your potential on our team. Let me know what you decide and thanks."

More often than not, "Gary" doesn't need to think it over further and immediately accepts the assignment. To some people this might seem like a trick, but it's the essence of motivation and you can tap into that energy—as long as you are sincere and truly do have the best interests of the employee at heart.

Training Is a Top Development Opportunity

Employees are the most important asset a company can have, for without them, a business simply cannot succeed. Employees can make or break a company, so developing their skills is extremely important. Their strengths can be the determining factor in how or if a company is able to remain a step ahead of the competition. One of the best ways to keep your workforce strong is through training.

The Container Store has been selected numerous times by *Fortune* magazine as one of the 100 Best Companies to Work For. Not only do they pay their employees above-average salaries, they strongly believe that their employee training programs are one of the major factors in their high staff retention rate and overall success. During their first year of employment, new employees can expect to receive 185 hours of training, about 26 percent more than any other retailer in the industry. Such practices have helped the Container Store continually grow at a level of almost 20 percent per year over the past two decades.

Though the temptation is great, cutting back on employee training should be one of the last things employers do. Bernie

Marcus, the Home Depot founder, holds fast to the belief that training is the key to establishing initiative and drive among employees. In fact, he attributes the success of his company to the long-standing practice of continuous training and rewarding for results.

According to a survey I conducted among employees working in industries across the nation, more than half the respondents stated a strong desire for managers to support their learning of new skills. Doing so lets employees know that their development and career advancement are important and that they're not in it alone. Pursuing additional training is decidedly difficult without the support of managers. Whether training is internal or external, employees are looking for guidance as to what training programs to pursue and as to working them into their schedules, especially if time out of the workday is required.

One of the primary concerns managers have regarding training is the massive travel expense often associated with it. Organizations are looking for ways to continue with training and development without breaking the bank. Over the last decade a large portion of training has been made available online or through other technological venues. Hours dedicated to technology-based training options have more than doubled in recent years as online options are becoming more and more popular, typically taking place as "webinars" or other modes of online presentation.

To keep costs down, some companies have embraced the idea of in-house training led by senior management or top executives. All employees can benefit from career development, and learning from those who know them and their roles the best is an ideal training situation. Programs can be a combination of general topics as well as topics that are company specific. Developing employees is much more than practical, on-the-job experience; it is imparting the wisdom of those who are more experienced, as well as reinforcing the company's goals and values.

Training on a Shoestring

- When training budgets are reduced, innovation is required. If space and dollars are limited, select top performers to participate in the training you provide. When times are tough, those with the most potential tend to shine even brighter and should be the first to be developed.
- Review existing training programs and evaluate which proved to be the most valuable and engendered the most return on investment. Cut those that have the least amount of benefits.
- Take into consideration the effectiveness of current programs. Are they truly necessary and making the most of employees' time? Perhaps, rather than holding yet another sales program, find a more innovative topic that can help performance, such as time management, organizational skills, networking, and so on.

Like most airlines, Southwest Airlines faced economic struggles after the events of September 11. With changes being made throughout the entire industry, the airline decided that all employees had to increase their ability to adapt to internal and external changes. So, rather than slash training, as was the norm in the industry at the time, Southwest increased it.

Canon USA, Inc., recently established Canon Academy in hopes of expanding leadership development. Utilizing the Internet and online courses, new managers have access to top-notch training geared toward strategic decision making.

———

Philips Electronics offers a training program called Inspire, reserved for carefully selected employees who show the greatest potential. Employees who are selected are placed in groups and assigned a business-related project.

———

The tax and advisory firm KPMG offers training and educational programs to employees and, more recently, webinars on financial planning and surviving a down economy. They have also added two seminars on stress and weight management, with personal coaches to help employees establish goals and stick to them. The cost of keeping these programs operating is exceptionally low, especially considering the tremendous benefit to the employees and the company. Employees were extremely appreciative of the forward thinking exhibited by the company regarding their health and well-being, and as a result, productivity and positive attitudes increased drastically.

Cross-Training Can Expand Employee Horizons

Cross-trained employees combat boredom and complacency while benefitting the company. If staff size is slim, employees who are versed in multiple roles can help in times of layoffs or other reductions. Make the most of your employees; take time to explore their other interests within the company. For example, a member of the technology department could have had a former career in marketing or sales and vice versa. Or they could simply have a strong interest in another part of the company. Utilize managers to provide or discover this information and use it to develop effective cross-training programs.

USAA began a cross-training program for call center reps in 2007. Agents who previously specialized in and handled only financial inquiries are now trained in insurance-related matters and can effectively handle both sets of customers. Previously, transferring calls between agents increased the operating costs of their call centers and had a negative impact on productivity.

Also, by cross-training their reps, USAA greatly increased productivity and improved customer service by reducing wait times. What's more, when the economic crisis hit, along with Hurricane Ike, USAA was able to continue operating without increasing staff, something most of its competitors found inevitable.

———

Charles Schwab assembled a group of employees from all departments within the organization and dubbed them the "Flex Force." When market activity was high, so was Schwab's call volume. This team of employees was on hand to field the additional calls and was provided adequate training to do so. Likewise, JW Marriott cross-trains administrative assistants to double as banquet servers when they are short staffed. In both cases, the companies have seen an increase in productivity and performance, as well as significant cost savings. In short, employees are often the most underutilized resources in a company yet are also one of the best options during a downturn.

———

The Glass Doctor in Florida encourages its salespeople to make in-person calls on customers rather than sit on the phone all day. Most salespeople are specialized in a certain type of glass: residential, auto, or commercial. The company developed a program at its training facility to train its salespeople on all of the products. Role-playing sessions designed to provide realistic sales scenarios also helped give the employees honest feedback on their approach and sales strategies.

The goal of the program was to position the company in the marketplace as a comprehensive distributor in the glass industry, sharpen customer service, and increase sales. The result was an added insight into untapped leads and a polished sales force that has helped the company increase sales and revenue.

———

During the recession of 2001–2003, Toyota shut down a plant for ten months but kept all employees and trained them. Toyota discovered that once it reopened, that plant had the highest global productivity and quality ratings, which helped secure a higher market share.

Cross-trained employees benefit the company as well as its employees, in good times and in bad. Toyota's unique approach of using a downturn to develop employees helped them establish procedures that aided even when things turned around. Not only that, employees found that they had acquired new skills that could help them in their current jobs and that they could use in other roles as well.

———

Debbie Stutts, customer service manager for Spectrum Chemicals & Laboratory Products in Gardena, CA, has sales representatives take turns working in other departments to learn, firsthand, the journey of an order through the company.

AT&T has a program called "Resource Link" that lets employees from diverse backgrounds and with varied management, technical, or professional skills "sell" their abilities to different departments for short-term assignments. It has greatly increased retention and employee satisfaction.

Allow Employees Opportunities to Explore New Roles

Another unique approach is to give employees an opportunity to experience different roles. For example, networking company 3Com believes that allowing those who work behind the scenes—especially engineers—to get out and sell to or visit customers gives them a greater appreciation for the value of the work they do. Salespeople especially are constantly on the front lines—they see how customers use products and hear firsthand what they need, what they think can be improved, and what simply isn't working. Those on the development side receive the information second- or thirdhand and rarely, if ever, have the opportunity to sit down with a customer and get the whole story. It's beneficial for them to engage in a dialogue that will help them do their job better and not feel as though they are operating in the dark with piecemeal information. Furthermore, when positive customer feedback is passed along, it means much more when it is conveyed in person and in greater detail.

Reassigning Employees Helps to Generate Enthusiasm

Identifying experienced employees and allowing them the opportunity to assume different or additional roles shows trust, confidence, and interest in your employees. Changes in the business necessitate changes in the roles and responsibilities of all employees. Reaching out to existing employees and giving them the first option to take on new tasks, needs, and opportunities benefits the company as well as the employees.

Employees like to increase their level of worth to the organization. In addition, current employees already have an understanding of the company culture, know policies and procedures, and have established relationships, so they can have a greater impact faster in achieving what needs to be done.

Before merging with PanEnergy and the Cinergy Corporation, Duke Power, the energy company based in Charlotte, NC, let employees—who were doing well but feeling bored with their jobs—post a message on the company's electronic bulletin board. If another employee with comparable pay and work skills wanted the job, the two employees could, with their supervisors' approval, swap jobs.

Involving employees from the very beginning of a project is important to building morale. Rather than bring employees into a project once the plan is fully formed, seek their input during the planning stages to help enhance their motivation and increase the chances that the projects will be successful and seen through to completion. When employees are empowered by their managers, the tendency is to work harder, better, and longer.

Hiring and training a new employee can take up to a year

and costs anywhere from 20 to 40 percent of the person's salary. So you can see why reassigning employees or expanding their responsibilities, if possible, is the better option. Employees view a company that makes the effort to reassign workers as one that truly values its employees, which is likely to have a positive impact on low morale or commitment—a critical component of turning an organization around. When employees are trusted with new roles and responsibilities, their sense of commitment and ownership increases—as does their positive view of the company and those in charge.

———

R ecently the state of Massachusetts dealt budget cuts that threatened its welfare-to-work program. Rather than lay off nearly 40 career counselors, the state reassigned them to call centers in need of additional clerks to help with the onslaught of unemployment claims being filed. They were all transferred at the same pay rate they earned in their previous job. The state benefitted because even though a month of training was required, the counselors were familiar with the system and had experience in working with the unemployed. The job itself was stressful, but the existing employees were well versed in handling the pressures. Whereas five employees hired from the outside quit within a few months, the reassigned workers remained.

———

L ocated in Lexington, KY, VistaPrint has made a practice of reassigning employees even when business is good. Their primary goal was to help employees better understand the business as it was rapidly growing. When hiring slowed but the need for more employees did not, the company focused on reassigning employees to roles that would directly benefit their bottom line. Recruiters were trained in sales and now work directly with potential customers. As a result, VistaPrint has been able to sustain its growth, increase revenue, and expand its hold on the marketplace. The reassigned employees were left with a sense of helping the company as well as an opportunity to grow professionally.

———

Luxury Retreats in Montreal, Quebec, has decided to take advantage of its existing employees to fill gaps in staffing rather than endure the expense of hiring from the outside. Some employees have been reassigned, while others are paid their regular salary, although their hours have been cut, to help in emergencies or to take classes further developing their skills. Offering career and development training to existing employees greatly reduces the need for, and cost of, future hiring efforts. By reinforcing the employees you have on hand and tapping into their skills and abilities, you are able to develop a workforce that is ready and able to step up to the plate when times get tough.

Mentorship Programs Serve as Useful Training Alternative

Providing mentorship programs, or simply encouraging employees to assume a mentorship role, allows employees who have grown within the company or who have significant career experience to pass on their learnings to other employees. Many times, individuals in entry-level or mid-level roles are promising or aspiring leaders, they only lack the guidance and direction to achieve their goals. Employees with a desire to further develop their skills and career path are eager to learn and welcome new opportunities, something that serves any company well, especially in a downturn.

PCL Construction ranked 28 on the 2009 100 Best Companies to Work For list for two very important reasons: their training program and their promote-from-within policy. The company has developed a "Pre-Con Boot Camp" that is designed to train employees in creating and maintaining strong customer relationships. The program is offered once a year to employees who have a desire to move into the preconstruction services area. PCL promotes a culture of employee ownership within the company and does so by focusing on promoting existing employees. In fact, in just one year close to 10 percent of employees were moved into higher-ranking positions. In an effort to make promoted employees successful in their new positions, PCL encourages mentoring by senior managers.

———

S. C. Johnson has developed a Mentoring Steering Committee responsible for pairing mentors and mentees according to similarities in work experience, interest, and skills. Over a period of 18 months, pairs contribute a total of 45 hours to the commitment. All participants in the program, mentors and mentees alike, have reported a positive experience that left them with a sense of personal and professional growth.

———

Newly graduated nurses often face culture shock when moving into a full-time role in a hospital environment. To ease this transition, and ensure the success of newly hired nurses, some hospitals have made adjustments to their entry programs, many of which can be modified to fit nearly any industry or company. Here are some of their ideas:

- Provide online evaluation systems to track progress.
- Establish regular meetings with a mentor to discuss the evaluation.
- Develop an easily accessible curriculum program.
- Select individuals from various departments to conduct training so that newly hired employees establish relationships outside those with people with whom they work directly.
- Recruit volunteers, especially previous or retired employees, to serve as mentors if existing employees cannot afford to take the time.

Hospitals that adopted all or some of the above strategies for ensuring success have reported exceedingly positive results. These include a drastic reduction in new-hire turnover, a reported increase in on-the-job confidence among new nurses, and an ability to attract qualified applicants from the outside because of their employer's growing reputation in the industry.

The learning and development team at Banner Health works alongside the executive office to develop mentorship programs for leaders. The result has been two effective programs that have produced hundreds of leaders:

1. NEW LEADER EXPERIENCE: *Every month, this three-day seminar is held at the company's headquarters and introduces new managers to the company's overall goals. In addition, the managers are presented with resources on how to guide employees effectively.*

2. LEADERSHIP SYMPOSIUMS: *These weeklong development programs give leaders the chance to renew their skills and interact with other leaders in the organization.*

Stronger managers can help move a company from middle of the road to great, and they can be even more beneficial when a sweeping recovery is needed. Investing in programs that provide leadership development is an effective strategy in the long and short term. If cuts to training budgets are necessary, concentrate on eliminating training for skills that can be attained through other means and concentrate specifically on leadership.

Internship Programs

In addition to or instead of mentorship programs, some companies have developed internship programs for employees. Especially in a large company, where options for a career path are numerous, allowing employees the ability to experience a behind-the-scenes look at a new role or department can help guide them in their development. For a predetermined period of time, allow employees who have expressed interest in moving to another role or division the opportunity to work alongside someone who is currently in the desired position or department. During this period they do not relinquish their existing jobs and are assured of being able to return to their original roles when the internship is complete. Even if an opening does not exist, or the specific role is currently occupied, when vacancies do occur the employee who has completed an internship and acquired the necessary skills and knowledge is likely to emerge as a prime internal candidate. This saves the company time and money in conducting an external search to fill open positions.

MITRE, ranked 66 on the 2009 100 Best Companies to Work For list, has taken a concentrated approach to its internship program. Known within the company as "shadowing," the program is open primarily to women who are interested in growing their career. Throughout the program, MITRE's female employees meet regularly with their shadow and participate in select meetings to which they otherwise would not have been invited.

Shadowing programs can be particularly effective in the development of unlikely relationships among employees. Companies that already have such programs in place have reported a relationship among shadows/shadowers that extends beyond the duration of the program. These connections, especially when spread across departments, do tremendous things for morale, communication, and commitment to the company. Employees no longer feel isolated in their roles or departments and begin to develop a greater sense of belonging.

Young employees in particular are ideal candidates for shadowing or mentoring programs, especially if their current role does not match their education or desired career path. Many times, young employees or new graduates will pursue an opportunity with a company in the hopes of moving up or on to a job or department that better suits their background and interest. This approach has been particularly successful in companies or organizations that must deal with frequent shortages of adequately skilled candidates.

Development of managers, or development of employees to *become* managers, is best achieved by combining personal and professional development. Each person should be focused on key factors of their personal life, as well as their career, including how they have contributed to their environments, how they interact with individuals they encounter, what their values and beliefs are, and what they need to acquire in order to get where they would like to be. Yet the motivation to explore and expand on each of these has to start with a goal and a targeted focus.

Learning Opportunities Can be Personal, Too

Training shouldn't end at job-related tasks and knowledge. At a time when employees will become more interested in the financial health of the company, it is important for them to understand the information being presented. Making additional training available to all employees regarding financial matters will not only aid in their understanding of the company's financial situation, but will help encourage a commitment to turning things around. If employees feel as though they are a part of the process by understanding how their jobs contribute to the overall performance of the company, they are far more likely to jump aboard and work that much harder to contribute.

GlaxoSmithKline offers a seminar focused on personal resilience to teach employees ways to prevent stress and succeed in their jobs. A group of employees is assigned the task of pointing out work-related pressures within their departments and presenting suggestions as to how they might be combated. The aim of the program is to address life pressures as well, with the belief that for employees to be successful they must be happy, which has to begin at home. Since its inception, GSK's stress management program has reduced work-related and stress-induced illnesses in employees by nearly 60 percent, which also resulted in a 29 percent decrease in absenteeism for health reasons.

Similarly, the financial services company Ernst & Young has offered stress management programs to employees for nearly 20 years. Known as EY/Assist, the program has been responsible for

LEARNING & MENTORING TIPS

➡ Give certificates highlighting employees' achievements when they use a technique learned in a training program.

➡ Ask an employee to represent you in a meeting or represent your company in a community outreach program.

➡ Ask an employee to help you with a project that presents a real challenge to both of you.

➡ Allow employees to select and attend a training course of their choice. Discuss what you hope they will learn from the course. After they attend it, meet with them to see how they will apply their new knowledge.

➡ Offer tuition reimbursement for college courses.

➡ Let an employee exchange positions with someone else in the company.

the development of policies such as allowing employees to take their children along on business trips and offering company-provided consultation services. Most recently, sponsors of the program developed a blog wherein employees can exchange tips for effective stress management. Among Ernst & Young employees, 76 percent reported stress levels at moderate to great before taking advantage of the stress management program. The same employees were surveyed again after enrolling in the program, and 50 percent stated that they had seen a marked improvement in their stress levels, with 62 percent feeling their productivity had improved.

The best learning cultures promote learning of all types, not just job-specific training. Offering programs that speak to employees' emotional and mental well-being is one way of showing you have their best interests at heart. For example, if company financial goals are being revised, chances are that employees' personal finances will be impacted, as well. Providing access to information (webcasts, online seminars, and so on) regarding financial management or investments is a great way to help employees plan for their future, as well as be more open to changes within the company. Helping employees learn how to properly manage their finances will help reduce stress levels and teach financial planning skills that can help them at work, especially when financial restructuring is necessary.

Offering such programs to employees can aid them in sorting out worries that are most likely at the forefront of their minds: investments, insurance, and general retirement planning. A better understanding of their financial situation can help employees focus more on long-term plans for their career. These days, employees are no longer relying on their 401(k)s for retirement savings and are looking for alternate means by which their future can be secured. Taking steps to ease such worries is beneficial to the company, and it requires very little cost or effort.

MetLife, one of the largest providers of employee benefits, offers retirement education seminars in various companies. The workshops are free and are presented by Certified Financial Planners offering advice and instruction for employees of all ages on financing retirement. At the end of each seminar, close to half of the attendees chose to take advantage of the opportunity to meet with a retirement specialist.

Assuming an active role in helping employees plan for the future shows a company's concern for all aspects of its employees' lives. Frequently, seminars can include discussions that go beyond financing retirement to planning activities when work is no longer part of the daily routine. An opportunity for employees to ask questions that they might not get answered elsewhere can set the wheels in motion for proper goal setting.

Fidelity Investments offers Web-based seminars that allow employees to participate from their office or computer. Or, if their work schedules do not allow, they can access an online tutorial at their convenience. Fidelity has found that of all attendees at its seminars, half make some kind of change to their retirement goals within a couple of weeks. A concentration on education and making it simple for employees to revise their goals and plans has made programs such as these very successful in the workplace.

———

New York City–based advertising agency ID Media offers monthly hour-long training programs on industry issues, and another New York City–based firm, Rand Engineering & Architecture, provides in-house professional-education programs. Heavy Construction Systems Specialists (HCSS), a Houston-area software developer based in Sugar Land, TX, occasionally brings in experts to teach employees important life skills, such as personal finance and public speaking.

———

Based in Foster City, CA, Bailard, Inc., a private investment firm, pays for employee development and encourages junior staffers to create ideas and pursue projects that have personal interest, resulting in an average employee tenure of 13 years.

———

Technical employees at 3M, the St. Paul, MN, science-based products company, spend an average of 15 percent of their time pursuing ideas of their own.

———

The Health Alliance, a hospital consortium (and the second-largest employer) in Cincinnati, OH, uses a scavenger hunt to orient new employees. During the hunt, they meet and learn about others in their department and what they do. Then they fill out specific information about their coworkers and share their findings in the weekly staff meeting. Mercer Management Consulting, headquartered in New York City, uses a scavenger hunt to orient team members who travel to new cities. They are asked to visit client offices, large hotels, and the convention center when they arrive, bringing back "proof" of their visits to each location.

Marriott International Case Study: A Tradition of Opportunities to Learn and Grow

In 2007 at the age of 74, J. W. (Bill) Marriott Jr. started a blog to create a direct line of communication with both customers and employees. "More than anything else, a blog is a way to put a personal face on the company," he explains. "They're coming to the blog to find out what you think. They want to know about you as a person. That's why I talk about my golden retriever, my grandchildren, and so many fun things we do as a family." Personal anecdotes have helped to make his blog, *Marriott on the Move*, a big hit with employees and customers.

The blog exemplifies Marriott's dedication to the personal growth and development he seeks from and inspires in every one of the 150,000+ associates working at more than 3,000 Marriott properties in over 60 countries around the world.

"Many of our senior managers and general managers have come up the ranks," he shares with pride. "Our head of North American lodging operations—with more than 2,000 hotels— started as a waiter. The head of all international hotels started as a security guard. I started working in the kitchen in Salt Lake City for four years. Almost all our senior people have gone through the trenches. So, opportunity is very important; innovation is very important to us. You can't just rest on your laurels. You really have to be looking for a better way.

"People feel the same around the world: They want to be recognized, they want to be taken care of, they want to get fair pay, they want an opportunity. We provide opportunities for people to grow. There are very few core values, and the most important one is that we do our best to take care of our people. If we take care of our customers, they come back. It's very simple, easily translated, and it's really become very global."

Perhaps the most important value to Marriott is opportunity. "We've employed literally hundreds of thousands of people. Everywhere I go I meet people who have worked for us, somewhere, sometime, someplace. And we give people the opportunity to learn. Giving people these opportunities has just been wonderful, and to continue to do that makes me feel that we have really contributed to their lives, their livelihood, and helped them advance and grow."

According to a study conducted by the Greensboro, NC–based Center for Creative Leadership, a nonprofit institution that does research and training on the topic of leadership, there are five ways to create new challenges for your employees without assigning them to entirely new jobs.

1. Assign small projects and start-ups that require learning new tasks, working under time pressure, and dealing with new groups of people.

2. Assign small-scope jumps and fix-its that emphasize team building, individual responsibility, dealing with the boss, encouraging subordinates, and managing time pressures.

3. Make small, strategic assignments that emphasize presentation and analytical skills.

4. Have your employees do course work and/or take on coaching assignments that require learning something new and are intellectually challenging, both of which can lead to heightened self-awareness.

5. Have your employees undertake activities away from work that emphasize individual leadership skills, working with new people, and learning to influence and persuade.

Mentoring & Career Development

At AIPSO, a 400-employee nonprofit in the auto insurance industry and based in Johnston, RI, there is a "buddy" program through which new hires get a mentor in the company. AIPSO has found that mentoring eliminates the period of new-employee awkwardness and engenders loyalty from the start. AIPSO reports that 40 percent of its employees were positively affected by the recognition program.

———

The Cleveland, OH, office of accounting firm KPMG rolled out a senior leadership mentor program. Senior leaders meet with mentees once a month to allay career stability concerns and build partnerships. KPMG also gave each employee a box of thank-you notes to use and send to fellow workers to recognize good work.

———

As part of a commitment to groom leaders at every level of the organization, the Ontario (Canada) Municipal Employees Retirement System (OMERS) strengthened its staff development programs—by mentoring, for example—so that when career opportunities arrive, the individual is ready for it. Elisa Freedman, a team leader in the pension accounting group, joined OMERS in 2003 and was proud of her employer and excited by future opportunities. OMERS provided her with an education-assistance package that paid tuition for the Certified Management Accountant accreditation and allowed her study time. The right opportunity arrived for Freedman when she was promoted to manager of pension accounting. "I've been able to advance and I've been nurtured in a way that I appreciate," she says.

———

At Cox Financial Corporation, based in Cincinnati, employees are encouraged to set their own goals. The goal-setting process begins with identifying what employees want to achieve in their personal lives, and then specifically how to achieve them. Cox examines their motivators further by having them rate certain achievements such as prestige, money, power, self-esteem, and helping others. "If goals originate from those personal priorities and then spiral outward, commitment is automatic," says Phillip R. Cox, president and CEO. "I can't make the goals for them or they're artificial." Employees are encouraged to enlist coworkers and family members as personal accountability partners. Cox posts everyone's results in the office, which often triggers self-correction. Rewards are personalized by pulling from the priorities on which each employee initially based their goals.

———

Woodmeister Master Builders, Inc., a family owned high-end residential construction business based in Holden, MA, promotes people based on talent and ambition, not birthright. The company launched an intense leadership-training initiative to assess and develop the leadership abilities of its staff. It spends about $60,000 annually—or $6,000 a participant—to put ten employees from a cross section of the company through its Next Level Leadership program. Employees nominate others or themselves and are selected by the company president and a leadership committee. They work one-on-one with a leadership coach, and all participants meet together monthly to discuss progress toward leadership goals. Says founder and CEO Ted Goodnow, who officially calls himself Chief Eternal Optimist, "We're not going to have this company run by our kids unless they decide they want to be actively involved and [our employees] think they are good leaders."

———

With more than 1,000 branches and 50,000 staffers in Canada, the large size of TD Bank helps the organization and employees adapt to change. "We get to offer the chance to do different and challenging things over a long career," says Peter McAdam, vice president of employee experience, "whereas a lot of companies think you just go in and that's your job." No changes, just routine. So thought Joanne Choi, manager of a branch in northern Toronto. Choi started in 1977 and, with opportunities, has worked almost every position in retail banking. Her peers—TD's longest-serving employees—report they get the greatest sense of accomplishment from their work. TD offers policies and programs to support development at every stage in a career. Choi has a district vice president as a mentor and takes pride in performing that role for staff at her branch. Each TD employee also has opportunities for training and has a personal development plan that formalizes goals and spells out what needs to be done. "I've been a manager for a long time, and I'm still learning," she says. "At the end of every day, I think, 'What did I learn today?' There's always something to learn."

———

To encourage front-line initiative and decision making, Railroad Associates Corp., a railroad engineering and contracting firm based in Hershey, PA, provides extensive on-the-job training to new employees, along with on-site mentoring and various courses. Employees access job budgets and scheduling information by laptop via the company intranet. The company offers employee stock-ownership, through which nonmanagement employees own about 40 percent of company stock. Employees are eligible for an annual individual bonus capped at 50 percent of their pay, based on customer feedback, safety records, and meeting deadlines. The exemplary employee relations, empowerment, and accountability seem to work. Company president Michael Kennedy estimates that the company saves $500,000 annually in salaries and other overhead costs.

———

HOK, an international architectural design firm in St. Louis, MO, offers extensive training to its employees. Employees are compensated for the time they spend in training. Staff members are asked to complete 40 hours of additional training in a calendar year.

———

Showing you care about where an employee's career is headed shows a long-term respect for the individual. Managing Personal Growth, an employee development program created by Princeton, NJ–based organizational development firm Blessing/White, helps employees take responsibility for their own job satisfaction, job performance, and career development. Each employee and his or her manager define the employee's job responsibilities and the skills required, and they chart a development plan, including several formal check-in meetings. The program has been highly successful for motivating employees, versus more traditional performance evaluation programs, because employees have a stake in the results.

The U.S. Army offers a mentoring program for its civilian employees.

Strategy #6: Recognize & Reward High Performance

The final strategy for increasing engagement with employees today is the overall topic of this book: recognition and rewards. The most proven driver of desired behavior and performance known to mankind is the concept of positive reinforcement, simply stated as "You get what you reward." As a manager in any organization, you will get more of the desired performance you want from your employees by taking the time to notice, recognize, and reward them when they excel in their work.

In my research I've found that it's almost universal that today's employees want and expect to be recognized when they do good work, although very few (12 percent) report that they are consistently recognized in ways that are important to them and three times as many (34 percent) are not recognized in ways they find meaningful. Some 85 percent of employees say they feel overworked and underappreciated where they work today.

Driving performance of any kind is a function of its consequences, and positive consequences such as employee recognition are needed to systematically reinforce successes and desired behavior when they occur. Positive consequences bring about positive results, and what you do doesn't have to cost a lot of money to be effective. When budgets don't allow for lavish celebrations, incentive trips, or expensive rewards, you can still find meaningful ways to recognize employees.

In fact, during challenging times the need for employees to feel valued increases greatly, and timely, sincere, and specific forms of appreciation should be more frequently expressed for a job well done. Managers need to increase their focus on employee recognition, exploring more ways to get creative in showing employees that what they do matters. More than anything, employees need to feel valued in today's business climate, and they tend to be more responsive to intangible and interpersonal recognition with little, if any, financial cost.

When cash flows freely, many companies don't hold back on the rewards, incentives, and perks for employees. During the good times, such rewards are often an essential retention and motivation strategy. However, during challenging times, many companies have found that they can't afford to reward employees as they did before, but they also can't afford *not* to reward them. Research by Accountemps found that 19 percent of its clientele reported that "recognition programs" served as one of the best remedies for low employee morale. Thirteen percent of executives reported that offering financial rewards was an important strategy for improving employee morale in tough times, followed closely by "unexpected rewards."

Organizations can successfully create a culture of recognition by freely and readily recognizing employees' contributions. They must make employees feel trusted, respected, and excited about their own successes and the successes of others in the organization. In return, they will get employees who are accountable for their actions and committed to making a difference.

Sometimes the money simply isn't there for cash rewards or high-dollar items. That doesn't mean that there aren't still options for showing employees that their time and work is valued and appreciated. Even something as simple as an ice-cream social, company-sponsored lunch on site, or doughnuts in the morning can make employees feel valued.

Here are a few categories to consider when you next want to thank your employees:

LOW-END REWARDS

This can include such items as gift cards from Starbucks or Amazon.com, gas cards, car wash or discount restaurant coupons, gift certificates, a pizza, or even a bouquet of flowers. For example, Jeanette Pagliaro, co-owner of Visiting Angels, an elder-care service, often receives positive feedback from clients or supervisors about her employees. Employees who receive such pointed recognition are given "Angel Bucks," which can be used to buy prizes at an auction sponsored by the company.

SYMBOLIC RECOGNITION

This can be tokens, pins, ribbons, a certificate or plaque that has special meaning. Core Creative in Milwaukee was recognized by *The Business Journal* as one of the Best Places to Work. At the end of every summer, the company sets aside time to find some creative way in which to recognize exceptional employees. From those who are simply performing well, to those who have gone above and beyond for clients, employees are celebrated and rewarded. Another company in the Midwest consistently distributes personal notes from vice presidents and managers, as well as posting feature articles on the intranet highlighting outstanding employees.

TIME OFF

Time itself can be used as an award, for instance, in the form of a voucher for a long lunch, an afternoon, or an additional day off. At Greenough Communications in Boston, high-performing employees are rewarded by being able to leave at 3 P.M. on Friday. The Corcoran Group, a top real estate agency in New York City, takes a unique approach to its policies during slow times. Founder Barbara Corcoran instituted a practice of giving salespeople an extra few weeks of vacation when sales are down. With not much going on, it's easier to be short staffed and allow employees some time to restore morale and alleviate stress. So far, this practice has been effective in that salespeople return refreshed with a renewed and positive attitude.

EMPLOYEE PERKS

Simple low-cost benefits that are available to all employees, such as soft drinks, coffee, bottled water, snacks, or the use of a company fitness room, are great for company morale. Best, Best and Krieger, a law firm in Los Angeles and Washington, DC, has held fast to simple employee perks such as "Bagel and Donut Friday" and retained the holiday party as a way to bring employees together in a social setting. Another California-based company, public relations firm Kiner Communications, continued to enjoy baskets of fresh fruit, attended a company-sponsored holiday party, and didn't miss out on bonuses.

Google, topping the list of *Fortune*'s 100 Best Companies to Work For, is the gold standard for employee perks. Employees get three free meals each day, and are able to save time and money by staying on site when they take a break to eat. Eating at the company cafeteria allows employees to interact with one another, which can create a sense of community and idea sharing. Washing cars and changing the oil are things everyone must do, and many times employees spend their lunch hours or take time away from work to do so. Providing these services on-site to employees allows them to scratch one item off their to-do list without disrupting the workday or weekend. The added benefit of stress reduction also makes employees that much more productive and less distracted.

PART II

Using
Recognition
& Rewards

DAY-TO-DAY RECOGNITION

In my doctoral research on why managers use or don't use recognition with their employees, I found that the top variable distinguishing those managers who use recognition was that they felt it was their responsibility—not corporate's or Human Resources'—to create the motivational environment for *their* people. They truly believed that recognizing their deserving employees played an integral part in how those workers felt about their jobs.

This finding coincides with what my research shows are the most important ways that employees prefer to be recognized when they do good work—that is, simple day-to-day behaviors that any managers can express with their employees, the most important of which is praise.

Praise & Recognition

The best praise is done soon, specifically, sincerely, personally, positively, and proactively. In a matter of seconds, a simple praise conveys "I saw what you did. I appreciate it, here's why it's important, and here's how it makes me feel"—a lot of punch in a small package.

Four of the top ten categories of motivators reported by employees in my research are forms of praise, and these categories make up the four sections in Part I: personal praise, written praise, electronic praise, and public praise. Now, you might say, "Are these really different types of praise? Don't they all have the same effect?" This was my initial thought, too, but I learned that these types of praise are in fact distinct from one another. Praising someone in person means something different to that person than what writing him or her a note means, and these forms of praise are both different from praising the person in public. To get the maximum impact out of this simple behavior, vary the forms you use and use them all frequently.

Research by Dr. Gerald Graham of Wichita State University supports these observations. In multiple studies, he found that employees preferred personalized, instant recognition from their direct supervisors more than any other kind of motivation. In fact, in another survey of American workers, 63 percent of the respondents ranked "a pat on the back" as a meaningful incentive.

In Graham's studies of employees' perceptions, manager-initiated rewards for performance were used least often, and company-initiated rewards for presence (that is, rewards based simply on being in the organization) occurred most often. Dr. Graham concluded, "It appears that the techniques that have the greatest motivational

> **"I've been reading literature on psychology for as far back as 25 years, and everything I've read says incentives are an effective way to tap a worker's intrinsic motivation, his inherent desire to do a job well."**—Tom Peters, *Author and Management Consultant*

impact are practiced the least, even though they are easier and less expensive to use."

Graham's study determined the top five motivating techniques reported by employees to be:

1. The manager personally congratulates employees who do a good job.

2. The manager writes personal notes about good performance.

3. The organization uses performance as the basis for promotion.

4. The manager publicly recognizes employees for good performance.

5. The manager holds morale-building meetings to celebrate success.

Ideally you should vary the ways you recognize your staff while still trying to do things on a day-to-day basis. For example, Robin Horder-Koop, vice president of corporate relations at Amway Corporation, the distributor of house- and personal-care products and other goods in Ada, MI, uses these inexpensive ways to recognize the 200 people who work for her on a day-to-day basis:

- On days when some workloads are light, the department's employees help workers in other departments. After accumulating eight hours of such work, employees get a thank-you note from Horder-Koop. Additional time earns a luncheon with company officials in the executive dining room.

- All workers are recognized on a rotating basis. Each month, photos of different employees are displayed on a bulletin board along with comments from their coworkers about why they are good colleagues.
- Horder-Koop sends thank-you notes to employees' homes when they do outstanding work. When someone works a lot of overtime or travels extensively, she sends a note to the family thanking them for their support.
- At corporate meetings, employees play games such as Win, Lose, or Draw and The Price Is Right, using questions about the company's products. Winners get prizes such as tote bags and T-shirts.

Other inexpensive ideas Horder-Koop uses to recognize employees include giving flowers to employees who are commended in customers' letters, having supervisors park employees' cars one day a month, and designating days when workers can come in late or wear casual clothes to the office.

According to Harvard professor and management consultant Rosabeth Moss Kanter, "Recognition—saying thank you in public and perhaps giving a tangible gift along with the words— has multiple functions beyond simple human courtesy. To the employee, recognition signifies that someone noticed and someone cares. To the rest of the organization, recognition creates role models—heroes—and communicates the standards, saying: 'These are the kinds of things that constitute great performance around here.'" Following are some guidelines Kanter offers for successfully recognizing employees:

PRINCIPLE 1: Emphasize success rather than failure. You tend to miss the positives if you are busily searching for the negatives.

PRINCIPLE 2: Deliver recognition and reward in an open and publicized way. If not made public, recognition loses much of its impact and much of the purpose for which it is provided.

PRINCIPLE 3: Deliver recognition in a personal and honest manner. Avoid providing recognition that is too "slick" or overproduced.

PRINCIPLE 4: Tailor your recognition and reward to the unique needs of the people involved. Having many recognition and reward options will enable management to acknowledge accomplishment in ways that are appropriate to the particulars of a given situation.

PRINCIPLE 5: Timing is crucial. Recognize contribution throughout a project. Reward contribution close to the time an achievement is realized. Delays weaken the impact of most rewards.

PRINCIPLE 6: Strive for a clear, unambiguous, and well-communicated connection between accomplishments and rewards. Be sure people understand why they receive awards and the criteria used to determine awards.

PRINCIPLE 7: Recognize recognition. That is, recognize people who recognize others for doing what is best for the company.

Personal Praise & Recognition

The most important type of recognition is that which occurs on a day-to-day basis—where the rubber meets the road. In my research with employees, 99.4 percent reported it was somewhat, very, or extremely important for them to be recognized by their managers when they did good work, and 73 percent expected recognition to occur either immediately or soon thereafter. *Personal* praise is generally considered to be the most important, and employees rank four forms of personal praise thus: "being personally thanked for doing good work" (88 percent); "being given a verbal praising" (86 percent); "being sought out by a manager to be commended" (82 percent); and "praising an employee for good work in front of another person" (61 percent).

The gap between the amount of praise managers think they give their employees and the amount employees report receiving is unfortunately wide. Bob Levoy, former president of Success Dynamics, Inc., reports: "I've asked more than 2,500 doctors to rank on a scale of 1 to 5 (1 = never, 5 = always) the following statement: 'I let my employees know when they're doing a good job.' Their average response is 4.4. I then asked their staff members to rank this statement: 'The doctor lets me know when I'm doing a good job,' and their average response is only 1.7. This difference between what doctors say they give and what employees say they get is often the underlying cause of employee resentment, diminished productivity, and turnover. This 'feedback gap' is present in almost every manager-employee relationship."

How do you close that gap? Management consultant Marshall Goldsmith offers the following advice:

> **One of my clients who was using 360-degree feedback scored very low in the area of "Provides Adequate Positive Recognition." What he did to improve was a great strategy for leaders everywhere.**
>
> **First, he listed the key groups of people that impacted his life: his friends, family, direct reports, colleagues,**

and customers. Then he listed the names of each of the people who were in that group. Then twice a week, once on Wednesday and once on Friday, he would look at the list and ask himself, "Did anyone on this page do anything I should recognize?" If they did, he'd send them a little note, an e-mail, or a voice mail to say thank you. He didn't do anything that took more than a couple of minutes. If nobody on the list did something he should recognize, he did nothing. He didn't want to appear to be false, to be a phony.

By following this simple technique, in one year he went from a 6 percentile in giving recognition to a 94 percentile. I have recommended this strategy to many leaders and have never seen it *not* work. It can help you, too, to do a great job in providing more positive recognition to those that are most important to you in your life.

It's the daily interactions that add up to define our relationships at work. It's the little things that managers do or do not do that can end up making a big difference in how others feel about working with and for them and about being a part of the organization. A systematic focus on the positives serves as a foundation and buffer to negative challenges—problems, complaints, stress, and so on.

> **"I can live for two weeks on a good compliment."**
> —Mark Twain

Although most positive day-to-day interactions are apt to be smaller in focus, with little or no cost, with some thought and planning you can be prepared to do more significant things, as well. For example, if someone closes a big sale or finishes a significant project, you can ask your president or CEO to phone the person to personally thank him or her. While you might not be able to do that every day, it's an out-of-the-ordinary yet simple form of special thanks you can call upon.

Remember: The best personal praise is timely, sincere, and specific. Create time to connect with each of your employees—even if it's over coffee or lunch—to see how they are doing and to thank them for all they've done. You could even, on occasion, personally praise each of your employees when your staff gets together for a meeting. (If you use this tactic, make sure you find something positive to say about everyone present so that no one feels left out.)

You can praise employees directly, in front of others, or when they are not around (a concept known as "positive gossip") knowing that this indirect praise will get back to them. For some employees, indirect recognition is the most credible because it is done without any expectation in return. It essentially says: "My boss must have thought what I did was important to have brought it up to the entire management team!"

Try working sincere thanks into your daily activities. For example, make it a habit to greet people with 100 percent focus, as if you had all the time in the world for them, even if you only have a few minutes. Give them your undivided attention; if that is not possible, tell them that you're distracted and would like to get back to them when you can better focus on them, their needs, and your conversation.

When people leave the office at the end of the day, say good-bye and thank them for the effort they made that day. When asking employees about great managers they have worked for, more than one person has told me how such a manager would

PERSONAL RECOGNITION TIPS

➡ Verbally thank the employee: Call them into your office; in a break or meeting room; at employee's work area—in front of peers; in the lobby prior to leaving.

➡ Shake hands with the employee.

➡ Arrange for employee to receive a congratulatory phone call from senior management.

thank them for being there every day before they went home. A simple courtesy, yes, but one that employees noted and valued. Nothing beats simple, day-to-day recognition for building a foundation of trust and goodwill.

A survey by the Minnesota Department of Natural Resources found that recognition activities contributed significantly to employees' job satisfaction. Most respondents said they highly valued day-to-day recognition from their supervisors, peers, and team members. Other findings from the survey include:

- 68 percent of the respondents said it was important to believe that their work was appreciated by others.
- 67 percent agreed that most people need appreciation for their work.
- 63 percent agreed that most people would like more recognition for their work.
- Only 8 percent thought that people should not look for praise for their work efforts.

Nancy Branton, of People Potential Group, Inc., in Woodbury, MN, and project manager for the survey, says, "Recognition is more important now than in the past. Employees increasingly believe that their job satisfaction depends on acknowledgment of work performance as well as on adequate salary. This is especially true of employees who are highly interested in their work and take satisfaction in their achievements."

Managers at Yell UK, the print-, online-, and phone-based product and service provider based in Reading, show immediate appreciation by saying thank you to employees for doing a good job.

———

Hugh Fleming of Chick-fil-A's Spotsylvania Mall restaurant in Fredricksburg, VA, tries to catch people doing something right every day and praise them on the spot.

———

At Domino's Pizza headquarters in Ann Arbor, MI, Eric Schmaltz tries to acknowledge at least five people every day, whether an employee or customer.

———

Nikki Burns, a manager at Miami Valley Hospital in Dayton, OH, says she tries to say thank you to every employee as he or she leaves for the day.

———

Organizations can greatly influence the use of positive recognition on a daily basis by providing training, tools, activities, and programs to foster that behavior, examples of which are provided throughout this book.

———

The Tennant Company, a manufacturer in Minneapolis, has a Positive Feedback Committee that each year sponsors a Positive Feedback Day, on which all employees receive "That-A-Way" notepads, pens printed with the phrase "Positive Strokes Only," balloons, and signs. At holiday time, the committee sponsors an open house with cider and cookies and invites employees to drop by at scheduled breaks.

———

ASAP-CUBED:
GUIDELINES FOR EFFECTIVE PRAISE

As Soon
As Sincere
As Specific
As Personal
As Positive
As Practical
. . . as possible!

When Greg Peel, a zone manager for Paychex in Dallas, TX, sees an employee working really hard, he calls that person's mother and thanks her.

———

Hyler Bracey, former president and CEO of the Atlanta Consulting Group, places five coins in one of his pockets each day. During the day, he transfers a coin to his other pocket every time he recognizes an employee for good work. That technique has helped him make praise a habit.

———

One store manager for CVS Drug Stores, based in Woonsocket, RI, brings a silver dollar to work on Monday mornings and gives it to a supervisor, who is asked to praise one of his employees and then hand the coin off to another supervisor. If the coin gets around to all the supervisors by the end of the week, the manager brings in doughnuts to the supervisors' meeting.

———

> **"The way positive reinforcement is carried out is more important than the amount."**
> —B. F. Skinner,
> *Psychologist*

Top officers in several branches of the military use coin medallions as personal recognition items. One bank president gold plates quarters and hands them to deserving employees. Other companies have used wooden nickels, regular nickels, or even green glass pebbles as symbolic recognition items for work well done.

———

A task-oriented, top manager at Qwest Communications in Denver reminds himself to recognize others by listing his employees' names on his to-do list each week. Then he crosses names off the list when he has had a chance to acknowledge those people for some aspect of their performance or behavior, such as reaching project milestones or delivering exceptional customer service. He says it's his way to "turn the people aspect of my job into manageable tasks I can focus on each week."

> **"Recognition is so easy to do and so inexpensive to distribute that there is simply no excuse for not doing it."**
> —Rosabeth Moss Kanter, *Professor, Harvard Business School*

———

Former Baltimore Orioles manager Ray Miller didn't get much personalized attention from his coaches as a minor league pitcher back in the '60s and '70s. "The way I was treated hurt me," he recalls. Miller learned from experience that paying attention to players is important, whether they are performing well or not. To be sure that he communicates with all players, he keeps a "talk-to" list on a yellow legal pad. "Just talking really matters," he says. "Take Cal Ripken. If he is playing great and for some reason you don't talk for four or five days, he looks at you and says, 'What's wrong?'" Miller has learned an important lesson: Feedback and recognition go a long way.

Store managers at the recently closed St. Ann-Macy's department store, in St. Louis, MO, used to go to each employee at the end of the day to see what went well for them that day, rather than wait for a weekly or monthly report. Those positive items were worked into the next morning's store rally. "It was a very effective way to reinforce good news on a timely basis and charge employees up to do their best every single day," said Dan Eppler, merchandise sales manager for the company.

Joe DeLuce, director of recreation for Champaign Park District in Champaign, IL, says it's important to bring up the topic of praise with your staff: "In our department staff meetings we recently asked everyone to say when they last thanked someone. Every one of the 30 people in the room talked about how they had thanked one of their staff or someone else in our department that day or within the last week. One staff member talked about one of her staff members going above and beyond, and since that staff person was in the room, it became very emotional. We talked about how important it is to thank people for doing outstanding work and that we want to be a department that appreciates others."

Robert Maurer, in his book *One Small Step Can Change Your Life*, describes working with a reluctant manager, Michael, to get him to start praising his employees:

"I asked him to imagine giving a person from his department a specific, detailed compliment

PERSONAL RECOGNITION TIPS

➡ Arrange for someone in upper management to visit employee's work area to acknowledge or thank the individual.

➡ Hand out chocolate kisses or hearts.

➡ Give an employee a single pink rose.

➡ Give lottery tickets and attach a note: "We hit the jackpot when we hired you!"

in an enthusiastic tone of voice, as if there were no problems at all with this person's work. He was to imagine how he would stand in front of the person, how it would feel to approach the person with a relaxed, open posture, how his voice would sound, and what any ambient sounds or smells there might be.

"I wanted Michael to start with compliments for a couple of reasons. Like most people, Michael found it easier to give criticism than compliments. But I also knew that a likely result of letting trouble in his department percolate for too long was that Michael would see his employees as nothing but a collection of problems. And from another perspective, psychological research clearly shows that people who feel underappreciated tend to resent criticism and ignore the advice they're given. By practicing giving compliments, Michael was not only learning to feel comfortable doing something that felt unnatural to him. He was also developing a skill that would increase the satisfaction and productivity of his employees.

"The small, active steps of mental rehearsal taught Michael a new set of skills, as well as a sense of the ease and reward of offering praise. At the end of three months, Michael found himself frequently stopping in hallways to give 15- or 20-second recognition to deserving employees."

———

According to Phebe Farrow Port, senior vice president of Estee Lauder, founder Leonard Lauder spent a limited amount of time with executives on store visits, preferring to meet with floor people. Phebe says, "One day, I saw him reach across a counter and say, 'Sorry to interrupt. My name is Leonard Lauder. I hear you are one of the beauty advisors. Thank you for everything you are doing for Estee Lauder.'" As they walked away on one such occasion, Phebe said, "Mr. Lauder, you're so good at this." He said, "I put myself on a quota of three thank yous a day years ago. I suggest you do the same." Phebe adds, "Everywhere the man goes, he writes a personal note to whomever he meets."

Written Praise & Recognition

Written praise, considered by employees to be the next most valued type of praise, comes in several varieties. Here is how employees ranked different forms in terms of importance: "letters of praise are placed in the employee's personnel file" (72 percent); "being given written praise" (61 percent); "being given a written note of thanks" (59 percent); and "being given a thank-you card" (48 percent).

A survey by the International Association of Administrative Professionals revealed that as many as 30 percent of professional secretaries would be happy with a simple letter of appreciation from their managers, but only 7 percent of respondents reported having ever received such a letter. In another study, positive written communication was found to be very important in motivating employees; however, this technique was used by only 24 percent of managers.

WRITTEN RECOGNITION TIPS

➡ Write a thank-you note and send to recipient's family, personally deliver it, or post in employee's work space.

➡ Have CEO write P&R letter to employee.

➡ Have everyone in the recipient's department make and sign a homemade P&R card.

➡ Write a welcome letter to new employee.

As part of its "Fat Cat Award," First Data Resources, a data processing services company in Omaha, NE, includes a letter of appreciation from the CEO and senior management, e-mails, and notes from peers.

SAY IT IN WRITING

- Make a thank-you card by hand.
- Post a thank-you note on the employee's office door.
- Write a "letter of praise" to employees to recognize their specific contributions and accomplishments; send a copy to your boss or higher managers and to the personnel department.
- Provide managers with specially printed packets of thank-you cards to hand out to employees who do exceptional work.
- Ask your boss, a very senior manager, or the CEO to send a letter of acknowledgment or thanks to individuals or groups who make significant contributions.

Hallmark Financial, a Dallas-based insurance firm, prints recognition cards listing company values, and gives them to management to give to employees "on the spot" when the employees have demonstrated the values in action. The cards have space for the names of the giver and receiver, the date, and an explanation of why the card was given.

Premier Travel Inn, located in London, UK, sends a postcard to individuals and teams after they have achieved great results or have demonstrated desired behaviors. One is "You're a Star," which is handwritten so that it is personal. Another is "The Great Leap Forward Award," given to a team member or a hotel that has made significant improvements in the business. The national operations director gives the letter to the individual, along with a toy kangaroo.

Sheryl Currao, proprietor of Bella Vita Salon & Day Spa in North Andover, MA—one of the fastest-growing salons/spas in America—doesn't get her employees together very often, but when she does, she takes time to write one paragraph about each one stating what she most values about that person. She reads each message in front of the entire staff.

———

When an employee leaves Alberta Health Services in Calgary, Alberta, leaders encourage colleagues to share farewell wishes in keepsake cards—including stories, humorous thoughts, quotes, or reflections of years past—to be placed in a commemorative leather box and presented to the departing employee.

———

> **"There is no verbal vitamin more potent than praise."**
> —Frederick B. Harris

Writing notes at the end of the day to employees who have performed well is an effective recognition strategy, claims Steve Wittert, general manager and COO of Fairbanks Ranch Country Club in San Diego. Wittert finds that his days are so busy that he seldom has time to personally recognize his staff. Instead, he keeps a stack of note cards on his desk, and when the pace slows down at the end of the day, he takes a few minutes to jot personal notes to the individuals who made a difference that day.

"At the end of each year, I write an individual letter to each of my employees, specifically listing highlights of their performance that I was proud of over the past year. This takes less time than you might think, and the impact on employees is more significant than you might imagine!"

———

Joe Floren, former communications manager for Tektronix, Inc., a manufacturer of oscilloscopes and other electronic instruments, located in Beaverton, OR, likes to tell the story of the "You Done Good Award." Floren recalls having coffee a number of years ago with his boss, a vice president. The boss said he'd been mulling over a problem stemming from the company's rapid growth. He thought the company was getting so big that it needed a formal recognition program. He had read some personnel handbooks on the subject and began telling Floren about several variations on the gold watch traditionally given for good work.

The boss's proposition sounded ludicrous to Floren. So he challenged Floren to come up with something better. Floren suggested drawing up a card called the "You Done Good Award" and letting employees give it to fellow employees.

To his surprise, the vice president agreed. Floren had some note cards printed and started distributing them. They caught on, and the informal awards have become part of life in the company. "Even though people say nice things to you," Floren says, "it means something more when people take the time to write their name on a piece of paper and say it. Employees usually post them next to their desks."

———

Janis Allen, owner of Performance Leadership Consulting in Brevard, NC, tells the story of a group of officers she was training in the Department of the Army. One person in

> **"Recognition is the most inexpensive, easy-to-use motivational technique available to management. Yet the degree to which this essential improvement tool is underused by most otherwise intelligent managers is bewildering."**
> —Jim Clemmer, *Author and President, The Clemmer Group*

particular, a colonel, showed great resistance to the use of any reinforcers. A week or so after the seminar, the colonel's manager—a general—wanted to praise him for his handling of an important presentation. The general found a piece of yellow construction paper, folded it in half, and wrote "Bravo" on the front. Then he wrote his reinforcing remarks inside.

The colonel was called in, praised, and given the card. "He took it and read it," Allen says, "and didn't even look up when he finished. He just stood up abruptly without making eye contact, turned, and walked out of the office." The general thought, "Wow, I've done something wrong now." He thought maybe he had offended the colonel.

However, when the general later went to check on the colonel, he found that he had stopped at every office on the way out and was showing off the "Bravo" card. He was smiling and everybody was congratulating him.

The colonel subsequently printed his own recognition cards with "Wonderful" on the front. They became his signature reinforcers.

A t Sea World San Diego, team leaders give "spotlight cards" to employees when they see them doing something well. They write down what they observed and what they liked about it, get at least two other leaders or supervisors to sign the card, and then present it to the employee. A copy is also posted on the employee bulletin board.

———

When Kelly McNamara worked for Raytheon Aircraft Company, now a part of Hawker Beechcraft, she wanted to cut down on all the red tape involved in rewarding an employee. So she and her team brought back an award— employee-to-employee thank-you notes featuring the "Beechcraft Busy Bee" cartoon (used many years ago by Beechcraft, a company that Raytheon acquired in the early 1980s)—which could be given to anyone by anyone in the company with no approval required.

———

In Marietta, GA, Wellstar Health System created a simple peer-to-peer leadership recognition program called "The Seven Attributes of Stars." According to Wellstar, these attributes are: communicating, global thinking, people-developing, lifelong learning, innovating, goal-achieving, and service-leading. Managers are given printed notepads and asked to check off the attributes that are embodied by fellow leaders and describe why they should be recognized for them. Any leader who is recognized for five or more attributes is publicly acknowledged at the next quarterly leadership meeting and gets to select a book from among five choices.

> **"Recognition is something a manager should be doing all the time; it's a running dialogue with people."**
> —Ron Zemke, *Senior Editor,* Training *magazine*

A Case Study in Written Praise

When it comes to recognizing employees, most companies have trouble holding their managers accountable. After all, how can you force people to be nice to their employees? Plus, if you do make them do something they don't want to do, won't they resent it and undermine your effort anyway?

They didn't think so at Bronson Healthcare Group in Kalamazoo, MI, once ranked as one of the Best Companies to Work For by *Fortune* magazine. The organization decided to stop focusing on the small number of people who do not conform to their expectations and to start focusing on, recognizing, and rewarding the 95 percent who are doing good work. It took some four years to ingrain this philosophy, but a systematic focus on their recognition practices has clearly made them an employer of choice.

For example, they asked all managers to write 12 thank-you notes per quarter, and to show them to their own managers as proof that they were indeed recognizing their employees. Additionally, human resources did random spot-checks on managers, asking to see copies of thank-you notes, and if a manager didn't have them, he or she was asked to schedule a "little talk" with the senior leader of the group. They've never had

MAKE USE OF NEWSPAPERS TO PRAISE EMPLOYEES PUBLICLY

- Write and publish a personal ad or publicity article in the local newspaper or company publication praising the person for a job well done.
- Send information about an accomplishment to the appropriate trade publication and the individual's hometown newspaper.
- Take out a full-page advertisement in a local newspaper every year and thank every employee by name for his or her contribution.

to schedule more than one talk before managers quickly got the message that the organization was serious about this activity.

Better yet, managers who started writing notes quickly discovered that they were being rewarded by their employees for those very notes. Now, new leaders in the organization are oriented to the practice from the very start of their jobs.

The thank-you note program has since expanded so that managers now send notes to employees' families or even to their children (sometimes with coupons for ice cream so they can take their parents out), and employees are increasingly writing more thank-you notes to their peers. As a result of all this focus (and related activities), Bronson Healthcare Group's turnover has dropped drastically, and they now have a waiting list for employees who want to work at the hospital. They have also been named a "best practice" in several national databases for nurse retention, as well as listed on the Working Mother 100 Best Companies lists.

Following are other real-life examples of effective written recognition.

> **"In the most innovative companies, there is a significantly higher volume of thank-you's than in companies of low innovation."**
> —Rosabeth Moss Kanter, *Professor, Harvard Business School*

Markeeta Graban, Health Services access manager for Washtenaw (MI) Community Health Organization, reports: "It's really true that anything can be a significant form of recognition. Over three years ago I drew a star on a piece of scrap paper, colored it, and gave it to someone for helping me out that day. They in turn gave it to someone else. It took on special significance with each use. Now we have it on a magnetic backing and pass it on to someone who has helped or is having a rough day. People love it!"

———

"**W**e tried to emphasize peer-to-peer recognition on our Organizational Development Team," reports Debbie Liles, former supervisor of OD at EMC Mortgage Corporation, and now director of corporate education at Carter BloodCare in Bedford, TX. One of the ways they did it was by using a form called the Appreciation/Recognition Form. Teammates completed the form when they observed someone exhibiting the behavior(s) the company valued. These were deposited in a beautifully decorated box throughout the month. At every monthly team meeting, all the certificates were read aloud. Certificate recipients got to pick their favorite candy bars or healthy snacks from the reward grab bag.

———

> **"Men and women want to do a good job, a creative job, and if they are provided the proper environment, they will do so."**
> —Bill Hewlett,
> *Cofounder,*
> *Hewlett-Packard*

A more informal way that they recognized/appreciated team members was through "Notes to My Terrific Teammate." They posted notes on colored paper on their teammates' walls when they were not around, so they would be pleasantly surprised by the latest "fan mail." When the sheets were filled up, more sheets were passed out.

———

CalPERS, the California Public Employees' Retirement System, based in Sacramento, uses rock-shaped "Steady as a Rock" note cards as well as mounted pass-around rocks to recognize behind-the-scenes daily performance by coworkers.

The New England Aquarium allows employees to recognize coworkers with a "thank-you cod" (a card shaped like a codfish)—a play on the New England accent. "Half the card goes to the employee and the other half goes into a quarterly lottery for gift certificates for paid time off, the company store, and local restaurants," reports Linda Hower Bates, learning technologist for Gilbane Building Company in Providence, RI.

———

Ginny Heard, supervisor of member correspondence at an AARP office in Lakewood, CA, has a simple yet effective recognition technique she developed when previously employed by Airborne Express. She cut an apple out of construction paper, wrote "Look for Teachable Moments" on it, and used the note as an icebreaker for discussing learning points or lessons in an employee's job performance. The award became very popular, and many other managers followed her lead. Everyone liked receiving the apples, and the notes became collectibles.

> **"If human beings are perceived as potentials rather than problems, as possessing strengths instead of weaknesses, as unlimited rather than dull and unresponsive then they thrive and grow to their capabilities."**
> —Robert Conklin,
> *American Teacher,*
> *Author & Speaker*

———

If one of Marty Stowe's employees at the New England Regional Office for Paychex in Boston was working extremely hard, Stowe—now a vice president for Paychex in Rochester, NY—sent a handwritten note to inform his or her spouse. If this employee really outdid him- or herself, Stowe gave the husband and wife a gift certificate for dinner for two.

———

**WRITTEN
RECOGNITION TIPS**

➡ Give "Certificates of Achievement" for areas of performance (e.g., company values, sales, major projects).

➡ Give customized achievement certificates (templates can be purchased from Successories, Baudeville).

➡ Send (or ask upper-level manager to send) a P&R letter to employee.

➡ Write, frame, and read a poem about employee to that employee.

➡ Write a P&R note and attach to candy bar, paycheck, or report.

➡ Write a formal P&R letter for employee's personnel file and give copy to recipient.

At Lands' End in Dodgeville, WI, former CEO Mike Smith personally reviewed all his mail. If he found a letter from a customer who mentioned an employee by name, he jotted a simple note to the employee and forwarded a copy of the letter to him or her. Employees loved these personal kudos from the CEO and posted them in their work cubicles.

Jimmy Collins, former president of Chick-fil-A, the Atlanta-based restaurant chain, writes personal notes of thanks on P&L sheets that he returns to owner-operators.

Doubt that little acts of recognition mean a lot? In her book *What I Saw at the Revolution*, President Ronald Reagan's speechwriter Peggy Noonan writes about a personal note she received from the president. She had been writing for him for four months, and had not yet met him, when one day President Reagan wrote "Very Good" on one of her speech drafts. First she stared at it. Then she took a pair of scissors and cut it off and taped it to her blouse, like a second-grader with a star. All day, people noticed it and looked at her and she beamed back at them.

Joan Padgett, Ph.D., of the Office of Workforce Development & Training at Veterans' Medical Center in Dayton, OH, reports, "I recently decided to take the time to give a welcome card to a new employee and wrote a personal note, saying, 'At the end of some days you'll feel elated; after some you'll feel completely drained; but may you always leave your office knowing you contributed to our organization.' The employee was thrilled and said she would keep the card always. Her emotional response convinced me of the value of giving cards to thank, congratulate, welcome, and celebrate employees."

A ngela Gann, the national administrator of compliance for Kaiser Permanente in Oakland, CA, sends personal notes to anyone she interviews for a job, but saves a really special greeting for the new hire, decorating the person's workstation on the first morning with glitter stars or banners.

T he *San Francisco Business Times* had paper tablets printed with different headlines, such as "Saved the Day," "Bit the Bullet," and "Went Above and Beyond," which they gave to employees who did an exceptional job. Soon, everyone had lots of the notes, and people were feeling more appreciated.

J ohn Plunkett, director of employment and training for Cobb Electric Membership Corporation in Marietta, GA, says, "People love to collect other people's business cards. Simply carry a supply of your cards with you and as you

> "In the twenty years I have been doing this . . . the number one thing employees say to us is 'We don't even care about the money; if my boss would just say thank you, if he or she would just acknowledge that I exist. The only time I ever hear anything is when I screw up. I never hear when I do a good job.'"
> —Catherine Meek, *Executive Director, School on Wheels*

'catch people doing something right,' immediately write 'Thanks,' 'Good job,' 'Keep it up,' and what they specifically did in two to three words. Put the person's name on the card and sign it."

"**A**n engineer on my staff spent an extended amount of time on the road doing environmental evaluations of companies," reports Michael L. Horvath, director of special projects for FirstEnergy Corporation, headquartered in Akron, OH. "I sent a letter to his three school-age children explaining why their dad was gone so much lately and that he was doing special 'secret agent' work that was very important for our company. His wife called the next day to say how excited their kids were that Dad was a 'secret agent!'"

"I try to remember that people—good, intelligent, capable people—may actually need day-to-day praise and thanks for the job they do. I try to remember to get up out of my chair, turn off my computer, go sit or stand next to them and see what they're doing, ask about the challenges, find out if they need additional help, offer that help if possible, and most of all, tell them in all honesty that what they are doing is important: to me, to the company, and to our customers." —John Ball, *Service Training Manager, American Honda Motor Company*

The "Reward of Excellence" program at Herbalife, the health and nutrition company based in Los Angeles, uses two-part cards, called "WOW!" cards, to recognize employees. Employees fill them out to praise coworkers for service, teamwork, and so on. One part goes to the honoree, the other goes into a recognition box, and the contents are reviewed each month by a six-member recognition committee. The committee selects the best "WOW!" card employee and posts the card on the "WOW!" bulletin board. The winner then gets points toward merchandise purchases, as well as raffle tickets for a cruise drawing, which is held at the end of every six months. All honorees are also automatically entered in the company's "All Star" program for additional recognition and visibility.

To make the program as successful as possible, Herbalife started with a three-month trial period, during which they collected feedback and suggestions. For example, when they discovered that employees didn't like paying shipping and handling for the merchandise they selected, the company built those amounts into the awards and slightly increased the number of points required. Besides increasing recognition, other benefits emerged, as well. Ana Franklin, senior manager of the Order Support Department, identified three: (1) the program helped employees set more specific goals and provided systematic tracking of results; (2) it costs less than previous programs, yet has a longer-term impact, replacing what had previously been a hit-and-miss approach (such as occasional distribution of gas cards and gift certificates); and (3) employees can now include their families in selecting merchandise, which is an added motivational incentive.

———

Jeffrey S. Wells, former senior vice president of Human Resources for Circuit City Stores, Inc., had his administrative assistant place note cards on his desk each month for him to write personal notes to employees who had anniversaries with the company. Don Eggleston, VP, Mission Values at SSM Health Care in St. Louis, MO, says, "I mark my calendar and then send cards or flowers to employees on the anniversary of important events in

> **"The more high technology around us, the more the need for the human touch."**
> —John Naisbitt,
> *Author*, Megatrends

their lives. For example, I've sent cards on the anniversary of a parent's death or for a child's graduation or birthday. These are subtle ways of letting employees know I'm interested without prying into their lives. After all, we're working with human beings, and we can all be more effective and sensitive if we understand one another better."

Electronic Praise & Recognition

Electronic praise is similar to written praise, but it is transmitted more readily and often with less effort than the latter. Praising via e-mail, voice mail, cell phone, pager, fax, or other forms of technology is increasingly important to today's employees, who are spending more and more time on "electronic leashes," interfacing more with their computers and less with their bosses or coworkers. Although today's office technology can make us more efficient, it also tends to have an alienating effect, creating more distance in work relationships and more stress as we are increasingly expected to be "available" 24/7.

> **"I consider my ability to arouse enthusiasm among men the greatest asset I possess. The way to develop the best that is in a man is by appreciation and encouragement."**
> —Charles Schwab, *Founder, The Charles Schwab Corporation*

A recent study by Pitney Bowes on messaging tools and practices reveals that U.S. workers are now receiving over 200 messages per day—more than ever before. What's the impact of this constant bombardment of messages and increased use of office technology? How can managers best recognize employee performance when an employee may not even have physical contact with his or her manager for weeks or months at a time?

Managers must take a proactive role in fostering a sense of teamwork by establishing regular, mutually agreed-upon communication times. Telephone calls, e-mail, teleconferences, videoconferences, and chat areas can all be conducted at an agreed-upon time. Additionally, message boards can be used for ongoing communication about progress on critical aspects of teamwork. Communicating in these ways gives virtual employees the opportunity to exchange ideas with team members, talk about problems, discuss ways to improve, evaluate the team's progress, share ideas, get feedback, brainstorm new ideas, discuss strategies, and acknowledge success.

For these reasons, it is increasingly important to use technology in positive ways to reinforce good work and encourage the human spirit. Employees increasingly perceive electronic praise as a critical motivator in their jobs. For example, in research I've conducted, over 70 percent of employees indicate that having a positive e-mail forwarded to them is very or extremely important to them, followed by "being copied on positive e-mail messages" (65 percent); "being given a praising via e-mail" (43 percent); and "being given a praising on voice mail" (26 percent).

Here's some additional advice that can help keep the human element at work even as we make a greater use of technology:

1. GET TO KNOW PEOPLE BEFORE YOU COMMUNICATE ELECTRONICALLY. *All rapport comes from shared experiences. Trust and respect are difficult to establish through the exclusive use of electronic exchanges. Since an estimated 90 percent of all communication occurs at the nonverbal level, what you don't see in your interactions might hurt your relationships.*

2. BE AWARE OF TECHNOLOGY'S LIMITATIONS WHEN YOU COMMUNICATE. *Don't have electronic communication replace a* *personal meeting just for the efficiency of it. Think of when it works well to use voice mail or e-mail, for example, and when a personal meeting would be better. Avoid the use of electronic communication for dealing with sensitive or complex issues, which would be better dealt with in face-to-face interaction.*

3. USE ELECTRONIC COMMUNICATION TO ENHANCE RELATIONSHIPS. *I know one manager who makes a point of using his cell phone to leave thank-you voice mails for others as he commutes home every evening, reflecting on the day's events. He keeps his messages 100 percent positive and avoids rolling them over into work problems or additional assignments. I know another manager who copies his manager on all complimentary e-mails he sends to any of his employees. When it comes time for performance reviews and salary actions, his manager always agrees with his recommendations because he's been kept in the loop the entire year.*

4. USE TECHNOLOGY TO EXPAND YOUR SCOPE OF RECOGNITION. *In discussions and decision making, technology can help you include others who might have been cumbersome to incorporate in the past. For example, Home Depot has weekly satellite feeds to every store that they call "Breakfast with Bernie and Arthur," their chairman and CEO. It's a chance for everyone to hear what's new and how things are going. A .G. Edwards, the financial services company, has a weekly audio conference that includes every employee online. I know of another company that audiotapes a monthly message to employees, which they can listen to at their convenience. Web chats, message boards, and dedicated phone lines for employee access to top management are other possibilities companies are using today to keep employees more connected and to allow them to play an integral role in their organizations.*

5. USE THE POWER OF TECHNOLOGY TO AMPLIFY GOOD NEWS. *Find ways to pass on positive information to your staff, such as forwarding them the news or publicly thanking them via e-mail. At a Hughes Network Systems office in San Diego, for example, they use an "Applause" electronic pop-up bulletin board on their intranet system, to which any employee can post thanks and recognition to any other employee. Employees get to see the latest praise each time they log on to their computers. In these days of relentless pressure and change in most organizations, hearing what's going well becomes a salve to relieve our stress and frustrations. Use technology to highlight any good news as it occurs, and don't forget to use e-mail and voice mail to leave a positive word of thanks.*

> **"We can all invest all the money on Wall Street in new technologies, but we can't realize the benefits of improved productivity until companies rediscover the value of human loyalty."**—Frederick Reichheld, *Director, Bain & Co.*

Since there tends to be a fine line between stress and excitement in most jobs today, a positive use of technology can go a long way toward creating more positive work relationships and a more human and supportive work environment.

When Katherine A. Kawamoto directed the contract management group at NCR, a technology company based in Duluth, GA, she planned when and to whom to send electronic anniversary and birthday cards up to a year in advance.

———

At a division of General Mills in Plymouth, MN, photos of top achievers are posted on their website as "champions."

Chris Higgins, senior vice president of project planning at Bank of America's Services Division in Virginia, says, "It is so important to give everyone credit. I always try to find out who is going above and beyond the call of duty. My team is usually spread out over the country, so I wander over the telephone wires or pop in unexpectedly on conference calls. It is not a huge effort; it mainly takes discipline, but has tremendous payoff."

ELECTRONIC RECOGNITION TIPS

➡ Put employee's story on company intranet.

➡ Set up a blog to praise employees.

➡ Put employee's name on electronic sign.

➡ Set up a recognition page on the company's website.

➡ E-mail, text, fax, or forward a praising to employee and his or her manager.

At *Business First* in Louisville, KY, the newspaper's advertising department sends a broadcast voice mail daily with a motivational message, joke, success story, or whatever helps the team get excited about its workday.

Edward Nickel, regional training and development manager for Nordstrom, Inc., in Oak Brook, IL, reports that some Nordstrom stores recognize employees over the store intercom system before the store opens by sharing great letters they have received from customers about exemplary service. Letters are then posted on an employee bulletin board for all to read. Each store manager has his or her own routine, but there is never a dearth of material, and hearing the examples motivates other employees to do the same.

Fargo Electronics, based in Eden Prairie, MN, uses an electronic newsletter to keep in touch with employees. Information about sales and production figures, customer feedback, and profit-sharing updates with employees are shared daily. At the end of each workday, department heads send information into the company's e-mail system.

Public Praise & Recognition

In my research, *public* praise was ranked as one of the top recognition preferences by today's employees. This included the following items being ranked as either very or extremely important to them: "customer letters are publicly shared or posted" (62 percent); "employee is praised in a department/ company meeting" (54 percent); "employee is recognized at a company awards ceremony" (46 percent); and "employee is acknowledged in the company newsletter" (39 percent). This supports other research that indicates that 76 percent of American workers rank recognition at a company meeting as a meaningful incentive.

Most employees perceive the use of public recognition as highly desirable. Performance management consultant Janis Allen notes that it's easy to leverage positive feedback when you hear it by passing it on to others. "When someone says something good about another person and I tell that person about it," Allen says, "she seems to get more reinforcement value from it than if she had received the compliment firsthand."

There is almost an endless variety of ways to acknowledge employees publicly. Sharing good news such as positive letters

> **PUBLIC RECOGNITION TIPS**
>
> ➡ Start off each meeting with employee recognition.
>
> ➡ Praise an employee during a department/all-company meeting.
>
> ➡ Give an employee a standing ovation during a company meeting.
>
> ➡ Recognize employee at a company awards ceremony.
>
> ➡ Announce an employee's achievement over the PA system.

from customers at the beginning of a staff meeting or posting them on a "Good News Bulletin Board" along with other positive information from members of the department can be effective. For example, at the end of staff meetings, employees of Mom's Landscaping & Design in Chanhassen, MN, share a "Well Done" about someone who has helped them.

Merchant Alliance Group, a wholesale merchant services company based in Columbia, MD, has a large dry-erase board hanging in the office, and each time a team member signs a new account, their name is added to the board.

———

Yell UK, the print-, online-, and phone-centered product and service provider based in Reading, UK, gives rewards or mementos at presentations in front of colleagues.

———

Sentinel Printing Co., Inc., of St. Cloud, MN, uses a fun and colorful wall display to recognize people's achievements. It's part of the "Great Catch" program. Names are put on the board with a "thanks for the great catch." Supervisors receive information about the employee, and some of those employees can become an "Employee of the Month."

> **"Outstanding leaders go out of their way to boost the self-esteem of their personnel. If people believe in themselves, it's amazing what they can accomplish."**
> —Sam Walton, *Founder, Walmart Stores, Inc.*

———

Camelback Hyundai-Kia dealership in Phoenix, AZ, focuses its monthly meetings on sharing goals and results, and on publicly recognizing employees who have been nominated by customers or other employees for good service. You could even bring in key customers to your organization to acknowledge deserving employees and send a powerful message about the importance of customer service.

———

D r. JoAnne Pitera Studer, president of Performance Consulting, in The Village, FL, suggests putting a flip chart next to the elevator door where people can list thank yous and successes for all to see. Pitera also recommends soliciting and announcing nominations for recognition awards for outstanding efforts at department meetings, perhaps in conjunction with a drawing for gifts or money.

———

Y ou can even create a "wall of fame" to show appreciation for top achievers, as they do at the headquarters of KPC. You can take time at the beginning of department or companywide meetings to recognize employees, as they do at Honeywell Inc.'s industrial fibers plant in Moncure, NC, where employees exchange public praising as part of morning plantwide meetings. Or you can use the end of meetings for employee recognition. Norman Groh, a regional manager at a Xerox Corporation office in Phoenix, AZ, ends his management staff meetings on a high note by asking that all managers share one thing they have done to thank their employees since they last met. Besides generating a surge of

> **PUBLIC RECOGNITION TIPS**
>
> ➡ Verbally thank the employee at their work area—in front of peers/ team.
>
> ➡ Introduce top management to employee who made significant contribution.
>
> ➡ Hold an appreciation day for an exceptional employee.
>
> ➡ Tie balloons to an employee's desk when he/she isn't around.
>
> ➡ Name a sandwich after a top employee.
>
> ➡ Develop and award a "Behind the Scenes" award for employees whose actions are not usually public.

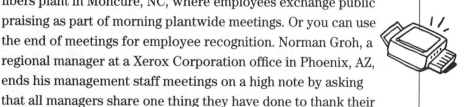

energy and an exchange of practical ideas, he gives them broader visibility by putting the stories in the employee newsletter.

———

Allowing employees to acknowledge one another at group meetings can also be very effective. Petro Canada, a large energy company based in Calgary, Alberta, hosts "bragging sessions" to allow employees to share with upper management progress they are making toward goals. The meetings have a fun and celebratory feel and generate high energy to continue efforts.

> **"It's up to you to decide how to speak to your people. Do you single out individuals for public praise and recognition? Make people who work for you feel important."**
> —Mary Kay Ash,
> *Founder, Mary Kay, Inc.*

Many companies have a year-end awards banquet, which of course provides lots of opportunities to spotlight individuals and groups. You can bring such ceremonies alive with stories about people's successes and the obstacles they had to overcome to achieve their goals. Tag on to any holiday celebrations you have planned some extra time to thank your staff for their dedication and performance. Look to the future as well, and share the signs you've seen of good things to come.

Most organizations also use company newsletters to recognize employees for a wide range of performance, to thank project teams, and even to share information about employee interests and hobbies.

———

A division of Hewlett-Packard in San Diego held a day of appreciation for an exceptional employee, computer scientist Jennifer Wallick. Fellow employees reserved ten-minute time slots to visit her, present her with flowers, and thank her for something she had done for them. She was praised every 15 minutes throughout the day.

———

Peter Economy reports that when he worked as a manager for the City of San Diego Housing Commission, all participants at weeklong management-training workshops would write down one positive thing on an index card for every other person in the session, an activity they called a "strength barrage." Each individual would then receive his or her index cards and read what everyone else had to say about them out loud.

———

Connie Maxwell, owner of Chez Connie's in Des Moines, IA, says of her prior work with the West Des Moines Community Schools, "I posted notes from other departments that had something positive to say about any of us; this way, people who worked with me were more inclined to write one to someone else, so there's a mutual sharing of thanks. It became a point of pride to have a note that one wrote posted."

———

When she worked for Time Warner in Milwaukee, Noelle Sment used an effective stress strategy: a "Bad Day Board," which was a list of everyone's names with a magnet that could be moved to indicate who was under a lot of stress, experiencing personal problems, struggling with difficult customers,

> **"In an environment where there is a shared vision of excellence, where people can be the best they can be on a daily basis, where they know what is expected of them, understand that reward is linked to performance, and believe they can make a difference because they will be heard, they will make a difference. They will go beyond our expectations and great things will start to happen."**
> —Frederick W. Smith, *CEO, FedEx Corporation*

etc. Initially meant to serve as a warning system for others, the group soon started cheering up anyone who was having a "bad day," and having a lot of fun in the process!

———

Xerox Corporation, headquartered in Norwalk, CT, gives Bellringer Awards: When an employee is recognized, a bell is rung in the corridor. Pacific Gas & Electric rings a ship's bell every time someone makes a noteworthy achievement. And the special markets department at Workman Publishing in New York City uses an inexpensive party noisemaker when any employee wants to share good news with the group. Everyone within earshot comes running.

> **"We realized that our largest asset was our workforce and that our growth would come from asset appreciation."**
> —Larry Colin, *President, Colin Service Systems*

———

Chris Giangrasso, VP of Human Resources and Communications for Arkema Inc., a Philadelphia, PA–based chemicals manufacturer, suggests organizing a day of appreciation for a worthy person. When he worked for Aramark, which provides food and leisure services and textile rentals, the company scheduled a day in honor of the person (for example, Bob Jones Day), and sent a notice to all employees announcing the date and the reason for the honor. The honoree enjoyed all sorts of frills, such as computer banners and a free lunch.

———

Chris Ortiz, at NASA's Ames Research Center, reports: "After reading *1001 Ways to Reward Employees*, I created an award for all my team members who helped me. I call it my Thanks-a-Million Award. It contains a thank-you note taped to ten

100 Grand candy bars. Recipients break them up and pass them on to others who have helped them."

———

The president of a teacher's union in Vancouver explains that when he worked in the construction industry, what started as a joke became a coveted honor each workday. One morning, a foreman placed a yellow rubber ducky on the desk of a person who had done a great job the previous day. The tradition continued and soon everyone looked forward to seeing who would receive the day's honor.

———

A government contractor based in Pensacola, FL, tells us, "I'm the maintenance manager supervising 64 jet mechanics for a company that contracts out to the U.S. Navy's flight school. These rough-and-tough men love it when I tape a pinwheel or a balloon

THE MOST BEAUTIFUL SOUND . . . YOUR NAME

- Use the person's first name when delivering a compliment.
- Greet employees by name when you pass their desks or in the hall.
- When discussing an employee's ideas with other people, make sure you credit the employee.
- Acknowledge individual achievements by using employees' names when preparing status reports.
- Name a continuing recognition award after an outstanding employee.
- Ask five people in your department or company to go up to the person during the day and say, "[Your name] asked me to thank you for [the task or achievement]. Good job!"

PUBLIC RECOGNITION TIPS

➡ Make a visible honor roll.

➡ Post employee pictures on a photo-sharing website.

➡ Create a video yearbook highlighting employee accomplishments.

➡ Create a "Best Practices" book filled with employee accomplishments.

➡ Publicly post positive customer feedback about employee.

➡ Put employee's name on public electronic sign.

➡ Place a P&R note in a local newspaper.

to a plane they're working on, signifying that the jet engine has passed every test with flying colors."

———

At San Francisco–based Jossey-Bass, Inc., a division of publisher John Wiley & Sons, all employees have nameplates from their first day on the job. They are made with an etching machine and slipped into a slot on the employee's door or desk. This not only makes newcomers feel welcome, but also helps their colleagues to remember their names.

———

Whenever possible, allow employees to connect their names with their work. Home Depot posts workers' names on signs, such as "This aisle maintained by Jerry Olson."

———

At a Bloomington, IN, hospital cafeteria, sandwiches are named in honor of the "Employees of the Month" and those who have received the most commendations from patients. Items stay on the menu for six months.

———

Wells Fargo Bank has developed some unusual no-cost rewards, such as renaming an item in the cafeteria after a deserving employee or presenting a bag of fertilizer supplied by the keepers of the Wells Fargo stagecoach horses.

———

All employees at Apple Computer in Cupertino, CA, who worked on the first Macintosh computer had their signatures placed on the inside of the product. Employees at Cooper Tire & Rubber Company of Findlay, OH, are allowed to stamp their names on the inside of the tires they produce so they can be recognized for their contributions.

———

When Southwest Airlines achieved the best on-time performance and baggage-handling, and the fewest complaints per customer for the fifth year in a row, it dedicated an airplane to all its 25,000 employees and placed all of their names on the outside of the overhead bins.

———

Federal Express in Memphis used to inscribe the name of an employee's child in large letters on the nose of each new airplane it purchased. The company held a lottery to select the name and flew the child's family to the manufacturing plant for the christening.

> **"Provide positive, immediate, and certain consequences for people's behaviors, and they will do what you want."** —Barcy Fox, *Vice President, Performance Systems, Maritz, Inc.*

———

Ford Motor Company, AT&T, and Meridian Health in New Jersey use their employees in commercials.

A Case Study in Public Recognition

In the Electro-Optics Division of Honeywell, Inc., in Minneapolis, financial difficulties were causing a serious dip in morale, which was leading to additional problems. The company needed to turn the situation around, but had to do so on a very low budget, given the state of the division. Seeking a creative solution, managers developed a recognition program called Great Performers. "The division was looking for top performance from its employees," says Deborah van Rooyen, program director, "and that got me thinking that top performance comes from top performers, and that got me thinking about top performers everyone is familiar with."

Van Rooyen spent a month in the local library researching the lives of great performers in politics, education, social work, business, science, and the arts. All the people she studied had one characteristic in common: They succeeded by overcoming obstacles.

Van Rooyen's idea was to put together a program in which these people's well-known accomplishments would be celebrated alongside those of division employees. She hoped that the possibility of being named a Great Performer would inspire employees to put forth their best efforts.

- Present "State of the Place" reports periodically to your employees, acknowledging the work and contributions of individuals and groups.
- Establish a place to display memos, posters, photos, and so on, recognizing progress toward goals and thanking individual employees for their help.

"Turnaround begins with small accomplishments," Van Rooyen says, "so we wanted to convey the idea that every job is important. For example, we wanted to encourage secretaries to type a letter only once, and to encourage employees in the shipping department to be careful enough that nothing would get broken, and so forth."

Management accepted the idea, and Van Rooyen worked with the division's staff to finalize the list of 40 celebrity Great Performers, being careful to include men, women, minorities, and teams.

A teaser campaign then followed featuring the celebrity Great Performers with memorable quotes. Employees were invited to nominate Great Performers in the company and were asked to explain the reasons for their nominations. A committee of volunteers reviewed the nominees. All were given pins in the shape of the letter *G* (for great) and the committee selected five employees they thought best exemplified the spirit of the program. These winners were interviewed, and stories were created to use on posters that looked just like the ones featuring the celebrities. Each included the employee's photo, a quote, and a description of the employee's achievements and contributions.

"The posters were a visible way to help boost self-esteem," says Chuck Madaglia, division public relations manager. "The idea was to catch employees doing something right and get them feeling good about themselves."

The response was overwhelmingly positive. The Great Performers became corporate celebrities overnight,

- Introduce top management to individuals and groups who have made significant contributions.
- Use charts or posters to show how well an employee or group is performing.
- Develop a Behind the Scenes Award for those whose actions are not usually in the limelight.
- Name a space after an employee and put up a sign (The Suzy Jones Corridor, for example).
- Honor peers who have helped you by recognizing them at meetings. Mention the outstanding work or idea brought to your attention by an employee during your staff meetings or at meetings with your peers and managers.
- Recognize people who recognize others.

and everyone wanted to be one. Many more individuals had the chance: Five new employees were selected each month during the year the program was in place. Morale improved dramatically, and the ongoing program encouraged employees to make changes in work habits, make successful proposal bids, begin recycling scrap, and improve quality control. Within six months, the division was in the black, thanks in part to the success of the program.

Bob Gaundi, Human Resources manager of Mental Health Systems in San Diego, says: "Certainly recognition from supervisors is important, but praise from fellow employees is of the highest order, so we allow employees to recognize coworkers through a monthly newsletter. We ask employees to write a short statement about laudable efforts they witness from fellow employees. All of the examples are published in a special section of our monthly newsletter. Employees always turn to this section first!"

———

At Stew Leonard's in Norwalk, CT, the company newsletter overflows with news of accomplishments, customer comments, and employee contests, such as the offer of a $5 reward to the first employee who deciphered the meaning of a performance chart that measured some aspect of the store's operation.

> **"Everyone who works gets paid— but not everyone gets recognition. That's why it means so much to people."**
> —Bob Nelson

———

Jackson, MI, Chick-fil-A marketing director Tara Hayes produces a newsletter highlighting individual accomplishments both at work and in the community. She also includes feature stories about deserving teams.

———

At Label House Group Limited, a medium-size brand identity and packaging solution company located in Trinidad and Tobago, one of the most frequent ways of recognizing employees is through the internal newsletter, under the heading "Caught You Doing Something Right," according to Shelly-Ann Jaggarnath, Human Resources officer for the company. On a quarterly basis, employees caught exhibiting the desired behaviors and attitudes, or going beyond the call of duty, are profiled in the newsletter and given small tokens of recognition, such as cooler bags.

———

The H. J. Heinz food company, based in Pittsburgh, PA, routinely shares information about employees at all levels of the organization in its internal publications and annual reports, including personal details about their lives, their off-the-job pursuits, and even their poetry. At Tandus Flooring, Inc., a carpet manufacturer in Dalton, GA, the company recognizes and lists the achievements of employees' children in its newsletter.

———

Publix Super Markets, based in Lakeland, FL, publishes a biweekly bulletin that lists the births, deaths, marriages, and serious illnesses of employees and their families. For more than 20 years, the president sent personalized cards to the families of everyone listed in the bulletin.

———

Chuck King of the East Longview and Longview Mall Chick-fil-A's in Longview, TX, highlights employee success in the local newspaper and offers Chick-fil-A sandwiches to all students who provide proof of perfect school attendance.

———

At Claire's in Wood Dale, IL, district managers reward a manager by working his or her store on a Saturday. The regional managers also have a traveling trophy cup, which they fill with goodies (and items related to the award) as it is passed from one district manager to another.

CAPTURE THE MOMENT

- Create a Hall of Fame wall with photos of outstanding employees.
- Take a photo of the person being congratulated by his or her boss's boss. Place photographs of top performers in the lobby.
- Make a photo collage about a successful project that shows the people who worked on it, its stages of development, and its completion and presentation.
- Create a "yearbook" to be displayed in the lobby that contains everybody's photograph, along with his or her best achievement of the year.
- Create a "Good Tries" booklet to recognize those whose innovations didn't achieve full potential. Be sure to include what was learned during the project so that this information can benefit others.

———

At Kragen Auto Parts, based in Phoenix, AZ, the president and other top executives served dinner to all store managers at their annual meeting as thanks for a job well done.

———

Resident Home Corporation, a nonprofit agency that supports individuals with developmental disabilities in Cincinnati, sets up a quarterly car wash for its 200 employees (and the general public) on a Friday when they are getting their paychecks. "We feel that this is a great motivating tool that the administrative team will take three hours of their day to serve them like they serve others," says Larry Mullins, Human Resources director. "We also feel this is a great way to show the general public around us that we are a great organization to work for, and it gives us time to discuss with them what we are about—important aspects for a nonprofit agency that depends on financial and volunteer support from the local community." RHC also hosts "Massage Days" twice a year, when they bring in a massage therapist and allow employees to sign up for I5-minute slots.

———

When Norwest Banks (now a part of Wells Fargo) hosted a sales and service conference in Orlando, FL, all the executives lined up on the sidewalk and applauded employees as they disembarked from the buses and entered the resort. "It really made everyone feel very special," reported Victoria Gomez, a bank vice president from Columbia, MD.

Public Recognition & Social Rewards

The use of personal and social reinforcers is reported as being highly desirable by most employees. As performance management

---

PUBLIC RECOGNITION TIPS

➡ Honor peers who have helped you by recognizing them at meetings. During your staff meetings or at meetings with your peers and management, mention the outstanding work or idea brought to your attention by an employee.

➡ Introduce peers and management to individuals and groups that have been making significant contributions as a way of acknowledging their work.

➡ Nominate employees for any of the company's formal award programs.

➡ Recognize (and thank) people who recognize others. Make it clear that making everyone a hero is an important principle in your department.

consultant Janis Allen says, "Surprisingly, many people say they wish their organizations would give fewer tangibles and use more social reinforcers. Most people are hungry for somebody to simply look them in the eye and say, 'I like the way you do that.'"

PUBLIC RECOGNITION TIPS

➡ Publicly announce bonuses and raises.

➡ Establish a place to display information, posters, pictures, and so on, praising progress against goals and thanking individual employees for their help.

➡ Invite employees to your home for a special celebration, and recognize them in front of their colleagues and spouses.

She goes on to state: "If people receive social reinforcement on the 4:1 ratio (a minimum of four socials to one tangible) and receive reinforcers for behaviors, not only results, they will view the tangible as a symbolic representation of appreciation. Then tangibles become items which serve as reminders of the social reinforcement they have already received. A tangible reinforcer carries the most impact when it symbolizes the recognized behavior or result."

Recognition at a company meeting was ranked by 76 percent of American workers in a recent survey as a positive, meaningful incentive and was deemed most important by workers aged 24–34 and 35–44.

At GreenPages, a technology solutions provider in Kittery, ME, each sales team picks a support person of the month and each support team picks a salesperson of the month. Then members of each team speak a few words about the person they have selected at their monthly meeting.

Employees at Oregon-based Flying Pie Pizzeria restaurants complete a Verbal Comment Card when they hear or have a particularly energetic or successful conversation, usually, but not always, with a customer. The best of these conversations are published in a flyer stapled to paychecks, and are featured in the margins of the restaurant's 16-page menu.

———

SGI and Netscape, high technology companies, in Mountain View, CA, have employee "rant" websites and newsgroups that their CEOs view every day. American Express Travel in Philadelphia, PA, has an employee hotline so employees can leave messages for the CEO.

———

Every four to five years, new store managers of J. C. Penney Corporation, headquartered in Dallas, TX, are "affirmed" in a ceremony of store managers held at over a dozen locations across the country. During the ceremony a pledge is given to the founding principles of the company, and at the conclusion each newly affirmed associate receives an HCSC pin, standing for Honor, Confidence, Service, and Cooperation.

———

According to Robert Voyles, vice president for marketing services for Carlson Marketing Group in Minneapolis, "One way of ensuring that people are happier at work is to make sure they have friends at the company." That is one of the reasons for the company's referral program for new hires. Workers are offered a small reward when someone they referred is hired, then a larger one when the new person completes several months on the job. "When someone recommends someone else, they take pride in—and feel responsible for—that person's work. If the new person messes up, it's a reflection on the person that recommended them," says Voyles.

As part of Chicago-based Hyatt Hotel Corporation's "In Touch Day," all 375-plus headquarters employees—from mail room to executive suite—went to Hyatt properties around the country to provide guest services. Jim Evans, vice president of sales, spent several hours hailing taxis, loading luggage, and collecting tips at the front door of the Hyatt Regency Chicago, and Darryl Hartley-Leonard, president of Hyatt, served lunch in the employee cafeteria, hailed cabs, checked in guests at the front desk, and tended bar. Said Hartley-Leonard: "We're all working toward the same goal, but we corporate people forget what it's like. After a day like this, we know what on-line workers really go through."

———

One day a year all white-collar manufacturing employees work on the production lines at Mary Kay, Inc.

———

> **"We spend an extraordinary amount of time just worrying about the environment and the people in it."**
> —Lewis T. Preston,
> *Chairman, J.P. Morgan*

To demonstrate their trust in employees, once a year all managers at Quad/Graphics in Pewaukee, WI, left the plant for 24 hours for the "Spring Fling and Management Sneak," leaving normal printing operations to continue without the presence of any managers. The managers held meetings and then went to the Milwaukee Art Museum. The company subsequently expanded the event into a two-day, three-evening affair, including seminars that were offered for managers at a local college. During the entire period of time, none of the managers is to set foot inside the printing plants unless an employee makes a request for emergency help. No manager has ever been called in.

One night a year during the Christmas holiday, The Walt Disney Company opens Disneyland to employees and their families only. Concessions and rides are run by upper management, who dress in costumes. In addition to being a lot of fun, this practice allows employees to experience the theme park from the customers' perspective. There are a multitude of other programs designed to build a sense of camaraderie and of identification with the organization, including peer recognition programs and root beer floats at informal recognition parties. Such practices and philosophies have made employee and customer satisfaction among the highest in the industry and are the cornerstone of the company's success.

No-Cost Recognition Ideas & Praisings

Some of the best forms of recognition cost nothing at all! A sincere word of thanks from the right person at the right time can mean more to most employees than a raise, a formal award, or an entire collection of certificates or plaques. Part of the power of such rewards comes from the fact that someone took the time to care—not only to notice the achievement, but to seek out the person and personally deliver a praising in a timely manner.

> **"Workers have always known how to work smarter, and when management isn't watching, they do. Then they use the time to create a halfway pleasant social experience—discussing last Sunday's football game or Betsy's wedding shower or just working at an easier pace. If companies want people to give that up, they're going to have to offer something valuable in trade—something that meets basic human needs for social interaction and financial well-being."** —John Zalusky, *Economist, AFL-CIO*

Research by Dr. Gerald Graham throughout the U.S. revealed that the type of reward most preferred by employees was personalized, "spur-of-the-moment recognition from their direct supervisors."

Since several studies on employees have shown that the greatest influence on job satisfaction is the supervisor, any manager has all the ingredients for achieving a high degree of satisfaction—and corresponding level of performance—with his or her employees.

NO-COST RECOGNITION TIPS

➡ Post a thank-you note on the person's door.

➡ Give a token—a specially designed coin, for example—to be used for a future favor.

➡ Personally clean and vacuum the person's car.

➡ Say hello to employees when you pass by their desks or pass them in the hall.

➡ A good way to personalize any reinforcer is to use the person's first name when delivering the comment. Tell him or her why the behavior or result is important to you.

➡ Acknowledge individual and team achievements by using their name(s) when preparing status reports.

Instead of giving toys or trinkets for recognition, the IRS Service Center in Nashville, TN, acknowledges contributions with a simple thank you and handshake at Employee Recognition events.

———

At Sprint, the telecommunications firm based in Overland Park, KS, some executives use noncash awards to motivate sales representatives to sell a new product or try a new sales approach.

———

Katie Freeland, executive director at Stones Crossing Senior Living Community in Greenwood, IN, does not return to her office from walking around the workplace until she has noticed at least five things that her staff has done well and has acknowledged them for those things. After each praising, she closes a finger on one hand to track her progress and returns to her office only after she has made a fist.

———

Lori Schaper, Sports Area manager for Disney Sports Attractions in Lake Buena Vista, FL, starts each staff meeting by polling the group for three things that are going well. They don't go on to the next item on their agenda until three positive items are identified.

———

Todd Atwood, training manager at Rally's Hamburgers, Inc., the fast-food restaurant chain based in Tampa, FL, makes a point of introducing himself to and learning the names of every employee in each branch he visits.

———

Dion McInnis takes a "morning walk-around" through his department at the University of Houston–Clear Lake (TX), briefly visiting each person, saying a simple hello, asking a question about work, or chatting about what is going on in their lives. "It reminds them that I appreciate who they are," says McInnis, an associate vice president of fund-raising and relationship building. On annual reviews, he states his appreciation for each person's work. He also uses meetings and e-mails to offer personalized thank yous.

> **"Knowing that what you do is important and appreciated is the best reward."**
> —John Ball, *Service Training Manager, American Honda Motor Company*

———

Sara Cohen, Activities Coordinator for Brentmoor Retirement Community in St. Louis, MO, has a technique that keeps her continuously focused on recognition: Every evening she makes a list of the individuals she thanked that day. This practice makes her reflect on her interactions and helps identify ongoing opportunities to acknowledge others.

———

Sierra View District Hospital in Porterville, CA, initially provided recognition tools for managers to use for a year. During the second year, they required managers to use a certain number of them. Bronson Healthcare Group in Kalamazoo, MI, requires every manager to use a dozen thank-you notes each quarter and provide copies of those notes to their managers. HR conducts "spot checks" and if a manager is behind, they set up a meeting with the manager's senior leader. They have never had to set up a second meeting with any manager. AAA of Southern California uses 360-degree feedback from employees to rate managers on how well they provide recognition and encouragement. The quantitative scores translate into how one third of the managers' annual bonuses are calculated.

> "The ratio [of feedback] should be four-to-one, positive to negative."
> —Chuck Powell,
> *Regional Manager,*
> *Preston Trucking*

———

At Allied Signal's Industrial Fibers plant in Moncure, NC, every piece of large equipment—including mammoth steam boilers and air compressors—is assigned an employee "owner." Ownership is acknowledged by large signs attached to each machine that spell out in large letters "This steam boiler owned by . . ." with the employee's name added.

———

When the Marriott Marquis in Times Square, New York, asked its 400 housekeepers how management could better recognize them for the great job they do, one of the top responses was, "Have managers use our names."

Flight attendant Sandy Poole remembers meeting then Southwest Airlines president Herb Kelleher one day and speaking with him for a few minutes. Said Poole, "Six months later I was walking down the hall at headquarters and he said, 'Hi, Sandy Poole. How's the new job?' And that was just so flabbergasting. And you do feel important, it really makes a difference."

Capital One's credit card call center in Tampa, FL, recognizes employees' birthdays and anniversaries by placing Styrofoam cakes above the people's cubicles during the month of the celebration.

Agencies of QSource, the Memphis-based nonprofit health care management expert, post thank-you letters from patients on a "Brag Board." They have also painted a bare-branched tree on a wall. Every time someone does something exceptional or receives a letter of thanks from a patient or family, that staff member's name and the date are put onto a golden leaf and attached to a branch.

NO-COST RECOGNITION TIPS

➡ When discussing an employee's or group's ideas with other people, peers, or higher management, make sure you give them credit.

➡ Create an ongoing recognition award named after a particularly outstanding employee.

➡ Call the person into your office just to thank him or her; don't discuss any other issue.

Josh Parker, a regional manager for the Newark, CA, branch of Pro Staff Personnel Services, said he would disco dance on the desktop if the staff met specific quarterly goals. They met the goal, and he danced as promised. Marcia Amant, Call Center supervisor in the customer care division of VSP, the country's leading vision service provider based in Rancho Cordova, CA, "does a little dance" to thank employees for something special they have done. For both Parker and Amant, dancing at work has become a tradition.

———

To recognize those who take extra effort to cover for vacationing coworkers, the Donaghey Student Center at the University of Arkansas in Little Rock, AR, gives a special award for "going above and beyond the call of duty to see that this office did not collapse in the absence of [vacationing employee's name]. We recognize his/her contributions to the successful and smooth operation of this office."

———

Many service providers who want to sell their services to the general public are willing to give short previews to company employees for little or no cost. For example, at Tassani Communications, Inc., in Chicago, employees can attend "Food for Thought" brown-bag lunches and listen to lectures on topics such as stress management, time management, or crime prevention. San Diego–based Great American Bank reserved a conference room for its own employees and those of neighboring businesses to attend Weight Watchers and Smoke Enders programs.

———

Alexandra Watkins, founder and creative director of Eat My Words, a "naming" firm in San Francisco, bartered with clients and collected products that would make suitable gifts for the holidays. "Many of our smaller clients were cash-poor," says Ms. Watkins, who in lieu of payments took bottles of vodka, bags of coffee, and gift cards, which she in turn gave to other clients. Watkins accepted 25 percent of her payments through in-kind trade that year, up 5 percent from the previous year.

———

When Ricki Snider worked for life insurance company Fortis Advisors, now known as Ageas, they used the "Keys to Excellence" to thank people for doing a good job. The keys were made of construction paper. The recipient received the key with a "thanks" written on it; the giver would save a tab from the key and submit his or her name and that of the recipient to Human Resources. There were separate monthly drawings for all key recipients and for all key givers. Nominal prizes, such as a $50 gift certificate, were awarded, but the buzz was about the keys themselves, which were visibly lined up in people's offices.

NO-COST RECOGNITION TIPS

➡ Create a "Best Accomplishments of the Year" booklet, and include everyone's picture, name, and statement of their best achievement.

➡ Get your employees' pictures in the company newspaper.

➡ Say thanks to your boss, your peers, and employees when they have done something well or have done something to help you.

———

Managers in the diagnostic imaging department of Presbyterian Hospital in Greenville, TX, use a Top 2 format—similar to the Top 10 made famous by late-night TV host David Letterman—to praise staff members via e-mail. Every day, managers e-mail "Two things we love about you" to staff members.

NO-COST RECOGNITION TIPS

➜ Agree to answer the person's telephone for a day.

➜ Wash the person's car in the parking lot during lunch.

➜ Ask five people in your department/company to go up to the person some time during the day and say "(Your name) asked me to thank you for (the task or achievement). Good job!"

➜ Write five or more Post-it notes thanking the person for a job well done and hide them randomly among the papers on his/her desk.

➜ Dedicate the parking space closest to the company entrance for the outstanding employee of the month.

Ray Williams, an employee of the San Diego County Fair, remembers a practice in business in which someone would praise another person by saying, "I've got a GL for you." The GL stood for "Good Last." The idea was that the first person would say something positive they had heard about the second person in exchange for the second person saying something positive they had heard about the first person.

———

Amy Watner-Freeman, director of Human Resources for Community Health Alliance of Pasadena, in Pasadena, CA, was once promoted and found herself managing a man who felt he should have gotten the promotion. "He made my life miserable, constantly interrupting and undermining everything I was trying to do." After several weeks of this, Amy found a solution: She wrote a letter to the man's wife telling her how honored she was to be working with her husband, how much knowledge and experience he had, and how much she looked forward to working with and learning from him. She also expressed what an important role he played on the team and how much she valued his being a part of the group. "The day after sending this letter, the man brought in a plate of chocolate chip cookies that his wife had baked and I never had a single problem with him thereafter!"

———

According to Sonya Parham, assistant manager for Human Resources Development at Busch Gardens in Tampa, FL, they give a "pat on the back" award to employees who do an outstanding job (and they send a notice of the award to the employee's file). They also award breakfast on Fridays for the employee of the month and for excellent service recognition and other notable deeds.

———

"People love to collect others' business cards," John Plunkett, director of employment and training for Cobb Electric Membership Corporation in Marietta, GA, says. "Simply carry a supply of your cards with you and as you 'catch people doing something right,' immediately write 'Thanks,' 'Good job,' 'Keep it up' and specifically what they did in two to three words. Put the person's name on the card and sign it."

> **"If you're going to help people reach their potential, they need to be recognized and rewarded. Everyone needs that."**—Jacqueline Norcel, *Principal, Tashua Elementary School, Trumbull, CT*

———

Put a top performer's name in lights. At Metro Auto in Pomona, CA, the name of the employee of the month is put up on the electronic billboard over the dealership. A similar idea was used at a downtown Philadelphia skyscraper with an electric message board on all four sides that takes up the top third of the building, which honored the head of the local school system: "Philadelphia congrats Dr. Constance Clayton on 10 years."

———

Bell Atlantic's cellular telephone division in Philadelphia, PA, names cell sites after top employees.

———

NO-COST RECOGNITION TIPS

➡ Make a thank-you card.

➡ Have coffee or lunch with an employee or a group of employees that you do not normally see.

➡ Volunteer to do another person's least desirable work task for that day.

Sam Colin, founder of Colin Service Systems located in White Plains, NY, used to go around handing out Life Savers candy to employees. That early tradition has developed into a lasting philosophy of recognizing employees that today includes the selection by coworkers of such distinctions as "most helpful employee" and "nicest employee." Coworkers vote for the employees they think should win those awards, and presentations are made by executives.

At General Electric's Medical Group some managers call their version of frequent recognition an "attaboy" system.

The Marriott Corporation, based in Washington, DC, honors 15 to 20 people a year with its J. Willard Marriott Award of Excellence, an engraved medallion bearing the likeness of Mr. Marriott and the words expressing the basic values of the company: dedication, achievement, character, ideals, effort, and perseverance. According to Gerald C. Baumer, vice president of employee communications and creative services, selection is based on remarks made by the nominator and on the individual's length of service. Award winners represent a cross section of Marriott's workforce: dishwashers, chefs, housekeepers, merchandise managers, and so on. The Marriott award is presented at an annual awards banquet in Washington, DC, attended by honorees,

"With so many ways to reward people, you may ask, 'How do I decide how to reward each person?' The answer is simple: Ask them." —Michael LeBoeuf, *Author*, The Greatest Management Principle in the World

spouses, nominators, and top executives. "We want other employees to look up to these people," Baumer says.

———

At General Mills, headquartered in Minneapolis, new employees can pick a work of art for their own office from a large collection. Similarly, those who work in individual offices pick their own furnishings and works of art at Mary Kay, Inc.

Low-Cost Rewards & Recognition Ideas

As was evident in the last section, there are many highly effective forms of recognition that cost nothing. If you expand the available budget from nothing to a nominal amount (say, under $20), the number of potential reinforcers greatly increases. If the amount available increases to $50, an even wider range of reinforcers are possible. For a modest amount of time, energy, and thoughtfulness, any manager can deliver a unique and truly memorable employee reward. This section provides a collection of effective low-budget, low-cost rewards.

When employees close a deal at United Franchise Connection, the franchise consulting company based in the greater Philadelphia, PA, area, they push the Easy Button to alert and remind people in the office that "that was easy." The buttons are available from Staples Office Supplies at a minimal cost.

William Pickens, owner of Pool Covers, Inc., in Richmond, CA, often hangs a number on the wall and rewards employees who know how it

LOW-COST REWARD TIPS

➡ Discount coupons

➡ Holiday/birthday cards

➡ Coupon for a free haircut

➡ Entertainment book, gift catalog

➡ Newspaper, magazine, Netflix subscriptions

➡ Desk amenities/tools

➡ Disaster/survival kit

is related to the business. For example, 22.5 is the average miles per gallon of the delivery truck fleet, and those who knew that received a $10 prize. Pickens says this game gets employees to think about the business and also creates camaraderie.

LOW-COST REWARD TIPS

➡ Swiss Army knife, watch, charm bracelet

➡ Montblanc, Cross, or Waterman pen

➡ Travel/tote bag

➡ Gym bag, sports water bottle, personalized golf balls

➡ Bottle of wine, decanter

➡ Laptop case, computer game, iPod, iPad, iAnything

➡ Professional portrait of employee and family

When newcomers start at Employers Resource Council in Mayfield Village, OH, they are asked to make their "Favorites" list. The list includes desserts, hobbies, music, sports, vacations, and so on. It's a great way for managers to personalize giving out rewards and recognition. Similarly, when first joining RTC Relationship Marketing in Washington, DC, new employees make a wish list of things they would like to be rewarded with throughout the year. It's called the Kudos program. When someone uses the program, they submit what they did— for whom, and why they did it—to Human Resources. Then they receive their item. The program has been used for several years and is popular with employees.

System Improvements in Knoxville, TN, devised a fun way to incentivize timely returns from breaks during daylong meetings. At the end of each hourly break period, everyone who returns on time gets a playing card. At the end of a day, an attendee might have five to seven playing cards. They all play a round of poker, allowing people to discard cards—if they have them to discard—to improve their hands. They award nominal prizes (T-shirts, pocketknives, watches, for example) for the high hand and the low hand. Everyone has a chance to win. To simplify the process for large meetings and conferences, they reward promptness with tickets that are used in a lottery for prizes.

_____

VPs and other top administrators from Quincy (MA) Medical Center showed up early one morning to welcome employees to work with handshakes, smiles, and hot coffee. They did so in response to a recruiting effort by a rival hospital. "It's just employee recognition," said Quincy Medical chief executive Dr. Gary Gibbons, who stood outside the employee entrance from 6:30 to 8:30 A.M.

_____

Sharon Quinn, claims division manager for Blue Cross Blue Shield of Massachusetts, asks each of her employees what their favorite flower and color is and then, on their birthdays, gives each of them that flower in their favorite color. "It's a simple, personal thing to do that they really seem to like," Quinn says. "I'm on my second year of doing it and recently asked them if they'd like me to do something different, but they said, 'No, we like the flowers!'"

_____

Yell UK, the print-, online-, and phone-based product and service provider based in Reading, UK, rewards with small gifts. Brainstorm Marketing in Des Moines, IA, rewards employees with movie tickets.

_____

LOW-COST REWARD TIPS

➡ Create a "Hall of Fame" wall and place pictures of outstanding employees on it.

➡ Make a photo collage of the achievement, showing people who worked on a project, different stages of development, the final completion, and the presentation.

➡ Inscribe a favorite book as a gift.

Atlanta-based Corporate Resource Development, a sales and marketing company, sets off a siren to let all its coworkers know when special goals are met.

LOW-COST REWARD TIPS

➡ Bring the person bagged lunches for a week.

➡ Take the person to a movie at lunchtime.

➡ Buy lunch for the person and three coworkers of his or her choice.

➡ Tape a candy bar for the typist in the middle of a long report being typed, with a note: "Halfway there!"

➡ Make and deliver a fruit basket to the person.

➡ Find out what the person's favorite music is and make CD/DVD "YouTube" clips of that music for him or her.

Sarah Santos, compensation analyst for International Data Group, the Boston-based technology media firm, created an award by gluing an unopened can of Busch Lite on a gold-painted block of wood that was initially given to someone who had gone "above and beyond." The award has been passed around for years and is now considered a great honor.

A Case Study in Informal Recognition

Elsie Tamayo explained how she turned around the morale, pride, and productivity of the training department when she was training director for the County of San Diego Department of Social Services. When she first started, employee morale was low and the group's identity in the organization was weak.

Elsie met with the 13 employees in her department and asked how they wanted to be perceived by the organization. The group created its own identity as the "Training and Development Center," created a logo, and painted it on the outside and in the lobby of their building. Everyone also got business cards for the first time with the new department logo on those cards.

Elsie then said they were going to spend one half day a month as a Reward and Recognition Day (R&R Day) in which the group would come up with things they wanted to do together. In subsequent months they did such things as taking the train to Los Angeles to visit a museum, going shopping in Tijuana, going to the zoo, and so forth. They had no budget for activities, so initially any expenses were paid for by the employees.

At each department meeting she solicited the help of one employee to come up with some type of fun way of rewarding another employee in the group. For example, to announce one employee's promotion, the group paraded through the building; another employee was presented with an Energizer Bunny "because they kept going and going and going, helping others when needed"; someone who worked fast was awarded a toy roadrunner. She also started each department meeting by reading letters written to her praising the department or the people in it. At all times, she gave the group the latest information she had about developments in the organization.

Elsie used numbers as recognition to increase the visibility of achievements of the group. For example, the number of employees trained each month was tracked, as were cost-saving ideas, and progress was communicated throughout the organization. In the department, flip charts were hung publicly, tracking progress toward different goals, and "masters degrees" were awarded to trainers and managers who trained for 1,000 hours.

LOW-COST REWARD TIPS

➡ Find out the person's hobby and give a gift that relates to that activity.

➡ Leave a card with a note that it is redeemable for a lunch date at the employee's discretion.

➡ Bake a batch of chocolate chip cookies for the person.

➡ Give employees copies of the latest management/business bestselling book or a subscription to a business journal.

➡ Rent a sports car for the individual to drive for a week.

> **"Compensation is a right; recognition is a gift."** —Rosabeth Moss Kanter, *Harvard Professor & Management Consultant*

She bartered her training services with other training companies to get training slots for her group members or facilities for an off-site retreat. She also started a self-development library and positioned use of it as a reward.

She used extensive spontaneous rewards, such as quick handwritten notes or a note on a flip chart that read "you really handled the meeting well yesterday," with specifics and why the activity was important, and then posted the flip chart on the person's door. She often let people come in late the day after finishing a training session.

Once a week, every person was given an hour to meet with her to talk about anything they wanted to discuss. Initially many of the meetings took less than ten minutes, but over time everyone came to use the full hour. Employees would discuss results from a training session and how they could improve, problems they were having with other employees, ways to improve their skills and career potential, and so on.

She hosted a fake "marathon" with all project members, which included T-shirts and awarded "records"—actual LPs with new labels and jackets to fit the achievements of individuals in the group that were handed out during a mock marathon celebration.

All these activities were conducted with little or no budget, and throughout employees knew they still had to put in the hours needed to get their job done. Within several months the morale, excitement, pride, and energy of the department skyrocketed and the group was viewed with greater esteem by the rest of the organization.

Stew Leonard's in Norwalk, CT, has an Out-to-Dinner program for employees, in which dinners for two are awarded for doing something special, like coming in on one's day off or working through a break. All the managers are authorized to award similar things, whenever they want to; some walk around with lunch coupons in their pockets so they can hand them out on the spot if they feel like it. Stew personally writes notes of gratitude to employees for jobs particularly well done and sometimes slips extra dollars in their pay envelopes.

During Administrative Professionals' Week all secretaries get flowers at Mary Kay, Inc.

At Claire's Boutiques in Wood Dale, IL, district managers work a store for a manager on a Saturday if that person is being rewarded. The regional managers have a traveling trophy cup that they fill with goodies (and items related to the award) as it is passed from one district manager to another.

A Hewlett-Packard engineer burst into his manager's office in Palo Alto, CA, to announce he'd just found the solution to a problem the group had been struggling with for many weeks. His manager quickly groped around his desk for

LOW-COST REWARD TIPS

➡ Buy the person a rose or a bouquet of flowers.

➡ Cover the person's desk with balloons.

➡ Give employees notepads tailored to their personalities.

➡ Arrange for the employee to have lunch with the company president.

➡ Take a photo of the person being congratulated by her boss's boss. Place photographs of top performers in the building lobby.

some item to acknowledge the accomplishment and ended up handing the employee a banana from his lunch, with the words "Well done, congratulations!" The employee was initially puzzled, but over time the "Golden Banana Award" became one of the most prestigious honors bestowed upon an inventive employee.

———

LOW-COST REWARD TIPS

➡ Pay an employee's mortgage one month.

➡ To congratulate an employee, rent a billboard and feature his or her picture and name.

➡ Give the person a round of golf.

➡ When employees or managers travel to different parts of the country, have them visit local branches of the company.

Tom Tate, program manager in the personnel and management training division of the Federal Government's Office of Personnel Management in Washington, DC, tells the story of the "Wingspread" award. A beautiful engraved plaque was first given to the division's "special performer" by the department head. Later, that person passed the award to another person who he felt truly deserved the award. The award came to take on great value and prestige because it came from one's peers. A recipient can keep it as long as he or she wants or until that person discovers another "special performer." When the award is about to be passed on, a ceremony and lunch are planned.

———

Noreen Wahl, manager of Human Resources for Sherpa Corporation in San Jose, CA, emphasizes that it's not the award as much as the recognition. "We purchased an old bowling trophy that was ugly, gaudy, and huge from a pawnshop to use as a 'pass around' award for spectacular results achieved. Each recipient proudly displayed it while it was theirs."

Manager-Initiated Reward and Recognition Ideas

The following list of items was generated by sales managers at American President Lines in Oakland, CA, and submitted by Laird D. Matthews, director of sales training and development for that company. Most of the items are designed to cost less than $100 and are in the complete control of local management (thus not needing corporate buyoff). Some are intended to provide a bit of humor.

Letters from manager, managing director, vice president, president

Personal phone calls from managing director, vice president, president

Parking spot for top sales rep of the month

Day off, half-day off, Friday off

Magazine subscription

Monthly rep certificate with name on plaque

Meal with staff member, vice president, or president

E-mail acknowledgment

Promotional gift, special memento

Birthday card, cake, gift

Award pins

Team dinner, team outing

Videotape of interview for training as subject matter expert

Sales rep of the month, quarter, year award

Acting sales manager

Conference attendance

Tickets to events

Bottle of wine, champagne

Training award/ attendance

National accounts trip as "award-winning employee"

Tour of West Coast

Trip with account representative

Weekend trips

Open praise

Letters of recognition

Sales giveaway

Recognition lunch

Publication of recognition

Leader of the month (e.g. meetings)

Plum assignment

Increased territory

Transfer nonproducing account

One month of shoe shines

Contribution to favorite charity

Bulletin board notice

Flowers/balloons/ bouquet

One-month club membership

Dinner/night on the town with spouse

Represent company at an industry event (salesperson's choice)

A training session at new location of choice

Overseas training trip

Sports jacket/suit

Upgrade CRT

Sales meeting acknowledgment

Top performer takes everyone to lunch

Group day-off event

Massage/facial/manicure

Round of golf

Dinner with managing director

Hot-air balloon ride

Limousine ride

Upgrade the company car

Ship ride, harbor tour

Company logo tattoo!

Gift certificate

Own office

Better office location/arrangements

Champagne brunch

$50 cash

Case of beer

Toys for kids

Select employees for presentation to visiting executives

Invite staff to home

Submit articles about staff to various company newsletters

Exposure to top management through task force or committee

Relieve personal chores for sales rep (e.g., wash car, cut lawn)

Recognition Activities

Often, effective forms of recognition are events, one-time occurrences that commemorate a significant achievement or milestone. Such activities need to be planned in advance so as to be timely and pertinent to the situation and person being recognized.

On a very cold, wet, and snowy day, Awards.com, a recognition and rewards product company in Lyndhurst, NJ, hired high school students to scrape ice off the windshields of their employees' cars and then handed each employee a bottle of Heet as they left for the day.

———

Meet with the president of the company!

- Hunter Simpson, the president of Physio-Control, makes it a point to spend one hour with every new employee, no matter what level.
- Each new employee group at Viking Freight System spends an hour with the president or one of the other top officers of the company during a one-day orientation.
- Everyone who joins the company meets with Mary Kay Ash, the founder of Mary Kay, Inc., during their first month of employment.

> **"People who feel appreciated by their employers identify with the organization and are more willing to give their best to the job."**—Peggy Stuart, *Assistant Editor*, Personnel Journal

———

Give a special "VIP Pass" that would allow the individual free privileges for a certain period of time (one month or one quarter), as is done at Management 21 in Nashville, TN, according to Cheryle Jaggers, training coordinator. They could receive free lunches in the cafeteria, free membership in the company's fitness center, free parking in the parking garage, and much more.

———

Joan Cawley, director of Human Resources at Advanta Corporation in Horsham, PA, reports using the following forms of recognition: surprising internal service departments such as payroll and switchboard/receptionists with treats like doughnuts or candy; treating female staff members to a lunchtime manicure during an especially hectic period; buying Ninja Turtle decorations for an employee who was busy and had to plan a child's upcoming five-year-old birthday party; presenting a monogrammed canvas briefcase to commemorate a staff member's promotion to management; surprising her staff with a picnic at a local park, complete with champagne and strawberry shortcake she had made, in place of a regularly scheduled Friday staff meeting; presenting a "life saver" award—a dozen packs of Life Savers candies and a gift certificate to a local department store to recognize an employee's efforts in filling two jobs during a period of transition.

> **"Anytime you make people feel better about themselves, you are building strong motivation."**
> —Rebecca Boyle,
> *Manager, Training Services, Empire of America Federal Savings*

———

Catherine Meek, a compensation consultant based in Los Angeles, reports of a hospital she worked with in California: "At any one time they had 12 to 15 employee recognition programs going, each developed by employees." The janitorial and housekeeping staff came up with the Golden Broom Award.

They have little cards made up with a golden broom on them, and if someone is seen picking up trash (other than a janitor), then they get this award. After someone receives ten cards they get something else—nothing really expensive or big, but it gets the message across.

> "A good motivator finds out what his or her employees' hot buttons are—and then pushes them."
> —Stew Leonard,
> *Founder, Stew Leonard's*

"Another program is called the Guaranteed Service Program. It refunds a patient's money for non-surgical procedures if the patient is not totally satisfied with the services. If a patient does not feel they were provided with the appropriate service, then his or her bill is refunded. This hospital has a fund for this and every quarter what is not returned to patients is raffled off to employees. So what that does is [it] focuses employees on providing the best possible patient care because the better the care, the higher the fund and the more likely they are going to get more money in their pockets.

"Yet another program they have is called Caught in the Act of Caring. If an employee, vendor or anyone catches you in the act of caring, you get a little card that says 'I was caught in the act of caring.' After you get a certain number of these cards, you can trade them in for various merchandise.

> "Once employees see that what they do makes a difference to the organization and is valued, they will perform at higher levels."
> —Rita Numerof,
> *President,*
> *Numerof & Associates*

"None of this really takes all that much time as long as you have employees involved in these various programs. They [the hospital] don't even really think of the time, it's just the way they do business. It's an attitude that exists in that organization."

At South Carolina Federal in Columbia, SC, the president and other top managers serve employees lunch or dinner as a reward for a job well done.

Organize a recognition week for a key category of employee. Empire of America Federal Savings Bank in Buffalo, NY, announced a Teller Recognition Week in which tellers were showered with such acknowledgment tokens as carnations, boutonnieres, candy; certificates of appreciation; a breakfast in their honor; specially printed T-shirts; and a recognition party.

Patricia L. Keeley, training manager for Spectrum Emergency Care in St. Louis, MO, recommends having an employee's dry cleaning picked up and delivered to the office for one month or having a catering service bring lunch to an employee every day for a week.

Carla Levy, training specialist for Indianapolis Power & Light Company, recommends paying an employee's parking fees for a month or a year.

At McDonald's the company has different motivational activities for its distinct categories of workers, such as teenagers and older workers. "Thirty years ago, having an employee softball team was enough to satisfy workers," says Dan Gillen, staff director of store employment. "Today, we have to tailor our incentives to the specific nature of our work force."

For its teenage workers, the company has established a flexible scheduling policy to accommodate student schedules, exams, and papers. During the prom, workers might be brought in from other areas to cover for students who are at the dance.

For its senior employees, a district might hold a "senior prom," a chance for its older workers to meet one another and socialize outside the work setting, or stage a potluck supper in the restaurant or at a manager's home.

———

Warren F. Doane, senior vice president for Founders Title Company in Redwood City, CA, suggests a wide variety of recognition rewards, including limo rides to lunch and dinner, a stay at a bed-and-breakfast, a weekend in Tahoe, a cruise on the bay, a train ride to Reno, a baseball night for all employees, and tux-clad managers who serve employees lunch.

———

> **"If you give a little recognition to your casual business acquaintances—the order-processing clerks, permit-review people, receptionists, etc.—you'd be amazed to find out how much it means to them. . . . I want our people to be able to see the people with whom they work."** —Jack Nolan, *CEO, Nolan Scott, Inc., Towson, MD*

*The Ten Best Ways to Reward Good Work
by Michael LeBoeuf*

Reward #1: *Money*

Reward #2: *Recognition*

Reward #3: *Time off*

Reward #4: *A piece of the action*

Reward #5: *Favorite work*

Reward #6: *Advancement*

Reward #7: *Freedom*

Reward #8: *Personal growth*

Reward #9: *Fun*

Reward #10: *Prizes*

Cash, Cash Substitutes & Gift Certificates

C ash and cash substitutes, such as gift certificates, rank among the top ten ways employees say they'd like to be recognized when they do good work. Employees ranked the following items as either very or extremely important to them: "employee receives a gift certificate or voucher" (48 percent); "employee receives a nominal cash award" (46 percent); "manager gives the employee dinner out for two" (43 percent); and "employee receives entertainment tickets" (39 percent). This is supported by research showing that 95 percent of respondents considered a cash bonus a positive and meaningful incentive. Almost 15 percent of respondents in a survey by *Workforce Management* give cash awards to their employees and 2 percent give savings bonds as part of their organization's incentive programs.

Most people enjoy getting extra spending money—especially around the holidays or when they have unexpected financial needs. Although cash offers maximum flexibility to an employee in terms of how the money is spent, the problem with giving cash is that it often comes to be expected. If you give a $500 holiday bonus three years in a row, employees will count on receiving it the fourth year, as well. The other challenge with using cash is that it has no "trophy value," that is, no lasting value as a reminder of achievement. Money is often spent on bills and then quickly forgotten.

Cash substitutes (such as gift certificates, coupons, or points that can be traded for products) do, however, possess some trophy value. The products employees choose will help remind them of their achievements. Gift certificates have the joint advantage of quick fulfillment and flexible dollar amounts and expiration dates, and carry no shipping costs. They can be redeemed in a wide variety of places for a broad range of merchandise, from gourmet food to lawn mowers. Cash substitutes can provide an effective compromise between giving an employee money that is quickly spent and forgotten, and a fixed gift or reward that they perhaps do not want or need.

> **"There's nothing wrong with a cash award, but then it's spent. Seemingly small gestures—a parking spot, a plaque, bulletin boards with pictures of employees—can be as effective as banquets and travel."**
> —Donald Gagnon, *Training Coordinator, Brunswick Mining and Smelting Corp.*

Harbor Court Hotel in San Francisco gives $2 poker chips to employees for behaviors such as exceptional guest service and teamwork. The chips can be redeemed by the end of the month for gift cards.

Lewis-Goetz and Company, Inc., an industrial products manufacturer based in Pittsburgh, PA, sent $5 Dairy Queen gift certificates directly to the homes of their employees, along with a note to their children. The note said, "It has been a long hot summer and we have asked a lot out of your mom/dad. Please take the time to enjoy an ice cream with them and let them know how much not only you appreciate them, but how much our company appreciates their work ethic and commitment to our organization." The idea went over extremely well. "We actually received thank-you letters back from the children," says general manager John E. Veon.

———

At Atria Senior Living Group, operator of three senior living complexes in Tucson, AZ, when the whole staff scores well on twice-a-year customer satisfaction surveys and corporate inspections, every employee gets a gift card. "It helps to give our employees an incentive to keep our residents happy," said Donna Jacobs, senior executive director at Bell Court Gardens, where turnover was a low 25 percent.

———

Marlene Herman, owner of two Aamco Transmission & Complete Car Care franchises in the Cleveland, OH, area, issued gas cards and gift cards to her ten employees.

———

CASH & CASH SUBSTITUTE TIPS

➡ Recommend a bonus.

➡ Give a spontaneous/unexpected "on the spot" cash award.

➡ Give a cash bonus.

➡ Give cash on the spot.

➡ Give cash for employee to spend at company store.

➡ Give cash and take employees to the mall; stage a show-and-tell afterward of what everyone bought.

➡ Give a savings bond.

The chemical specialties group of W. R. Grace in Atlanta, GA, were given scratch-off lottery tickets as incentive to create improvement suggestions. When implemented, the workers' ideas helped the company save a documented $175,000 per year.

———

Several years ago, Infosurv, a market-research firm in Atlanta, GA, began awarding a $150 restaurant gift card every quarter to the employee with the best business idea. One employee won for developing a technology innovation that helped the company retain a major client that was about to leave. They have since added a second contest in which the company's 15 employees must identify a total of 100 innovative ideas by year's end to each receive a $100 reward. The program has paid for itself: In cost savings, revenue enhancement, and efficiencies, it is in the six-figure range.

———

Mike Hall, chief executive of Borrego Solar Systems in San Diego, introduced two quarterly employee contests for innovation, each with a $500 prize. One contest seeks the best business innovation, which must be formalized on paper to include the problem the idea solves, as well as its costs, risks, and benefits. The other competition rewards the best "knowledge brief," which requires employees to share valuable information that can benefit the company as a whole. For example, one worker won for creating a glossary of acronyms in the solar industry. Winners are determined by a companywide secret ballot.

———

Benco Dental, the U.S.'s largest privately held, full-service dental distributor based in Wilkes-Barre, PA, provides a

$300 cash bonus to employees who refer a new hire. The new employee must work for six months before the bonus is paid.

———

Heartland Dental Care in Effingham, IL, gives team members gift cards for exceeding sales goals. They can choose cards from SAM's Club, Walmart, Target, Best Buy, Eddie Bauer, or Citgo.

———

Wyoming Valley Health Care System in Wilkes-Barre, PA, offers up to $6,000 to a select group of prospective highly sought after employees: registered and graduate nurses; physical, occupational, and respiratory therapists; pharmacists; and imaging technologists. They must commit to work for a specified time period or return the money upon their departure.

———

One recent December, David Hall, owner of several Overflow discount stores in Queensland, Australia, gave his 60 staff members $30,000 in incentives, including gifts, cash, and vouchers. He gave $300 cash rewards to seven staff members, along with several $100 monthly customer service awards. Several long-term employees received prizes, including a $2,000 travel voucher and $200 and $100 gift cards. Hall gave every shop manager a $1,000 shopping voucher and a $500 voucher for a selected staff member. Throughout the year he had given them $50,000 in incentives. Over the last seven years, staff size has doubled from 30 to 60 and the multi-million-dollar business is booming. "I can't do it without them," the 37-year-old Hall says.

———

Dr. Bob Shillman, CEO of Cognex, a Boston, MA–based machine vision systems provider, has been known to give cash bonuses of up to $10,000 from a Brinks truck and to subsidize employee vacations to one of the Seven Wonders of the World.

The Vermont (US) Healthcare Association awarded cash prizes to assisted-living facilities for making innovative changes to their operations over the prior year. The Bel Aire Center, for example, changed their interview process so that direct-care workers would both interview and make the hiring decisions of their peers. Not only did the change improve employee morale, but turnover was cut in half.

Spotlight on Intuit, Inc.: A Case Study

Research shows that formal recognition and reward programs become stale over time. Like many organizations, Intuit, Inc., a Mountain View, CA–based tax and financial software provider, has been challenged to keep employee recognition effective over time. Recognition was left up to individual managers who did very little to recognize their employees. The company's initial attempts in using cash and merchandise to recognize employees each had their limitations.

In 2000 the company set out to improve their employee recognition. Jim Grenier, vice president of Human Resources,

GIFT CERTIFICATE TIPS

➡ Give a gift certificate for dinner.

➡ Give a home-improvement store gift card.

➡ Upgrade an employee's home Internet speed.

➡ Provide free postage for one year.

➡ Give a public transportation pass.

➡ Give coupons for car wash/detail, oil change, gas.

➡ Give certificates for music, book, pet, or grocery stores.

➡ Give coupons for retail stores, museums, tourist attractions, movies.

CASH SUBSTITUTE TIPS

➡ Coupons for free dessert

➡ Employee's favorite snack, beverage, food, dessert

➡ Free snacks in the office for a week

➡ Pancake breakfast, parking lot lunch

➡ Picnics—outside the office, on rooftop

➡ Barbecue, potluck dinner; high tea

said, "We want to let people know they are doing a good job and, at the same time, reinforce the same messages about where the business is going and what's important." The company created the Spotlight program to recognize performance, innovation, and service dedication.

Performance awards are given for specific behavior that meets certain award criteria; innovation awards are for patent disclosures, patent filings, and issued patents; and service awards are for milestone anniversaries. Most performance awards are given immediately, providing instant recognition. These awards are both monetary and nonmonetary, such as "Take a Bow," which can be given by anyone in the company to anyone else. Managers and higher-level individual contributors can give awards with monetary value to any employee in any part of the company. Some engineering leaders give "ship trips" to their teams. When a new product is shipped or a new software version is released, the leader takes the development team to an event. Intuit budgets 1 percent of its payroll for recognition, well under the 2.7 percent of payroll that average companies spend on recognition according to a national survey by the Society of Human Resource Management.

The impact of the Spotlight program has been significant. Use of the program initially increased from 5,500 to 20,000 awardees in the second year and then rose to 26,000 awardees by the third year. Within two years almost 95 percent of all eligible employees had received at least one award offered by the program. In a 2007 survey with eight categories, Intuit ranked number one in half of them: people management, social responsibility, quality of management, and quality of products and services. By 2008, *Fortune* listed Intuit as the most admired software company in the United States and one of the Best Companies to Work For.

STRENGTHS OF
CASH INCENTIVE AWARDS

- Desirable
- Easy to administer and simple to handle
- Understood by everyone
- Can provide an extra boost to a long-term program

Lowell G. Rein, chairman of LGR Consultants in McMurray, PA, offers ideas for rewards that involve relatively small amounts of cash:

- Offer silver dollars or gold coins for good work, a good safety record, or perfect attendance.
- Periodically give $20 bills to employees (or groups of employees) who excel.
- Place small cash awards with personal thank-you notes inside employees' calendars or desk drawers.
- Choose an outstanding employee to receive a small (but permanent) pay raise.
- Offer unexpected cash bonuses.

In Portland, OR, REI employees who come to work on a moment's notice because of understaffing get $5 gift cards to Starbucks.

Rocky Laverty, president and CEO of Farmer Bros. Company, a coffee producer in Torrance, CA, awards "Rocky Dollars" for outstanding performance. The award consists of a silver dollar mounted on a certificate, presented personally by the president with public congratulations.

Newell Rubbermaid, Inc., based in Atlanta, GA, rewards employees with "rubber bucks" for a job well done, redeemable for company products at a company store.

CASH SUBSTITUTE TIPS

➡ Specialty Food Day for a team, department, or the whole company (free ice cream, soft pretzels, ethnic foods)

➡ Coffee; gourmet coffee assortment

➡ Holiday basket; seafood sampler basket; exotic cheeses, spices

➡ Home-delivered steaks

➡ Fresh fruits and vegetables (farmers' market)

Burger King rewards workers with cash when they recruit management-level employees. Also, for finding entry-level workers, employees receive "burger bucks" redeemable for gift certificates from local stores.

At National Office Furniture in Jasper, IN, fake cash is awarded during meetings held to test product knowledge. At the end of the meeting, employees use the money to bid for prizes. Tickets for college football games and the Grand Ole Opry are also given to top performers. When a companywide slogan contest was held, winning teams received jackets.

Kyle Illman, managing director of Messages on Hold in Perth, Australia, shares: "Our client contact is over the phone, so we need our people to impress those clients to overcome the distance factor. I read compliments of employees out loud in team meetings and ask the honorees to pick from a deck of playing cards. For cards 2 through 9, they receive the same amount in dollars. For a 10 or picture card, they receive $10, and for an ace, $20. It's fun, and spurs all the reps to wow the clients."

> **"Economic incentives are becoming rights rather than rewards."**
> —Peter F. Drucker,
> *Author and Management Guru*

The *Dallas Business Journal* keeps a supply of gold-colored tokens in $10 and $20 denominations, redeemable at any store in a local mall. Managers provide the coins to employees for meeting weekly goals or making large sales. The paper also gives out movie passes, small cash bonuses, and certificates for in-office back massages.

Pitney Bowes, headquartered in Stamford, CT, awards a $25 savings bond for the best oral and written questions submitted at the annual stockholders' meeting.

Sandy Edwards, Human Resources representative for Great Western Drilling Company in Midland, TX, says the company offers a $25 savings bond to the employee who poses the most challenging question to the president at company communication meetings.

Great Western also hosts an employee appreciation banquet with a twist: Each employee receives $200 in play money to use at an auction. As part of the auction, managers take bids on services such as washing cars, baby-sitting, house-sitting, baking a cake, cooking a meal, and doing an employee's job for six hours. Employees also receive two gold pieces and a sit-down dinner.

CASH SUBSTITUTE TIPS

➡ Provide tickets to a sporting, musical, or cultural event, depending on the employee's preference.

➡ At an employee meeting, tape gift certificates to the bottom of chairs in the first three rows.

———

Coupons worth $35 are given to employees at Wells Fargo Bank in San Francisco for "extra effort" and "a job well done." They are redeemable for gifts such as season tickets to a sporting event, a pedigreed puppy, five shares of company stock, Rose Parade tickets, shopping sprees, a one-month mortgage payment, and paid days off.

———

Quad/Graphics printing company in Sussex, WI, pays employees $30 to attend a seminar devoted to quitting smoking and gives $200 to anyone who quits for a year.

———

At Celestial Seasonings, the packager of herbal teas in Boulder, CO, every employee receives a $25 check on his or her birthday, a $50 check at Thanksgiving, and a $100 check at Christmas.

———

Employees at the Naval Publications and Forms Center in Philadelphia, PA, nominate coworkers for the Wilbur Award, named after a longtime employee, which comes with $25.

Workers have the chance to earn a top award of $35,000 for an outstanding suggestion.

***

At Anchor Communications in Lancaster, VA, everyone receives a $50 gift certificate when they meet their quarterly cash flow target. Anchor also asks employees to try to conserve resources. As part of this effort, management puts up posters of the quarterly cash balance target all over the building and updates them daily. Those who guess the current cash balance in a pop quiz are given travel certificates for $1,500.

***

G. S. Schwartz and Company Inc., a public relations firm in New York, holds a "Hit Parade" contest in which it awards $50 a week to the PR representative who demonstrates the best method of getting coverage of an event or generating a story for a client. Winners receive one point toward a $100 quarterly prize, and runners-up are awarded half a point.

***

When Mary Jo Stuesser-Yafchak was president of Accudata in Fort Myers, FL, she held a monthly drawing for $50 and entered the names of everyone who had attended monthly after-hours training sessions into a drawing for $1,000 of travel credit at year's end.

***

Every other year, employees are offered selections from a gift catalog in lieu of a year-end bonus at Hatfield Quality Meats in Hatfield, PA. Every employee receives the same

> **"Money is not going to have the same impact with upper level management as it does with lower salaried employees. However, everyone appreciates recognition."**
> —Martha Holstein,
> *Associate Director,*
> *American Society on*
> *Aging*

monetary amount and can select an expensive item or several less expensive ones.

———

American Express Company's "Be My Guest" plan treats an employee sales incentive winner to dinner at the company's expense. The employee receives a certificate redeemable for a meal at a participating restaurant. The certificate charges the meal to the gift-giver's account.

WEAKNESSES OF CASH INCENTIVE AWARDS

- No trophy (i.e., lasting) value
- Not exotic
- Can't be enhanced
- Tends to become an "expected" award

At Pfeiffer & Company, a publisher now part of John Wiley & Sons, employees were financially rewarded for prolonging their business trips by an extra day or so to save the company money. For example, a plane ticket with a return on Sunday night might be $150 cheaper than one with a Friday return, so they would give the employee $75 of that savings. "It turned out to be a great way for employees to bond with clients, vendors, or coworkers in the other city when there simply had been no time during the normal work week for social activities," reports Marion Mettler, former CEO of the company.

———

A manager at Gap, Inc., headquartered in San Francisco, wanted to thank everyone for working madly to meet a big deadline. She gave them gift certificates from a spa for a facial or a massage. It was a much-appreciated treat to help employees calm down and relax after a tough time.

S teve Ettridge, president of Randstad Professionals US, a temporary-employment service based in Wakefield, MA, had a problem with young workers who would not admit having done something wrong. "Most of the mistakes could have been fixed or minimized, but I never found out about them until they blew up," Ettridge says. "One day I pulled out $500 in cash, and I told them about a mistake I'd made that week. I said that whoever could top it would get the money. Of course, they were afraid it was a trick." One employee finally admitted to a data-entry error that had caused a $2 million paycheck to be printed and almost mailed out. He got the $500. Since then the company gives out quarterly $100 awards to employees who admit mistakes they have made on the job. Ettridge says the award is designed to allow people to be human and to encourage risk taking.

T he late Victor Kiam, president of Remington Products in Atlanta, GA, maintained a $25,000 discretionary fund to give instant cash recognition to workers who had been spotted by their supervisors doing an exceptional job. Kiam called these people into his office and handed out checks ranging from $200 to $500.

> **"Greed is still a great motivator."**
> —Tom Staffkamp,
> *General Manager for Large-Car Operations, Chrysler*

At the Internal Revenue Service, cash awards of at least $100 are given for ideas (some go as high as $4,000). Workers who score well on their performance evaluations get cash bonuses averaging $500.

***

When J. Pierpont Morgan, founder of the JP Morgan Bank, died in 1912, he bequeathed one year's salary to each member of his staff.

A Case Study in Cash Incentives

Before being acquired by Byron, MN–based Schmidt Printing Company, Solar Communications, a Naperville, IL, direct-mail and packaging business, evolved a system of cash bonuses over the years. Initially cash bonuses were casual, even paternalistic. At the end of most months, founder John F. Hudetz would hand out checks—usually $20 to $60—with everyone getting the same amount.

When the company reached $2 million in sales, the owners wanted to try a more clearly defined program. Employees were assigned to specific machines and divided into work teams of four or five; the more a team produced during a given month, the bigger the bonus for each member.

The new incentive system had an immediate effect. The packaging machines ran faster than ever as employees jockeyed for larger and larger payments. In many cases, production rates doubled. In good months, team members in the top group would see bonuses of about $250, while their counterparts might receive a quarter

CASH SUBSTITUTE TIPS

➡ Sports equipment

➡ Consumer electronics

➡ Power tools

➡ Furniture

➡ Clothing, shoes, jewelry, sunglasses, cosmetics

of that. Because of the pressure to produce, however, other problems occurred, such as machine breakdowns caused by a failure to carry out regular maintenance.

PUT YOUR MONEY WHERE YOUR HEART IS

- Offer a cash bonus with taxes prepaid.
- If an employee works overtime, send a $20, $50, or $100 bill to a spouse with a thank-you note for his or her support.
- Give employees who recruit new workers a cash bonus.
- Buy the person a gift certificate.
- Pay for the tutoring of an employee's child.
- Pay an employee's parking or traffic ticket.
- Pay an employee's mortgage for one month.
- Pay for a housecleaning service for an employee's home.

Then the company rewarded everyone for bottom-line results according to the clear-cut formula: Every quarter, managers set a target for profitability based on what they thought was within reach. Assuming the company met the goal—the numbers were openly discussed within the company—25 percent of the incremental earnings went into a bonus pool. The pool was then divided in relation to a person's earnings during the previous quarter. If, for example, an employee earned 0.5 percent of the total payroll, he or she was entitled to 0.5 percent of the bonus pool, modified by two factors: It took two years to become fully vested in the program, and unexcused absences or tardiness could shrink a check.

Evolution of Solar Communication's Cash Incentive Program

INTERNAL BONUSES, COMPANYWIDE, 1977–84

Upside: *No promises, easy to administer*
Downside: *Employees didn't know what they were being rewarded for; no motivational effect*

PRODUCTION BONUSES, BY TEAM, 1984–88

Upside: *Stimulated output and creativity*
Downside: *Set off rivalries among departments and individuals; created equipment and quality problems; administrative nightmare*

PROFIT-SHARING BONUSES, COMPANYWIDE, 1987–PRESENT

Upside: *Simple to understand; emphasizes teamwork and interdepartmental coordination*
Downside: *More difficult for individuals to influence*

During especially busy periods, Nucor Corporation, a steel manufacturer in Charlotte, NC, has six-day workweeks, paying bonuses for the sixth day based on time-and-a-half pay.

———

In Green Bay, WI, WS Packaging Group holds monthly bonus meetings called STP (share the profit). The company shares information on every line item of its budget and shares profits that exceed its goals with employees. However, if there's a loss, it has to be made up before any additional bonuses can be paid.

———

The fibers department at E. I. du Pont de Nemours & Company in Wilmington, DE, has an Achievement Sharing Program in which all employees put 6 percent of their salaries at risk and are paid a sliding percentage of that amount based on how close their department comes to its annual goals. Less than 80 percent means no increase; 80 to 100 percent means a 3 to 6 percent increase; 101 to 150 percent means an increase of 7 to 19 percent.

———

The Works Bakery Cafe, based in Keene, NH, puts 23 percent of earnings over budget into a bonus pool every four weeks, to be shared by all employees.

———

At D'Agostino Supermarkets, based in Larchmont, NY, every employee, including part-time workers and delivery staff, is eligible for the gain-sharing program. The concept is simple: Stores that exceed their budgeted profit goals for the quarter share most of the excess with their employees. Gain-sharing funds are allocated by department—so if the meat department pulls in 25 percent of the excess business, its employees receive proportionally more than a department that pulls in less. "This is an incentive to work together to improve performance and also to push each department to its potential," said Roi R. Tucker, vice president of Human Resources, who is now with Zallie Supermarket in Philadelphia, PA.

———

CASH SUBSTITUTE TIPS

➜ Jam of the Month Club membership

➜ Wine, with customized labels

➜ Turkey for Thanksgiving

➜ Bagels, doughnuts, pastries; cookies; tubs of ice cream on a mobile cart

➜ Chocolates, jellybeans, popsicles; bubble gum machine

Wells Fargo Bank employees can make as much as 25 percent of their annual salary in bonuses if they achieve certain performance levels, and about 60 percent of employees receive bonuses each quarter. John Gavin, regional manager in Fort Worth,TX, says, "We found that a typical bonus was seen as just part of the salary. Now everyone is paid based on performance. The difference in employee behavior is significant."

———

Employees at Pacific Jaycraft, a manufacturer of precision components for aerospace applications in Spring Valley, CA, rewarded employees for a 50 percent increase in sales with a year-end bonus of 15 percent of salary. Marketing manager Doug Van Vechten explains: "Jaycraft has always held the belief that motivated and productive employees are the key to success."

———

Amsco Steel spends 30 to 40 percent of annual net income on incentives and bonuses for 60 employees, based on three separate financial thresholds.

Nominal Gifts, Merchandise & Food

Almost any type of product, merchandise, or food can be used as a form of recognition or reward. Employees reported the following items as being very or extremely important to receive when they do good work: "manager provides food to celebrate success" (39 percent); "employee is given flowers, a gift, or memento" (39 percent); "manager buys the employee lunch or dinner" (36 percent); "employee gets coupons for food, car wash, movies" (35 percent). In a survey of American workers by *Workforce Management*, 63 percent ranked merchandise incentives as meaningful. More than 50 percent of respondents reported using jewelry and 41 percent using watches as part of their organizations' recognition programs.

There are many advantages to the use of merchandise for recognition. Merchandise incentives are desirable and promotable, since a good selection can appeal to every taste and can be used to reward achievement at various levels and times. The best merchandise for incentive campaigns has lasting value, reflects the quality of the recipient's achievements, inspires pride of ownership, suits the recipient's lifestyle and tastes, projects a positive image of the company, can be fulfilled promptly and without hassle, and is guaranteed and exchangeable.

> **"The way we see it, spending $1 on something clever and unique is better than spending $50 on something ordinary and forgettable."**
> —Richard File, *Partner, Amrigon*

Fred Maurer, sales manager of special markets at Canon USA in Lake Success, NY, points out that with merchandise, people receive retail values while the company pays discount or wholesale prices. "This fact of life—that we offer people more for their money—is key to the incentive business, and it isn't publicized enough," Maurer says. Maurer's preference in incentive merchandise is "anything to do with home offices, fax machines and home copiers in particular. These items are not only nice to have, but also help make people that much more efficient."

Merchandise also offers trophy value to recipients and can be "drop-shipped" directly from the manufacturer. Items valued up to $400 for safety and length-of-service awards are tax deductible for the company. Finally, redemptions take place at the end of a program, so major costs are incurred after results are in. However, merchandise incentives require detailed administration and are inappropriate for participants who earn low wages.

According to a survey sponsored by Specialty Advertising Association International, the printable goods people most appreciate are clothing (T-shirts, jackets, caps), desk or office accessories, writing instruments, glassware and ceramics (including mugs), and calendars.

"I don't like cash because the cost-value relationship is one to one; I don't use travel because when dealers win, they have to use their vacation time to take the trip. Incentive travel can be self-defeating if it's a 'must' vacation. Merchandise, on the other hand, has a high perceived value and lots of flexibility. You must be sure to put quality into every decision, however. Don't cut corners on promotion or merchandise. With premiums, there is a very thick line between junk and quality."
—Rod Taylor, *Group Promotion, Manager of Paper Products, Procter & Gamble*

Dorchester Hotel in London, UK, has Employee of the Month and Instant Star recognition programs. Names of recognized employees go into a drawing for prizes such as a chauffeur-driven ride home, teas, product vouchers, and spa treatments.

The U.S. Postal Service: A Case Study

Perhaps the greatest benefit of recognition comes when employees face exceedingly tough, challenging times. Take the case of the post office in Orange, CA, that was able to achieve record success through a clear and systematic focus on recognizing its people.

"Going into the fiscal year," David L. Eng, postmaster for the Orange Post Office, says, "I knew it would be a tough year. Our budget was significantly reduced and there was pessimism about achieving the goals." Eng's team had been ranked in the top 20 percent of the largest post offices in the district, but Eng felt they could achieve more. He asked his leaders what it would take to become the best large office in the Santa Ana district. They said they would each like to have a jacket like the one Eng had on. Eng wore a nice leather jacket with a USPS emblem on it. "If we earn the top ranking," he responded, "I'll see that you each get a jacket like this!"

The team identified a short list of items that could have the greatest impact on the organization's goals and metrics, focusing on activities that were each preventive, proactive, and positive. Each of these goals was discussed in daily meetings, and metrics were tracked monthly. Along the way the focus was always on the positive. For example, each month Eng asked every supervisor to nominate two or more employees that had gone "above and beyond" in contributing to the group's goals. Each of those employees received a certificate of achievement from his or her supervisor and a nominal gift. During the third quarter, as an incentive to get every employee involved in reaching the organization's goal, Eng held a raffle to create momentum for the final quarter.

The goal, focus, and recognition paid off when Orange was ranked the number one large post office in the Santa Ana district. The group achieved a $634,799 increase in revenue and a $476,851 savings in expenses, for a net $1,111,650 contribution. To celebrate, Eng and his supervisors took each shift of employees to breakfast where the leaders served the employees and thanked them for a job well done. Then, as promised, Eng gave leather jackets to the supervisors.

Chevron U.S.A., headquartered in San Ramon, CA, keeps a large box, secured with a padlock, brimming with all sorts of gifts. An employee being recognized on the spot for some accomplishment is brought to the Treasure Chest by his or her supervisor, who holds the keys. The employee gets to choose an item from the box: a coffee mug, pen-and-pencil set, gift certificate, coupon for lunch or dinner, or movie tickets. Recognition can come from peers as well. At Boardroom, Inc., in Stamford, CT, CEO Martin Edelston keeps a closetful of fun recognition items any manager can use to quickly acknowledge a deserving employee.

———

Managers at Bronson Healthcare Group in Kalamazoo, MI, set up "toolboxes" filled with $150 worth of recognition items suggested by employees, such as movie tickets and coupons for ice cream, time off, valet parking, and restaurants. The items are used to recognize employees when they do a good job, and the toolbox is replenished as needed.

———

One recent January, the snow was really coming down at Valassis Communications' corporate headquarters in Livonia, MI. CEO Al Schultz wanted to thank employees who made the long trek into the office and were hard at work despite the inclement weather outside, so he ordered pizza and soft drinks for everyone at all three Michigan locations and joined employees in the auditorium at corporate headquarters for an impromptu lunch while the snow fell.

———

When Dave Baldwin, senior partner with Pathwise, a training and consulting firm, was with Abbott Laboratories in Abbott Park, IL, he gave a bouquet of flowers held together with a watch to an associate who delayed her vacation and "took the time" to help when needed in the department. The employee wears the watch as a badge of honor to this day. In another instance, Abbott honored an employee who set up an off-site management meeting by having each senior executive give her a flower with a personalized word of thanks at the beginning of the event. She reported that although she had received flowers before, the personalized thanks by the company's senior executives made this recognition event the most meaningful of all.

———

The Maritz, Inc., office in Fenton, MO, has a "Thanks a Bunch" program in which a bouquet of flowers is given to an employee in appreciation of special favors or jobs well done. That employee then passes on the reward to someone else, and so on and so forth. Each recipient also gets a thank-you card. At certain intervals, the cards are entered into a drawing for rewards such as binoculars or logoed jackets. The program is used during periods of especially heavy workloads or other stressful times.

———

The Hartford Steam Boiler Inspection and Insurance Company in Hartford, CT, spends up to $50 per year per administrative employee on gifts tailored to various interests, including dinners for two, tickets to movies and sporting events, gift certificates, and coffee for a month. There are four requirements for the award: The employee must be a team player, take initiative to solve problems, provide leadership in supporting company goals, and show an attitude that inspires others to do their best.

> **"There's no knowing what any given employee will value as a reward. That's why, with noncash items, we recommend offering employees a wide range of rewards. Let them choose whatever is to their personal liking."**
> —Barcy Fox, *Vice President, Performance Systems, Maritz, Inc.*

Spokesperson Karen Block says, "I believe that when the final results are in, the investment will be returned to us many times over."

———

"It's not the gift itself but the idea behind it. It's nice to walk around the house and see an item and think, 'Oh, yeah, that's from 1984; I remember what I did for that one.' The memory the item gives you is so much better than money. Cash is here today, then it's gone."—Barion Mills Jr., *Agency Manager, State Farm Insurance*

David Walling, training coordinator for the Natural Resources Conservation Service office in Champaign, IL, reports using "spot awards"—specially designed coffee mugs, watches, and pen-and-pencil sets—to recognize good work.

———

As an exciting alternative to employees selecting merchandise from a catalog, some companies host shopping sprees, allowing award winners to go on a rampage through a warehouse that stocks appropriate prizes. Carlson Marketing Group has opened its Dayton, OR, distribution center to employees of Mobil, Toyota, and Nabisco.

Carlson marketers fly their employees to Dayton for a pre-spree party the night before the appointed date. On the day of the event, employees walk the winners through the warehouse, pointing out where the most valuable goods are. The 200,000-square-foot warehouse contains about 4,500 items, including electronics, glassware, golf clubs, and vacuum cleaners.

Carlson recommends that sponsors limit the run-through to two minutes. According to Michael Barga, director of distribution in Dayton, "More than two minutes becomes a struggle for the participant, who's dashing down the aisles and throwing items

MOTIVATING MERCHANDISE

ELECTRONICS
Tools help people improve their efficiency: multimedia cell phones, fax machines, and wireless laptop computers.

APPLIANCES
Compact appliances save space: combo washer-dryers, under-the-counter can openers, TVs, and radios.

SERVICES
Services help people save time: a housecleaner for a year, baby-sitting coupons, spa visits, and facials.

UNIQUE GIFTS
Customized gifts add special meaning: special-edition lithographs, first-edition books, antiques, and company-imprinted credit cards.

into a big shopping cart." On average, winners accumulate about $3,500 worth of goods per minute.

———

The Smurfit-Stone Container Corporation in Chicago topped a profitable year in which it gave every employee a television set by giving everyone a VCR (retailing for several hundred dollars at the time) the next year; 24,000 were distributed. To announce the gift, the company made a ten-minute video with two actors impersonating Roger Ebert and the late Gene Siskel. The characters reviewed the company's year, and footage of the various facilities was shown. CEO Roger Stone then appeared, gave the two-thumbs-up sign, and announced the gift. At the end of the presentation, each employee received a certificate resembling a movie ticket, which was used to claim the VCR.

Recognition items can be generated around a theme such as summer. Towels, umbrellas, rafts, chairs, and coolers work well as standard promotional beach items. For a barbecue theme, options include grills, cooking utensils, hats, and aprons—even a custom-built barbecue pit and patio furniture. Floats, boats, and inner tubes can also be customized; for larger prizes, companies can use canoes and dinghies. Recent users of such items are Pepsi, Sunkist Soda, and Moosehead Beer.

In Dresden, Ontario, where winters are harsh, manager Craig Bullen of TD Canada Trust decided to thank his employees in a weather-wise way. A winter storm was in effect, and as the snow accumulated, Craig sent out a note to all of his employees: "To celebrate our year-to-date branch results, I've placed a little treat in each of your vehicles to help keep your path clear and safe. The three items are:

1. A jug of washer fluid to keep your vision clear

2. A snowbrush to help you stay on the journey ahead

3. A lock deicer to provide a warm, comfortable experience."

In Mary Kay, Inc.'s Career Apparel Program, sales consultants who reach specific goals become eligible to buy specific outfits. Once someone qualifies to become a director, for example, she is invited to attend Mary Kay's management conference and, while there, is

GIFT & MERCHANDISE TIPS

➡ Find out the person's hobby and give an appropriate gift.

➡ Buy the person something for his or her child.

➡ Give an employee a copy of the latest bestselling management or business book.

➡ Inscribe a favorite book as a gift.

MOST POPULAR SPECIALTY ITEMS

- Wearables
- Writing instruments
- Desk and office accessories
- Glassware and ceramics
- Calendars
- Sporting goods
- Buttons, badges, and ribbons
- Auto accessories
- Houseware and tools

fitted for a director's suit at the expense of the company. The style changes every year. Laura Whittier, manager of affinity programs, says, "Our directors love the suits because they are functional and provide a visual symbol of their success. Qualifying to buy the suit indicates high status; wearing it results in a more professional look and instant recognition of success."

Six Ways to Customize an Apparel Award

1. Design an eye-catching graphic featuring your company name, logo, or popular product name and place it prominently on the apparel.

2. Opt for a subtler placement by sewing a tag with your name or logo onto a sleeve or cuff.

3. Create a special label to appear inside the cap or garment.

4. Place a crest with your logo on the pocket of a shirt, using a color slightly darker than that of the shirt.

5. For loyal long-term employees, offer a very high-quality brand-name item without your company name or logo, and present it with a special card conveying your sincere appreciation for their hard work and support.

6. Make the centerpiece of your graphics a hot license that can be linked to your promotional campaign or company image.

———

"**E**veryone eats," says Rick Farone, product and program coordinator for Royal Appliance Manufacturing Company, based in Glenwillow, OH. "When you reward people with food, you know it's something they'll use. Food makes people happy." An almost infinite variety of food gifts can be used to reward employees, including fruit baskets; fruit-of-the-month clubs; home-delivered steak, seafood, or lobster; jelly and jam; and spices.

———

DDB Worldwide Communications Group, an advertising agency located in New York City, gives bottles of champagne to employees who develop great ideas.

———

At the Angus Barn Restaurant in Raleigh, NC, an employee "caught in the act of caring" gets a choice of entree from the restaurant's menu.

———

PERSONALIZE IT

- Give a personalized company coffee cup or belt buckle.
- Have a pen-and-pencil set engraved for the person.
- Personalize the label on a wine bottle with a message of thanks.

"When it becomes extremely hot during the summer months, I carry an ice chest full of freezer pops around and give them out to employees who are working in areas that are not air-conditioned," reports Cynthia M. Wood, team manager at an International Paper office in Eastover, SC. "You should see their faces light up!"

———

At Long's Drugs, the drugstore chain now a part of CVS Caremark, based in Woonsocket, RI, employees who worked late into the night to stock shelves for holiday sales were given certificates for free pizza and soft drinks and time off later the same week so they could be with their families.

———

MetaSolv Software, of Plano, TX, and now a part of Redwood City, CA–based Oracle, uses keg parties to introduce new employees to the rest of the 350-person fast-growth company. The new employee works the tap and gets to meet everyone.

———

Persistence Software in San Mateo, CA, and now a part of Progress Software, based in Bedford, MA, brings in a breakfast tray and places it near a new person's desk on his or her first day and then invites the other 110 employees to meet their colleague. Most people come by to grab a bagel or muffin, introduce themselves, and chat.

Liz Claiborne's HR department celebrates "Bagel Fridays," where employees take turns bringing in bagels and cream cheese for the office. It's a great way for everyone to take off 15–20 minutes each Friday morning, come together in a common meeting area, and chat about work, life, and other issues. What started out as just a bag of bagels and some spreads has exploded into an all-out Food Fest, in which the food shopper of the week thinks about a theme, buys tablecloths, knickknacks, and decorations, and then gets not only bagels, but usually coffee, juice, and other goodies. The themes often coincide with holidays; seasons, such as "Summer Fun in the Sun"; or events, like the "Super Super Bowl." Employees assigned a Bagel Friday usually start thinking about it two to three weeks in advance, racking their brains as to how to outdo the person from the week before.

> **"One reason food is a good motivator is that it provides the winner with an experience with family and friends. Food is a social gift."**
> —Jeffrey Gibeault,
> *Sales Manager, Business Incentive Department, Omaha Steaks International*

One manager at American Express Financial Advisors treats employees to lunch by sending someone to Taco Bell or White Castle.

Once a week, a different staff member at the Rock and Roll Hall of Fame in Cleveland cooks and serves breakfast for the rest of the staff. This is a great morale booster for everyone and gives people some downtime to discuss the week's business.

Oscar Mayer in Northfield, IL, holds an event called "Team Lunch," in which researchers have lunch together. They eat Oscar Mayer products, work on problems, and tell stories about

UNUSUAL SPECIALTY ITEMS

- Boxer shorts
- "Mick Jagger lips" alarm clock
- Jalapeño lollipops
- Portable picnic table and benches
- A Spanish-language calculator
- Desktop toy train
- Coffee cups imprinted with a message that appears— or disappears—when they're filled

one another. People about whom enough stories are told have become company legends.

———

At Electronic Data Systems in Plano, TX, managers are encouraged to get to know their employees' tastes, hobbies, and interests, so deserving staff members can be rewarded with appropriate incentives, such as tickets to a sports event, the opera, or a dinner for the family at a restaurant. Molly Edwards, EDS's manager of recognition services, says one employee in Dallas was even given a washer and dryer for a particularly good performance. Another employee in Michigan returned from vacation to find that her kitchen had been completely remodeled.

Recognition Items, Trophies & Plaques

Recognition items are similar to general merchandise except that the items are somehow customized or personalized to the individual, company, or event, making them potentially more valuable as motivators, since they can serve for some time as reminders to the employee of the achievement or event.

In a recent survey of subscribers of *Personnel Journal*, almost two thirds include plaques and certificates in their awards programs. Almost 15 percent give cash awards and 2 percent give savings bonds. More than half use accessory jewelry and 41 percent use watches.

Merchandise of any type is used by 41 percent of the organizations surveyed. Rings—along with travel—seem to be an integral part of sales incentive programs. Another 11 percent indicated they used travel incentives and 17 percent said they gave sales incentives in general. Trophies are awarded by 12 percent; ribbons are awarded by 2 percent.

According to one recent poll, the imprintable goods people most appreciate are:

1. Clothing (T-shirts, jackets, and caps)

2. Desk or office accessories

3. Writing instruments

4. Glassware and ceramics (including mugs)

5. Calendars

The travelers polled were also asked to name the most unusual imprinted product they had ever received, according to the Specialty Advertising Association International, sponsor of the survey. Among their most interesting answers were: a flyswatter, flower seeds, a

> **"We don't just give someone a plaque. We have our costumed animal characters bring balloons to them. Fellow workers gather around, and we present the plaque right on the floor of the store. We take their picture, put it in *Stew's News* (the company newsletter), and we also mount it on a walnut plaque hung right on the Avenue of the Stars (an entire picture-covered wall of the store). Every day you see your picture, and you feel good forever."**
>
> —Stew Leonard,
> *Founder, Stew Leonard's*

broom holder, a rock, underwear, an athletic supporter, a brick trophy, and a scarf from an Elvis impersonator.

Aquascape, a St. Charles, IL, landscaping firm, rewards employees with humble gifts like "bobblehead dolls." The president of a teacher's union in Vancouver, Canada, explained that when he worked in the construction industry, what started as a joke became a coveted honor each workday. One morning a foreman placed a yellow "rubber ducky" on the desk of the person who had done a great job the previous day. The tradition continued and soon everyone looked forward to seeing who received the day's honor. Employees at the Child Support Enforcement Division of the Minnesota Department of Health Services give each other Yogi the Bear, a traveling award for great internal customer service—being nicer than the average bear. They write up the reason for the award and present the paper award, along with Yogi, a stuffed brown bear, to the honoree. Yogi stays in the honoree's cubicle until he is awarded to someone else in the unit. As part of its Great Leap Forward Award, Premier Travel Inn, located in London, UK, gives the award winner a stuffed kangaroo.

> **RECOGNITION ITEMS TIPS**
>
> ➡ "You Measure Up" ruler
>
> ➡ Traveling awards that get passed on from winner to winner
>
> ➡ "Big Dog" (rawhide bone) award
>
> ➡ "Helping Hand" (work/construction gloves) award
>
> ➡ Merit badges

Tandy Corporation in Ft. Worth, TX, uses a 3½ foot toy gorilla to recognize initiative and innovation. The gorilla visits and stays with a person who had a useful idea until the next good idea comes along. The person who has the most ideas in a quarter receives another prize. Liz Dawson, district sales manager for The

Body Shop in Florida, painted a fish platter gold and awarded it to an employee for something spectacular that person had done. Over the years the award evolved to recognize only exceptional achievements.

———

First Data Resources, a data processing services company in Omaha, NE, rewards employees with University of Nebraska football tickets, gift certificates, pens, plaques, mugs, and other items. As part of its "Fat Cat Award," the company has a professional portrait of the winning employee done and gives it to that person.

———

Atria Senior Living Group, which operates three senior living complexes in Tucson, AZ, rolled out a new employee rewards program along with $63,000 in big cardboard checks.

———

Employees of the Los Angeles Dodgers receive the same gifts and promotional items—Dodger caps, jackets, bats, and so on— that are given to fans during the baseball season.

———

The Soil Conservation Service in Champaign, IL, rewards employees by giving them special framed prints of wildlife or ones on various other topics, depending on the preferences of the recipient.

———

RECOGNITION ITEMS TIPS

➡ Award personalized gifts, such as rewards that recognize people's distinctive interests or hobbies, etc., to all those involved with an innovation.

➡ Design and present a plaque commemorating the achievement.

➡ Personalize the label on a wine bottle(s) with a message of special thanks or achievement.

The City of Decatur, IL, gave each employee a "company jacket" with the city's logo on the front of the jacket, according to Susan Nordquist, Personnel Specialist for the city.

Bill Nesbit, vice president of quality systems for Central Telephone Company of Illinois, relates two recognition stories. After a heavy ice storm, five workers were sent out to do overnight repairs—on Valentine's Day. As a form of thanks, each of the employees' spouses were sent a box of chocolates with a card expressing the company's appreciation for their husbands' efforts.

> **"Simple observation suggests that most of us are trinket freaks— if they represent a genuine thanks for a genuine assist."**
> —Tom Peters, *Author and Management Consultant*

In another instance, heavy water damage caused chaos with telephone cables that took more than 49 people to set straight. The supervisor sent each a lottery ticket with a note that read "I never gamble when I count on you." Bill notes that both stories are significant because the company's past culture caused them to be overly cautious in recognizing employees for fear of overlooking someone or having to recognize so many people that it was often easier not to recognize anyone.

Nonmonetary Rewards

Weekend trips to resorts	Boardroom luncheons	"Traveling" awards (monthly)
Days/time off	Publicity (company)	Plaques
Banquets	Publicity (external)	Special parking space
Luncheons	Publicity (hometown)	Free parking (in large cities)
Tickets to local events	Certificates of recognition	Shopping spree

Books/CDs/DVDs

Family photo session

Trophies

Redeemable "atta-boys/-girls"

Briefcase

"Boss of the Day"

President's Medallion

Free meals (on-the-spot)

Cookouts

Attendance at outside training seminars or conferences

Photo session with company president

POPULAR COMPANY LOGO ITEMS

T-shirts

Gym bags

Coffee mugs

Pen-and-pencil sets

Jackets

Stadium chairs

Ice chests

Umbrellas

Thermos jugs

Paperweights

Desk pen sets

Leather goods

—K. H. "Skip" Wilson, *Senior Training Specialist, Mississippi Power & Light Company*

Books can be personalized to highlight an achievement. The Houghton Mifflin Company, as well as other publishers, customizes books to fit specific occasions. Books can be customized in several ways:

- Have the CEO personalize a book with an inscription to commemorate an occasion or achievement.
- Incorporate a company's logo on the front or back covers or on the spine.
- Alter a book's title to feature a brand or a company. Warner Books, for instance changed *How to Talk to Your Cat* to *The Meow Mix Guide to Cat Talk*.
- Insert product allusions into a book's text. For example, in a pet-care book, a manufacturer could alter the sentence

"Veterinarians recommend giving a dog food that is high in protein" to "Veterinarians recommend giving a dog food that is high in protein, such as Brand X." Book publishers note that this is usually possible only on large orders and if the product is appropriate to the text.

- Feature a letter or brief message from a company on a separate page before the title page.
- Excerpt an appropriate chapter from an original work and create an entirely new book.

T he Sterling Optical Company based in Woodbury, NY, awards savings bonds, certificates, and plaques to employees for attaining branch sales targets, as well as for individual performance for outstanding service to patients and to the branch.

N orthern Telecom commissioned an original limited-edition sculpture by the Kirk Stieff Company to recognize the exceptional achievement of its Honor Circle winners. Pins, award certificates, and travel prizes, as well as a theme video, a program brochure, posters, and promotional mailings complemented the merchandise campaign. Of 12,000 people eligible to participate in the program, 534 (34 percent more than expected) achieved their sales goals, and the company outdid its previous year's performance with a 13.4 percent boost in sales and a 3 percent increase in market share.

RECOGNITION ITEMS TIPS

➡ Make "achievement" decals/badges/emblems for uniforms, hard hats, T-shirts, etc.

➡ Purchase a unique pen to serve as a memento for a task well done.

➡ Give a personalized or company coffee cup.

➡ Award a gold banana pin for an outstanding achievement.

➡ Give a personalized belt buckle.

SECTION 5

GROUP RECOGNITION, REWARDS & ACTIVITIES

We know recognition works with individuals, but it can be just as effective with groups. This section discusses forms of effective group recognition, rewards, and activities, from group-based recognition programs to specific team awards to fun activities, games, contests, celebrations, parties, special events, and travel.

As with recognizing the achievements of individuals, some of the best forms of team recognition are informal and intangible, such as a manager thanking group members for their involvement, suggestions, and initiatives, or sending a letter to all team members thanking them for their contributions. Team spirit and group morale can also be bolstered by informal reviews throughout a project or by hosting a lunch celebration with project teams once they've completed interim findings. At the end of the project, let the group celebrate as it chooses.

The task of recognizing teams does present a dilemma, however, in balancing the team's collective effort and acknowledging the individual contributions of its members. You run the risk of slighting those members who contributed most to the group's success and reinforcing other members who might have barely made it to the meetings. "Jelly bean motivation"—giving equal recognition for unequal performance—is detrimental to the group's sustained productivity and morale.

One way to mitigate this dilemma is to be sure the team leader recognizes the contribution of individual members as the team makes progress, and encourages group members to do the same. As the group becomes a team, its productivity and morale is shaped by specific behaviors of any member of the group, not just the designated group leader. To develop a team that functions well, it's important for members to feed off each other's success; to support each other in various, explicit ways such as acknowledging productive contributions, new ideas, or suggestions by others; and to create positive interventions, such as volunteering for a group assignment or assisting another member of the group with his or her assignment.

Managers must also learn to couple individual performance with group output. Research by Deborah Crown of the University of Alabama shows that a combination of individual goals coupled with overall group goals results in team performance 36 percent greater than what would happen otherwise. "It might be as simple as changing to rewarding people for the percentage of goals to which they contribute," says Crown. "You're more likely to have success if you give people a goal and direct their action where you want it directed, rather than hoping over time they'll try to do the right thing because they identify with the group."

Eight Ways to Praise Teams

1. Have an upper manager stop in at the first meeting of a special project team and express his or her appreciation of the members' involvement.

2. When individuals present an idea or suggestion, thank them for their initiative and contribution. Encourage involvement in the group's goal-setting process, problem-solving, brainstorming, etc.

3. Celebrate progress, interim findings, and final results, letting team members decide how to celebrate.

4. Open the floor for team members to praise anyone at the beginning or end of the meeting. Provide a "praising barrage" by the team for one or more of its members.

5. Have members of the team create awards for each other. Invest in team mementos and symbols of a team's work together, such as T-shirts or coffee cups with a team motto or company logo.

6. Conduct team-building activities and field trips, such as bowling, laser tag, a visit to a state fair, a "popcorn lunch," or a team challenge or contest against a group goal or another team.

7. Invite upper management to attend a meeting with the team during which individuals ask questions and the group is thanked for its efforts.

8. Send letters or e-mails to every team member at the conclusion of a project, thanking them for their contribution. Consider thanking the team members' families, as well, if the team effort was significant.

Group Recognition & Rewards

T he important thing to remember about group recognition is that the entire team needs to be recognized. If only the manager or highest performer of a group is recognized, the group may lose motivation.

Employees are applauded for doing a great job at the Kansas City Symphony.

———

Ron Sutton, CEO of Standard Auto Parts in Baltimore, MD, asked each of his managers to submit a recent positive achievement their group accomplished and that they were proud of. He said that after they submitted an item, he would give them tickets to attend a special meeting. At the meeting, as people started to applaud each example that was shared, Sutton challenged the group to make the response to each item louder than the previous one. Soon the entire group was standing and cheering—sending a positive surge that spread throughout the company.

> **"What's important to me is getting together with all the others who achieved that [same] goal, and the pride I take in satisfying a goal the company has set."**
> —Barion Mills Jr.,
> *Agency Manager,*
> *State Farm Insurance*

———

Debbie Stutts, customer service manager for Spectrum Chemicals & Laboratory Products in Gardena, CA, asked employees to bring in their favorite CD to play while people work.

———

At the Proforma Worldwide Support Center, a printing and promotional products franchise in Cleveland, OH, executives scraped the snow off all 100 employees' cars at least once a month during winter. They have also rotated a guest parking space—the closest to the building—among employees recognized by their peers, and treat workers to breakfast once a month.

> **"Nothing, not even the most advanced technology, is as formidable as people working together enthusiastically toward a shared goal. Whether as a nation, an army, or a corporation—people become unstoppable when they are moved by a common vision, and have the power and tools to achieve it."** —United Technologies Corporate Brochure

Michelle Steinbeck, a project manager for West Corporation, a customer relations management provider in Omaha, NE, reports that Senior Vice President Jill Vacek hosts a holiday lunch party each year for all employees in her department. Vacek reviews the year, highlighting each group's contribution and mentions many by name, their years of service, and any promotions they may have received. New members are also recognized. At the end she has a drawing for door prizes. "What everyone realizes is that everyone wins a prize. While presenting the prize, she shakes hands with each person, recognizing and thanking them personally. If a person receiving a prize was not mentioned in her review, Jill usually has something specific to mention about them, highlighting their contribution," says Steinbeck. "I totally appreciate all the planning and effort that goes into the party each year—it would be so easy just to have a lunch, but what Jill turns the 90 minutes into is so much more."

———

At MicroAge Computer in Tempe, AZ, managers fine individuals who come late to company meetings and pass the money out to people who arrive on time.

———

When Randy Dorr was a supervisor at MCI, now a part of New York–based Verizon Communications, he motivated a team of low-performing telemarketers by calling their mothers to tell them how great the employees were every time they met their performance goals. As a result, the group became the top-performing team in the company.

***

At Advanced Micro Devices in Sunnyvale, CA, photos of work teams often appear in company publications.

***

Terry Horn, Human Resources director at Household Automotive Finance in San Diego, and now a part of Dallas, TX–based Santander Consumer USA, Inc., wanted to thank all the employees in his department for their great work in meeting financial goals. The group was all women, except for one man, who was very health conscious and ate a banana every day on his break. Horn gave each of the women a bunch of flowers and the guy a bunch of bananas. They all really appreciated the gesture.

***

To energize their teams, laboratory managers at a Kaiser Permanente office in Pasadena, CA, collaborated to convert a little-used conference room into a Strategy Center, purchasing furniture and equipment and decorating the room to make it conducive to creative thinking and brainstorming sessions.

***

Montefiore Nursing Home in Beachwood, OH, a 500-employee nonprofit facility, started a "Keys to Our Commitment" program, in which teams promise to uphold certain

> ## GROUP RECOGNITION TIPS
>
> ➡ Let a team/department write a song and perform at a company event.
>
> ➡ Start a spontaneous celebration in the office (conga line, karaoke, dance party, confetti).
>
> ➡ Throw a unique food theme/international potluck luncheon or dinner.
>
> ➡ Give the team the afternoon off.
>
> ➡ Treat the team to an upscale brunch or seafood dinner buffet.

values, such as helping one another, serving patient needs, or being helpful to relatives. Basically, workers are challenged never to say "I don't know." Staff members who embody a value are awarded paper keys by fellow staff members. They can then trade them for pins, from bronze to gold; for instance, ten paper keys equal one bronze pin. The program has helped employees to work more cooperatively, share information with management, and feel more supported. Turnover has been cut in half.

TIPS FOR BUILDING AN EFFECTIVE TEAM

- When hiring, look for people who work well with others. You want employees who can handle the collective process.
- Set a good example for your staff. For instance, leave at a reasonable hour so that they know it's okay to do the same.
- Encourage one-to-one discussions between staff rather than structured meetings. Personal relationships build trust.
- Hold informal retreats to foster communication and set goals.
- Reward collective accomplishment whenever possible, even if the reward is only juice and bagels.

New store managers of J. C. Penney Corporation, headquartered in Plano, TX, make a pledge to the founding principles of the company at a ceremony, and are presented with a pin to mark the occasion.

———

At Delta Air Lines, based in Atlanta, GA, employees fill out Team Recognition Cards to give to teams that they feel have gone "above and beyond." Cards are entered in a drawing for a prize of $500, to be donated to a charity or civic organization of the team's choice.

At the Good Samaritan Society–West Union nursing home in West Union, IA, teams are recognized for the compliments they receive from patients, relatives, and administrators. Comment cards are read out loud and posted on the central bulletin board, and administrators bring baked goods or flowers to recognize the team with the most favorable comments.

> **"There's nothing more important than making certain that each employee feels respected and valued."**
> —Robert Crandall,
> *Former CEO,*
> *American Airlines*

Grinnell College, located in the heart of Iowa, recently held a recognition initiative entitled "Above & Beyond" for departments and individuals who demonstrated positive attitude, innovation, and outstanding service to others. A traveling trophy was passed from one deserving office to another, departments formed teams to compete onstage in "Family Feud: Customer Service," and Excellence Award forms were widely distributed around campus so that staff, faculty, students, and college visitors could share memorable campus service experiences. Those recognized were also featured prominently in each issue of the college's employee newsletter.

BlueCross BlueShield of North Carolina uses several forms of group recognition:

- One department has three teams working on different projects, each with specific deadlines. To motivate the employees, they allow teams to wear jeans for a week if they meet the previous week's goals. Everyone pushes to make sure they are not wearing business casual when another team is wearing jeans.

- A team composed of project managers and business analysts (PMBA) recognizes accomplishments every month by awarding a stuffed "Pumbaa" (from Disney's *The Lion King*) to the team member with the most significant accomplishments.

- A team manager reports: "For one project, I awarded each team member various items to represent their contribution to the project: a giant bottle of glue for the team member who held us together with sales, a jar of jam for the team member who 'hand jammed' (aka manually entered) enrollment data, a set of pom-poms for our always positive cheerleader, etc."

- One special projects group is involved in a major, multiyear, enterprisewide effort that crosses multiple divisions within the company. Participants are eligible for the "Most Valuable Ant" recognition award. The award is a 6-inch-high custom-painted ant figurine with a personalized certificate attached.

- In the I.S. department, any member can nominate any other member for a "Golden Graeme" award. The awards are given for going the extra mile in ensuring the success of the department, putting in long hours to get the work done against a tight deadline, improving processes to better ensure success and/or quality, improving a business relationship, taking on a very challenging assignment and achieving desired results, and so forth. The award is given out quarterly at an all-hands meeting.

- In another division, the senior vice president, nicknamed "Bob," presents pins for "Bending Over Backwards" at quarterly departmental meetings. Employees nominate coworkers who have "bent over backwards" to achieve department goals. Photos of the presentation are posted on bulletin boards in the department.

———

James Allchin, the retired head software guru at the Microsoft Corporation in Redmond, WA, rewarded programmers for meeting a key milestone on a project code-named "Cairo" by bringing a camel into the office. The camel was an immediate hit with the Cairo team, who petted it and had their pictures taken with it.

———

Team members get pins when they complete a project at the Naval Publications and Forms Center in Philadelphia, PA. Employees also received a $500 bonus when the agency won the government's quality improvement award.

———

Merck & Company's Wilson, NC, plant has a rewards program called "Reasons to Celebrate" and a unit incentive program called "Pay for Performance." Teams can nominate fellow teams or team members for gift certificates of up to $300 for individuals and $500 for teams.

———

"If you have to have a program to do recognition, you've missed the point. In our culture, someone is thanked or recognized every two minutes. It's a part of who we are and the sincere mutual respect, caring, and empowerment we have for one another."—Audrey Robertson, *Director, Public Relations, The Container Store*

At *Business First,* in Columbus, OH, team members receive $500 each if the team reaches a certain goal: If it reaches a higher goal, they receive $1,000 each. To be eligible for team bonuses, members must make at least 90 percent of their individual goals.

————

At Great Plains Software in Fargo, ND, where projects could last as long as nine months, project leaders celebrated along the way with dinners, picnics, and other forms of informal recognition as they reached preset goals. The company, now a part of Microsoft Dynamics GP in Redmond, WA, used a two-part bonus program to spur on its project teams. Team members received half the bonus when they hit the product's target release date, and the other half 90 days after the release, based on the performance of the product. At the conclusion of projects, the teams created a "Friends List" to recognize nonteam members who supported them along the way. Friends received gift certificates and thank-you letters.

————

In the team program at Wright Business Graphics in Chino, CA, everyone can win, but one team wins big. "We're using a combination spoilage/attendance program," says marketing manager Richard S. Calhoun. "[One year, we] put forty thousand dollars into a special fund, and every time a mistake was made, we deducted from the forty thousand dollars. We ended up

> **"Each employee has to be asked, 'What should we hold you accountable for? What information do you need?' and, in turn, 'What information do you owe the rest of us?' This means that each worker has to be a participant in decisions as to what equipment is needed; how the work should be scheduled; indeed, what the basic policy of the entire company should be."**—Peter F. Drucker, *Author, Post-Capitalist Society*

giving out about seven thousand dollars." The next year the 36 employees were divided into four teams, with a prize kitty of 1.25 percent of shipments. One quarter of a percent was credited to each team, and spoilage by any team member was deducted. At the end of the program, the team with the lowest spoilage also got the leftover .25 percent. A Chicago hospital took the same approach, creating a $100,000 cash pool that was used to satisfy billing or customer service complaints. Whatever was left in the pool at the end of the year was distributed to employees.

A Case Study in Group Motivation

When Richard Nicolosi—now CEO of Nicolosi Advisors based in Sarasota, FL—became the head of the paper products division of Procter & Gamble, headquartered in Cincinnati, competition had taken its toll. The company's market share for disposable diapers had eroded from 75 percent to 52 percent in less than ten years. Nicolosi found a highly bureaucratic and centralized organization that was overly preoccupied with internal functional goals and projects. Almost all information about customers came through highly quantitative market research. Moreover, the technical people were rewarded for cost savings; the commercial people focused on volume and share; and the two groups nearly always worked in opposition.

Nicolosi immediately began to stress the need for the division to become more creative and market-driven instead of just trying to be a low-cost producer. "I had to make it very clear," he later reported, "that the rules of the game had changed."

The new direction included much greater stress on teamwork and multiple leaders. Nicolosi pushed a strategy of using groups to manage the division and its specific products. Two months later, he and his team designated themselves the paper division's "board" and began meeting first monthly and then weekly. The next month they established "category teams" to manage their major brand groups (diapers, tissues, towels) and started pushing responsibility down to these teams.

He asked the marketing manager of diapers to report directly to him, eliminating a layer in the hierarchy. He also talked more to the people who were working on new products.

A month after that, Nicolosi's board announced a new organizational structure that included not only category teams but also new-brand business teams. Within four months, the board was ready to plan an important motivational event to communicate the new paper products vision to as many people as possible. All the Cincinnati-based personnel in the paper division, as well as district management and paper plant managers—several thousand people in all—met in the local Masonic temple. Nicolosi and other board members described their vision of an organization in which "each of us is a leader." The event was videotaped, and an edited tape was sent to all sales offices and plants.

All these events helped create an entrepreneurial environment in which large numbers of people were motivated to realize the new vision. Most innovations came from people dealing with new products, but other employee initiatives were oriented more toward a functional area, and some even came from the bottom of the hierarchy. For example, a few of

> **"To make it to the future, you have to think about what employees owe the company—their best efforts to secure its success—as well as what the company owes its people—a first rate learning experience, a purpose higher than a paycheck and a chance to be part of a winning team."**
> —Nancy K. Austin, *"Letting People Bloom,"* Incentive *Magazine*

the division's secretaries developed a Secretaries' Network, which established subcommittees on training, rewards and recognition, and the "secretary of the future." Echoing the sentiments of many of her peers, one paper products secretary said, "I don't see why we too can't contribute to the division's new direction."

Within four years, revenues at the paper products division were up 40 percent and profits were up 66 percent—while the company's competition continued to get tougher.

———

Anita Nimtz at Iowa State University in Ames, IA, celebrated Administrative Assistants' Week with a variety of freebies, including potted plants on Monday, lotto tickets on Tuesday, boxes of Band-Aids on Wednesday, and Crunch 'n Munch snacks on Thursday. Her staff loved it and still calls her the "greatest" manager.

———

The Carmel Clay Public Library in Carmel, IN, celebrated Staff Appreciation Week with the following activities, all planned and executed by the library's 12-member management team. None of the details were divulged in advance, so each day brought surprises.

MONDAY

- An appreciation display consisting of a banner, balloons, and photographs of staff members at work was set up in the lobby and remained throughout the week so that patrons could help celebrate and say "thank you" to the employees.
- Upon arrival at work, each staff member received either an electronic thank-you card or a handwritten note from a manager from another department.

TUESDAY

- Each staff member was given a commemorative bookplate with his or her name and invited to insert it into a favorite title at the library. This allowed people to be remembered and appreciated each time a patron checked out their books.

WEDNESDAY

- The library published a 4-by-5-inch ad in the local newspaper inviting the public to join the management team "in recognizing the 135 CCPL staff members who serve our community with professionalism and dedication on a daily basis."
- The independent coffee shop in the library gave a 20 percent discount to all library employees for the entire day.

THURSDAY

- Managers baked or purchased cookies, brownies, muffins, fruit, chips, and other treats and delivered them to each department via a snack cart in the morning and again in the afternoon.

FRIDAY

- Employees were given a bonus casual dress day (usually limited to the last working day of the month).
- Each employee received rolls of Life Savers labeled "We Appreciate You."
- "We received extremely favorable feedback on our efforts," reported Cindy Wenz, Human Resources manager for the library. "With the exception of the $150 ad, which was paid for with funds provided by the Friends of the Carmel Clay

Public Library, all of the items were no-cost or low-cost, with the latter absorbed by the members of the management team."

Fun, Games & Contests

Fun is a great motivator, making work go faster and creating a buffer to stress. Increasingly important, given that 40 percent of today's employees say their jobs are very or extremely stressful and 25 percent view their jobs as the number one stressor in their lives today, according to the National Institute for Occupational Safety & Health. Having fun can also lead directly to increased productivity. At the Colorado Health Sciences Center in Denver, employees who viewed humorous training films and attended fun workshops showed a 25 percent decrease in downtime and a 60 percent increase in job satisfaction.

Fun can also achieve more serious objectives, such as communicating critical information or encouraging desired behaviors or performance. A good way to do this is to couch those goals in a game or contest. The relevant information or behavior becomes highlighted in the process, and a general sense of excitement is created along the way. Keys to a successful employee contest include:

- Promoting the program and its purpose
- Setting realistic, achievable, and measurable goals
- Limiting the contest to a brief period
- Keeping contest rules uncomplicated
- Ensuring that prizes are desirable to employees

> **"The best thing you can say to your workers is 'You are valuable, you are my most important asset.'"**—Phyllis Eisen, *Senior Policy Director, National Association of Manufacturers*

- Linking rewards directly to performance
- Giving rewards and recognition promptly

If you systematically do things that encourage a fun work environment, the morale of your group will directly benefit. Being thoughtful about planning activities that are fun for your group can also serve as a powerful source of team building.

> **"If you show people you don't care, they'll return the favor. Show them you care about them, they'll reciprocate."**
> —Lee G. Bolman and Terrence E. Deal, *Authors*, Leading with Soul: An Uncommon Journey of Spirit

When its Xbox 360 gaming system launched Kinect, Microsoft, the Redmond, WA–based computer giant, invited all its employees to try it out. Daxko, the Birmingham, AL–based software company, has a work/play lounge that features a Wii and a big screen television.

The Family Learning Program at Blue Gargoyle Community Services in South Chicago gives employees a tool to cope with the extreme rigors of work. It's a Chicken Hat, a colorful felt headpiece with dangling legs that says without words that you should not be trifled with. Jane Hough says, "When things get too serious or laborious, you simply don the Chicken Hat and enter an entirely different state of mind. What better way to say, 'I've got one nerve left and you're on it!' to those around you?" The hat is available from www.orientaltrading.com for about the cost of a bottle of aspirin.

Agencies of QSource, the Memphis-based nonprofit health care management expert, invite field staff to eat lunch between 11 A.M. and 2 P.M. Managers set up grills in the parking lot and cook hot dogs and hamburgers for the staff while other managers and members of the office staff wash the staff's cars. At Parrott Creek Child and Family Services in Marylhurst, OR, employees sat in the shade and drank iced tea while their managers washed the employees' cars.

Undertone, the New York City–based digital advertising experts, offers twice-yearly team-building events, "Company Weeks," to reinforce collegiality. Activities range from scavenger hunts to picnics. Undertone's revenues have jumped 40 percent since it began holding these events.

The University of Iowa Hospitals & Clinics in Iowa City occasionally turn staff meetings into Teddy Bear Picnics, where everyone brings a stuffed animal that has special meaning to them. "As each staff person explains the significance of their animal," says Michele O'Connor, PHR, Human Resources generalist, "we get to see the 'softer' side of our coworkers and appreciate the side we see at work is often one-dimensional."

> **"I think it's important to have fun at work—and not just at holiday time."**
> —Ellen Jackofsky, *Assistant Professor, Southern Methodist University*

At Bell South's call center in Charlotte, NC, the manager unexpectedly served ice cream to call center employees while on a tour of the center.

At OOP!, a specialty store in Providence, RI, employees choose offbeat special "holidays" to celebrate, such as National Hug Month or Willie Nelson's birthday, taken from Chase's Calendar of Events. The employees dress to suit the occasion, have a good time, and it costs the store nothing. The fun times also attract customers. One company in St. Louis, MO, has "Dress Your Supervisor Day," in which employees get even with the boss—in a fun and stress-reducing way.

ACTIVITY TIPS

➡ Olympics-themed office competition and party

➡ Friendly rivalries: With a prize on the line, pit departments/branches against each other

➡ Tournaments and games: bocce ball, croquet, horseshoes, basketball, H-O-R-S-E, dodgeball, soccer, softball, bingo, "paper-football," garbage can basketball, 9-hole miniature golf course, cards

➡ Game room in the office, with pool and Ping-Pong tables, CD jukebox, pinball, and video game system

Neiman Marcus, the luxury department store in Dallas, formed an ad hoc team to increase fun and excitement at work. They involved employees in the planning process from the start, not just as representatives on the team, but to seek participation in every activity. The team created Project Smile, and planned four "big" events for the year, with sign-up sheets to get help from employees. They also hosted smaller, more spontaneous activities as individuals or teams warranted special attention for their achievements. For example, they produced an "Accounting Olympics" where people competed in a variety of metric activities, while increasing their learning and understanding of the accounting function.

Jennifer Zuri, the marketing communications manager of Aquascape, a St. Charles, IL, landscaping firm, helped put on a lunchtime "wallyball" tournament at the company fitness center, printing and framing the winner's certificates. Months later, employees are still regularly playing, and Zuri is planning an office Olympics for the end of summer.

———

Sausalito, CA, accounting software developer SBT Corporation (now a part of Irvine, CA–based Sage Software, Inc.) gave receptionists petty cash to stock the front desk with yo-yos, candy, and toys. The company knew that laughter and fun are infectious, and that if their receptionists were relaxed and happy, then clients would be in good spirits as well.

> **"People are going to be most creative and productive when they're doing something they're really interested in. So having fun isn't an outrageous idea at all. It's a very sensible one."**—John Sculley, *Former Chairman, Apple Computer*

———

Schwartz Communications, a public relations firm in Waltham, MA, feels like a big family, with employees' kids—and a company dog—on-site most days. The company has a game room, creativity training, sports teams, and four well-stocked kitchens. It also doles out cash on the spot for special accomplishments and shares profits with employees. When clients renew contracts, the team that services the contract receives a percentage of the annual retainer fee. Says cofounder Paula Mae Schwartz, "People are motivated to perform every day because they know we'll reward them emotionally, educationally, or monetarily. I don't think people give their all unless you give yours to them."

———

During the summer, Rich Willis of Paychex's Cherry Hill, NJ, office bought tubs of ice cream, put them on a cart, and wheeled them around so employees could help themselves. He is now doing the same in Albuquerque, NM.

———

Once a month, employees who play musical instruments at KFC Corporation in Louisville, KY, are asked to bring them to work. This motley crew of musicians is then given a list of the month's top performers and asked to serenade those individuals. The recognition activity has been so successful that the company has initiated a second musical serenade, performed by a string quartet.

———

> **"A business has to be involving, it has to be fun, and it has to exercise your creative instincts."**
> —Richard Branson, *Founder, Virgin Music Group and Virgin Atlantic Airways*

To lighten the atmosphere, one California company gave different Page-A-Day calendars to staff members and encouraged them to share their daily page with others. Calendars included jokes, crossword puzzles, vocabulary words, and gardening tips.

———

In Georgia, the Augusta Technical College wanted to create a highly interactive and fun exercise to help team members get to know one another. Participants had to answer questions such as "What is the name of a person you'd like to meet?" and "What is the most exciting place you've ever visited?" Answers were written on colored paper and hung as a mosaic in the hallway.

———

Charleston Memorial Hospital in Fall River, MA, asked employees to bring in pictures of their pets and had them posted on a lunchroom bulletin board. Everyone had a lot of fun trying to guess which employees the pets belonged to. Jossey-

Bass Publishers in San Francisco used a similar idea to help new employees become acquainted with the staff: Veteran employees were asked to post family pictures, along with cute captions, in the work areas.

———

Ben & Jerry's has a permanent committee for planning fun activities, known as the "Joy Gang." Over the years, various people have assumed the title of "Grand Poo-bah," as they led the committee in generating fun ideas for the workplace. Perkins Coie LLP has a "Happiness Committee" that consists of five anonymous employees who can initiate fun activities for the organization.

———

Employees at a Capital One Financial Corporation office in Tampa, FL, created a fun environment by forming "scream teams" to recognize peers and celebrate such important occasions as birthdays and holidays. The team also developed theme days for people to dress up and bring food, and sponsors a quarterly picnic and the "Wacky Olympics" competitions.

> • Create humorous awards or certificates related to each achievement and a special outfit or hat to wear when they are presented.

———

Employees at Pacific Power in Portland, OR, use Frisbees to deliver memos on "Frisbee Memo Day."

———

> **"**Small things work, even seemingly corny things like putting cartoons above your desk or having everyone bring in pictures of themselves from the sixties. You don't have to be a comedian to display a light touch.**"**—Malcolm Kushner, *President, Malcolm Kushner and Associates*

Rebecca Rogers at University Health Care System in Augusta, GA, does a fun activity she calls "communal captions." She posts photos from newspapers and magazines over the copy machine and invites staff members to write funny captions for them, making copy-making time more interesting.

> **"We want people who enjoy what they're doing and for whom work is an extension of themselves."**
> —Emily Ericsen,
> *Vice President of Human Resources, Starbucks Coffee Company*

One of the greatest honors employees can receive at Microsoft is a sodded office: While they are away, fellow employees remove all the furniture and lay down a wall-to-wall layer of sod. This became such a popular prank that a memo was distributed: "Whoever wants to sod someone's office, call this number and we'll do it." Legitimizing the prank, however, made it less fun, so the sodding was soon replaced by other high jinks, such as filling offices with Styrofoam peanuts or popcorn. In one memorable case, a manager returned from a business trip to find his office door removed and the space Sheetrocked over and painted to perfectly match the corridor wall.

Suzy Armstrong of State Farm Insurance in Tulsa, OK, watched a video filled with cute songs and silly exercises with her employees, and led the 15-member team of underwriters in aerobics exercises in the common area.

"For eight minutes every afternoon, I have department heads lead their employees in stretching exercises at their desks," says Pam Wiseman, training coordinator for Designer

Checks in Colorado Springs, CO. "It's a little silly, but it's fun, and it gives everyone a break. I think we're more productive because of it and we feel better, too."

———

Merle Norman Cosmetics in Los Angeles buys its female employees makeovers. The company also sponsors an Employee Night every other Saturday at the San Sylmar container manufacturing facility located in the San Fernando Valley outside Los Angeles. First-run movies are shown for employees, who may bring as many as six friends. After the movie, employees and their guests can make their own free ice-cream sundaes.

———

Linda L. Miles, president of Miles & Associates, a seminar-planning firm in Gig Harbor, WA, treated her staff of six women to a pedicure as a reward that came to be called "Happy Feet Day."

———

The Bank of America offices in San Francisco have a "Laugh-A-Day Challenge" for one month. Each employee tries to make coworkers laugh the whole day with cartoons and jokes. Winners receive T-shirts and books containing the best jokes and cartoons.

> **"Take your work seriously and yourself lightly."**—Bob Nelson

———

Matt Weinstein of Playfair, a Nicasio, CA, company that offers humor seminars, has several suggestions for keeping the work environment fun. He recommends giving "joy breaks," during which employees can look at cartoons or listen to CDs.

He also suggests getting everyone together on the floor for childhood games, like marbles and penny-pitching. Other ideas from Matt:

- Give your employees a casual dress day, such as Hawaiian Day or Suspender Friday.
- Plan a surprise picnic for your employees in the parking garage or lot.
- Make campaign buttons out of employees' baby pictures. Have them wear one another's buttons and try to figure out who's who.
- Put rubber fish in the watercooler.
- Staple Kleenex tissues to potentially stressful memos.
- Glue chocolate Kisses to boring memos.

Ritch Davidson, "senior vice emperor" at the company, adds:

- Designate days when anyone who makes a negative comment forks over a small sum of money—25 or 50 cents—and use the money to start a Fun Committee fund.
- Instead of giving out holiday bonuses in checks, give out cash, close a few hours early, and take everyone to a shopping mall. After the spree, stage a show-and-tell.
- Hold fun contests—Nerf basketball, volleyball, or bubble-blowing competitions—or play cooperative games, such as charades and treasure hunts.
- Have a party for no reason at all.

During a recent canning season, overtime had climbed so high at the Dole Food Company plant in Springfield, OR, that workers wondered if they were going to go crazy. As one technician said, "I couldn't look at another bag of lettuce!" To prevent burnout, manager Donna Lynn Johnson started a kazoo band. At first, the 325 plant employees were skeptical, but they soon got into the spirit of things and started smiling more.

At Eastman Kodak in Rochester, NY, an executive formed a Humor Task Force to gather Monty Python videos, Woody Allen books, plastic chattering teeth, and other props for a "Humor Room."

Children's Hospital of The King's Daughters in Norfolk, VA, hosts a stress-relief fair for employees with booths (dunk tank, Velcro dartboards, massages) and food.

> **"The most important thing I learned from big companies is that creativity gets stifled when everyone's got to follow the rules."**
> —David M. Kelley, *Founder, IDEO Product Development*

IBM, Coca-Cola, Ford, Monsanto, and Nikon all purchase gold-sealed Star Certificates declaring employees' ownership of actual stars, with a star album containing a sky chart and star verification record. Star certificates are available for $45 from the International Star Registry in Ingleside, IL.

Iteris, Inc., based in Santa Ana, CA, has its own Fun Committee, which launched Project Girth. For every pound an employee lost, a dollar would be sent to his or her favorite charity. Iteris also sponsored a "Guess the Stock Price on March 31" contest in which the winner got a free lunch at a hoagie shop. Finally, the plant's conference room has an exact replica of the space shuttle *Columbia* made out of Budweiser beer cans.

———

"In my experience, there are two great motivators in life. One is fear. The other is love. You can manage an organization by fear, but if you do you will ensure that people don't perform up to their real capabilities. People are not willing to take risks when they feel afraid or threatened. But if you manage people by love—that is, if you show them respect and trust—they start to perform up to their real capabilities. Because, in that kind of atmosphere, they dare to take risks."—Jan Carlzon, *CEO, SAS*

M CI, now a part of New York–based Verizon Communications, had top management work together to shoot a movie. Famous scenes from movies such as *Raiders of the Lost Ark* were filmed, using team members in the roles of the actors and actresses. The project was a great team-building experience. The completed movie was shown to all employees at a company meeting.

———

S mall teams of food service executives received a Kodak K12 camera and a list of captions at a recent Society for Foodservice Management conference in San Francisco. After a 20-minute lesson covering the basic points of photography, they had two hours to snap pictures of their teams to match captions, such as "to boldly go" and "team spirit." Claudia O'Mahoney, executive vice president of the association, says, "The cameras made the meeting successful because they allowed people to be their most creative."

———

At Mid-States Technical Staffing Services (now owned by AccuStaff), in Davenport, IA, teams of employees competed to produce the most accurate time sheets (which originally had a 38 percent error rate). Within three weeks, time sheets were 100 percent accurate. The teams only competed for ten weeks, but time sheets were still 99.6 percent accurate at year-end.

Robert Marn of the Chilcote Company in Cleveland, OH, used a bingo game to teach workers proper procedures, to lower injury rates, and to cut compensation claims against the company. Accidents decreased by 56 percent the following year, with a savings of $21,000.

> **"If you want to thrive and remain competitive in a work that is changing radically and relentlessly, you need the fluidity and flexibility of humor."**—C. W. Metcalf, *President, Metcalf & Associates*

At Valassis Communications, a marketing company headquartered in Livonia, MI, employees were given cards and stampers to play bingo at work. Numbers were called out hourly over the PA system from morning until about two in the afternoon, with a break for lunch. Winning cards were placed in a drawing for one of five prizes, which were tied into a theme, such as Fourth of July, movie night, summer, or winter.

During staff meetings at the *Phoenix Business Journal,* an employee is chosen to read the mission statement; then the publisher quizzes people on what it means for them. Token prizes are handed out for correct answers.

Memtron Input Components in Frankenmuth, MI, now a part of Esterline Corporation, created its own version of Monopoly, called Memtronopoly. Managers supply caricatures of themselves to serve as game pieces and submit lists of problems that are made into "Process" and "Systems" cards. Players roll a die, draw a card, and discuss problems or hand out employee recognition as they progress around the board.

———

One health services company in Oakland, CA, holds bowling games during Friday afternoon breaks. They set up the pins in a long hallway and award prizes for the winners. It ends the week on a lighter note.

———

As a break for busy assembly or warehouse workers who are meeting quota or ahead of schedule, some firms in Silicon Valley call for a surprise 15-minute basketball break, although Ping-Pong or pool works, as well. At Microsoft, it's not uncommon for employees to take a break to throw a Frisbee.

- Hold a raffle for members of an outstanding work group, giving away a night on the town, a resort weekend, or a home computer.

A Case Study in Fun & Games

Fun and games are an important aspect of work at Robert W. Baird, a financial services company located in Milwaukee. Some departments have "humor rooms" where associates can unwind with puzzles and games.

At one branch, sales associates were told to reserve time on their schedules for a mandatory compliance meeting, where they were to watch a compliance video. When they arrived, they were treated to a comedy movie and junk food instead, while brokers covered their phones. Everyone appreciated the opportunity to drop what they were doing, relax, laugh, and enjoy the afternoon.

Another branch celebrates Christmas in July. One year, families were invited to a bowling alley, where the branch manager showed up in a summertime Santa suit complete with red shirt, suspenders, red gym shorts, red high-top Converses, white hair, and a beard.

The company also hosts numerous contests. The public finance group held a "Talk Like a Pirate" week during which associates wore pirate hats to work and were judged on their performance. The information technology department held a three-legged race in which the winning team was allowed to leave early. And in celebration of a record month, one branch closed the office early and held a putt-putt match. Teams played on a makeshift golf course built from two-by-fours, toy windmills, and bridges, which snaked in and out of offices and cubicles. After nine holes, everyone wanted to play another nine.

> **"Laughter is the shortest distance between two people."**
> —Victor Borge,
> *Musical Humorist*

The U.S. Postal Service sponsored a national contest to sell the greatest number of first-class phone cards in one month. The winner of the $1,000 prize was the Rio Linda, CA, post office, with average sales of $25.58 per employee per day—well above the $22 figure achieved by the runner-up. Employees planned to use the money to buy a refrigerator to store their food.

Remington Products, Inc., the personal care products maker based in Atlanta, GA, held a company contest tied to the theme "What Makes Remington Good." Prizes included a trip to Acapulco, won by an employee who submitted a poem about the company.

> **"Incentives help continue momentum in terms of employee morale."**—Patricia Schod, *Manager of Media Relations, Motorola*

———

Southwest Airlines, based in Dallas, TX, has a Halloween costume contest, a Thanksgiving poem contest, and a design contest for the year-end newsletter. The firm also has an annual chili cook-off.

———

Truck drivers with FedEx Freight Corporation in San Jose, CA, participate in truck-driving championships, competing in events such as maneuvering a tractor trailer through a barrel course. State winners receive special recognition, a trip to "boot camp" to prepare them for the national championships, and a trip to the national championships itself. The Chairman's Challenge gives national winners a number of opportunities, including a choice of several vacation options, including a seven-day, all-expenses-paid cruise in the Caribbean or a trip to a major sporting event, such as the NFL Pro Bowl in Hawaii.

———

Hardee's Food Systems, the fast-food chain headquartered in St. Louis, MO, held a Competition for Excellence, in which three-person teams from each of more than 2,000 restaurants competed against other Hardee's in their districts. The teams were judged by regional managers on the three basic qualifications for fast-food employees—service, product makeup, and work area cleanliness—as well as on how well they worked together. Winning teams advanced to the regional competition, and seven finalists were flown to the company's headquarters. Cash awards were given at each level, with the winners of the national competition receiving $1,500 each. All the national finalists flew in on the company jet, were whisked around the city by limousine, and were generally treated like VIPs.

In a competition called "Bonus Bucks," employees "caught in the act of doing something right" were awarded bonus points. At the end of each quarter, each district (five to seven restaurants) held a party at which workers used their collected points to bid on items like T-shirts and televisions.

———

For every job listing a graduate passes on to the Career Planning and Placement office at Fordham University in New York, a piece of paper bearing his or her name is entered in a lottery. A random drawing, held every three months starting in October, selects a winner, who is then featured in the *Fordham* magazine. Prizes consist of season tickets to Fordham sports events, dinners at local restaurants, and vacations to spots like historic Tarrytown, NY.

> **"Our main employee incentive program has raised the average level of performance considerably. Teamwork and interdepartmental relationships have been enhanced."**
> —Daniel J. Wildermuth, *Director of Marketing, Mirassou Vineyards*

———

QuizMaster Productions, a quiz show company focused on team training based in Roswell, GA, holds contests modeled after TV game shows, such as *Jeopardy*, *Wheel of Fortune*, and *Win, Lose, or Draw*. Employees play in teams, answering questions about company products and operations.

To promote product knowledge, BI Performance, a Minneapolis-based performance improvement company, has foreign and domestic car salespeople call an 800-number and take a product knowledge test over the phone. During the test, a computer randomly chooses 15 to 20 questions out of a pool of about 200. Salespeople who answer 80 percent of the questions correctly win instant merchandise.

———

> **"I've come to the conclusion that there's no such thing as a bad cap program. Caps always go over really well, as do T-shirts, jackets, and sweats. People seem to take great pride in displaying their company name and logo on their clothes."** —Jim Turner, *Director of Safety and Loss Prevention, ANR Freight System, Inc., Denver, CO*

Teams of custodians at Texas A&M University in College Station hold their own annual "Olympics" to test their proficiency with everything from dust mops to floor waxers. Just as in the real Olympics, participants hold preliminary meets, in key events such as the "Peanut Push" and the "Obstacle Course."

———

Domino's Pizza, Inc., based in Ann Arbor, MI, holds an annual companywide "Olympics" in which it promotes events ranging from accounting to dough making, vegetable slicing, truck loading, dough catching, and tray scraping. The Domino's Olympics awards $4,000 to national champions in each of 16 categories. The team leader who supervises the most "gold medalists" wins a free vacation.

———

The Hotel Association of New York City hosted a "Hotel Olympics" to recognize employees. Chefs had to prepare a

Caesar salad and an appetizer of their choice; bartenders were asked to make a Manhattan and an original drink recipe; maids were timed for bed-making speed as well as tautness of the sheets; and waiters and waitresses had four minutes to carry a tray of champagne-filled glasses 800 feet, spilling as little as possible. All entrants received cash prizes, tote bags, and soft drinks. In addition, first-place winners won cameras and trips to Las Vegas and California, second-place winners received TVs, and third-place winners got his-and-hers Bulova watches.

CUNO, a maker of water filtration and purification systems in Meriden, CT, knew wholesalers would not sell its products if they knew nothing about them. To change this, managers mailed 5,000 training guides about water-quality problems with a 50-question multiple-choice test. Wholesalers were asked to review the manual, dial a toll-free number, and answer 10 randomly asked questions from the list of 50. A wholesaler who scored 80 percent or better received a customized baseball cap, a mug, a bumper sticker, and a certificate naming him or her as a water filtration specialist. A total of 1,900 wholesalers enrolled, and 1,000 earned certificates.

To encourage participation, distributors who returned their enrollment cards were entered in a sweepstakes that offered 82 prizes, including RCA TVs and VCRs, radios, and pen-and-pencil sets. The company also tracked those who did not call and encouraged them to read the manual and take the test. Once certified, wholesalers could qualify for a second-level award. Anyone who sold 15 of the company's products in 45 days won a nylon jacket imprinted with his or her name and the company's logo; 140 jackets were distributed.

Finally, the company placed 15 "mystery" calls during the promotional period to ask distributors to name the water purification system they carried. All 15 wholesalers answered correctly and won $100 each.

———

Tupperware, based in Orlando, FL, holds four-month contests and two-to-three-week challenges throughout the year. Both reward high sales or recruiting efforts through points that can be redeemed for catalog merchandise. Meeting or exceeding sales quotas can earn dealers a week for two in Puerto Vallarta, Mexico, or a seven-day cruise.

To combat high turnover among its approximately 90,000 dealers, the company developed an incentive recruiting program. Dealers who recruit at least one new dealer in September, when turnover reaches a peak, receive a porcelain doll. Tupperware gained some 3,000 more dealers than expected through such efforts. Hostesses whose parties generate a minimum of $61 in party sales qualify for gifts or merchandise from the Tupperware collection. Managers who reach sales quotas or a combination of sales and dealer recruiting goals qualify for the use of a car, which can be turned in for a new model every two years, or cash.

> **"Now and then it's good to pause in our pursuit of happiness and just be happy."**
> —Guillaume Apollinaire, *French Poet and Critic*

———

Don Lundberg, CFO of Peoples National Bank of Kewanee, IL, describes a contest for the marketing of new MasterCard and Visa cards in which employees receive gifts tied to the number of new accounts they open. For each of the first four accounts, they receive a flower; for every five additional accounts, they win the following items in succession: a $5 gift certificate for Dairy

Queen, a waiver for card fees, a $15 gift certificate at a local restaurant, a $50 savings bond, a day off with pay, a riverboat ticket, and $25.

———

First Capital Life, now a part of Pacific Life Insurance based in Newport Beach, CA, held an offbeat sales contest called "Murder in Montreux," in which marketers got monthly clues to try to determine who of eight possible suspects was guilty of "murder." To entice marketers to play along, a special grand-prize drawing was held in Switzerland for those who solved the mystery.

———

USMotivation, an incentives firm in Atlanta, GA, persuaded the king and queen of Sweden to sponsor a sales contest for a group of American employees of a Swedish-owned vinyl manufacturer. During the contest, the king and queen sent the employees letters concerning royal etiquette, autographed pictures, and gifts like Swedish crystal to those who were meeting their goals. At an awards dinner outside Stockholm, the king and queen presented the awards, and the ceremony was videotaped.

Celebrations, Parties, Birthdays & Special Events

Celebrations, parties, and special events are more organized forms of public recognition. While it is often traditional for companies to host holiday or year-end celebrations, group celebrations are more effective when they are linked to the *performance* of the group or organization. With a little forethought and planning, you can make any group event a meaningful form of recognition. Celebrating birthdays is another important, and more personal, way for companies to honor their employees, and a few examples are included here.

At Welch's, the Concord, MA–based fruit products giant, CEO Dave Lukiewski serves his staffers lunch in the company cafeteria during special employee recognition days. "I have always been motivated by 'attaboys,' but I try to formalize that and make it more of our culture," says Lukiewski. Surveys have found a nearly 7 percent improvement in positive responses due to the recognition efforts.

SPECIAL EVENT TIPS

➡ Buy a piñata for the office.

➡ Have a popcorn party.

➡ Treat them to a movie during or after work.

➡ Let them make a team/department video.

➡ Have them create a "celebratory" banner.

Led by CEO Kent Murdock, 1,600 employees of Salt Lake City–based O. C. Tanner Co., a jewelry store, gathered in the company cafeteria to dance the "O. C. Tanner Adulation Jiggity-Jig," a group dance that was led by Kent in honor of National Employee Appreciation Day. After the employees participated in the group dance session on Friday, the company treated them to a free lunch. CHG Healthcare, also headquartered in Salt Lake City, honors employees on a day other than the official National Employee Appreciation Day. CHG designates a week in June as Employee Appreciation Week. It has given employees free massages, sponsored a health fair, and had managers run errands for employees. CHG spokeswoman Mary Biljanic says, "Since implementing an employee recognition program, our company has seen lower turnover rates."

Mary Swank, owner of Simply Swank hair salon in Hudson, OH—one of the fastest-growing salon/spas in America—celebrates each employee's birthday. She finds out what kind of cake they want and then bakes it from scratch.

———

At Dean College in Franklin, MA, senior managers surprised the staff with a visit from a local ice-cream vendor to thank them for their hard work during a student orientation session.

———

At Clausen Nursing Home in Iowa City, IA, owner Gordon Clausen and his family treat their six employees, mostly students from a local university, to a home-cooked meal with the family during the holiday season.

———

SME Vista Optics, a contact lens products manufacturer based in Widnes, Cheshire, UK, recognizes its 20 employees with curry and beer evenings; visits to the theater; thank-you mentions at weekly team lunches; bottles of wine; a director treating the team to an evening out to celebrate success; and taking the entire company to an overseas trade fair to meet customers.

———

Wequassett Resort and Golf Club in Chatham on Cape Cod, MA, hosts clambakes, croquet matches, and themed events for employees of the resort. In-home care provider Right at Home, in Bloomington, MN, traditionally treats more than 200 employees to an annual meal and show at the Chanhassen Dinner Theatres. Camden Property Trust, a real estate investment trust in Houston, TX, and Fairfield Resorts, the time-share unit of Cendant Corporation in Central Florida, host annual Halloween parties for employees and their children. The entire staff at MMI Associates, a marketing firm in Raleigh, NC, spent a recent Friday at a local spa.

———

Oregon-based Flying Pie Pizzeria restaurants maintain a tip fund that pays for concerts, parties, paycheck stuffers, recognition, enhancements like a nicer stereo system, and an annual raft trip. Starwood Vacation Ownership, with 1,900 Central Florida employees, rewards employees with a variety of family-oriented events.

———

David Hall, owner of several Overflow discount stores in Queensland, Australia, hosted a top-notch Christmas party. It had a 5-star buffet dinner, an open bar, music, and presents. He gave every shop manager a voucher for a shopping expedition. The expedition started with champagne breakfast, included lunch, a cocktail party, and $100 for hotel accommodations.

———

Employees of Vicinity Media Group, a publishing company that produces regional lifestyle and business magazines and is based in Fairfield, NJ, attended a joint holiday party with other small businesses. CEO David Black purchased tickets for his 19 employees to attend a "Bring Your Own Business" party in early December hosted by Jersey Street Furniture Rental, a party decorations company in West Orange, NJ. At the event, his workers drank, danced, and mingled with other small-business employees. Black says he spent 25 percent less on the joint party than he would have spent on the company's annual holiday dinner, which normally takes place at an upscale restaurant.

The Container Store, a Case Study: National We Love Our Employees Day

On Valentine's Day, The Container Store, the nation's leading retailer of storage and organization products, based in Dallas, TX, surprised its 4,000 employees across the country by declaring "National We Love Our Employees Day." That day and in the following week, employees were treated to special celebrations and recognition at the company's stores, home office, and distribution center. The company supported its recognition effort with ads in *The New York Times* and *The Dallas Morning News* (the hometown paper), customer e-mails, a social-media campaign, outdoor and online messaging, in-store signage, and messaging through the stores' music systems.

"While we appreciate and recognize our employees every day of the year, we thought it fun on this Valentine's Day to publicly thank them for their diligence, positive attitude, perseverance, and commitment to helping our customers and ensuring our special company remains strong despite a tough economy," said Kip Tindell, chairman and CEO. "We also encourage other companies to adopt Feb. 14 as a day to recognize their own employees' contributions and successes." Successful, this company is: For the past 11 years, the retailer has been named to *Fortune* magazine's annual list of 100 Best Companies to Work For.

SPECIAL EVENT TIPS

➡ In an employee meeting, tape gift certificates to the bottom of chairs in the first three rows.

➡ Provide tickets to a sporting, musical, or cultural event (depending on the employee's preference).

➡ Coordinate a surprise celebration of the achievements of an employee or group of employees.

➡ Have birthday lunches at a restaurant, such as Benihana, which provides a photo memento of the occasion.

- Turnover of less than 10 percent (compared to retail industry average of more than 100 percent)
- Strong financial performance, including a double-digit, year-after-year compounded growth rate
- National recognition as an employer-of-choice, driving such interest that only 3 percent of applicants are hired into the organization
- Ongoing commitment to laying no one off

> **"There is a great creative void in most of corporate America. When you inject a level of humor and playfulness, employees find a common ground. They're reminded that they're all working on the same side."**—Carl Robinson, *Vice President, Organizational Psychologists LLC*

The Container Store attributes its success to its values-based business philosophies focused on its entire interdependent group of stakeholders, beginning with employees and also including its vendors, customers, and shareholders. In doing so, the retailer finds that employees take better care of customers, which ultimately ensures a prosperous bottom line even in a challenging economy. "We strive for excellence, to be special, to be different and to be more than just another retail store. That has always meant putting our employees first and in doing that, they truly take care of the customer," says Tindell.

———

At Minnesota-based Wilson Learning Corporation, each employee is given a Mickey Mouse watch on their first day of work as a reminder that they should always have fun while working for the company.

———

Hewlett-Packard uses informal beer busts in the afternoons to mark special events.

_____

At Dow Corning, in Midland, MI, management hosted an ice-cream social in which managers made and served ice-cream sundaes to employees to thank them for an accomplishment, reports George K. Stevenson, Human Resources specialist for the company.

_____

Don Coyhis describes how a humor seminar helped when he was district manager for Digital Equipment Corporation's Colorado customer support center: "We taught everyone to juggle beanbags; if employees felt uptight after a call, they were encouraged to juggle to break the tension and prepare for the next call. We also instituted a 'grouch patrol,' which was empowered to tell grouchy people to take a break. We found that if we systematically took breaks, productivity improved."

_____

Give a personalized cartoon for an employee award. Nichecartoons.com can create a fully customized comic strip including the recipient's name and work achievement.

_____

Alissa Meredith, lead physical therapist for Scripps Memorial Hospital in Encinitas, CA, instituted a "Margarita Award" for the therapist who had to work with the toughest client that week

SPECIAL EVENT TIPS

➡ Ask a friend of the employee to find out something that he or she might like or like to do.

➡ Plan a roast of the person at a company meeting.

➡ Let any employee request a "Dream Day" to go to the beach and contemplate their job, life, and future. Have the person report any insights when he or she returns.

➡ Have an appreciation and welcome party whenever an employee leaves or joins your work unit.

or month. The awardee was then treated by the group to a margarita happy hour.

———

The morning after a product passed a crucial test at Odetics, a company that makes robots and spaceborne tape recorders in Anaheim, CA, a mariachi band paraded through the plant, followed by some girls from the local Baskin-Robbins franchise offering free ice cream.

———

Advanta Corporation in Horsham, PA, has its senior management host a "grill your boss" cookout in which they dress up as chefs and cook hamburgers and hot dogs for all employees, reports Joan Cawley, director of Human Resources for the company.

———

First Chicago Bank gives out "Felix" and "Oscar" awards for the employees with the neatest and messiest work areas.

———

At a recent quarterly meeting, Apple executives used kazoos instead of applause to indicate their approval of speakers.

———

At Domino's corporate offices in Ann Arbor, MI, everyone from the president to the receptionist wears a red, white, and blue Domino's uniform once a week. Employees are invited to bring their pets with them to work on Fridays.

———

L iebert Corporation in Columbus, OH, which manufactures air-conditioning and power-supply systems for computer rooms, offers free popcorn to employees all day long.

———

P arties are always breaking out for almost any occasion at Time Warner in New York City. For example, when *Money* magazine moved from the 29th to the 33rd floor of the Time & Life Building in Rockefeller Center, *Money* held a block party. The best employee parties are reportedly held at Advanced Micro Devices, Apple Computer, Leo Burnett, Hewlett-Packard, Odetics, Tandem Computers, and Time Warner.

Easy Office Morale Boosters

15 suggestions for relieving office gloom:

1. Order pizza or a huge submarine sandwich for a communal lunch.

2. Designate a bulletin board as a place for employees to post favorite jokes, cartoons, etc.

3. Attach cartoons or humorous anecdotes to the more mundane memos that need to be circulated.

4. Schedule a staff meeting off-site in a congenial atmosphere; if possible, follow up with a casual social event.

5. Schedule an "Ugly Tie" (or Crazy Sweater or Silly Socks) Day with a joke prize for the winner.

6. Hold betting pools for such high-profile events as the Super Bowl, Kentucky Derby, Oscars, Emmys, and the World Series.

7. Take a daily humor break; designate someone to share a joke or funny story with the rest of the staff.

8. During a lunch break, screen a funny film or television show in a conference room or one of the larger offices.

9. Bring a camera to work. Take candid shots of employees and post the results throughout the office.

10. Make a point to smile and say hello to office mates.

11. Give everyone an opportunity to arrive or leave an hour early one day a week.

12. Never take anything too seriously. Keep reminding yourselves, "This isn't brain surgery." (Unless, of course, it *is* brain surgery.)

13. Trace the history of employees' family names and post on bulletin boards.

14. Create a baby pictures bulletin board: of employees or of their children.

15. Create a Facebook page for employee vacation pictures.

MORALE TIPS

➡ Team, department, or companywide bike rides/hikes

➡ A karaoke afternoon or an after-work party

➡ Scavenger/treasure hunt for new hires

➡ Carnival, including a dunk tank for executives

➡ Ice-cream truck to come to the office

➡ Car wash

Marion Laboratories, Inc., takes all its employees and their spouses or guests (some 2,500 people) to see the Kansas City Royals play baseball once a year. Everyone wears a baseball cap or T-shirt with a big *M* on it, and top executives of the company go up and down the aisles handing out free drinks and other refreshments.

———

At Space Camp in Cannes, France, employees can train much the way astronauts do, learning about satellite deployment, aerodynamics, and astronomy, as well as working in simulated weightlessness and training in other space environments, such as hypergravity. The program culminates in a simulated space flight. French operations of Microsoft and Aerospatiale both did this.

———

First Pennsylvania Bank in Philadelphia arranges a once-a-year banquet for employees (and their families) who "take that extra step."

———

West Texas Utilities in Abilene, allows employees to celebrate their birthdays or special occasions by bringing in cakes or doughnuts to share with others during breaks. This gives them control over whether or not to celebrate, and costs the company nothing. Most employees participate.

———

When SI Ventures founder Manny Fernandez was CEO of Gartner, Inc., a Stamford, CT, technology consulting and research firm, he would call every employee on his or her birthday. Said Fernandez, "It used to be a lot easier when we were small. Now I sometimes make 12 calls a day, but it's a great way to keep in touch with what's going on in the company and employees seem to enjoy it."

———

Martin Edelston, chairman and CEO of Boardroom, Inc., in Greenwich, CT, personally signs a "Happy Birthday" card to each of his 85 employees and drops by to sing to them on their special day.

The president of Merle Norman Cosmetics keeps track of everyone's birthday and makes a point of seeking out people to wish them well on that day. The company chef also bakes a birthday cake for the employee.

> • Engrave on a plaque the names of the employees who have reached 10, 15, 20, or more years of service. Acknowledge individual achievements during a company meeting each quarter.

Personal letters and cards are sent from headquarters in Laval, Quebec, to the stores of Dairy Mart (now part of Circle K, based in Tempe, AZ) on people's birthdays and wedding anniversaries.

Compass Bank in Birmingham, AL, plans a lunch outing for each birthday person. He or she gets to select the restaurant, and the manager picks up the tab. All other staffers are invited to attend on a "Dutch treat" basis.

When associates at Robert W. Baird turn 40, they receive a "birthday rock" to keep on their desks until the next person turns 40. The rock has been making its way around the firm from desk to desk for years. One Baird manager lets associates leave a couple of hours early, as well.

"**O**ne thing we do that is an especially big hit with the employees' families is sending flowers or cookie-grams to the place of business or to the home of all spouses on their birthdays and anniversaries," says Michael L. Finn, chairman and CRO (chief remover of obstacles) at Fortress Safe & Lock in Cincinnati, OH. Every child (up to age 16) is also sent a birthday card with $20 in movie tickets. "Including the families has meant a lot to everyone," Finn concludes.

———

Employees pick random birthdays and give that person a cake and celebration at Windsor Shirt Company.

———

Have a birthday committee in charge of thinking up new and creative ways to celebrate birthdays. Once, when four employees had birthdays on the same day at Porterville Development Center, they blindfolded them and drove them to a restaurant, put signs on their backs that read "It's my party," and everyone in the restaurant stood and sang "Happy Birthday" to them.

> **"Celebrate what you want to see more of."**
> —Tom Peters, *Author and Management Consultant*

———

There's a birthday album at the spaceborne products plant of Odetics, Inc. (now Iteris, Inc.), where everybody's picture appears on his or her birth date on a huge calendar hung along a wall.

———

H. B. Fuller and Recreational Equipment, Inc. (REI) give employees the day off on their birthdays. Lowe's Companies offers them a free lunch, and all Mary Kay, Inc., employees receive a birthday card and a voucher for a free lunch for two.

———

Spouses of employees at Black & Decker in Anaheim, CA, get flowers on the employee's birthday, thanking them for their support, reports Bill Paolillo, district manager for the western region. Flowers can also be given to the spouses of employees who travel a lot to show appreciation for the sacrifice.

———

At the Veteran's Administration Philadelphia (PA) Regional Office and Insurance Center, during the month of his or her birthday, each employee has the privilege of giving a coworker the office's Extra Step Award, a $30 cash award given annually to employees who go out of their way to satisfy their internal customers, i.e., other workers they serve.

———

On a person's birthday at San Diego–based Four Pi Systems, Inc., coworkers individually delivered a single flower every 15 minutes throughout the day.

———

Employees at The SCOOTER Store throw spontaneous celebrations for colleagues who do something exceptional. This typically involves giving them pats on the back, throwing confetti, and making lots of racket with horns and noisemakers. The guests of honor feel great about their jobs and company, and the "combusters" (the individuals offering the "spontaneous combustion") appreciate the opportunity to play around. The store's Insurance Verification Department also held a contest in which, if it achieved a certain record, the male manager would come to work in a dress picked out by the supervisors, and one of the team members would do his makeup. Not only did they meet the goal, but they exceeded it.

———

BlueCross BlueShield of North Carolina hosted a "parking lot lunch" with a tent and barbecue to thank staff for their hard work on a major corporatewide initiative.

———

When Jennifer Wallick, a computer software manager, worked for a subsidiary of Hewlett-Packard in San Diego, she rewarded her work group after finishing a demanding project by giving them a "popcorn lunch"—that is, taking them to see a movie over lunch hour. As she explains, "It meant a slightly longer lunch hour, but it was a great break and a lot of fun!"

———

To recognize the accomplishment of a team goal, Nancy Lauterbach, owner of Five Star Speakers & Trainers in Overland Park, KS, closed the office for half a day and took the entire staff to the movies and to a restaurant for coffee afterward. At the movie, everyone received money for snacks. On other occasions, the company offered employees a casual dress day to reward extra effort.

———

Jon Holmes at the Anderson Mall & Clemson Boulevard Chick-fil-A restaurants in Anderson, SC, throws an annual banquet for his team, during which he gives each person a present. He believes the key to employee retention is to show you care by attending team functions, ball games, and cheerleading competitions.

———

> **"I prefer things that are spontaneous. Things I hate the most are the routine, expected things like an annual company picnic. I think it's important for there to be an element of humor, laughter. It adds to the company. It's one more thing that makes you want to get up in the morning and go to work."**—Joel Slutzky, *Chairman, Iteris, Inc.*

Firmani & Associates, a public relations firm in Seattle, closes one day per quarter so employees can go to a movie. Besides being a fun stress reducer, the outing promotes camaraderie. Owner Mark Firmani also tries to create a fun atmosphere with perks, such as a casual dress code, weekly staff lunches, and supplies of juice, soda, and candy.

At the Fayetteville, AR, Crabtree Mall, manager Charlie Kerr throws midnight bowling parties to recognize his entire Chick-fil-A team for meeting performance goals.

> • Invite employees to your home (or a special celebration), and recognize them in front of their colleagues and spouses.

Radio rating surveyor Arbitron celebrates the achievement of significant milestones with appropriate dinners and parties. When the company completed a phase of its Mexico project, there was a taco bar, music, and sombreros. Additionally, the finance department gets together every year to recognize individuals with the "Top Dollar Award": They get a fun gift that changes from year to year, and their names are engraved on a plaque. Work groups and departments often use recognition as an icebreaker or a welcome break from meetings.

Lone Star Park in Grand Prairie, TX, threw a party for 400 full-time employees and their families. Children were given small gifts, and employees drew tickets in a raffle for gifts from the park's gift shops, as well as larger electronic items such as TVs.

S oftware developer McAfee, Inc., transformed a hotel ballroom into a winter wonderland, complete with 6,100 tiny white lights strung on 49 white birch and fir trees, giant ice sculptures, cotton snowdrifts, and a dance floor made to look like an ice-skating rink.

———

A laska Airlines has an annual Children's Holiday Party in one of its airplane hangars. Employees transform it into a winter wonderland filled with decorations, pizza, cookies, cotton candy, popcorn, inflatable toys, face painters, and clowns. The best part, however, is when the hangar doors open and one of the planes (with the nose repainted as a reindeer) rolls up from the "North Pole." An employee dressed as Santa jumps out with all of his elves, and the crowd of 2,500 employees and family members goes crazy.

———

S ince Robert W. Baird's headquarters is located in sometimes-frigid Milwaukee, one department held a post-holiday ice-skating party for associates and their families. A mock skating "code of etiquette" was circulated, with requirements such as "absolutely no laughing at someone else's fall until you're sure nothing is broken." At the end of the night, surprise trophies were presented in the following categories:

- Skating as a Weapon of Mass Destruction
- Most Artistic Fall vs. Ugliest Technique
- Most Vertically Challenged
- Most Original Style

Each year, Baird associates and family members also enjoy exclusive access to the Milwaukee Zoo for an evening that includes dinner, refreshments, entertainment, and special animal shows. Approximately 3,000 people attend.

————

Advertising giant DDB's Sydney, Australia, office throws terrific holiday parties, complete with truckloads of decorations, live bands, theme cocktails, and gourmet finger food. According to former senior media group head Greg Tremain, DDB "announced the Agency Person of the Year and had a joke award ceremony and a video of all the commercials made throughout the year. It was a big morale builder."

————

Guests at a corporate Christmas party at Wembley's Conference and Exhibition Center in London were treated to a Cinderella Ball, complete with costumed characters, waltzing, and a Christmas feast.

- Give the employee a round of golf.
- Rent a sports car for the employee for a week.
- Rent a billboard and put up a message featuring the employee's picture and name.

————

Kaiser Permanente's corporate offices in Oakland, CA, join together for a team-building activity every December; they built gingerbread hospitals one year. This type of activity not only reinforces the roles people play at work, but gives everyone a chance to sit down together for a treat after they're finished.

A Case Study in Celebrations

Lands' End, the Wisconsin-based clothing and merchandise retailer, defines the standard for zany and fun celebrations. Here's a snapshot of some of the activities in a recent year:

GOING FOR THE GOLD

The company has used the theme of "Going for the Gold" throughout the year in events and activities ranging from company meetings, a 40th anniversary celebration, the Lands' End Summer Olympics, "Golden" Customer Service Week, and "Golden" Service Stories (customer letters).

WORLD'S LARGEST PILLOW FIGHT

On September 29, 2004, employees and their families, retirees, community members, and local students, 2,776 in all, joined Lands' End for the "World's Largest Pillow Fight." Following the fight, pillows and pillowcases embroidered with "Sweet Dreams from Lands' End," worth a total of almost $100,000, were donated to the Association of Hole in the Wall Camps. Coverage of the event spanned from New York to California, including MSNBC and a national spot on NBC's *Today* show.

SUMMER OLYMPICS GOLDEN GAMES

The Lands' End "Summer Olympics" were hosted July 13–August 21, and featured events such as marshmallow golf, a beach ball throw, the plank walk, a free-throw contest, and the gurney push. The top team for each event was awarded a traveling trophy and the honor, fame, and status that goes with being an "Olympic" champion. The event included opening and closing ceremonies, and all finalists were honored at the company picnic, which featured games, rides, bingo, and entertainment for all ages, including a game show, the Lands' End Alumni Band "Kids from Wisconsin," and an award-winning entertainer, Neal McCoy.

TORCH SIGHTINGS

No Olympics is complete without a torch. So "torches" were sent to various departments in the company, and each department had to submit a photo of its torch in a unique location. It ended up in Rome, Japan, the Lands' End swimming pool, a roof, a tractor, and many other places. The division that most creatively displayed its torch received extra credit toward the Lands' End Olympics. (Incidentally, the torch picture did end up swaying the Lands' End Olympics results, allowing a merchandising team to win by a hair.)

———

The Portland, OR, REI displayed its employees' artwork one year by showing it in conjunction with the Portland Pearl District's First Thursday Art Walk event.

———

At Dow Chemical Company in Midland, MI, management hosted an ice-cream social where they made and served sundaes to their employees to generously thank them for their accomplishments.

———

The Texas Rangers baseball club treated 150 employees to a serenade by the Hamilton Park Men's Choir.

———

Lucian LaBarba, former president of American FoodService, now a part of Houston, TX–based FreshPoint, said he wanted to hold an event that all associates and their families would enjoy, so he asked his daughters what they thought might work. They both suggested the circus, so he planned the event, dubbing it "The Greatest Food Service Show on Earth." It was the most successful event the company had ever held. They repeated it the following year, purchasing over 500 tickets. Each person also got $5 in "circus bucks" to spend that day.

———

ACCESS Destination Services in Long Beach, CA, offers many unique themed events. For example, Safaris, Inc., re-creates Hollywood's golden age at the former home of mogul Darryl F. Zanuck. A Hollywood marquee emblazoned with the company's name greets guests, floral arrangements and candles float in the pool, and Chinese lanterns hang outside the pool-house-turned-casino. Five hundred people dine, play croquet and no-stakes casino games, and dance to a jazz trio at the lavish estate.

> **"Pay geared to performance is important, but so is 'rah-rah.'"**
> —Daniel Finkelman, *Principal, McKinsey & Company*

The company also arranges Indian-Western barbecues at Indian Canyon, a desert oasis with towering palms in the foothills of the Santa Rosa Mountains near Palm Springs. Authentic Cahuilla Indian dancers and singers perform at the barbecue while potters, weavers, and silversmiths demonstrate their crafts at an Indian marketplace where participants can shop. Stuntmen stage a gunfight, and guests—who wear cowboy hats and bandannas—two-step to a country-and-western band.

The company sometimes arranges other events, like a "Field of Dreams" evening at Dodger Stadium, where retired ballplayers in vintage uniforms play ball with participants.

———

Recently, Mana, Allison & Associates temporarily took over Napa's Inglenook winery and staged a Renaissance Fair, barbecue, and winery tours for 850 people. Mimes, jugglers, and musicians entertained the group.

Viacom in New York City has its own version of the Academy Awards in various categories, such as customer service, leadership, innovation, and teamwork. Nominations can come from employees at any level.

Field Trips & Travel

In a recent survey of American workers, 77 percent ranked a trip to a desirable destination with a spouse or guest as a positive incentive. Travel incentive rewards have a number of advantages: They are extremely desirable and promotable; they provide an exclusive venue for fostering team spirit and education; and they have "bragging value." There are, however, disadvantages: They are too costly for many applications; travelers are out of the office during the trip; it takes extensive effort and experience to create a high-quality travel program; and typically only a few employees can get the reward.

> **"One of the most important reasons for a company to have an incentive trip is to foster loyalty and good feeling toward the company."**
> —Jennifer Juergens,
> *Former Editor in Chief,*
> Incentive *Magazine*

Keurig, a Reading, MA–based coffee machine maker, sends high-performing employees on a five-day "Origin Trip" to Central and South America to see where the company and its owner, Green Mountain Coffee Roasters, get their coffee. The trips are meant to inspire, to reward for good work, to deepen relationships with the company, to meet the farmers, and to live the company's environmental mission of sustainability.

TOP INCENTIVE TRAVEL DESTINATIONS

(ranked in order of popularity)

WESTERN HEMISPHERE

1. HAWAII
2. CARIBBEAN ISLANDS
3. CALIFORNIA
4. FLORIDA
5. MEXICO
6. NEVADA
7. ARIZONA
8. NEW YORK
9. CANADA, BERMUDA
10. PUERTO RICO, CHICAGO

Every other year, Rudi's Organic Bakery, a private company based in Boulder, CO, rewards its outside sales representatives who meet sales goals with trips. Employco USA, based in Westmont, IL, also recognizes its employees with free trips.

———

At Stew Leonard's, proceeds from vending machines in the employee lunchroom are used to subsidize trips and outings for employees.

———

Tina Berres Filipski, editor and director of publications for Meeting Planners International in Dallas, TX, took her staff of eight to the Texas State Fair one Friday afternoon, paying for their admission.

———

Jeff Alexander, a dentist in Oakland, CA, took his staff on a field trip to a shopping mall and gave each an envelope with $200 (all in ones!), stipulating that they buy at least five things and that he would take back any money they had left after two hours. At their next staff meeting, employees had a show-and-tell.

———

Shane Benson, manager at the University Place Town Center Chick-fil-A restaurant in Charlotte, NC, takes team members on a ski trip each year. On the bus, they hold "rolling award" banquets, during which awardees walk the aisle to receive prizes.

TOP INCENTIVE TRAVEL DESTINATIONS

(ranked in order of popularity)

OVERSEAS

1. FRANCE

2. SPAIN, ENGLAND, GERMANY, ITALY

3. AUSTRALIA

4. PORTUGAL, MONACO, AUSTRIA, SWITZERLAND, HONG KONG

5. IRELAND, SINGAPORE, BALI, THAILAND, ISRAEL

At monthly P&L review meetings, employees at PSS World Medical in Jacksonville, FL, go off-site to amusement parks, bowling alleys, miniature golf courses, or play a business version of *Family Feud*.

———

Panache Destination Management took a group of several hundred people to the Hacienda Winery in Sonoma and staged an *I Love Lucy*-style grape-stomping competition, followed by lunch.

———

Incentives To Intrigue, a firm based in San Francisco, provides a staff of writers, producers, and actors who come up with a script for a murder mystery or treasure hunt. One such event was staged for a group of employees during a dinner on the Napa Valley Wine Train. The costumes, decoration of the train cars, and events took participants back to the First International Wine Tasting during World War I. Another murder mystery weekend took 66 employees of Ford Motor Company through Chinatown, Union Square, and the financial district to solve the mystery.

Kaiser Permanente in Oakland, CA, encourages work groups to use their cash rewards as a group. Winning groups have purchased box seats at a baseball game and taken a train trip to Napa Valley's wine country, both on workdays.

> **"Companies in industries large and small have long tapped the power of incentive travel to increase productivity and performance in the workplace."**
> —*Incentive* Magazine

Brier & Dunn stages jungle-theme dinners at the lions' den of the San Francisco Zoo, with lots of plants and jungle music. The company also arranges private yacht-club dinners, preceded by a regatta or cocktail cruise, and black-tie dinners in historic mansions; and it offers the Great American Rolling Treasure Hunt, which has teams exploring the city's neighborhoods by streetcar to discover local landmarks.

Dick Eaton, chief energizing officer of Leapfrog Innovations, based in Medford, MA, knows how to structure fun. Eaton hosts scavenger hunts in the city for corporate clients, designed

FIELD TRIP TIPS

→ Hike

→ Go-cart excursion

→ Paintball game

→ Racetrack or casino

→ Harbor, lake, bay, or river cruise

→ Amusement park, dude ranch

→ Fishing, cabin in the woods

→ Company headquarters

→ Supplier site

to promote teamwork and build morale. Mercer, Inc., headquartered in New York City, also uses a scavenger hunt to orient team members who travel to new cities. They are asked to visit client offices, large hotels, and the convention center when they arrive, bringing back "proof" of their visits to each location.

———

When Nelson Motivation, Inc., in San Diego achieved quarterly revenue goals, it packed everyone into a limo driven by an Elvis impersonator and drove to Disneyland for the day. On other occasions, the company sent employees horseback riding on the beach, gave them a day at a spa, and flew all staff and spouses or significant others to New York City to celebrate for a week.

———

Tegrant Corporation, based in DeKalb, IL, has a novel way of rewarding senior managers who demonstrate successful leadership. They win a trip to the company's manufacturing plant in Bowling Green, KY, to spend a day with line workers there. Likewise, plant workers who are especially productive or offer innovative, money-saving ideas win a trip to any of the company's sales offices in the United States or Canada. Those who have taken part in the exchange have gone back totally pumped.

———

The Container Store awards top-performing employees a week at the CEO's mountain cabin in Colorado.

———

PricewaterhouseCoopers, the financial consulting company, rewards its top ten professional and administrative employees with monetary awards and five-day trips to New York City.

> **"When basic compensation is adequate, it takes something extra and something tangible to motivate people to greater performance."**
> —*Incentive* Magazine

———

Every dollar that marketing staffers save on airfare, hotel bills, and meals while on the road earns them points toward a resort vacation for two at the Dr Pepper Snapple Group, based in Plano, TX. The two people who collect the most points by year's end win the weeklong vacations. Travelers save money from their travel allotments by taking connecting rather than nonstop flights, flying on weekends, staying in more modest hotels, and dining in less swanky restaurants.

———

Molson Coors Brewing Company took 325 people from more than 80 of its distributorships across the country on a houseboat excursion. Winners attended an informal dinner with coworkers at a resort, where they were given a brief introduction to houseboat safety and handling. Then everyone headed for the houseboats, which slept from six to ten people. The next five or six days were spent meandering on a lake; optional activities, such as tours of nearby parks and group rafting,

> **"If you're going to dangle something in front of them, why limit yourself to carrots?"**—from an advertisement for Norwegian Cruise Lines

- For a thrilling adventure, give a skydiving package that includes a six-hour introductory course, complete with a written test and first jump. Such packages can be found all across the country at smaller airports, particularly in warmer areas such as California, Texas, and southern Florida.
- Sailplane or glider rides also appeal to the adventurous, as does hot-air ballooning. These trips usually begin in the early morning and last about an hour.
- White-water rafting is popular across the country, especially in Pennsylvania, northern New York, Idaho, California, Oregon, and Alaska. Give a one-day experience, a weekend camping trip, or a weekend stay at a lodge or hotel.

were also worked into the schedule. The last day included a Farewell Fish Fry, after which winners were shuttled back to the airport. The price for the excursion was about $300 a week per person.

Since every distributor "won" a houseboat, each decided whom to send—a salesperson and his or her family (up to six people) or a group of salespeople. Rick Clay, vice president of sales, says, "Houseboating's a great form of relaxation because it's one of the few places where there aren't any telephones. This type of setup really allows you the opportunity to talk and listen to each other."

———

Dogsled treks across marked, groomed trails are available in various parts of the American snowbelt. Lewis Elin, president of The Topps Company, Inc., the maker of baseball cards in New York City, has been mushing with friends, customers, and suppliers for several years. "It gives you a totally different perspective on winter and the great outdoors," Elin reports, "while offering a really challenging experience as well."

———

The Travelers Companies, headquartered in New York City, sent winning agents to the Masters golf tournament each year. They were flown on the company jet and wined and dined at the event. Each agent received a bag of customized merchandise—from cookbooks to visors and suntan oil. They mailed a Masters scratch-off game card to other key brokers, who have to follow the tournament to win. Prizes ranged from a trip to London to imprinted visors. Richard Brown, second vice president for advertising marketing services for the insurance company, reported a 23 percent response rate on the card. For nonsales employees, a putting contest was held one week prior to the Masters. For three days, the home office set up a golf turf and challenged its employees to make a hole in one. Golf shirts and balls were awarded to winners, who were also entered in a drawing for eight golf-related prizes ranging from warm-up suits to windbreakers.

> **TRAVEL TIPS**
>
> ➡ Travel upgrade
>
> ➡ First-class seat when flying for business
>
> ➡ Tickets to employee's favorite TV show
>
> ➡ Airline tickets to destination of employee's choice

———

For a truly unique experience—especially for car lovers—there is racing school. At Road Atlanta, a two-and-a-half-mile Grand Prix track in Braselton, GA, individuals can attend a one-day racing school to learn handling techniques such as braking, skid padding, and heel-toe downshifting. They then spend another day racing around the track. The Valvoline Company organized this incentive trip for six buyers from distributorships around the country.

———

All managers at Quad/Graphics, Inc., printers in Sussex, WI, are entitled to a free trip to New York City. The company picks up the airfare for two and lets them use its apartment on 57th Street. About 20 managers a year take advantage of this opportunity.

———

When Leo Burnett Worldwide reached $1 billion in advertising revenues, every employee in the New York and Hollywood offices was flown first-class to the Chicago headquarters for the company's annual breakfast celebration.

———

TRAVEL TIPS

➡ One night at luxury hotel

➡ Bed-and-breakfast

➡ 3-day getaway to a resort

➡ Extravagant trip to Europe

➡ Caribbean/Bahamas/Hawaii/Tahiti vacation

➡ Around-the-world cruise

REWARDS FOR SPECIFIC ACHIEVEMENTS

"You get what you reward! Know what you want to get and reward or recognize people in some way to get it."
—Bob Nelson

While everything discussed so far can be used to drive a wide range of behavior, this section looks at examples that were used to elicit *specific* types of performance: sales revenues, customer service, employee suggestions, productivity and quality, and attendance and safety. Many of the examples contain multiple aspects or performance goals, and tend to be part of a formal program.

As stated earlier, formal programs have several advantages. They tap into the power of public recognition, which is a significant motivator to many employees. They tend to be ongoing, offering a stability that employees can come to rely upon. If the programs have clear, objective criteria, they can avoid elements of subjectivity and favoritism that sometimes mar more informal forms of recognition.

The downside of formal programs is that they tend to become

stale, predictable, and boring over time, unless they are kept fresh and relevant through periodic changes and improvements—or an influx of new people with new energy and ideas running the programs. Because formal programs are so public, there is greater damage when something goes wrong, such as when a deserving person or group is left out, promised rewards are not delivered or are delivered too late, or upper management is not actively involved with or supportive of the programs.

> **"We covet recognition that we earn by dint of our own hard effort."**
> —Dennis LaMountain, *Management Consultant*

In an article in *Workforce Management*, Philip C. Grant stresses that corporate reward systems need constant attention. The mere existence of such programs does not guarantee that they will be valued or that they will have any impact on employee motivation and satisfaction. Therefore, managers must manage them. There are several ways to do this:

- Tie rewards to needs. Because each employee has different needs, reward systems must be flexible. If feasible, rewards should be adapted to each employee.
- Ensure the rewards' fairness. Every employee must be satisfied that, in relation to the demands of the job and to what workers in similar jobs outside the company are receiving, the rewards they receive are just.
- Make sure timing is proper. It's best to schedule frequent presentations of rewards so that employees receive them shortly after the achievement being recognized.
- Present rewards in a public forum. Rewards are not meant to be presented in the privacy of an office. Schedule a special meeting for the occasion, and don't camouflage the rewards.

They must stand out and be highlighted; don't squeeze praise among a dozen other topics of conversation.

- Talk up the value of rewards. If managers show enthusiasm for a reward at the time it's presented, they add to its perceived value. However, be sure not to oversell them. Constant talk about how great a reward is can start to make it sound ridiculous.

Outstanding Employee & Achievement Awards

Traditional forms of recognition typically include outstanding employee and achievement awards, which are often accompanied by recognition items such as trophies, plaques, or certificates. In my research, 54 percent of employees rank a "special achievement award" as very or extremely important to them, and 43 percent cite "certificates of achievement" as having similar importance. Outstanding employee awards are often based on a formal selection process to ensure as much objectivity as possible, and can be given for a single exceptional achievement or employee performance over time. Awards tend to be more meaningful when they have been selected by one's peers, not just by management, and when there is no quota on the number of recipients.

David Hall, owner of several Overflow discount stores in Queensland, Australia, gave diamond earrings to Employee of the Year Fiona Walker.

> **"Human beings need to be recognized and rewarded for special efforts. You don't even have to give them much. What they want is tangible proof that you really care about the job they do. The reward is really just a symbol of that."**—Tom Cash, *Senior Vice President, American Express*

A couple of years ago, Norm Kane, vice president of Synovate, a global market intelligence company based in Chicago, started issuing "Golden Pencil" awards to coworkers who had done exemplary work. The award is a gold-colored #2 pencil engraved with the words *Norm Kane's Golden Pencil Award*. It's simple and sincere, and is a token of thanks that Norm and his group can give out fairly often—and they do.

——

A regional manager for Hallmark created achievement certificates for each member of his team, citing a key attribute that personified each individual, such as: "for consistent follow-through without having to be asked," "for being able to close the really big account," or "for pitching in to help others—and always with a smile." He read them out loud at an end-of-the-year celebration, where employees had to guess whom they referred to. It was a fun team-building experience for everyone.

——

G eneral John M. Loh, U.S. Air Force (Retired), rewarded his team members at the Tactical Air Command with certificates for solving their own problems.

——

A t Citibank in Oakland, CA, customers (and other employees) can reward and thank employees with Thumbs-Up certificates, which can be exchanged for merchandise. Early in

- Create a special award for specific major accomplishments and name it (a Gorilla Award, for example).
- Create an ABCD (Above and Beyond the Call of Duty) Award for employees who exceed the requirements of their jobs. Give them a polo shirt emblazoned with "ABCD Award."
- Have employees vote for the top Manager, Supervisor, Employee, and Rookie of the Year.
- Dedicate the parking space closest to the company entrance to the outstanding Employee of the Month.

the program, many workers were so pleased by the recognition that instead of redeeming the certificates immediately, they proudly displayed them on their walls.

———

Lands' End uses the Big Bean Award to recognize people for using their "beans," such as assisting with a last-minute task, staying late to help with a project, or finding a great employment candidate. Each month, employees attending the employee services divisional meeting get to nominate someone by placing nomination slips in a ballot box. (They can also complete an online nomination form in advance of the meeting.) At the end of the meeting, one name is drawn from the box, and that lucky person gets to play "Bean Machine," otherwise known as Plinko, where he or she gets the chance to win great prizes such as a Lands' End beanbag chair or a gift card to the "Dry Bean"—or some not-so-great prizes, such as pork and beans, kidney beans, or a beanie hat. Everyone nominated is sent a copy of the nomination, along with a special bean prize, and all nominations are displayed for one month on the employee services website.

———

*T*he *Charlotte Observer* in North Carolina has used FUIEE awards, which stands for Fun-Urgent-Informative-Energetic-and-Essential, for innovative employees, such as a reporter with a great story or a staff member with an idea for cutting costs or improving customer service. The newspaper also gives prizes based on employee nominations. Each week, a rotating committee reviews nominations and announces three winners, who receive one of the following items: $50 cash, movie tickets, or use of a preferred parking space. All nominations (including those for nonwinners) are e-mailed to employees to read and enjoy.

> **"Compensation is what you give people for doing the job they were hired to do. Recognition, on the other hand, celebrates an effort beyond the call of duty."**—from "How to Profit from Merchandise Incentives," *Special Supplement,* Incentive *Magazine*

*F*edEx Freight Corporation has numerous recognition programs, ranging from the EZTDBW (Easy to Do Business With) Award, which is a small gift and a certificate of recognition, to the Extra Mile Award, which is a larger monetary award for exceptional performance. These straightforward award programs allow employees at all levels to recognize one another spontaneously.

*T*o create group rapport and to recognize success, The Phelps Group in Santa Monica, CA, gives out "Atta Boy"/"Atta Girl" awards after weekly staff meetings. The simple plaques, presented with great fanfare, are passed from old to new winners.

*S*yncrude Canada Ltd., one of Canada's largest energy companies, based north of Edmonton, Alberta, works hard to keep recognition fresh, personal, and meaningful. For example, John Thomas, manager of operations, recently initiated a "Pay It Forward" award, a plaque that is passed from employee to employee for exemplary work. Each recipient is honored twice, both in receiving the award and in selecting and presenting it to the next winner. Feedback has been very positive.

———

Employees who go the extra mile at KFC Corporation, headquartered in Louisville, KY, are presented with a "Floppy Chicken Award," a thank-you note, and a $100 gift certificate. Former president and CEO David Novak started the program when he flew into an awardee's city and personally presented him with a rubber chicken that he pulled out of a crumpled brown-paper sack. A photo of the presentation is on permanent display at the "Walk of Leaders," which is a prominent area at corporate headquarters.

> "People want to learn new things, to feel they've made a contribution—that they are doing worthwhile work. Few people are motivated only by money. People want to feel that what they do makes a difference in the world." —Frances Hesselbein, *President, The Leader-to-Leader Foundation*

———

The most popular award at Synovus is the quarterly Standing Tall Award, for employees who go beyond the scope of their jobs. They are nominated by coworkers, and winners are chosen by a special committee. The awards are presented at a luncheon, by the CEO and other senior officers, and each recipient gets $100, a day of paid vacation, and a tacky pink flamingo with a bow tie, which costs only $3.47. Employees proudly display the flamingos in their cubicles, encouraging others to earn the award as well.

———

Timberland's John Lewis Award, named in honor of U.S. congressman and longtime civil rights activist John Lewis of Georgia, is given to one outstanding member of the sales team each year. This individual must manifest Timberland's core values—humanity, humility, integrity, and excellence—by making a significant impact on his or her community through advocacy and volunteer service. The award is a $5,000 grant to the nonprofit organization of the winner's choice, a day in Washington, DC, with Congressman Lewis, and a commemorative plaque. In 2004 John Lewis himself made the award presentation.

Employees at Robert W. Baird, a financial services company located in Milwaukee, give fellow associates the Blue Chip Award to show appreciation for good work. Recipients receive a short note from the associate and a small "Baird Blue Chip" with the words *In recognition of a job well done*. These awards are typically presented by the manager during a department meeting so other coworkers can join in applauding the recipients. Many associates display Blue Chips on their desks, and some departments have wall space dedicated to hanging the award notes. The top 2 percent of Blue Chip recipients are recognized each year at the annual meeting for all associates. Baird also has an "Associate of the Month" program, which provides recognition for associates who consistently make superior contributions both to their clients and to the company. Nominations come from coworkers, and the monthly winner receives flowers, $100 in cash, a certificate for dinner for two, an item of Baird clothing, an

> **"Because of our incentive programs, we know that we will be here in the future and that it is because of our hard work now."**—Charles Gehl, *Coordinator, Frank Implement Company*

Associate of the Month certificate, and a traveling trophy to keep on his or her desk for the month. The award is usually presented by a group of fellow associates and Human Resources personnel, and the winner is featured in an "eBriefs" story in the company's online newsletter.

———

The REI store in Ventura, CA, always gives out "appreciation awards" during its store meetings. One day, after it had given out the usual awards, it called attention to two employees who deserved a little more credit than usual. They were each presented with the Pineapple Award—a fresh pineapple with a healthy crown of leaves.

> **"High achievers love to be measured, when you come down to it, because otherwise they can't prove to themselves that they are achieving."**
> —Dr. Robert N. Noyce, *Cofounder, Intel Corporation*

———

A Tualatin, OR, REI store rewards staff members with the Golden Hanger Award for going above and beyond their responsibilities in providing support to salespeople. It's a plain clothes hanger spray-painted gold; recipients are nominated by peers and are presented the awards at store meetings. There's an award presentation at each and every meeting. REI also has a peer-nominated and peer-selected formal recognition program called the Anderson Award (named for founders Lloyd and Mary Anderson). Recipients are selected once a year from every department and store, and receive certificates and engraved bricks on a pathway at the headquarters' campus. They are also eligible for the President's Award, which is given to the top ten employees in the company. Those winners are invited (with their partners or spouses) on an adventure-travel trip with REI's president.

Emerson Process Management Power and Water Solutions allows employees to give the Rising Star Award to fellow employees for good work. They type up a brief description of the awardee's accomplishments on the Rising Star page on the company intranet, and an award sheet is sent electronically, with the nomination description, to the employee with a copy to his or her supervisor. The employee gets to choose one of a number of $5–$12 prizes, such as movie tickets, car washes, gas or video rental cards, and restaurant or mall certificates; or he or she can receive a Rising Star pin, which many pin to their cubicles or work spaces as badges of honor.

————

Each year, CEDRA, a bioanalytical chemistry company, gives out the "Buttkicker Award" to employees who have the attitude and potential for leadership. They have to have been nominated by existing Buttkickers and approved by management in accordance with strict selection criteria. They each get their names added to a pedestal (in the lobby) with a wooden boot on top, a gold and diamond boot pin or tie tack, and a trip with the company's president to the local western-wear store to pick out a pair of boots.

————

The Legend Award is the highest honor an Alaska Airlines employee can receive. He or she must exhibit a unique blend of spirit, resourcefulness, integrity, professionalism, and caring. Once a year, each new class of honorees (approximately 8 to 12 employees) is inducted into the Alaska Airlines Hall of Fame and invited to a luncheon celebration with guests, coworkers, and senior management. In recent years, the award presentation has taken place at the Chateau Ste. Michelle Winery. "Legends" are first

flown to Alaska Airlines corporate headquarters to unveil the engraving of their names on marble pillars, and then taken by bus to the *Spirit of Washington* Dinner Train, which takes them to the chateau. Each "Legend" also receives a hand-painted sphere trophy.

Microsoft Dynamics GP in Redmond, WA, used to hold a celebration every year called Pioneer Day, where they presented awards to employees who had distinguished themselves in some way: a Jesse James Award for tolerating eccentricity, a Sodbuster Award for innovation, a Heritage Award for customer service, and several awards for excellence in various technical areas. The winners were held up as mentors, and others were encouraged to learn from them.

> **"What makes employees come to work is a sense of pride, recognition and achievement. Workers committed to their jobs and recognized for their work will work whatever hours it takes to get the job done."**—Thomas Kelley, *Chairman of the Board, Society for Human Resource Development*

Avis Rent A Car has several recognition programs, such as the Destination Excellence Award, which is given to employees who reflect Avis's values in dealing with customers and who have made some significant, quantifiable impact on the business. The highest award is the Milestone Achievement Award, which is presented by the executive committee to the employee who has made the most significant contribution to the company.

Beverly Cronin, a book manager at a Hastings Books, Music, and Entertainment store in Rio Rancho, NM, recalls receiving

> **"Once employees see that what they do makes a difference to the organization and is valued, they will perform at higher levels."**
>
> —Rita Numerof,
> *President, Numerof & Associates*

a "Spark Plug" award in the 1960s, which was a spark plug painted gold and hung on a ribbon, from a department store manager in Akron, OR. In giving it to her, he said, "This is for you, because you add a spark to our workplace." She still keeps the award in her jewelry box to commemorate the first time she was recognized for doing a good job.

———

The La Jolla, CA, office of New York–based Ziff Davis media and publishing company gives out "Daredevil" awards, a distinction granted to anyone who is caught doing something innovative or helpful beyond the call of duty. Award recipients are regularly announced via e-mail to the entire company.

———

CUNA Mutual Group created the Big Bone Award to play on a theme of "Big Dogs" that it was using for its formal recognition program at the time. A large (four-foot) rawhide dog bone was passed around (à la Stanley Cup) to outstanding members of the leadership team. The winners were chosen by their bosses and the award was presented at one of the three face-to-face meetings held every year. "If you won, you got to sign the bone, bring it home as an airplane carry-on (a lot of people fly to the meeting location), and display it in your work area," explains Eileen Doyle Julien, division manager of administration for the northwest marketing division of CUNA in Latham, NY. "As far as reliving the reception of this award, it was great!" says Eileen. "How can someone who sees this large bone in a business or airport setting not ask about it?!"

BlueCross BlueShield Association in Chicago gives "People Are Tops" awards, which include balloons tied to the person's desk, belly dancers, and a song or message delivered by someone in a gorilla suit. The company also recognizes outstanding employees four times a year with "Superstar" awards. Each Superstar gets a $500 savings bond, a star, and a sweatshirt.

At the annual profit-sharing banquet, management at the Angus Bam Restaurant in Raleigh, NC, gives out achievement awards to the top ten all-around employees. The restaurant also recognizes performers with the People's Choice Award, which is given by coworkers.

Walmart Stores, Inc., headquartered in Bentonville, AR, offers extensive award programs such as Regional All-Star Teams, the Special Divisions' All-Star Departmental Honor Roll, the VPI (Volume Producing Item) Contest, the Department Sales Honor Roll, and the Shrinkage Incentive Program. Award winners' names and pictures appear in the company newspaper.

> **"When people are treated as the main engine rather than interchangeable parts of a corporate machine, motivation, creativity, quality, and commitment to implementation well up."**—Robert H. Waterman, *Director of The Waterman Group*, *Coauthor*, In Search of Excellence

---

Nelly Attwater, former supervisor for training and development for El Torito Restaurants in Cypress, CA, shared how the restaurants used the "Be a Star" program. "When a manager or supervisor caught someone doing something right—or above and beyond—that employee was given a 'Star Buck,' which served as a cash substitute. Each restaurant had a drawing at the end of the month for prizes (cash, TV, etc.), and each region had a drawing for prizes also ($1,000 cash, TV, VCR, etc.). Each employee could have numerous stars for the drawings."

> **"All behavior is a function of its consequences."**
> —Bob Nelson

Nordstrom, Inc., the Seattle-based department store chain, offers the Pacesetter Award to employees who have exceeded goals by a considerable margin. As a Pacesetter, an employee receives a certificate, a new business card that reads "Pacesetter," and a lavish evening of dining, dancing, and entertainment to share with a guest. For the next year, the Pacesetter enjoys a 33 percent discount on all Nordstrom merchandise, which is 13 percent greater than the standard employee discount.

At Ceramics Process Systems Corporation, a technical ceramics manufacturer in Chartley, MA, the Extra Mile Award is given each December to several people who have gone above and beyond. Peter Loconto, former president of the company, says, "We were struggling to improve yield and productivity. One person took it upon himself to document all the issues involved and set out the problems so that management could clearly see where the obstacles were." Another person, faced with what management considered overly stringent (even unreasonable) requirements on a particular job from one customer, worked day and night—unasked—to accommodate the client's wishes. The employee got the job done on time. "When we announced the person's name, everyone in the company stood up and cheered," Loconto says. "That was a true validation of the person's hard work." Winners' names are engraved on a plaque that hangs in the company's lobby, and the chosen employees also receive either cash or equity in the company.

———

At TD Insurance Meloche Monnex, an insurance banking company in Montreal, Quebec, top performers receive a personal letter from the president, congratulating them on their achievement. They also receive an annual salary increase double the average. A portion of the increase is paid in one lump sum when the employee's salary is in the high range. These employees also get priority in the choice of additional responsibilities and training.

A Case Study in Recognizing Outstanding Employees

At Stew Leonard's, the ABCD (Above and Beyond the Call of Duty) Award goes to employees who exceed the requirements of their jobs. They receive a polo shirt emblazoned with the words *ABCD Award*. The store also has a "Superstar of the Month" program, in which one person in each department is elected by peers on the basis of different departmental criteria—cleanliness, safety, etc. His or her one month of superstardom commences with considerable fanfare, including a photo for the Avenue of Stars (a picture-covered wall in the store), balloons, and cheering by coworkers. Trophies, gifts, gift certificates, and cash are generously dispensed to recognize accomplishment.

> **"Next to excellence is the appreciation of it."**—William Makepeace Thackeray

Each year, "Stewie" awards recognize the top manager, supervisor, employee, and "rookie of the year"—based on employee ballots. The manager with the lowest turnover also wins an award. Outstanding performance awards are presented yearly to 3 top employees from among 20 or so nominated by the president and selected by previous winners. Banquets are held to present the honors.

> **"Motivation is based on what you bring to it as an individual. What is motivational to one person isn't motivational to another."**—Crystal Jackson, *Personnel Manager, Companion Life Insurance Co.*

Southwest Airlines allows station managers to reward "Star of the Quarter" employees with celebrations. At one station, the honoree invites a group of people to a lunch or dinner featuring a menu of his or her choice. The station managers do all the shopping, preparation, and serving for the event. Instead of an added hassle, this has become a team-building activity as managers work together to coordinate everything. This is just one reason why it is now harder (based on the percentage of accepted applicants) to get a job working at Southwest Airlines than it is to get into Harvard University!

At *Business First* in Columbus, OH, an employee of the month is recognized at each staff meeting, where the publisher praises his or her achievements. The company also gives out the "Ugly Ben Award," a new $100 bill, which has Benjamin Franklin's picture on it, to the person who "finds a way to meet the monthly sales budget against all odds."

At Home Depot, Inc., the home improvement supply center headquartered in Atlanta, GA, each store picks an Employee of the Month: someone who has given time to an area of the store that technically lies outside his or her responsibility. The honoree gets $100, a merit badge (collecting five badges earns an extra $50), and a special badge to wear on his or her apron. In addition, the employee's name is engraved on a plaque at the front of the store.

———

A t ICI Pharmaceuticals Group in Wilmington, DE, now a part of Chicago-based Akzo Nobel, the Performance Excellence Award is given to employees for any idea that helps the business and to employees who go above and beyond the call of duty. The winner receives $300. Employees can be nominated for this award by anyone in the company.

———

A t Gregerson's Foods, a retail grocery chain in Gadsden, AL, outstanding employees are named Associates of the Month at each store location. They receive silver name tags inscribed with that title and with the month and year of the award, to wear as long as they work for the company. The employees' names are also listed on plaques at each store.

———

M anagers at D'Agostino Supermarkets, a supermarket chain based in Larchmont, NY, name employees All-Stars when they go beyond the call of duty. At least one All-Star is chosen each month from each store, up to 24 people per year per store.

———

T he Carlson-Himmelman Award given by Westin Hotels, headquartered in White Plains, NY, is presented annually for outstanding management achievement. Recipients get a trip around the world.

At Valassis Communications, the "Innovator," "Collaborator," "Risk-Taker," and "Employee of the Year" award recipients receive 100 to 200 shares of company stock, crystal trophies, and coveted parking spaces. Recipients are nominated by peers, who simply complete a form, and are selected by a volunteer review and selection committee. In 2003 the CEO also gave away an "Integrator Award," which was a one-week trip for two aboard the *Queen Mary II*, and in 2004 gave the "Global Thinker Award," which was a trip to the destination of the winner's choice, along with $3,000.

Once a month at Meridian Travel, Inc., in Cleveland, OH, CEO Cynthia Bender has the company's 62 employees write in their vote for who should be Employee of the Month. "Managers always have their favorites, but the employees know who pitches in and helps out," says Bender. "It's important different departments don't become isolated," she says. "This makes employees notice others more and develops camaraderie."

The Golden Falcon awards at Federal Express include a gold uniform pin, a congratulatory phone call from one of the company's senior executives—and ten shares of stock.

At the Unitog Company, a leading maker of industrial uniforms and business clothing based in Kansas City, MO, top executives visit each plant to present the Wonder Worker award, as nominated by coworkers. The Wonder Worker of the year at each location receives a cash award, a personalized plaque that remains on view at the plant for the entire year, and a crystal trophy with the Unitog logo embedded inside. A typical award for a quarterly winner might be a Unitog sweater and a day off with pay.

———

Federal Express has a host of awards to reward individual and team quality efforts:

- The Circle of Excellence award, presented monthly to the best-performing Federal Express station, underscores teamwork.
- The Bravo Zulu (Navy talk for "well done") program gives managers the prerogative of awarding a dinner, theater tickets, or cash to any employee who has done an outstanding job.
- The Quality Achievement Award, presented annually, is the company's highest award.

———

Phil Hughes, director of Human Resources for Acapulco Restaurants, Inc., in Long Beach, CA, reports how hourly and salaried employees are rewarded. The company rewards its hourly employees in the following ways:

$100 for hourly referrals after 90 days

$300 for management referrals after 90 days

Employee of the month receives $50 cash, one day off, and a door-front parking space for 30 days.

Bright Ideas Program Awards up to $1,000 for ideas for saving money that are adopted

President's Award plaque and check for up to $2,500 for an act of outstanding service, signed and presented by the company president

Lunch from the department head for a job well done

Breakfast prepared by the management staff for the line staff

Theme days throughout the year (Cinco de Mayo, 4th of July, Halloween, Christmas), with various giveaways, trips, cash, limo rides, etc.

Casual dress in the office every Friday and all week from Memorial Day to Labor Day

Monthly cash contests in the restaurants for the best server, bartender, busser, etc.

The company rewards its salaried employees as follows:

Average check contest: $16,000/car grand prize

Quality Service Control Monthly Award for Highest Score: $1,000

Quality Service Control Award for 95 percent or better: $100 each month

Safety Lotto (restaurant must remain accident free that month to be eligible): $500 each month

General Manager referral: $1,000 per referral

General Manager of the Year: $5,500 + trip + one week of vacation

President's Club: Plaque + recognition in company publication

President's Honor Roll: Plaque + recognition in company publication

———

There's only one reserved parking spot at Odetics, Inc., and that's for the person selected as the "Associate of the Month."

———

Sales Revenue

One of the more easily quantifiable achievements in most companies is the attainment of sales goals, and it's no secret that salespeople tend to be highly motivated by recognition as well as money. For that reason, sales reinforcers are fairly commonplace. But how you reinforce sales success can vary greatly.

MRE Communications, a branding company based in Baltimore, MD, gives employees an extra week of vacation during the Christmas holiday as a reward for helping the company reach its financial goal.

———

Austin Taylor, a fine men's clothier in Anaheim, CA, offers a Dress for Success incentive program for its sales teams, where salespeople receive custom clothing items for making their goals.

> **"There's nothing like a good contest to get sales cranking."**
> —Tom Webb, *Chief Economist, National Automobile Dealers Association*

———

Although they had to make cuts in other areas due to the slow economy, technology vendor CDW, based in Vernon Hills, IL, still hosts a sales recognition dinner and annual trip for top sales employees to plan strategy with senior executives.

———

To respond to a complaint that customer service representatives were underappreciated compared to salespeople, a mobile camera business in Houston, TX, gives its salespeople blue poker chips every month to award to a customer service clerk who was instrumental in helping to close a sale or satisfy a customer. Recipients then get to a pull a prize out of a hat.

> **"Informal day-to-day acknowledgements mean a lot. Especially welcome are the spontaneous calls from upper management congratulating me when I exceed a sales goal. Without the personal touch, this job would just be money, and money can only motivate you so much. Recognition gives me personal pride and means something."**
>
> —Irene Elliott, *Account Executive, United Postal Savings Associates*

In its efforts to keep employees engaged, equipment and supplies distributor Restaurant Equipment World (REW) of Orlando, FL, hosts million-dollar parties for everyone in the company when a department reaches $1 million in sales. REW treats employees to ventures outside the office to avoid workday interruptions, as well as to give employees a greater opportunity to bond. Behind-the-scenes employees are included and recognized, too. "We want our people to work as a team so that customers get the same level of service no matter how little or how much they spend," says Vice President Patty Nuzo. REW spends just under $50 per person for its recognition events, about $500 to $1,000 per party. "It's nice to see them do things as a group where everyone is equal, regardless of their role in the company. We have been able to retain a lot of great people because of the friendships they make at work."

Hewlett-Packard marketers send pistachio nuts to salespeople who excel or who close an important sale.

Chilton Ellett, a telemarketing consultant based in Chapin, SC, suggests giving a penny for every three deals a telephone sales representative closes. The penny is then dropped into a gumball machine, and the individual is paid different amounts depending on the color of the gumball: 25 cents for a white gumball, $3 for red, and $10 for blue.

Paul Levine, general manager of Miller Nissan in Van Nuys, CA, awards $5 to the first and second salespeople to sell cars on a given day—then gives them $5 for every car sold by any other salesperson that day. The first person to make a sale can win $100 in a day just for selling one car, and as much as $200 or $300 if he or she sells more cars.

_____

At St. Louis, MO–based Nestlé Purina PetCare Company, members of sales teams that exceed annual goals in at least two of three categories receive trophies featuring a bronze dog and cat sitting on a company logo.

_____

When John Gurden made his monthly target of $125,000 in automated voice-processing system sales, David Woo, CEO of Automatic Answer (now owned by The Amanda Company) in San Diego, asked him what he would like as a reward. His response: designate a "John Day." Soon, John Day banners were plastered throughout the offices, and receptionists answered the phone with, "It is a good morning at Automatic Answer, where we are celebrating John Day." Woo also let Gurden use his office that entire day and gave him a special John Day photo album at a lunch in his honor.

> **"Nonsales employees feel that the sales people are always getting the perks and they think, 'Hey, they couldn't have made all those sales without me.'"**—Bob Carlton, *Incentive Program Planner, RJ Young Company*

_____

Whenever they exceed a monthly goal, Turbo Leadership Systems celebrates on Friday afternoons by taking the entire sales team on an outing, such as miniature golf, go-carting, or paintball. They always take pictures to display later on a bulletin board.

———

There is nothing like a good challenge to stimulate a team of workers. At a pizza party to celebrate a record sales month, Michael Phillips, director of sales for Seattle-based Korry Electronics, now a part of Everett, WA–based Esterline, told his sales force that if they beat their new record, he'd shave his head. Phillips reports: "Everybody got involved in trying to break the record, even the customers. Returns people were even booking extra rework and warranty sales." When it looked like the record-breaking was imminent, Phillips jokingly put up signs on computer monitors saying it couldn't be done because the computers were down. "That really fueled the fire," he says. To celebrate the "unbelievable" month, he brought in his own "Hair Terminator," who shaved his scalp in front of 565 employees at a rooftop party that celebrated Korry's 60th year in business. Reps who had contributed the most sales got first snips. Key customers and sales reps from around the world were also present.

> **"Incentive programs can make a difference, providing visible rewards that build up confidence and knowledge."**
> —Tom Mott, *National Practice Leader for Sales Compensation Services, Hewitt Associates*

———

Manish Mehta, president of ELetter in Portland, OR, said he would wear high heels to work for a day if his company met an ambitious sales target. He had to keep the promise, and now employees have suggested that he wear a dress if ELetter meets another milestone. Mehta explains, "You can match other companies' offers, but to make employees stay, you have to make work fun."

A former Paychex manager in Seattle created a sales lead contest in which payroll specialists would receive raffle tickets for every referral they received. At the end of each week, he held a drawing for prizes, which were usually solicited from current clients, such as a free manicure from someone's beauty salon or a small TV. Employees whose names were called during the drawing got to spin the prize wheel, which was colorfully decorated and about five feet in diameter.

"Though I'm self-motivated to a great extent, some motivation does come from outside. Recognition is great—and if the end result is a promotion, if I can further my career by being recognized as a top seller, that's great too."—Susan Charboneau, *Senior Sales Representative, United Services Automobile Association*

R ecently, The SCOOTER Store held a month-long program to recognize the top nine sales employees on a daily basis. These "Overachievers" took turns "stealing" an executive's chair for the day, in a program called "The Executive Chair Swap." The executives attended the ceremonies and took pictures with the Overachievers, which were then displayed on the company's Star Network. For the company's fourth and goal quarter, employees were featured in a mock-up *SCOOTER Illustrated* magazine cover when they scored personal touchdowns. Many of the covers still hang over their desks.

F or salespeople at Valassis Communications, a marketing company located in Livonia, MI, that produces inserts for newspapers worldwide, entry into the company's Hall of Fame is the most prestigious award. The honor is based on sales and leadership, and winners are selected by existing Hall of Fame members. Once selected, their photographs are hung in the Hall of Fame, which is at the company's global headquarters. The awards are presented at the annual Sales and Vision Awards, which attract about 600 employees each year.

———

To respond to a complaint from customer service clerks that they are unappreciated (compared to salespeople), Bruce Smith, CEO of Safety Vision, a mobile camera business located in Houston, TX, gives each salesperson a blue poker chip every month to award to someone for their effort in closing a sale or satisfying a customer. Each awardee gets to pull a prize—ranging from inexpensive dinners to Montblanc pens—out of a hat. Smith says, "It gets people a little more excited about what they do and provides some special recognition."

———

> **"Pretend that every single person you meet has a sign around his or her neck that says, 'Make me feel important.' Not only will you succeed in sales, you will succeed in life."**—Mary Kay Ash, *Founder, Mary Kay, Inc.*

At the *Phoenix Business Journal*, the sales team gets lattes or bagels in the morning when it sells twice the daily goal. At the *Milwaukee Business Journal*, everyone on the sales team receives a $25 gift certificate to a local store or restaurant when the team meets its goals for the week. If it makes 10 percent more, they get two certificates, and if it makes 20 percent more, they get three certificates. Employees create banners showing how much more is needed to meet the goals.

———

Patrick Dickerson of the Chick-fil-A Queensborough branch in Mt. Pleasant, SC, posts total drive-through sales each hour. When a record is broken, the entire shift receives "Doodle

Dollars" that can be exchanged for Chick-fil-A merchandise.

———

When Michigan-based Talking Book World was in business, the main office collected daily sales tallies from its various stores and circulated the results to all franchisees. The stores at the top of the list were called by the other stores and shared success stories with them, while everyone else tried to move up the list and be recognized as the number one store in the upcoming week.

———

Gail Herenda of Supercuts in Fort Lee, NJ, divided her staff into teams competing to sell hair care products. Each product sold is represented by an ant-shaped sticker, which is placed on the team banner. The team with the most ants at the end of the week wins a free lunch from Gail. Sale of hair care products is up.

———

At the *Atlanta Business Chronicle*, sales reps get quotas for each of four departments, and receive a $250 bonus if they meet all four. This helps them to focus on all aspects of the publication, rather than simply the total volume of ads sold.

———

The *Cincinnati Business Courier* offers various incentives to salespeople for achieving individual or group sales goals. Examples from the past include: an afternoon off for a movie or baseball game; maid service at home for the following month; and

---

SALES TIPS

➡ Cash bonus

➡ Humorous, handmade award

➡ Bicycle or motorcycle

➡ Golf clubs

➡ New or used car

➡ Vacation package

➡ An experience customized to his/her preference: special event, such as river rafting, bungee jumping, paintball, etc.

cash for an afternoon shopping spree with a show-and-tell at the end of the day.

———

As a sales manager for Westinghouse Electric Company in Los Angeles, Robert Partain threw a barbecue lunch for his sales staff the first time they made their team goal. He promised to do it each time they made their goal again. Seventeen months later, he had given 16 barbecues, missing only the month of the Northridge earthquake.

———

> **"Incentives are awards for working hard, an indulgence."**
> —Vicki Pritchard,
> *Sales Agent, Carlson Marketing Group*

Greenpages, in Kittery, ME, has each sales team pick a support person of the month and each support team pick a salesperson of the month. Then each team says a few words about the person they have selected at a monthly meeting.

———

At Coronet/MTI Film and Video in Deerfield, IL, now a part of Phoenix Learning Group based in St. Louis, MO, Mary Jo Scarpelli, sales director, brings the sales team bagels and cream cheese on the last Friday of each month.

———

For meeting team goals at WFAN-FM in New York City, the entire sales staff is treated to trips such as a daylong yacht cruise around Manhattan or a day in Atlantic City.

———

Richard Meyerson, president of Traveltrust Corporation in Encinitas, CA, offered to remodel a nursery in a sales manager's home to accommodate a newborn child if the manager made her sales goals. While the remodeling was taking place, she lived in a house owned by the corporation. On another occasion, the company rewarded a male employee with a fully paid paternity leave.

———

I try to put myself in their place," says Jennifer Hurwitz, who designs incentive programs for employees of LensCrafters, the one-hour eyewear stores based in Mason, OH. "I remember my retail store experience of working hard for 13 hours a day on my feet, and I try to design something that will make it a new and interesting day for our people each time they come to work." For example, newly opened stores with expectations of more than $100,000 in sales during their grand opening week are targeted for special attention to help them reach that goal. The whole company watches the daily figures as they are transmitted to every location by computer. On the final day, if the store is nearing its goal, Hurwitz says, "the president and key people from the home office are flown in on a company plane for the last few hours to cheer them on and help them out, and then everyone is taken out for dinner and a big party, with awards given out right then to every person who has contributed."

> **"My main motivation is the recognition. It's very competitive and tough to move ahead here, so going to the awards luncheons and meeting the VPs is a good way of gaining visibility. My main purpose is to move ahead in my job, not to win a prize. If being a top performer helps me get promoted, it's a means to an end."**
> —Sara Navarro, *Senior Sales Representative, United Services Automobile Association*

———

Advanced Micro Devices, a manufacturer and marketer of complex monolithic circuits in Sunnyvale, CA, launched an "American Dream" sales campaign as an incentive for reaching

$200 million in sales. The reward was nothing less than a house. Every employee's name went into a hat for a drawing in case the goal was reached. Jerry Sanders, president and founder, had local reporters accompany him on his unannounced visit to the home of the winner, Jocelyn Lleno, an AMD factory line worker. Lleno was handed a check for $1,000 and was to receive the same amount every month for the next 20 years to buy her house. Two other employees received Cadillac Sevilles.

A spectacular method for recognizing and motivating outstanding employees was created for Pitney Bowes, based in Stamford, CT, by Multi Image Productions, Inc., of San Diego, which produces shows incorporating slides, film, video, music, dancing, and spectacular lighting displays. Pitney Bowes's top sales producers were recognized during the show, produced and staged in Kona, Hawaii. "Our goal was to give them a type of business theater in which they would feel entertained as well as motivated to reach their goals for next year," said Multi Image Productions president and CEO Fredric W. Ashman. Budgets for these productions range from $10,000 to $1.5 million.

> - Host Employee of the Month awards for highest productivity, quality, or sales; most improvement; least absenteeism; or whatever you designate as most important. Display a photo of the employee in a prominent place, and honor him or her throughout the month at a series of lunches or other events.

M ary Kay, Inc., awards pink Cadillacs, mink coats, and diamond rings to leading independent sellers.

The life insurance industry uses an elite club, the Million Dollar Roundtable, to recognize and give status and special privileges to top salespeople.

———

When Levi Strauss & Co., headquartered in San Francisco, reached $1 billion in sales, its executives gave out more than $2 million in stock and cash to employees as rewards. When it passed the $2 billion level in 1979, employees once again received significant cash awards.

———

Paychex payroll services company in Rochester, NY, awarded gold rings to sales reps when they signed a career total of 300 new clients. The reps received a diamond for the ring at 500 clients and won additional diamonds after 1,000 and 2,000 clients. Gene Polisseni, vice president for marketing at the time, said the program rewarded those who may not have won annual sales contests but who consistently performed well.

———

If an operator of Chick-fil-A, the Atlanta-based restaurant chain, increases sales by 40 percent over the previous year's sales, he or she earns the right to drive a Lincoln Continental for one year. If the increase is repeated the following year, the operator gets the car for good. More than 100 operators have won Lincoln Continentals.

———

> **"Travel to exotic and/or foreign destinations is the single most sought-after prize by my sales force of 60. It gives them an escape from their normally hectic schedule and seems to make them feel that the effort they spent to get there was all worthwhile."**
> —John Franz, *President, Brasseler USA, Inc.*

Security systems manufacturer Checkpoint Systems in Thorofare, NJ, names its top eight salespeople to its President's Club. Club members act as an advisory council to the company's top executives and get a five-day group trip to such places as Bermuda and Acapulco.

———

Professional Salon Concepts, which sells hair care products and services in Joliet, IL, awards $200 gift certificates from Nordstrom to the two sellers who "touched the biggest number of current and prospective clients" in a month. That includes customer classes, cold calls, appointments, and visits.

———

IBM gets employees to help generate demand for new products by awarding medals for sales leads. Any employee who steers 15 potential customers to an IBM dealership for a demonstration of a new operating system software wins a bronze medal; additional leads earn silver and gold medals.

———

Chuck Piola, executive vice president of sales at NCO Financial Systems in Horsham, PA, tells how he started a new reward at his company for junior salespeople. "This guy was a year out of college, and one month he finally broke through— so I took him out and bought him a new suit." Piola also lent salespeople his Mercedes for a weekend so they could see how it felt to be a top salesperson at NCO.

———

Rexair in Troy, MI, offered running suits with the company logo to domestic distributors and salespeople who gave a predetermined number of in-home demonstrations of the company's cleaning system over a two-week period.

ACCO Brands, Inc., a Lincolnshire, IL, manufacturer of office products and supplies, recognizes outstanding salespeople through the President's Inner Circle, which is open to anyone who has completed one year in a commercial territory as a full-time direct company employee and reached a minimum dollar increase of 15 percent based on commissionable sales figures for the given fiscal year. The reward is a diamond-studded Inner Circle ring.

The Boise Office Products Division of Office World, Inc., headquartered in Boise, ID, annually recognizes its top 30 sales representatives with a sales executive's ring and a two-night, three-day, all-expense-paid trip to a meeting in a resort area. Recent meetings have been held in Palm Springs, San Antonio, Orlando, and New Orleans.

During a recent cross-selling promotion at United Commercial Bank in San Francisco, customer service and customer relations representatives were given "Hula Bucks" for every $100 in traveler's checks they cross-sold. At the end of the promotion a rally and auction were held so they could bid on prizes, including a trip to Hawaii.

> **"People work for the money, but go the extra mile for recognition, praise, and rewards."**
> —Stuart Levine, *CEO, Dale Carnegie and Associates*

The sales incentive program at The United Insurance Company of America, now known as Unitrin, Inc., provides a management-by-objectives guide, says Richard L. Lauderdale, director of marketing sales support for the Chicago-based firm. "Every salesperson, no matter what level of performance, can select a goal to strive for within the program. The single greatest result of the program is the growth of the people who strive to achieve it."

———

At Nelson Motivation, Inc., one sales consultant was 187 percent to goal in just seven months. I noticed that he often played with little sports cars when he was on the phone. So one day I called him and said, "Write down this phone number—I just rented you a Porsche Boxer for a week." Initially, the sales consultant replied, "Oh, Bob, that's very nice. You don't need to do that." But within 20 minutes he called back and almost screamed, "This is the nicest thing anybody has ever done for me in my entire life!" Coworkers took a photo of him in the car, which he ended up using as a screensaver for his computer monitor. On another occasion, I bought this same consultant a suit to thank him for exceeding his goals.

———

Group RCI, based in Parsippany, NJ, annually stages the RCI 500, a mock Indy 500 race in which agents compete to confirm as many time-share exchanges, subscription renewals to the company's magazine, and space reservation services as possible. With each transaction, the representatives' paper race cars are pushed up a certain number of spaces on an oval track drawn on a bedsheet tacked to a wall. Representatives dress as race car drivers, officials, or fans, and the office is decorated with streamers and checkered flags. The top producer is recognized, as are the highest-finishing Rookie of the Year, the Most Improved Driver, and the three Best-Dressed Drivers.

———

Xerox Corporation, headquartered in Norwalk, CT, used a sports car theme for its Fast Track sales motivation program, which also involved technical support employees and their managers. Everyone accrued points that were redeemable for either merchandise or cash rewards ranging from $10 to $10,000. Also distributed were battery-powered toy Ferraris and spark plugs "to spark new ideas."

> **"Keep the right goal in mind: don't look for money, look for applause. If you create something of value the sales will come."**
> —Robert Ronstadt, *CEO, Lord Publishing, Inc.*

———

Pentel of America in Torrance, CA, uses the Samurai Award to motivate salespeople to (1) increase sales over the previous year, (2) perform a certain amount of "end-user work" (contact and sales with the final user of the company's pens), and (3) submit sales and marketing reports (SAMs) on new techniques for promoting the company's products. Samurai winners receive a cash award, a Sales Master ring, a genuine Samurai sword, and a weeklong first-class trip for two to Japan, which includes a tour of the Pentel factory, as well as a ceremonial luncheon with several Japanese managers. The regional sales manager whose territory performs best in all three areas also wins a cash award, ring, and trip to Japan.

———

At KXKT-FM, a Top 40 station in Omaha, NE, cash, merchandise, and travel are offered to sales employees. Says Cathy Roach, general sales manager, "We've also done fun things, like have a wheel with cash ranging from ten dollars to one thousand dollars. For every piece of new business they bring in, they spin the wheel and win something. We've also blown up balloons containing cash and had people throw darts at them."

A Case Study in Sales Recognition

The "FasTrack" program at Morris Savings Bank (now a part of Wachovia Bank/Wells Fargo, headquartered in San Francisco) rewarded workers for landing new business, as well as for cross-selling to new and existing customers. Each salesperson had a quarterly quota of 45 cross-sale points, earning a point for each additional service they sold to a customer. Tellers had a quarterly quota of 15 referrals; when customers agreed to one of their suggestions, the tellers sent them over to the sales desk with a referral card. Each salesperson also got a $2 commission for every cross sale, and each teller got $2 per referral. A sales coordinator tracked each person's progress on a poster in the lunchroom.

Other awards were given out at quarterly meetings. The top salesperson of the quarter and the teller with the highest number of referrals each got $300, an extra vacation day, and an engraved pewter mug. The manager of the branch with the highest deposit level got a trophy and an engraved Cross pen, and that branch was treated to a party by the sales department.

Branch managers were eligible for bonuses as well. If 90 percent of the staff met the quota, the managers got the same bonus as the employees. They got double that amount if all the employees attained the quota and if the branch was awarded a certain number of "mystery shopper" points from the mystery shoppers who visited each branch at least once every quarter.

In the Gold Coin Club, employees were given 10 gold coins when they met their individual quarterly quotas; the top salesperson in each branch got an additional 5 coins; everyone got five coins if the entire branch met the quota, 24 coins for reaching the quota in all 4 quarters, and 3 coins for having a sales tip published in the newsletter. Coins were displayed on the salesperson's desk in a clear acrylic box with his or her name on it. At an awards banquet, employees used their coins to bid on prizes—including televisions and a trip to the Bahamas. The banquet featured an awards ceremony modeled after the Oscars. Award categories included Salesperson, Teller, and Branch Manager of the Year. Winners received SARAs (Sales and Recognition Awards), which are statuettes of *Winged Victory.*

One employee who has twice been a top teller says the program helped her. "I pay more attention to customers, and I try to offer more service, which can be more important than the product," says June Barbee, head teller at the Mendham Village branch. "And when I won the top teller award, that was really motivating."

———

The Miami Lakes, FL, cosmetics company Elizabeth Arden implemented a sales program in which staffers who increased their sales by at least 25 percent over those of the same five-month period in the previous year earned a weeklong Caribbean cruise for two. Besides increasing sales, the program reduced turnover. Cynthia Bloom, resident makeup artist at Bloomingdale's in New York City, says, "I've been offered jobs for more money with other companies, but I didn't take them. I'm loyal to this company—Arden's been good to me, so I'm good to them."

Customer Service

I t is said that it costs five times more to win a new customer than to keep an existing one. So satisfying customers is a goal most companies want to constantly recognize and reinforce. Here are some great reinforcers that companies have used to foster exceptional customer service.

> **"Our clients are the reason for our existence as a company, but to serve our clients best, we have to put our people first. People are a company's one true competitive measure."** —Hal Rosenbluth, *Former CEO, Rosenbluth International*

C IGNA, the global health services company headquartered in Philadelphia, PA, gives a life-saving ring called "Man Overboard" to employees who "go over and beyond" in serving customers.

O ne year, at the Buena Park, CA, Knott's Berry Farm, COO Jack Falfas challenged the employees who play "monsters," the ride operators, and the maze crews to improve their customer service during its annual Haunt. The teams that provided the best customer service would earn points for nightly recognition and get a chance to have their names engraved on the Golden Haunt trophies. Each night of the Haunt, Falfas and a crew of score-card-toting judges walked through the streets, mazes, and rides, looking for energy, creativity, and outstanding overall delivery in entertaining customers. Falfas said the incentives worked well. When he walked through the park late at night, employees would look for him and ask, "How'd I do? How was I tonight?"

At Indianapolis-based Mike's Carwash, with 37 locations in Indiana and Ohio, frontline workers earn points for providing strong customer service, and staffers at each location can be named "associate of the month" and win prizes of $25 or $50.

———

Starwood Hotels & Resorts Canada, which owns, operates, or franchises more than 50 hotels across the country, knows that people stay at their hotels because of the quality of service provided by their employees. Starwood offers both informal and formal praise and rewards. They ensure that staff cafeterias, change rooms, and prayer rooms are comfortable, and managers are encouraged to publicly laud staff for excellence just about every day, if they deserve it. Starwood has seen measurable improvements in guest satisfaction since implementing new service training initiatives. They have an annual employee turnover rate of only about 14 percent—one third the industry average.

> **"You have to treat your employees like your customers. When you treat them right, they will treat your outside customers right."**—Herb Kelleher, *Chairman, Southwest Airlines*

HOLD A SERVICE LOTTERY

- Award a silver pin or similar prize for positive customer comments.
- Whenever a service employee receives a letter of praise from a customer, enter his or her name in a weekly drawing. Offer a fun prize.

Ron Smith, now at the City of Sacramento Department of Public Works, says that years ago, when he owned a deli, he would ask all the servers to greet each customer as if that person were a favorite aunt or uncle. He promised that if they did, he would make up the difference if they received less than $75 per day in tips. He only had to do so once in ten years.

———

Several guests at the Walt Disney World Dolphin Hotel in Orlando, FL, were so impressed with one of their servers that when they returned to the hospital where they worked in Indiana, they named the "Jason Chestnut Customer Service Award" after him to recognize superior customer service in their own organization.

———

At Busch Gardens, Tampa, FL, employees who offer exceptional service to guests receive a scratch-off card. These cards are issued on the spot by the management staff and can be redeemed for a variety of rewards.

———

> **"Once people trust management, know they're responsible, and are given the training, it's astonishing what they can do for customers and ultimately for the stakeholders."**
> —James Henderson, *CEO, Cummins Engine Company, Inc.*

One manager of a cable installation company in North Carolina holds a weekly lottery for installers who were praised in customer letters. The winner gets to grab as many quarters as possible out of a fishbowl, with the average grab being about $30.

———

When John Kapp was general manager and president of an Atlanta, GA, Del Taco fast-food restaurant, he wanted to improve service by focusing on positive stories about customer service. So he asked his seven regional managers, and received 12. He then wrote a note to each employee praised in the stories. These stories were photocopied and put in the break areas in every store. One month later, he asked his managers for stories again, and this time, he received 65; the following month produced even more. By the fourth month, the group produced 125 pages of stories, and copies were distributed to all the stores— each with a note of thanks from John. Not only did good service skyrocket, but turnover of managers and assistant managers improved by more than 300 percent!

> **"The highest achievable level of service comes from the heart, so the company that reaches its people's hearts will provide the very best service."**
> —Hal Rosenbluth, *Former CEO, Rosenbluth International*

Doug Barnett, manager at Chick-fil-A in Perry, GA, runs a DOTS program (Delivering Outrageous and Tremendous Service). Team members accumulate dots on index cards for excellent performance in areas such as high check average and low deletions. The dots can be cashed in for meals or merchandise from local businesses.

The Eagle Award is used at SKF USA Inc., in Kulpsville, PA. Each employee of the industrial and automotive engineering firm is given two Eagle Award coins to give to other employees for outstanding customer service, along with a certificate briefly describing the service. Employees who receive five or more Eagle Awards are given a decorative display holder. Ten Eagle Awards can be exchanged for a $50 American Express Be My Guest certificate. The employee who receives the most Eagle

Awards in a six-month period is recognized with a trophy and a $250 American Express gift certificate at the president's semiannual State of the Company meeting. Jeff Minkoff, corporate quality assurance manager, reports that more than 1,500 Eagle Awards were given out in the first one and a half years of the program alone.

―――

Every year, the Robert W. Baird financial management firm celebrates Client Service Week to demonstrate its "clients come first" principle. Baird president and CEO Paul Purcell and managers at all levels work on the front lines as help-desk representatives, receptionists, client services representatives, mail and office services staff, and graphic designers in order to interact with clients. Baird also gives the G. Frederick Kasten Jr. Award, named after its chairman, to associates who provide outstanding service to their clients and continually strive to improve customer service. A winner is selected from each business unit, based on nominations by fellow associates, and awards are presented at the Annual Meeting for All Associates. Each winner receives a one-week, all-expenses-paid vacation anywhere in the United States.

―――

Employees can give one another "PEOPLE" awards at Parkview Health, a hospital system in Indiana, for providing exceptional customer service. PEOPLE stands for *P*atients and families; *E*mployees, physicians, and volunteers; *O*ur communities; *P*artnerships; *L*eadership; and *E*mpowerment. Anyone, whether inside or outside the organization, can nominate employees for awards. One copy of the small piece of paper is presented to the awardee, one to his or her manager, and one is sent to the PEOPLE Award department in HR. Accumulated awards can be traded for merchandise: 5 awards = a sticker for name badges, 10 awards = an umbrella, 25 awards = a duffel bag or blanket, 50 awards = a windbreaker or sweater, and 100 awards = a jacket. Yet another award is presented for every 50 awards accumulated beyond 100.

Doug Barnett of the Sam Nunn Boulevard Chick-fil-A in Perry, GA, gives POSSE (Positively Outrageous Service) buttons to team members when they receive positive customer comments on feedback cards. They're encouraged to wear them at all times and to uphold high standards, as members of an elite group.

> **"It's vital that you motivate your people—customers and employees— anyone who can contribute to the company's success."**—Robert Evans, *Director, Promotional Services, Gillette Company*

Donna Friedman, an employee at a Home Depot in Ft. Lauderdale, FL, received special recognition for returning a $3,000 bracelet to a customer. The customer gave her a pure silver bracelet, and the company gave her a special letter of praise for her personnel file and a watch of her choice.

Pioneer Eclipse, a manufacturer of floor-care machines based in Sparta, NC, takes customers to meet line workers who have worked on their products. Employees love to tell customers about their ideas and to listen to their suggestions.

Broward County Government in Ft. Lauderdale, FL, has a program called SUNsational Service to promote the way internal and external customers should be treated. Employees are nominated for embodying the organization's 10 Standards of Customer Service Excellence. Winners are chosen bimonthly by a group of employees called the "Prize Patrol," with music, dancing, and fanfare. Each recipient gets a basket containing a variety of prizes from the county store. The organization also hosts a customer service week, including an energy profile seminar, a customer service movie day, stress massages, and fun contests, such as an ugly tie contest, customer service *Jeopardy*, customer service quizzes, and word search puzzles.

Rhonda Lowe, publisher of the *Los Banos Enterprise* newspaper, found a way to thank loyal advertisers by creating "Thanks A Million" bouquets. Using a computer program that makes currency, she designed some $1 million bills. She then wrapped them around 25-cent suckers to look like petals on a flower. She bought some inexpensive potted plants and inserted the "flowers" into the potted plant, then added a bow and a sign that read "Thanks A Million For Being Our Customer." Sales representatives signed their names and personally delivered the awards to their top

- Create a Praising Board—a white board (or flip chart) where you post letters of appreciation from customers.
- When paychecks go out, write a note on the envelope recognizing an employee's accomplishment.
- Write five or more Post-it notes thanking the person for superior customer service and hide them amid the work on his or her desk.

accounts. It gave them the chance to be real heroes and to create a buzz—and clients prominently displayed the awards.

———

At Stew Leonard's, whenever a cashier thanks a customer by name, the customer drops a coupon with the cashier's name into a big box. Known as "The Name Game," the three cashiers who have thanked the most customers each week get $30 each. Employees also display "Ladder of Success" charts, mounted at cash registers, for customers to see each employee's progress. At Hecht's department stores, based in Arlington, VA, employees win points toward a shopping spree if managers hear them calling customers by name.

———

In "Today's Way Giveaway" at Dallas, TX–based Today's Office Professionals, every time a temporary employee exceeds a client's expectations, he or she is entered in an annual drawing for prizes. Clients rate them on evaluation cards, which are then submitted to the company. Approximately 950 prizes have been awarded over three years.

———

McDonald's owner/operators are given jewelry bearing the company's Golden Arches logo to distribute to employees who provide superior service.

———

CUSTOMER SERVICE TIPS

➡ "Quarter Grab"— fill a fishbowl with quarters and let honorees reach in and grab as many quarters as they can hold in a handful.

➡ Take photo of employee with customer.

➡ Give five minutes of free time or a candy bar if an employee uses a customer's name during interaction.

➡ Send honoree to visit a customer site.

Every month at the Nordstrom department store chain, based in Seattle, every store manager meets to pick a Customer Service All-Star—the person who has made the most striking contribution for that period. Managers draw from their own observations, customer comment sheets placed near every cash register, reports by "mystery shoppers," and letters from customers. The winner gets $100, "Customer Service All-Star" stamped on his or her business card, and a larger employee discount on store merchandise. A Customer Service All-Star store is also picked each month, with headquarters providing money for a storewide barbecue or pizza party.

> **"We will move mountains to let our employees and customers know we care. I've traveled 4,000 miles to spend five minutes with a customer, to let her know how important her business is to us. Caring is contagious, and we try to spread it around."** —Harvey MacKay, *President, Mackay Envelope Corp.*

The Omni Service Champions program of Omni Hotels recognizes employees who go out of their way to deliver extraordinary service with medals, ribbon pins for their uniforms, cash, dinner, recognition in the company's newspaper and on posters in each hotel, and, finally, a three-day celebration at an Omni hotel chosen by company executives. At the end of the year, the three employees from each hotel who receive the most commendations are awarded medals (gold, silver, and bronze) and cash ($1,000 for gold and $500 each for silver and bronze), and all attend a gala.

In New Jersey Transit's Customer Service Awards program, employees who serve the public directly earn awards for exemplary customer service, while internal workers, such as secretaries, maintenance people, and accountants, receive awards for service to other employees. Two months before the awards are announced at the end of each year, posters with ballots are placed in train stations and at bus stops. Both riders and employees can make nominations for the awards, as can vendors who sell supplies to the agency.

In a recent year, the agency received 300 nominations and chose 10 winners. The number of ballots a person receives is taken into account, but the quality of the nomination is more important. "If we have one nomination for a person, but it's outstanding, that person might win." A nominating committee made up of managers selects the winners. Among the criteria are exceptional customer service, especially to correct something that has gone wrong; demonstrated creativity or resourcefulness in assisting a customer; and development of new ways to solve problems.

The type of award varies each year. Past winners received savings bonds and a two-day trip to Atlantic City, and each recipient gets a plaque or trophy. Awards are given out at an annual companywide meeting held at a conference center.

The Good Samaritan Hospital in Cincinnati, OH, instituted a recognition and reward program to improve customer service that incorporates monthly drawings and internal publicity, but also uses continuing training to reinforce a list of ten performance standards on which the program is based. To make sure goals, criteria, and progress are being communicated constantly, all 3,200 employees attend a one-hour training session every other month.

> **"Our business is about technology, yes. But it's also about operations and customer relationships."**
> —Michael Dell,
> *President and Founder,*
> *Dell Computers*

Delta Air Lines has a "Feather in Your Cap Award" for customer service above and beyond the call of duty, such as that provided by the flight attendant who drove a passenger from Houston to Beaumont, TX, for a funeral she would otherwise have been unable to attend because she missed her connecting flight.

———

At The Andersons retail stores in Maumee, OH, store managers were given a certain number of silver dollars to give out when they observed or received comments about good customer service. Employees who received silver dollars were enrolled in the Silver Dollar Club and became eligible for monthly prize drawings.

———

> **"From the beginning I was empowered to take responsibility to deal with clients directly. It adds a lot of satisfaction to the job and, compared to what my peers tell me about their work, this is an oasis."**
> —Ian Harris, *Actuarial Consultant, Hewitt Associates*

At FMC Lithium in Charlotte, NC, managers take deserving employees on trips to visit customers or vendors. This not only recognizes operators for their efforts, but also educates them and builds a sense of ownership of their work and the company's products. The additional cost is more than repaid in increased motivation and overall business understanding.

———

LensCrafters optical stores, headquartered in Mason, OH, granted $100 bonus checks for outstanding customer service, with the top nine people getting $1,000 and a crystal memento.

———

American Airlines gives "You're Someone Special" notes to its top frequent fliers to give to American employees when they receive exceptional service. The employees receive credit toward their own travel, and customer comments are printed in the company newsletter. Continental Airlines mailed "Pride in Performance" certificates to its top 50,000 frequent fliers and asked them to pass them out to particularly helpful employees. Continental workers could redeem the certificates for dinners, luggage, hotel stays, flight passes, and other merchandise.

> **"We lead by being human. We do not lead by being corporate, professional or institutional."**
> —Paul Hawken,
> *Founder, Smith & Hawken*

For its Service Excellence Award, Citibank in New York City rewards employees at all levels, except senior management, who demonstrate outstanding customer service. An employee is nominated by his or her manager, then reviewed by management within the employee's division. Award winners usually get a gift certificate for up to $500 in merchandise.

The Service Leader Award program at the American Hospital Association in Chicago offers winners a $100 check, a certificate, and an engraved plaque at the monthly managers' meeting. A Service Leader of the Year is selected from the 12 monthly leaders. That person receives a $100 check and an engraved plaque.

In the Most Valuable Player program at Busch Stadium in St. Louis, MO, ten randomly selected fans are given two small

MVP cards, which they can give any two employees who show them some courtesy—defined as "a smile, a welcome, a way of handling a question or problem," says Vicki Hutchison, manager of special projects for the Civic Center Corporation. Employees then turn over the cards to supervisors; if the group of workers collects at least 15 of the 20 cards during the game, a drawing is held and the winner gets a $100 bill.

A monthly Outstanding Teamworker program encourages workers to nominate fellow All-Stars, who receive recognition in the form of a pregame, on-the-field ceremony; a lapel pin; their choice of merchandise from a catalog; and brunch in their honor.

———

At Park Lane Hotels International, based in Hong Kong, guests were asked to nominate hotel workers who provided outstanding service. The company rewarded all nominees with Sony personal electronics and held a grand-prize drawing for a TV; the guest who nominated the grand-prize winner received two free nights at the hotel.

———

MCI in Ashburn, VA, now a part of New York–based Verizon Communications, used picnic baskets from Harry and David in Medford, OR, to reward 50 of its customer service reps. "MCI wanted to recognize employees who saw a problem and stepped right in to solve it," says Jon Silver, a sales rep for Harry and David. A note of appreciation was tucked inside each basket.

———

Cellular One based in Bellevue, WA, has a bonus plan that awards employees $10 for every customer compliment they get (mostly on customer comments cards), and deducts $10 every time a customer complains about service. Customer compliments have tripled since the company began the reward program.

The San Diego Convention and Visitors Bureau awards the title "Cab Driver of the Year" to the driver who exemplifies outstanding hospitality. The winner is feted at the city's Annual Cab Driver Appreciation Day, and receives 500 business cards, an engraved dashboard plaque, and a magnetic sign for the cab that announces the award. One winner, Montag Plank, says he provides riders with extras, such as newspapers and information about local attractions. "No matter what your job is, if you're courteous and do the job right, people will respect you for it," he says.

> **"The deepest principle in human nature is the craving to be appreciated."**
> —William James,
> *Philosopher and Psychologist*

When Dick Radell, vice president of Human Resources for The Marcus Corporation in Milwaukee, receives exceptional service at one of the company's restaurants, he writes a short note on the back of his business card and gives it to the server immediately.

A Case Study in Customer Service

"We shared the dream to be recognized as the very best company when it came to delivering value to customers, employees, shareholders, and communities," says Kent B. Foster, former president of GTE Telephone Operations (now owned by New York–based Verizon Communications). To help reach that dream, the President's Quality Awards program recognizes employees in four categories: area and region, individual employees, teams, and vendors.

The company's 4 areas and 14 regions compete each year for Quality Champion Cups. Award recipients are selected directly by customers who are surveyed annually. The most improved region is also recognized with a trophy.

Individual employees are rewarded at three levels of achievement: The top ten employees receive $2,500 along with a personalized award and a letter of commendation from the division president. The 30 finalists receive $750 and a personalized award, and the 40 semifinalists receive $500 and a personalized award. One individual who has demonstrated exemplary commitment to quality is chosen for the Individual Quality Champions to receive the President's Distinctive Commendation. He or she receives a monetary award, a special medallion, and a letter of commendation from the president.

Team awards are given to two first-place Gold Award winners (one for external and one for internal customer service), two second-place Silver Award winners, and three Bronze Award winners for external efforts. Members of each team receive cash, a personalized award, and a letter of commendation from the president.

Employee Suggestions

Only 41 percent of employees believe the average company listens to their ideas. No wonder, then, that the average American worker makes 1.1 suggestions per year—one of the lowest among industrialized nations. Compare that with the 167 suggestions per employee in Japan, and you can see the untapped potential.

> **"We have to get everybody in the organization involved. If you do that right, the best ideas will rise to the top."**
> —Jack Welch, *Former Chairman, General Electric*

Bruce Power, based in Tiverton, Ontario, Canada, uses an innovation program where its employees get points for giving and championing ideas. They have identified $5 million in cost-saving ideas and are implementing ideas that save an additional $2 million.

———

Newell Rubbermaid, Inc., the organizing products giant based in Atlanta, GA, sends its employees to unique places, such as museums, hoping it will inspire them to come up with new product ideas. Similarly, Olin Corporation, the Clayton, MO, ammunitions and chemicals manufacturer, recruits and trains employees to become "idea scouts."

———

When Andrew Schuman bought Denver, CO–based Hammond's Candies in 2007, the company was operating in the red. Mr. Schuman soon learned that an assembly-line worker, rather than an executive, had designed

> **"An idea is a fragile thing. Turning it off is much easier than keeping it lit. Ideas shine because somebody had them and somebody helped them and nobody turned them off. Companies have to reward people for being creative, for coming up with new ideas."** —Tom Peters, *Author and Management Consultant*

445

the company's popular ribbon snowflake candy. "I thought, 'Wow, we have a lot of smart people back here, and we're not tapping their knowledge,'" said Schuman. He consequently offered a $50 bonus to assembly-line workers who came up with successful ideas to cut manufacturing costs. One worker suggested a minor change in a machine gear, which resulted in reducing the number of workers needed on an assembly line. Another employee devised a way to protect candy canes while en route to stores, resulting in a 4 percent reduction in breakage and helping the company to earn a profit that year.

———

Advanced Technology Institute, a private R&D management nonprofit based in North Charleston, SC, offers $500 bonuses to employees who refer people who are hired and stay at least six months. The bonus increased the number of referrals, including referrals of several employees' family members. Nearly 60 percent of all jobs are filled internally.

> **"Companies don't need management stars or heroes to thrive. What they absolutely do need is an effective system for getting and implementing ideas from the people who do the work."**
> —Martin Edelston,
> *CEO, Boardroom, Inc.*

———

Akron (OH) Children's Hospital uses Lean Six Sigma quality methods to engage and empower employees to maintain a culture of continuous improvement. To gain support the executive team created the Center for Operations Excellence, a system that allows employees to share ideas and get the resources to turn ideas into reality. Success stories are shared and celebrated during departmental meetings. One outstanding result: The waiting list for MRIs at the hospital was dramatically reduced. Through discussion with department employees and redistribution of the workload, the hospital was able to drop the wait time to three days or less.

———

Radio Shack, based in Fort Worth, TX, uses a four-foot stuffed gorilla to recognize initiative and innovation. The gorilla is given in turn to each employee with a useful idea. The person who has the most ideas in a given quarter receives yet another prize.

———

During a downturn in business, Rosenbluth International, a corporate travel agency in Philadelphia, PA, and now a part of New York–based American Express Travel Related Services, ran a program called "Operation Brainstorm," asking employees to think of ideas to cut costs. More than 400 were submitted, and the company was able to avoid laying off employees.

———

When Vic Anapolle was operations manager for a chemical specialties group at W. R. Grace & Company in Atlanta, GA, he set out to motivate employees to increase the number and quality of their suggestions: using "Starperks" scratch-off lottery tickets, he was able to obtain an average of 12 to 14 suggestions per employee, leading to cost savings of $175,000 per year. Each lottery ticket gave employees the chance to win various prizes and all tickets (winners' and losers') were used for an overall drawing for a trip.

———

SUGGESTION TIPS

➜ Pay employees 10 percent of any money saved based on their ideas.

➜ Publicly post the Best Suggestion of the Week (include suggester's name).

➜ Publish (hardcopy and/or online) every suggestion that was implemented, who submitted it, along with the result.

➜ Reply to every employee suggestion within a day of submission.

➜ Have CEO personally respond to employee suggestions.

The SCOOTER Store crowns employees "Superheroes" if they "come to the rescue" with revenue-generating ideas or implement cost-cutting programs and procedures. They are donned with red tablecloths closely resembling superhero capes.

———

Each year at FedEx Office and Print Services, the employee who submits the best suggestion wins an all-expense-paid trip to Disney World for his or her entire store. While they're away, top brass fill in.

———

Peavey Electronics Corporation in Meridian, MS, rewards hourly workers for their suggestions by paying them 8 percent of estimated first-year savings based on those suggestions.

———

The Office of Human Resources and Administration at the U.S. Department of Energy in Washington, DC, sponsored an "Ideas Day" for employees to think of ways to improve the way they worked. They collected 2,134 ideas, 68 percent of which were implemented.

———

At Kodak's Image Loops and Sundries Department in Rochester, NY, production is shut down when operators reach their weekly goals for each type of loop, so that they can work on other projects. Employees have used the extra time to develop ideas, which has resulted in improvements and great camaraderie.

———

INCREASING EMPLOYEE SUGGESTIONS

- For most people, simply using their suggestion is recognition enough.
- When an employee presents an idea or suggestion, thank the person for his or her concern and initiative.
- Make sure you respond to and actually try to use as many suggestions as possible.
- Widely publicize suggestions used, along with a description of their positive impact on the organization.

Arthur Hogling, executive director of the Developmental Disabilities Resource Center in Lakewood, CO, reports: "Employees who aggressively cut costs receive baseballs, signed by our management team, at monthly meetings. They have become a source of pride on people's desks."

———

A Deere & Company office in Dubuque, IA, doubled employee participation in an employee suggestion program by providing all participants with pocket protectors, magnetic calendars, and notepads with the slogan "Got an idea? Write it down!" Employees whose suggestions were implemented received awards.

———

Urban Bianchi, a machinist with Cleveland, OH–based Parker Hannifin Corporation, has turned in more than 800 cost-cutting proposals that his bosses have approved—so many that the *Los Angeles Times* has dubbed him "the undisputed king of the suggestion box." The company has rewarded him with a flood of appliances, coupons for free dinners, tools, and other gifts, with an estimated value of $17,000 in a four-year period.

"I've got so much stuff, it's unbelievable," Bianchi says. While he adds that for him doing a job well is what's motivating, he also admits that he gets a kick out of sharing his riches with family members. "When I gave them radios, they loved it," he says. "It meant more to them that I got a radio doing a good job, working hard, than if I'd bought it at a store."

> **"If workers cannot inform managers— and managers cannot learn and respond— workers' insights have no credibility, and the notion of their partnerships with management becomes empty verbiage."**
> —Dr. Mitchell Rabkin, *President, Beth Israel Hospital*

Ice-cream maker Ben & Jerry's distributes grants to departments at corporate headquarters if they come up with creative suggestions. They can use them to purchase merchandise such as popcorn makers or hot chocolate machines.

At Stew Leonard's, a suggestion program rewards employee ideas with retail gift certificates worth up to $500. The company's bimonthly newspaper reports on the ideas that are adopted.

Two county employees in San Diego have been awarded $10,000 each for suggestions that saved the county government more than $1.1 million. Ken Buccellato and Renee Sherrill received the bonuses through the Do-It-Better-By-Suggestion Program, which rewards employees for ideas that save money, improve safety, or increase efficiency.

In San Diego, 71 county employees came up with ideas that generated nearly $400,000 in savings. They were honored at a

year-end ceremony and received cash awards ranging from
$25 to nearly $5,000.

———

In three months, the American Achievers program at American
Airlines inspired nearly 3,500 seven-person teams to come
up with more than 1,600 ideas that were adopted, resulting in
more than $20 million in cost-saving or revenue-generating
improvements. Employees reaped $4.7 million
in merchandise prizes, each prize based on
the cash value of the idea implemented. More
important, employees wholeheartedly supported
the changes because they had designed them.
That success has led to a continuing system
called AAchievers that includes instant points-
for-merchandise rewards for good work by
individuals and groups.

The focus of the AAchievers program has
since expanded to recognize employees for
doing anything special, or for consistently
doing a good job. Managers, crew chiefs,
lead agents, and other supervisors can award
AAchiever points at any time to any employee.
For example, points can be awarded for
perfect attendance throughout a bad winter
or to a worker who helps a passenger with
an emergency. They are issued on certificates
that can be cashed in for travel benefits or
merchandise from a catalog compiled for the program.

———

SUGGESTION TIPS

➡ Over lunch, hold a
brainstorming session
for solving the company's
most intriguing
problems.

➡ Ask each of your
employees to turn in one
idea every two weeks.

➡ Give an "Innovation"
or "Bright Idea"
(flashlight) award.

➡ Encourage employees
to develop/present
ideas to management
team or CEO.

➡ Teach employees
how to develop ideas
and make powerful
presentations.

"Everyone Counts" is a program at toolmaker Black & Decker, headquartered in Towson, MD, that uses teams to brainstorm and develop ideas about training, communication, administration, and rewards. People from different departments are grouped into 39 teams, and 2 evaluation committees for managerial personnel receive ideas and judge their merit. The evaluation teams also note leadership potential in some employees when they make their presentations. A total of 200 ideas have been submitted and 59 approved, one of which was worth $700,000 in cost savings. The 12 ideas that have already been implemented deal mostly with improved operations that result in cost savings. The $700,000 idea concerned the substitution of a new material in one of the company's product lines. The program has also improved the company's vertical lines of communication.

_____

"Managers should realize the importance of each suggestion. Try to find what it is in each suggestion that has worth. Each suggestion and the reaction to each suggestion can build trust." —Shoichiro Toyoda, *President, Toyota Motor Co.*

The pharmaceuticals company Cyanamid Canada, now a part of Cargill, based in Winnipeg, Manitoba, has a "Key to Innovation" campaign that encourages workers to contribute ideas and become "Frequent Innovators." For productivity-enhancing ideas, employees receive 40 to 1,000 points, redeemable in an awards catalog for such prizes as glassware, radios, televisions, and weekend trips for two.

_____

Fel-Pro, a gasket manufacturer based in Southfield, MI, holds a $1,000 drawing once a year for all employees who participated in the firm's suggestion program.

A Case Study in Recognizing Employee Suggestions

IBM's suggestion program awards $50 to $150,000 for money-saving ideas or suggestions with benefits like enhanced health, safety, or customer service. The amount of the reward for an idea that leads to measurable savings is based on 25 percent of the first year's net material and labor savings. For awards of more than $200, the suggester also receives 25 percent of projected net savings for the second year, up to $150,000.

> **"We believe that most people have capabilities beyond those they are called on to demonstrate in their jobs."**—from a statement of philosophy printed by Hewitt Associates

Awards for suggestions that yield intangible benefits depend on such factors as the seriousness of the problem and the creativity and effectiveness of the solution. These awards usually range from $50 to $100, although the $150,000 maximum applies, as well. The program is open to all employees. In a recent year, IBM gave out eight $150,000 rewards, out of 153,000 ideas submitted by its 223,000 U.S. employees. Other programs include:

INVENTION PLAN ACHIEVEMENT AWARD

These awards recognize a significant record of invention. The first patent application the employee files under the provisions of the plan earns $1,500. Employees receive points for patent applications, as well as for other qualifying inventions that are created. At each 12-point plateau, the employee gets a certificate and $3,600. The first plateau also earns jewelry.

IBM DIVISION AWARD PLAN

This award recognizes and rewards achievements that have "outstanding value" to the company in terms of cost savings and the impact on the major mission of a specific division. Awards range from $1,500 to $25,000.

At the 10,000-person Honda of America factory in Marysville, OH, employees receive $100 for each accepted suggestion, but they also get anywhere from 1 to 12 V.I.P. points for each one. If they make a presentation to a quality circle meeting, they get an extra 50 points. When they accumulate 300 points, they get a plaque; 1,000 points nets $800. Higher-level prizes are a Honda Civic for 2,500 points; and an Accord, two extra weeks of vacation, and four weeks' pay for 5,000 points. The company received more than 10,000 suggestions in a recent year, resulting in savings of $5 million.

Productivity & Quality

In America, the current application of rewards to encourage productivity and production is unfortunately underused and ineffective. According to one study, only 40 percent of employees believe the average American company offers meaningful incentives to maximize quality and productivity. In Japan, on the other hand, 93 percent of workers felt certain they would benefit. Let's look at some other discouraging statistics about the American workplace:

- 89 percent of American workers think their companies would perform better if employees were given meaningful incentives to improve quality and productivity.
- 81 percent of workers believe they will not receive rewards for any increase in productivity.
- 60 percent of managers believe their compensation will not increase if their performance improves.

Agencies of QSource, the Memphis-based nonprofit health care management expert, divide the staff into teams to work on different performance outcomes. They have a large racetrack on the wall where each team has a car, which is moved forward as the team makes progress.

———

Pizza-making employees at Oregon-based Flying Pie Pizzeria restaurants can earn two special statuses that reflect how accurately and quickly they make pizzas. The first is "Quality . . . My Friend" Status: for people who successfully make three menu pizzas to specifications, without looking at the scale while making the pizza. A $25 prize and a lapel button are awarded to successful chefs. The second is "Fast . . . at Making Fourteens" Status: for people who can make a combo pizza in less than 60 seconds within weight tolerances. Winners get a $25 prize and a lapel button.

———

In an effort to reduce both turnover and expenses, The Daniels Company, a trucking firm in Springfield, MO, challenged its drivers to cut their fuel costs by improving mileage—then let them keep the difference. Since then, turnover has been cut by 25 percent and trucks are logging fewer miles, thus cutting overall costs.

———

Katzinger's Deli in Columbus, OH, made a deal with their employees that, if they reduced food costs, they would split the savings with employees. Their cost savings was $30,000, of which employees split $15,000.

———

ILove Rewards (ILR), a Toronto, Ontario–based employee recognition company, incentivizes employees to find ways to save money. As an alternative to cutting staff, its most recent program, The Recession Package, helps train employees to negotiate contracts, attain better prices from suppliers, or lower travel and shipping costs. "Every day when I go out and rent a car, order a catered meal for a meeting or travel for business, there's always an opportunity to get a better price," says founder and CEO Razor Suleman. "We help employees to think of it as their own [expense]; teach them how to ask for a better price." Since 2007, ILR has nearly doubled

> **"Those who give and get praise at work have increased productivity."**
> —findings from The Gallup Organization

the number of employees at its headquarters from 18 to 34, and collectively achieved savings of $106,000 in 2008.

———

Kathy Atkinson, a program manager for a nuclear clean-up facility located in Buffalo, NY, created the Bright Ideas Program to meet four improvement goals. It had two parts: (1) generation of new, bonafide original ideas, and (2) implementation of those ideas. For both parts, employees received scratch-off coupons for redeemable points for merchandise in a catalog. They submitted a narrative explaining an idea with an estimated cost, benefit, and savings. All recipients were eligible for a quarterly grand-prize drawing for a cruise. For a cost of $25,000 per year—less than half of what was budgeted—the program saved a documented $2.2 million in "cost avoidance'" over the first 18 months. The program was written up as an innovative best practice by the Department of Energy.

Wachovia's Proof Olympics: A Case Study

Wachovia, the Charlotte, NC–based financial services company recently acquired by Wells Fargo, has gone to Olympian heights to improve its operations. In 2006 Wachovia's Check Services Division led the industry in unit cost efficiency for the third straight year. A big reason for this accomplishment has been an incentive program called the Proof Olympics. Lisa Massiello, a Certified Recognition Professional (CRP) in Operations & Technology who heads up Employee Engagement & Recognition, shares details of what happened:

"For a long time, many people outside of our division thought that their financial centers completely processed all of the work they received. They didn't know that each center

> **"What the American worker is telling us is that the answer to increased productivity and motivation can be found inside their own companies and that meaningful rewards need to be offered to workers at every level in the organization."**
>
> —Patrick Delaney,
> *President, Society of Incentive Travel Executives (SITE)*

dispatches work to one of 15 encoding shops in Payment Services. Encoding not only forms the cornerstone of banking operations but also shapes the foundation of the global financial system," Massiello says. Without encoding, very little within financial services can move. "Yet encoding is still confusing to many employees; we needed to clarify the work and importance of this department to the rest of the enterprise. That's when we came up with the Proof Olympics, which after several years, has grown to become one of the most exciting and anticipated events in all of Item Processing."

The purpose of the Proof Olympics is to provide and support a long-term approach to increase encoder productivity, reward and recognize top encoders, cultivate encoder morale, and foster teamwork and partnerships between sites. During the month of September, each of Wachovia's 15 Encoding shops places its encoders into one of three production categories. September statistics are then evaluated to determine a site's medalists for all categories. A bronze medal gets $25 Top Dollar Award, silver gets $50, and gold $100. They also recognize encoders who increased their productivity the most during the month ($25). In November, the top encoder from each site goes to Atlanta, GA, to compete against their peers in the Proof Olympics. The Proof Olympics bronze medalist receives a $1,000 Star Award, the Silver a $2,000 award, and the Gold gets $3,000 along with the title "Best Wachovia Encoder."

However, the true measure and importance of the Proof Olympics is best expressed in the words of previous participants. Columbia, SC, champion Lucretia Profit said, "I'm amazed by the high ability of the other site champions," while Atlanta, GA, champion Jermaine Taylor added, "Holding the Proof Olympics showed how much Wachovia truly appreciates us." Charlotte, NC, champion—and Best Wachovia Encoder—Donald Anderson said proudly, "I just wanted to see how I compared with the top encoders from other sites."

Results—13 Million Reasons to Hold the Olympics. The program has helped to reduce proof unit costs to $.02 per item, and every fully established site has now reached that goal. The program has become a model for the divisions' other incentive programs that support their long-term approach to improving productivity. By the end of 2007 proof-unit cost reductions at Wachovia resulted in compounded annual savings in excess of $13,000,000.

PRODUCTIVITY TIPS

➡ Provide computer hardware/software/ upgrades or smartphone that will improve an employee's efficiency and productivity.

➡ Give a new tool cabinet filled with tools.

➡ Send employee on a multisite tour to see industry best practices at other companies.

At Worzalla Book Manufacturing in Stevens Point, WI, the quality services department exceeded its goal of 99.85 percent accuracy in customer specifications for five years in a row. Bill Downs, the quality supervisor and continuous improvement manager, wanted to celebrate, but he was limited to a budget of $20 per person. So he took the department to lunch and gave each member of the team a certificate of appreciation and a gift card for a movie rental and pizza. The group enjoyed the lunch and gift cards, but seemed to take even more pride in displaying the certificates in their offices and explaining their achievement to anyone who cared to listen.

———

When Jennifer Wallick was software development manager at Four Pi Systems, a developer of manufacturing test equipment in San Diego (now a part of Hewlett-Packard), she found that programmers did not like to bring up errors. To keep employees from getting frustrated when they found a bug in a new software product, she started the "Find a Bug, Win a Prize" program that awarded a candy bar to anyone who found a bug in the new software product. Jennifer says, "It certainly changed people's attitudes. It also improved the quality of the software because more bugs were reported and fixed sooner."

———

> **"I don't think it's possible to make a great quality product without having a great quality work environment. So it's linked—quality product, quality customer service, quality workplace, and quality of life for your employees."**
>
> —Yvon Chouinard, *CEO, Patagonia*

At Ryder System truck rental and leasing, based in Miami, FL, employees in quality action teams (work groups put together to come up with quality improvement suggestions) are encouraged with tangible incentives in addition to more traditional forms of appreciation. Jerry Riordan, vice president of quality, says, "We try to give them a quick response from the decision makers, as well as quick implementation for accepted ideas. Their incentive is the pleasure of getting changes made." The company is implementing a continuous improvement process that stresses response to ideas within ten days, as well as more formal recognition and reward procedures.

———

Bob Vassallo, manager of employee relations at the Thomas J. Lipton Company, maker of food products in Englewood Cliffs, NJ, reports having an Open Vending Machine Day in which employees are allowed free access to plant cafeteria vending machines for reaching certain manufacturing goals, such as productivity, quality, and safety.

———

Noncommission employees who have achieved peak performance at the *Portland Business Journal* in Portland, OR, are recognized monthly. Special voice-mail messages on the main switchboard announce their names, the high sales results, and the gains in circulation, and cash bonuses are distributed.

———

At 3M in St. Paul, MN, managers give the "Golden Step Award," inspired by the Greek god Hermes's winged slipper, to those who make a new line of business profitable, initiate a new product or service, or create a new market niche. These tacky, plastic, gold-colored shoes are highly valued by employees.

———

NCO Financial Systems in Horsham, PA, started a bonus system for data-entry clerks, encouraging them to work as a team to eliminate backlogs in paperwork. Each clerk receives a point for each day without backlog, and monthly prizes (up to $250 in value) are awarded based on the number of accumulated points. Those who don't win top

> **"What I absolutely believe is that honoring the people who do the work can produce stunning results for the company. If the people in the factory believe there's a real effort to help improve their skills, provide opportunities for advancement and job security, they can do things that will blow your mind."**
> —Sidney Harman, *CEO, Harmon International Industries, Inc.*

prizes are also entered in a random drawing for $100. Productivity has increased 25 percent with this system, with no drop in quality.

———

Motorola in Schaumburg, IL, has awards breakfasts at which factory workers who have met certain quality goals are recognized by senior managers.

———

The Outstanding Teller Service Award at the First-Knox National Bank in Mt. Vernon, OH, tries to tie productivity and customer service awards to measurable goals. The program selects one outstanding teller from each branch using a system based 33 percent on tellers' choice, 34 percent on customer satisfaction (selection cards are included in customers' bank statements), 11 percent on balancing record, 11 percent on number of transactions, and 11 percent on supervisory rating.

> **"The way managers treat subordinates is subtly influenced by what they expect of them. If managers' expectations are high, productivity is likely to be excellent. If their expectations are low, productivity is likely to be poor. It is as though there were a law that caused subordinates' performance to rise or fall to meet managers' expectations."**
>
> —J. Sterling Livingston, Harvard Business Review

A Case Study in Quality Improvement

The Tennant Company, a provider of nonresidential floor maintenance equipment, floor coatings, and related products based in Minneapolis, began its quality improvement push by defining an objective "to recognize superior quality performers in their organization." Because people respond differently to various kinds of rewards and recognition, they developed a three-dimensional program.

First is the formal awards program, in which honored employees (up to 2 percent of the workforce each year) receive a 10-karat gold and diamond ring and a plaque at an annual banquet. The peer-driven program has three rules governing the selection of award recipients:

1. The company's established criteria for selecting recognition recipients are printed on the nomination forms.

2. An employee can nominate anyone, with the exception of people he or she reports to directly.

3. Recognition recipients are selected by a committee of employees of different rank and from different departments of the company.

Second, an additional "formal" award grew out of employee feedback asking for more frequent recognition. Winners of the Koala T. Bear (a play on the word *quality*) are visited by a costumed bear and a recognition committee. Each recipient receives a stuffed Koala T. Bear and a certificate of his or her achievements. There's a less stringent nomination process, and the awards are presented monthly.

Third is the informal rewards program, designed to recognize people who meet specific goals. It is flexible and can be tailored to meet the needs and preferences of individuals and groups. Informal recognition is immediate recognition given by manager and supervisors to those employees doing something right.

While any one of these dimensions might be considered

> **"I thought, my God, if I can get people pumped up, wanting to come to work, what an edge that is! That's the whole secret to increasing productivity. I saw them push and accomplish things they never thought were possible. I saw satisfaction on a daily basis."**—Jack Stack, *CEO, SRC Corp.*

a complete program in many organizations, Tennant firmly believes that all three have to be present to maximize employee motivation and performance. According to former Human Resources manager Rita Maehling, "Like a three-legged stool, each dimension plays a critical role. Take away one leg of the stool and it falls."

A Case Study in Improved Performance

When Lou Gerstner became president of Travel Related Services (TRS) at New York–based American Express, the unit was facing one of its biggest challenges in AMEX's 130-year history. Hundreds of banks were offering or planning to introduce credit cards through Visa and MasterCard that would compete with the American Express card. And more than two dozen financial service firms were getting into the traveler's check business.

Within a week of his appointment, Gerstner brought together the people running the card organization and questioned all the principles by which they conducted their business. In particular, he challenged two widely shared beliefs—that the division should have only one product, the green card, and that this product was limited in potential for growth and innovation.

Gerstner also moved quickly to develop a more entrepreneurial culture, to hire and train people who would thrive in it, and to communicate clearly to them the organization's overall direction. He and other top managers rewarded intelligent risk-taking. To make entrepreneurship easier, they discouraged unnecessary bureaucracy. They also upgraded hiring standards and created the TRS Graduate Management program, which offered high-potential young people special training, an enriched set of experiences, and an unusual degree of exposure to people in top management. To encourage risk-taking among all TRS employees, Gerstner established a Great Performers program (similar to the program at Honeywell described earlier) to recognize and reward truly exceptional customer service, a central tenet of the organization's philosophy.

In the Great Performers program, life-size posters showing famous people with their greatest achievements were displayed throughout the facilities for many weeks. Then the company began to picture American Express employees on posters, with a statement of a major accomplishment by each employee. Afterward the employee could take the poster home.

Nominations were made by fellow employees, supervisors, and customers. Award winners were eligible to become Grand Award winners, named by the worldwide governing committee. There was no limit on how many people could win; in a recent year, 38 employees garnered the award. Prizes for Grand Award winners included an all-expense-paid trip for two to New York City, $4,000 in American Express traveler's checks, a platinum "GP" logo pin, and a framed certificate.

These initiatives quickly led to new markets, products, and services and resulted in an increase in TRS's net income of 500 percent in 11 years, or about an 18 percent annual compounded rate. With a return on equity of 28 percent, the business outperformed many so-called high-tech, high-growth companies, as well as most low-growth but high-profit businesses.

Managers at Katzinger's Delicatessen in Columbus, OH, made a deal with employees: If they reduced food costs, the company would split the savings with them. The company ended up saving $30,000, and the employees split $15,000 among themselves.

Attendance & Safety

In many ways, nothing is more important to a company than attendance and safety, especially in manufacturing firms. Offering effective attendance incentives to encourage employees to be prompt and not miss workdays, and effective safety incentives to ensure employee well-being and minimize accidents, is essential to the success of many companies.

Denny's Restaurant, based in Spartanburg, SC, ran a national advertisement to thank Amber Deahn and Linda Olson, their Coeur d'Alene, ID, employees who played an important role in the 2005 rescue of kidnapping victim Shasta Groene. "We knew we wanted to convey the enormous pride we had in these employees," said Denny's spokeswoman Debbie Atkins. "They certainly represent the best of the best at Denny's."

A McDonald's in St. Louis, MO, gives first choice of work schedules to employees with the best attendance records. This promotes better attendance and—because many employees are students—gives people a chance to coordinate work and class schedules.

Leone Ackerly, the owner of Mini Maid Service Company in Marietta, GA, gives employees an attendance bonus each pay period if they have come to work every day on time and in uniform.

> **"The main thing that makes me happy about getting up in the morning and coming to work is the fact that I like what I do and I have freedom. You're free to do your job, take complaints or recommendations to your supervisors, and they listen. It makes it a lot more pleasant to be in a job when it's like that and not just being crammed down your throat."**
> —Jerry Forsythe,
> *Senior Operator,*
> *Chaparral Steel*

General Electric, headquartered in Fairfield, CT, offers a cash bonus for every six months of perfect attendance.

The Atlantic Envelope Company in Atlanta, GA, now part of National Envelope Corporation of Uniondale, NY, awarded employees two hours' extra pay for every month of perfect attendance.

Rush-Copley Medical Center in Aurora, IL, rewarded 128 employees with a buffet lunch, a certificate of achievement, and a ceramic coffee mug inscribed with "Perfect Attendance" and the year. A special gift certificate went to the employee with the longest perfect attendance.

Pella Corporation in Pella, IA, awards a $100 savings bond and arranges coffee time with top management for employees with one year of perfect attendance. The company, which markets windows, even arranged a reception with the governor of Iowa for seven employees with 25 years' perfect attendance.

In the Instant Win Giveaway program at Todays Staffing, based in Dallas, TX, temporary employees who have worked during the previous six months are given a card with a scratch-off panel concealing the name of a prize. Prizes include a diamond watch, $100 or $50 cash, calculators, and six months of free long-distance telephone calls.

To recognize those with perfect attendance, Merle Norman Cosmetics, based in Los Angeles, offers the following gifts:

One year: *a gold engraved watch*
Two years: *a video game, cookware set, or stainless flatware*
Three years: *a stereo or portable TV*
Four years: *a food processor*
Five years: *a camera*
Six years: *personal electronics*
Seven years: *a TV*
Eight years: *a microwave oven*
Nine years: *a specially designed ring*
Ten years: *a two-week, all-expenses-paid trip to Hawaii for two*
Fifteen years: *a two-week, all-expenses-paid trip to anywhere in the world for the employee and his or her spouse, relative, or friend*

How well do these incentives work? In a given year, more than one-tenth of all hourly employees did not have a minute of absenteeism or tardiness, and eight employees had gone ten years without missing any time from work.

———

A large manufacturing firm with 7,500 hourly employees increased attendance by offering nonmonetary privileges, combined with progressive discipline for excessive absences.

———

In an effort to decrease absenteeism, New York Life Insurance Company holds a lottery for employees who have been at work every day each quarter. The first 10 employees to have their names drawn earn a $200 bond; the next 20 earn a $100 bond; and 70 more receive a paid day off. A special lottery is held for employees with perfect attendance records for the entire year. Prizes are two $1,000 bonds and ten more paid days off. The company estimates that absenteeism is 21 percent lower than during the same period the previous year.

———

At Toyota Motor Company of America, every employee who has perfect attendance for the year gets a coupon to enter a drawing for a free car. If an employee has two years of perfect attendance, he or she gets two tickets, for three years, three tickets, and so on. Six cars are awarded annually.

———

JP Morgan Chase & Company reported saving $820,000 in reduced absenteeism in one year alone by offering New York City employees backup child care. Employees are offered 20 free days of child care a year.

———

When Vic Anapolle was operations manager for a chemical specialties group at W. R. Grace & Company in Atlanta, GA, (now headquartered in Columbia, MD), he implemented a new system for employee motivation. Starting with a nominal budget of $100 per person per year and using "Starperks" scratch-off coupons to reward safety practices, he set a safety goal of one million man-hours without any injuries. Not only did he surpass the goal, motivating his group to exceed one and a half million man-hours without any injuries, but his group was able to

> **"Those who give and get praise at work have better safety records and fewer accidents on the job."**—findings from The Gallup Organization

pass a surprise OSHA hazardous chemical inspection with flying colors.

———

According to Dick Radell, vice president of Human Resources of The Marcus Corporation in Milwaukee, all the employees who work at a specific restaurant for one month without an accident are awarded a "Megabuck" from the state lottery, in a program that is quite popular with employees.

———

At FedEx Corporation, the express freight company headquartered in Memphis, safe workers and drivers receive a recognition gift (pins, watches, and rings, with diamonds added for continuous safety streaks) for safety milestones every five years. In addition, quarterly and annual President's Safety Awards in the form of cash and clothing, as well as a trip in the case of the annual winners, are given to four employees (one in each of four work groups) to recognize outstanding safety achievement. Contests are held for different locations, and winning work groups are recognized with barbecues or clothing.

———

Southern New England Telephone, in New Haven, CT, and now a part of Dallas, TX–based AT&T, rewarded employees who drove one calendar year without a preventable accident. To be eligible, an employee must have driven at least 12,000 miles annually or spent 25 percent or more of his or her work time operating or working out of a company vehicle. Employees amassed certificates that were redeemed for products from one supplier.

———

At Furst-McNess Company in Freeport, IL, which manufactures premixed animal foods, Mark S. Fryer, director of Human Resources, says the company gives $25 to all personnel who are assigned a company vehicle and receive no moving violations for a calendar year. If an employee goes three years without any violations, he or she gets an additional $100 award. Accidents with company cars have been greatly reduced.

———

As an incentive for safe behavior, APG Electric in Clearwater, FL, gave employees with good safety records a chance to win a prize from $6,500 worth of cash and gifts, as well as a shot at the grand prize—a $13,500 Chevrolet pickup truck.

———

Southern Wine & Spirits of America, a distributor of bottled waters, juices, and alcoholic beverages, has a recognition award that has helped reduce safety-related financial losses by 70 percent—from almost $1 million annually to only a few hundred thousand dollars per year. The award is a Super Bowl–style gold and diamond ring, presented to drivers who steer clear of safety-related problems for five years in a row. A 1-carat diamond is added to that ring for each year of continued safety. Driver Alex Barnes says proudly, "It's truly an honor to wear the ring."

———

> **"The recognition program, along with good training and supervision, helps keep safety on the minds of all our workers—including management and supervisors. It helps keep us focused as a team."**
> —Jim Rainsberger, *Superintendent, Pipeline Division Terminal. Quaker State*

SECTION 7

FORMAL REWARD TOOLS & PROGRAMS

The formal reward and recognition programs in this section are part of even more complex and structured systems than the ones for specific achievements. In this section, we look at multilevel reward programs and point systems, employee and company anniversaries, company benefits and perks, charity and community service programs, and company stock and ownership.

Tim Puffer, of Puffer & Associates marketing and public relations in St. Paul, MN, describes eight general guidelines for conducting a successful reward and recognition program: (1) define objectives, (2) lead by management example, (3) develop specific criteria, (4) use meaningful rewards, (5) involve employees, (6) keep communications clear, (7) reward teams, and (8) manage the long term.

Multilevel Reward Programs & Point Systems

Most companies have one or more formal reward programs for recognizing employee performance, often integrated to address the needs of different levels and types of employees. Although such programs typically recognize only a small number of people, the experience is significant and motivating, and the public example helps to shape the future aspirations of other employees.

Michael Stalbaum, founder of Unreal Marketing, an online advertising agency based in Narberth, PA, encourages employees to take "points" instead of cash by making the points worth 50 percent more than a cash payout. One employee used points to decorate her home using Pottery Barn gift certificates; another redeemed them for a night at a Ritz-Carlton hotel. Starwood Hotels & Resorts–Canada offers employees Westin gift points, which can be used at local retailers.

———

When Roger Jewett was president of Rare Method, a Calgary, Alberta–based interactive marketing firm, he realized he was accumulating more air miles than he could use. He started giving them to employees for a job well done. Dubbed Rare Miles, they set up a system where anyone could send e-mails with Rare Mile points attached to recipients who deserved them. After a time, workers with enough points went into a drawing for free flights and other prizes.

> **"Employees will be more receptive to formal, organization-wide programs if they believe that the company really cares about them on a personal, day-to-day basis."**—Rosalind Jeffries, *Rewards and Recognition Consultant*

———

Banister Shoe in White Plains, NY, uses a combination of programs to reward and recognize employees at all levels and for various achievements. Formal award programs include Manager of the Year; District Manager of the Year; the Leadership

Achievement Award, also known as the "eagle ring," in which an employee first receives an onyx ring and then diamonds for it with each additional recognition event; the Achievement Award or "pyramid pen"; and membership in the President's Club for store managers.

Less formal programs include "hero meetings," which are held once a month in the central office to announce achievements and encourage employees to praise one another, and also include spontaneous standing ovations for various achievements by individuals.

> **"When the number of awards is high, it makes the perceived possibility of winning something high as well. And then the average man will stretch to achieve."**
> —Thomas J. Peters and Robert H. Waterman, *Coauthors*, In Search of Excellence

Inspired by the slogan "At Ross, You're in the Company of Excellence," president Dick Gast decided that Ross Products, based in Columbus, OH, and recently acquired by Abbott Nutrition, needed a recognition program to enhance its tradition of providing superior products and services.

Since much excellence is subjective, Gast decided to put it into more concrete terms by allowing employees to participate in defining and recognizing it. He specified that the program be open to all 4,100 employees, from line workers to executives, and that it be employee-driven. All company employees should be eligible to win and participate in selecting winners.

The program designates three levels of achievement with rising prestige and increasingly valuable awards. At each facility, it is administered according to the number of people and their particular preferences. Any full-time Ross employee may nominate another full-time employee, whether subordinate or supervisor, for an award. Employees may even nominate themselves.

All nominations are considered by a screening committee of 12 to 25 workers in each area. The committee considers all nominations and selects the most deserving people to be voted on by employees in their area. Although managers can serve on the selection committee, they have no more clout than any other members in determining final selections. Service on the committee is voluntary and may not exceed two years.

The Award of Excellence program gives employees many chances for recognition. At the end of each quarter, the screening committee reviews all nominations submitted during that period. Nominees affirmed by the committee and verified by the personnel department as employees in good standing automatically become Level I winners. Their names are announced at a general meeting, during which they receive a two-ounce silver ingot engraved with the Ross Award of Excellence logo on the front and the original Ross milk truck logo on the back. The ingot is encased in a clear plastic base and can be used as a paperweight or desk ornament. The award costs approximately $50. The number of first-time winners varies depending on the number of area workers, although it is generally between 10 and 15 per quarter.

Each quarter, area employees select four Level II winners from among the Level I winners. Those four winners receive a five-ounce silver ingot with the same Level I imprints, but in the

> **"Create a dynamic work environment by varying load, having a formal job rotation program so people don't become stale in their current positions and by offering opportunities for personal and professional development."**
> —Ron Rosenberg, *Founder, Drive-You-Nuts.com*

shape of an Olympic-style medal, complete with a ribbon. The award is encased in a black-velvet-covered box and costs approximately $100. Level II winners also receive a letter of congratulation from the division president. At the end of the year, a recognition dinner is held at each Ross location for all Level II winners.

> **"Decision-makers for the incentive programs should be very careful not to impose their own personal choices on their audience."**
>
> —Bruce Tepper,
> *Associate, Joselyn, Tepper & Associates, Inc.*

At the end of the fourth quarter, an election is held to select Level III winners from among the Level II winners. Level III winners get together for a three-day trip to celebrate their achievements. Activities include a visit to the company's headquarters for a reception hosted by the president, a double-decker bus tour around the city and a free afternoon, followed by a president's celebration dinner. Each Level III winner is awarded a Waterford crystal decanter with six glasses, as well as a $250 gift certificate to be used toward his or her choice of merchandise from a catalog. The estimated cost of the Level III festivities is about $20,000.

"An excellent employee is someone other employees look forward to working with because that person is pleasant, easy to get along with, and does everything possible to make each working day a productive and pleasant experience for everyone," says Mike Strapp, director of marketing and financial services and Award of Excellence program chairman. "Fun is an important element in the definition of excellence.

"With any recognition program, the goal is to encourage other employees to strive for the same kind of excellence as those who are recognized. Recognition from your peers is a great motivator."

"If you feel appreciated, you're going to go out of your way, too," said Maria Rossi, the company's receptionist, who became one of the company's first 36 Level III winners. "I have always appreciated my job, but this made me feel appreciated back."

———

Radisson Hotels & Resorts, based in Omaha, NE, have a program designed to increase employee retention and to improve service. The hotels award points for being on time, providing good service to guests, improving quality in hotel operations, reaching department profit and production goals, and referring new employees. The points are awarded by managers; customer service points are also tabulated from comment cards and quarterly evaluations by supervisors. Managers are rewarded for reducing turnover and costs, increasing the return rate on guest comment cards, and implementing suggestions.

The highlight of the program is its prize structure. "We're offering standard merchandise prizes like TVs, toasters, and golf clubs," says Sue Gordon, vice president of Human Resources. But workers can also choose more practical rewards, such as bus passes, free child care at local day care centers, tuition reimbursement, and educational funds.

> **"A solid performance-improvement program pays for itself out of the profits it generates."**
> —The MBF Group, Inc.

———

Newstrack Executive Information Service in Pitman, NJ, uses an Employee Recognition Coupon system that helps foster teamwork, better morale, and employees' appreciation of one another's contributions.

Each employee receives 20 coupons. When he or she sees a coworker doing something extraordinary, the employee fills out the coupon with some words of praise and gives it to the coworker. Employees save the coupons (a maximum of 20 per year) and redeem them for special awards:

1 coupon: *certificate for free car wash*
5 coupons: *$25 gift certificate for dinner*
10 coupons: *$50 gift certificate for Macy's*
15 coupons: *one-night stay for two in Atlantic City*
20 coupons: *one-year membership at Four Seasons Health Spa*

A Case Study in Point Systems

A survey of employees at former farm equipment business Cascades Diamond in Thorndike, MA, indicated that 79 percent thought they were not being rewarded for good work, 65 percent believed management did not treat them respectfully, and 56 percent approached their work with pessimism.

To change these perceptions, the company developed a program called "The 100 Club," which stressed attendance, punctuality, and safety among the rank and file. An employee earned 25 points for a year of perfect attendance, 20 points for going through a year without formal disciplinary action, and 15 points for working a year without losing time due to an injury. For each day or partial day of absence, the company deducted points. A worker also earned points for making a cost-cutting or safety suggestion to management, as well as for community service, such as participation in a blood drive, the United Way, or Little League.

> **"It's not enough to tell people they should be happy to have a job here. At a time when people are asked to really stretch themselves with fewer resources, you want to reward them for that stretch."**
> —Bruce Donatuti, *Director of Human Resource Policy, Citibank*

When an employee reached 100 points, he or she got a nylon jacket with the Diamond logo and the words "The 100 Club." A teller at a local bank described a woman who came into the bank and modeled her baby-blue 100 Club jacket for customers and employees. She said, "My employer gave me this for doing a good job. It's the first time in the 18 years I've been there that they've recognized the things I do every day."

During those years she had earned $230,000 in wages, which had paid for cars, a home mortgage, food and other essentials, vacations, and college educations. In her mind, she had provided a service for her earnings. The money wasn't recognition for her work, but the 100 Club jacket was.

In the first year of the program, the division saved $5.2 million and increased productivity by 14.5 percent, and quality-related mistakes declined by 40 percent. In a later survey, 86 percent of employees reported that they thought the company and management considered them "important" or "very important"; 81 percent responded that they got "recognition by the company"; and 73 percent said the company showed "concern for them as people." On average, 79 percent said their own attitude toward work quality had improved.

A Case Study in Multilevel Recognition Programs

The MidMichigan Regional Medical Center in Midland has a number of formal recognition programs at the hospital and departmental levels.

> **"Well-constructed recognition settings provide the single most important opportunity to parade and reinforce the specific kinds of new behavior one hopes others will emulate."**
> —Tom Peters, *Author and Management Consultant*

> **"The best programs get participants 'hunting when the ducks are flying.'"**
> —*Incentive* Magazine

At the corporate level, employees, volunteers, and physicians at the Medical Center can nominate other employees, volunteers, or physicians for an Apple Award for anything they did that went beyond the normal scope of their jobs. These nominations go to a committee to ensure that they meet established criteria. When they are approved, nominees receive a red apple lapel pin. After an employee receives five red apples, he or she gets a silver apple; and after five silver apples, a gold apple is awarded. At the silver and gold levels, there are formal presentations and gift certificates.

An employee is chosen each month as Most Valuable Person from nominations by other employees. At the end of the year, the staff is asked to vote for one of the 12, who then becomes the Most Valuable Person of the Year. Each month, the MVPs' pictures are posted at the two main entrances to the Medical Center and write-ups appear in the Medical Center newsletter and the local newspaper.

At the departmental level, the Pharmacy Department has developed a "recognition sheet" that anyone can complete. It has space for an employee's name, the date, an explanation of the employee's activity or productivity, and the name of the person completing the sheet. The completed sheet is routed to the manager of the department. The recognition sheets are used to select an internal Employee of the Month chosen for what he or she did, not by the number of recognition sheets that were completed. The Employee of the Month receives a $25 gift

> **"Incentive awards are not compensation—they are recognition—a meaningful way to say thank you, while focusing attention on your company goals. Incentive awards are recognition for a job well done, a personal expression of gratitude. They must carry a hassle-free guarantee of satisfaction."**
> —The MBF Group, Inc.

certificate. Recognition sheets are also typed up in a summary report that is distributed at the monthly staff meeting. At the end of the year, a contest is held for Employee of the Year. Each of the 12 recognized employees has his or her picture on the wall in the department, and everyone votes. The winner receives a gift.

The business office keeps a Praise and Recognition Board. Praise and Recognition forms are available throughout the department. Employees are encouraged to take a minute to recognize their coworkers, and the forms are posted on the board if the employee chooses. All forms go into a drawing each month; the prize is a gift certificate.

The Family Practice Center uses numerous recognition methods. Each staff meeting starts with thanks among coworkers. When a staff person is noticed doing something well or performing a special task, a Family Practice Center Flower is delivered to that person with a preprinted card from the department. Staff lunches are also provided at intervals.

The Medical Records Department has a "Good Deed Slip" that employees are encouraged to fill out. Half the slip goes to the employee, and half goes into the suggestion box. The employee with the most slips that month becomes Employee of the Month; there is also an Employee of the Year. The department also hires new employees using an interview team. The manager and supervisors are on the team, and the remainder of the team is nominated and voted on by fellow employees. At the end of the interview process, the team is treated to lunch or dinner.

> **"We need to re-emphasize employee recognition programs to combat the negative impression people get when they read about thousands of layoffs in the country every day."**—Bob Hammer, *Corporate Vice President and Director of Strategic Management, Motorola*

SPECIAL PRIVILEGES TIPS

➡ Set up catalog-driven point system for redeemable merchandise, services, or experiences (I Love Rewards, etc.).

➡ Let employee pick their desired work location.

➡ Assign a temporary employee to help the honoree for a day.

➡ Give coupons for various household services.

➡ Give coupons for personal health and fitness services.

➡ Give a full/partial country club membership.

In the Information Resources Department, a Good News Reporter is assigned monthly to actively seek out information about good performance by interviewing customers and peers. The reporters have been very creative with their presentations: A professional singer was brought in to sing a rap song; children were videotaped announcing the good deeds of the month in a TV news format; a *National Enquirer* format was used to spread the news; and one session was modeled after the Emmys.

The Medical Center has many cross-functional and cross-departmental teams that are encouraged to celebrate their successes. Numerous departments and teams have lunches and pizza parties. After meeting for a year and a half, the Educator Resource Team had two major accomplishments. Its quarterly meeting became a surprise celebration at which each member received a mug that said he or she was a charter member of the team. Team members also received a letter signed by the president of the Medical Center, and the chairperson for the team congratulated them on their accomplishments and teamwork. The team leaders for the subgroups received gift certificates.

Company Benefits & Perks

In deciding on jobs, a company's benefits, such as health care or child care, are often significant factors. On the job, however, such benefits do little to motivate employees to perform at higher levels over the long term. Company perks described in this section (as opposed to the personal perks covered earlier in this part) are offered to all employees and involve a financial cost to the organization. Following are a variety of unusual organizational benefits and perks being offered today, which, if tied to desired employee behaviors or performance, can become important motivators.

YouDecide (formerly CFN), a voluntary benefits outsourcing firm based in Atlanta, GA, does the legwork for its employees looking for the cheapest rates on car, homeowner, or renter's insurance, mortgages, refinancing, or home equity loans. The service is free.

Joe Ball, owner of Ellis Well Drilling in Clermont, FL, lets his entire staff of four employees use company equipment on personal time, and when necessary, makes interest-free "small" employee loans. He is very lenient with family issues, encouraging employees to bring their children to work and giving paid time off for surgeries and emergencies. Twice a quarter at Fairfield Resorts, the time-share unit of Cendant Corporation in Central Florida, employees bring family members to work with them. They also get flexible work hours to help manage family demands.

> **"We used to call them 'fringe benefits,' but we quit using the term 'fringe' when we saw the magnitude of that figure."**—James Morris, *Director of Survey Research, U.S. Chamber of Commerce*

Sierra Cheese in Compton, CA, rewarded its employees with cost of living raises to thank them for staying with the company in hard times. The company had put money aside and had enough to reward its employees.

———

At the 5-star Dorchester Hotel in London, UK, all employees get 5-star treatment, starting with an employment package that offers pension programs, subsidized meals, sabbaticals, and discounts for eye care and rental cars. There is an employee helpline, for advice or just a listening ear for their troubles— housing, divorce, traumas, or medical problems. Since its launch, it has been used by about 10 percent of the hotel's workforce. Annual employee satisfaction surveys show that over 80 percent find the hotel fair and honest in handling complaints, up from 75 percent the previous year. About 96 percent say they are proud to work for the hotel.

———

Dell Computers, the information technology company based in Round Rock, TX, gives all its employees—factory workers to management—up to ten personal business days instead of calling them sick days. This is something that many small businesses are willing to do as well.

———

New York City–based American Express, the global financial services firm, employs on-site nurse practitioners, and employees can get prescriptions filled on-site. Employees can modify their schedules remotely to accommodate sick family members or doctor visits. Incremental hours can be traded with others across the workforce. Some locations offer discounts of up to 50 percent on certain fees for trips booked through the company, fee-free traveler's checks, and foreign currency exchange. Parsippany, NY–based resort and hotel operator Wyndham Worldwide has groceries delivered to its employees' desks at Wyndham Resorts, and employees receive "no-wait" medical appointments during lunch. Emerald Physicians of Hyannis, MA, has meals delivered to sick employees at their homes. They provide biweekly "healthy living luncheons," with guest speakers, and regular yoga classes, chair massages, and spa packages. Staff has free access to two vacation condos.

———

WellPoint, based in Indianapolis, IN, manages the BlueCross BlueShield health plan in several states and hosts a popular monthly wellness teleconference. Badger Mining Corporation, the mining and quarrying firm based in Berlin, WI, provides financial support for tobacco cessation programs and for hiring financial planners. Johnson, Inc., an insurance broker based in St. John's, Newfoundland, implemented a new health and wellness program.

———

Washburn Communication, a marketing and communications strategy firm in Bellevue, WA, provides either free parking or a free annual Metro bus pass; company-sponsored shared-car access for business use; short-term and long-term disability insurance, premium paid in full; up to 16 days of paid time off per year, 8 paid holidays; and inexpensive access to the fitness facility located in their office building. They host periodic happy hours and have lunches delivered to the office.

———

The New York City offices of Accenture, the global consulting firm, has a "7 to 7" travel policy in which nobody has to leave home before 7 A.M. Monday, and everyone is encouraged to schedule being home by 7 P.M. on Friday. Silverstein Properties, Inc., a nationwide real estate development and investment firm based in New York City, lets its workers start their weekends at 1 P.M. on Fridays.

COMPANY BENEFITS TIPS

➡ On-site dry cleaning drop-off/pickup

➡ Company dental plan

➡ On-site employee washer/dryer

➡ Body scans/in-depth physical examination

➡ Let employee pick an object to decorate/improve the office (e.g., aquarium, larger computer screen, chair)

At the Canton, MA, headquarters of Dunkin' Brands, a coffee and doughnut retailer, employees get to eat the company's products for free: Dunkin' Donuts and Baskin-Robbins ice cream. Washburn Communication, a marketing and communications strategy firm in Bellevue, WA, provides a kitchen with refrigerator, snacks, hot and cold filtered water, Starbucks coffee, tea, hot chocolate, biscotti, fruit bowl, and jars of candy. Analytical Graphics Inc., an aerospace and defense company based in Exton, PA, has free on-site meals for breakfast, lunch, and dinner. Other conveniences include washers and dryers for doing laundry, and a dry-cleaning service.

Facebook, the Palo Alto, CA–based online social networking giant, offers a broad range of cafeteria items including Thai curry. Celebrity chefs sometimes prepare menus, and cooking internships are offered to employees to spend a day with the 50-member kitchen staff and learn the finer points of the culinary arts. Google, in Mountain View, CA, provides a wide array of menu items. Uno, a restaurant chain based in West Roxbury,

MA, lets employees make their own lunches in one of two full kitchens. They can also order from a discount-priced employee menu. Coffee and soda are free. Durkee-Mower in Lynn, MA, provides peanut butter, bread, and an unlimited supply of its famed Marshmallow Fluff to its employees. Legal Sea Foods, the Boston-based seafood restaurant chain, serves employees free breakfast and lunch in its corporate cafeteria. Minneapolis-based Quality Bicycle Products hosts monthly breakfasts for bike commuters. Other companies that subsidize their employees' meals include Lucasfilm, the fully integrated entertainment company based in San Francisco; Autodesk, the building software firm based in San Rafael, CA; and Apple Computers, based in Cupertino, CA.

At Daxko, the Birmingham, AL, software firm, employees get 15 paid vacation days, a free YMCA membership, and 6 weeks paid parental leave.

Conductor, Inc., the New York City–based search engine optimization firm, provides extensive recreational activities, company-organized team sports, citywide scavenger hunts, and ice-cream parties. Between 2006 and 2009, revenues grew over 1,800 percent, reaching $10.5 million.

> **"The way positive reinforcement is carried out is more important than the amount."**
> —B. F. Skinner,
> *Psychologist*

At its Sugar Land, TX, headquarters, Heavy Construction Systems Specialists (HCSS), a Houston-area software developer, provides a robust wellness program, including a one-third-mile crushed-granite jogging trail, exercise room, game room, gym with a basketball court, and putting green. HCSS contracts with a company that provides employees with doctor consultations over the Internet from its offices. They also pay fitness and wellness trainers to counsel employees on nutrition and exercise and offer on-site yoga, pilates, and exercise classes. The Switzerland office of UBS, the financial services firm, installed a nap room to recharge employees during the day. One U.S. office provides a Friday beer cart to help employees socialize and relax.

———

Capital One, the bank holding company headquartered in Fairfax County, VA, offers employees a company gym, campus walking trails, and reduced-calorie entrees. In 2009 its on-site services saved employees $280,110 in copay amounts. Computer software firm Adobe Systems, based in San Jose, CA, provides on-site fitness facilities and bocce courts, and supports 80 recreational and hobby clubs. It has also brought in Shawn Anchor, author of *The Happiness Advantage*, to give a motivational speech to its employees. Food manufacturer General Mills, based in Golden Valley, MN, offers a complete gym, on-site personal trainers, and a physical therapist. Raytheon BBN Technologies in Cambridge, MA, encourages healthy behavior and hosts a summer fitness program and free workout classes in a company gym. At Ventura, CA–based Patagonia, the outdoor apparel store, employees are encouraged to walk, bike, or surf during lunch. Employees at its Reno facility can go fly-fishing.

———

Network Solutions, a Web design and support services company based in Herndon, VA, gives a $20 gasoline card to trainees who travel more than ten miles to the call center in Butler Township. Trainees get the gas bonus for six weeks. Network's expansive benefits package includes a 401(k) plan, health, dental and vision insurance coverage, homeowners and auto insurance, flex time, company training, paid time off to participate in community outreach programs, and employee recognition programs. The company provides debit cards and a package of services to set up a domain name on the Web with hosting. It also subsidizes the snack machines in the cafeteria with a one-price policy of 25 cents for chips, candy, and soft drinks. Railroad Associates Corp., a railroad engineering and contracting firm based in Hershey, PA, pays 100 percent of health-insurance costs for employees and their dependents.

———

Schaumburg, IL–based Convergint Technologies, a building safety and security system provider, gives $100 cash to each employee for a "fun and laughter personal day—to do something they really want to do." "If all 860 company employees take advantage of the perk," cofounder and president Greg Lernihan said, "it may cost us $86,000, but it's the best way I can think of to spend $86,000."

———

Indianapolis-based Mike's Carwash, with 37 locations in Indiana and Ohio, offers tuition reimbursement of up to $2,500 annually to everyone working at least 20 hours a week.

———

Employees at Autodesk, a San Rafael, CA, design software developer, have been bringing their companion animals—canine, feline, and other furry friends—to work since the early 1980s. Company spokeswoman Kathy Tom-Engle says, "It allows employees to be more productive. It's a nice stress reliever, and people don't have to worry so much about a pet that's home alone." Three other organizations—Periscope, the Minneapolis-based advertising agency, and two San Diego–based companies, Petco Animal Supplies, a pet store chain, and Critter Cleaners, a pet grooming company—encourage employees to bring their pets to work. Critter Cleaners will also groom them at no charge. Iams Company, the pet food maker in Mason, OH, allows employees to bring dogs to work on Fridays.

> **"In past eras when our motivational paradigm was pay and promotion, we built an overly layered and over paid structure. Not only were the side effects bad, but motivation wasn't so hot either. Today we need a motivational paradigm based on more fundamental motivational requirements like purpose, meaning, involvement and growth."**
> —from QualTeam, *a business consulting firm based in Colorado*

At London, UK–based Courier Service, a delivery company, employees can take paid sick leave for the death of a companion animal.

At Railroad Associates Corp., a Hershey, PA–based railroad engineering and contracting firm, employees are eligible for an annual individual bonus capped at 50 percent of their pay based on customer feedback, safety records, and meeting deadlines.

Westgate, one of the largest time-share resort operators in Central Florida, gives employees a subsidized way to balance the demands of work and family: on-site child care. Since opening in 2001, Westgate's Children's Learning and Development has been a boon for employees like cafeteria worker Sara Chisholm. Chisholm, an employee in Westgate Resorts'

Sand Lake Commons building, believes the ability to see her kids at a company day care center during the day adds immensely to her peace of mind. "Child care is extremely important," Chisholm says. "I need to work, but I'm also a mom. It's great to know that my kids are safe." Westgate also offers financial assistance to employees with expensive family emergencies. Other amenities include job sharing and flexible work hours.

———

SAS, the business analytics software firm based in Cary, NC, offers day care. Edward Jones, the financial investment firm based in St. Louis, MO, also provides day care and flexible schedules for people to adopt children. The South Mountain Company, a design and construction firm in West Tisbury, MA, helped an employee pay the costs of adopting a son. Pittsburgh, PA–based design firm Maya Design allows its employees to bring their newborns to work.

———

Genentech, the San Francisco–based founder of the biotechnology industry, provides day care for children. Graham Co., an insurance broker in Philadelphia, PA, provides a lactation room for nursing mothers. At TechTarget, a technology media firm in Newton, MA, there is no set policy on vacation or sick leave.

———

> **"Many employers of all sizes are exploring the next generation of full-blown flexible benefit plans, which I call life-cycle programs. These plans start with the premise that employees are best suited to tailor a benefit program to their own needs and at the same time work within employer-established parameters. The outcome can be a win–win, with employees utilizing a varying set of benefits throughout their worklife."**
> —Gary Kushner,
> *President, Kushner and Co.*

The staff at Epcor Utilities Inc., the Edmonton, Alberta–based utility company, get one extra Friday off a month to spend time with family, to travel or relax. Staff who work Fridays enjoy a quieter office and time to deal with e-mail and catch up on work or even get ahead.

———

Quill Corporation, office supplies and equipment provider in Lincolnshire, IL, tries to lower health care costs by rewarding employees. The company forecasts its health care costs for six months and places the money in a pool. If funds remain in the pool at the end of the six months, they are divided equally among participating employees. Health care costs for the company have declined approximately 35 percent in each of the first two years of the program.

———

At Paychex, the wellness program called "Well Power" is a long-running effort that publishes a quarterly newsletter, *Personal Best*, which has tips on health awareness, tests, exercise, nutrition, and obtaining good health care. More important, the company pays for a Health Risk Assessment performed by a mobile testing unit that visits each branch. Employees can call the Personal Wellness Coordinator for help in understanding the tests and their implications, researching related health issues, and building a health improvement plan. Almost half of Paychex's employees participate.

———

George MacLeod, a restaurant owner in Bucksport, ME, allows his employees to run the restaurant by themselves one Sunday every month and split the profits among themselves to help pay for their health insurance. Participating employees have made enough money to cover the entire cost of their insurance premiums. IKEA distributes all profits from the day's sales one day a year as a bonus to employees.

———

Hi-Tech Duravent, makers of flexible hoses and ducting products in Georgetown, MA, lumps all vacation time, holidays, and sick days into a single account. Employees can take time off whenever they need it.

———

IBM provides health classes and physical examinations. Employees at Johnson & Johnson have access to a large fitness center with an option to enroll in a comprehensive program that includes a physical examination and professionals that guide enrollees in a physical fitness regimen. As an incentive for staying healthy, Johnson Wax deposits $300 in every employee's flexible health plan at the beginning of each year to be used to pay for health care charges not covered by the company's health plan. Unused money in the account at the end of the year is paid to the employee in cash.

> **"By providing part-timers with insurance, we've helped bring turnover to below 50% in an industry where it typically runs more than 100% annually. Thanks to lower turnover, we've saved more in training costs than we've spent on insurance."**
> —Howard Schultz, *CEO, Starbucks Coffee Co.*

———

"It is not the dollar cost of the award, but sometimes the novelty of it," says Terry L. Curry, manager of Human Resources for Muscatine Power and Water in Muscatine, IA. Employees there take part in two rounds of "wellness" team events during the summer. First-round participants receive T-shirts. They receive shoelaces as well if they participate in both rounds. The company has also given away stadium cushions for participation in late summer or early fall wellness events.

––––––

Gail Sneed, resource coordinator for the City of Dallas, TX, suggests offering a Free Month of Wellness for employees who must otherwise pay to use fitness equipment and take classes.

––––––

Pioneer Natural Resources Company, an Irving, TX, oil and gas company, gives workers up to $700 a year in bonuses if they exercise three times a week, don't smoke, don't take sick days, and don't submit major medical claims. Since the program started, the company has cut health care costs to 25 percent below the industry average.

––––––

Westinghouse Electric Company in Monroeville, PA, gives $200 annual bonuses to workers who do ten minutes of aerobic exercise three times a week for at least nine months a year. The company estimates that it saves $1,715 annually on every fit employee.

––––––

Reader's Digest reimburses up to 50 percent (up to $250 per year) of the cost of health club memberships for its employees. Employees who choose to take sports instruction or participate in a sport can also be reimbursed for part of these fees. Time Inc. does the same if the club has a cardiovascular fitness program.

Steelcase, Inc., based in Grand Rapids, MI, has a mini hospital staffed by 19 nurses and 2 physicians. The company also employs a psychologist and two social workers to counsel people on their personal problems, at no cost, on company time or after hours.

PricewaterhouseCoopers provides a resource and referral program for employees who need child care information. One senior consultant used the service to find suitable care when her nanny quit just as she was closing a half-million-dollar deal. She was able to interview candidates immediately and not miss a day of work. The cost: $150. Nearly 30 PricewaterhouseCoopers offices provide subsidized weekend child care during the busy tax season.

Southern California Edison has 12 staff physicians and part-time specialists to take care of its employees. The company also gives employees 25 percent off their electric bills.

Ryder System runs a subsidized day care center across the street from its Miami headquarters to attract and retain talented employees who might have small children. Now the company is constructing a $5 million public charter elementary school next door. "We want to be the employer of choice in South Florida," says Anthony Burns, chief executive of the truck leasing and logistics firm. The proximity of the school will mean productivity gains for Ryder, since teacher conferences and soccer games will be right across the street. Ryder employees' children will have first claim to the school's 300 seats. As of 2005,

Florida is the only state that allows schools to give preference to a company's employees' children.

———

Motorola is constructing an on-site day care center near its facility in Boynton Beach, FL, to help workers with young families.

———

In Houston, TX, the Medical Center Charter School is adjacent to the hospital, clinics, and medical schools. Children of the medical center's employees account for nearly the entire enrollment, although it is open to the public.

———

> **"Our early emphasis on human relations was not motivated by altruism, but by the simple belief that if we respected our people and helped them respect themselves the company would make the most profit."**
> —Thomas J. Watson Jr., *Former CEO, IBM*

Nations Bank, acquired by Bank of America and headquartered in Charlotte, NC, provides five different on-site or nearby child care centers for its 100,000 employees. They also have a chartered public school for 150 students from kindergarten to third grade in Jacksonville, FL. Finally, new parents can work part-time for up to six months after maternity leave is over.

———

First International Bank & Trust in Watford City, ND, opens its conference room to employees' school-age children every afternoon. They are free to turn on the big-screen TV, have snacks, and start on their homework while their parents finish up the workday. It has been at least four or five years since anyone has quit the company.

———

Baxter International Inc., which sells health care products, systems, and services, provides priority access for its employees at over 150 day care centers around the country at a reduced rate. The company pays for up to a year's worth of counseling for employees.

———

Marriott International, based in Bethesda, MD, helps employees balance career and personal life through its Work–Life Program, which has established a child-development center; child care discounts; family care spending accounts; referral services for child, elderly, and family care issues; and many other innovative programs.

———

JP Morgan Chase & Co. recently opened a lactation room for nursing mothers on its Wall Street trading floor so they would be able to return to work sooner after maternity leave.

———

Leo Burnett Worldwide, Inc. provides up to $3,000 in adoption assistance; H. B. Fuller, Herman Miller, and Physio-Control provide $1,500; IBM and Procter & Gamble provide $1,000.

———

> **"How companies treat employees says worlds about the quality of their management. And quality management usually translates into companies with a long and successful financial story. Whether it is demonstrated through superior benefits, family-friendly policies, safety records or union relations, a strong record on employee relations is generally an indication of forward-thinking executives thinking creatively about running a business."**
> —Steven Lydenberg, *Research Director, Kinder, Lydenberg, Domini & Co.*

One night a year, Sears employees brought in immediate family members for a shopping spree using the employee discount.

———

Fel-Pro Inc., in Southfield, MI, provides an interest-free cash advance of up to $2,250 for full-time employees to buy computers, which they can repay within two years through payroll deductions. To date, Fel-Pro has financed computers for 367 employees.

———

Under Timberland's adoption assistance program, full- and part-time employees receive up to $10,000 ($12,000 for a special-needs child) to help defray the costs of adoption. They also receive two weeks' paid adoption leave and may take additional paid time off, using their "Lifestyle Leave" account.

———

At Apple Computer, based in Cupertino, CA, all employees— from assembly-line workers to vice presidents—are loaned a computer just two months after joining the company in a program called "Loan to Own." Ten months later, the computer is theirs, no strings attached. One Christmas, all employees received a solar-powered calculator; the next year, they received personal electronics.

———

Pharmaceutical house Eli Lilly & Company, headquartered in Indianapolis, IN, pays 100 percent of employees' prescriptions for any Eli Lilly drugs.

———

Benjamin Moore & Company, based in Montvale, NJ, lets employees buy paint at wholesale prices. The company also sends crews to two employees' homes each year to paint them for free.

———

At Nissan's Smyrna, TN, plant, any employee with 12 months of service qualifies to lease a Nissan car for $160 a month, which includes maintenance, tax, license, and insurance.

———

Robert Mondavi Winery in Oakville, CA, gives every employee a case of wine at the end of each quarter. Anyone who works for Anheuser-Busch Companies, based in St. Louis, MO, is entitled to two free cases of beer a month.

———

Sea World San Diego employees are given four free passes to the park per year, and are invited to bring friends and relatives to see the shows free once a year during "Employee Night."

Other companies that reward employees with their own products include:

General Cinema (now owned by AMC Entertainment): *$1 movie passes for employees and their guests*
Mirage Resort & Casino: *free tickets to Las Vegas shows; free lunch at the hotel's dining room once a month*
Southwest Airlines: *free standby air travel for employees and their families*
Ben & Jerry's: *three pints of ice cream per day for every worker*

———

At the Exxon Mobil Corporation, employees get a 10 percent reduction in the price of Exxon gas and 15 percent off the price of TBA (tires, batteries, and accessories) from Exxon service stations. Gas is also sold at cost at FedEx, Liebert Corporation, and Merle Norman Cosmetics, which sells its cosmetics at cost, as well.

———

> **"Years ago, 'employee perks' usually entailed a designated parking space close to the building and a gold watch, a bonus at retirement in addition to your pension. Today, those ideas aren't even considered perks. They're the norm."**
>
> —Kelly Williams, *OfficeSolutions*

At Delta Air Lines, employees and their spouses receive annual passes for unlimited travel anywhere on the Delta system, and reduced rates on other airlines after ten years of service. Employees at FedEx can fly free on the company's planes and at reduced rates on other airlines.

———

Random House offers all employees ten free books a year and a 50 percent discount on all Random House books.

———

REI (Recreational Equipment, Inc.), based in Kent, WA, allows employees to use rental equipment at no cost. It also gives first-edition, not yet released, pieces of REI gear or apparel as holiday gifts to each employee. Products are personally delivered by a member of the senior team to each store and department. The stores take this time to hold staff meetings, pancake breakfasts, and pizza dinners. They also set up "Let's Talk" sessions between store leaders and the senior staff member, and between the staff member and front-line employees.

———

Most employees of Westin Hotels receive free meals at work. Free rooms are also available to employees after one year's service. A ten-year employee and his immediate family can stay for 15 nights at a Westin Hotel, with 20 percent off the cost of meals. Other employees get 50 percent off any hotel room rate.

———

Employees at Valassis Communications receive holiday baskets at the end of each year. Recently, the gift had a back-in-time theme: It was a Radio Flyer red wagon filled with old-fashioned candy and toys. Other holiday "baskets" included coolers on wheels filled with barbecue tools, cookbooks, sauces, and foodstuffs; two-piece luggage sets; insulated bags filled with sports equipment; and large, decorative tin tubs filled with edibles.

A SAMPLING OF PERKS OFFERED BY TIME WARNER

- If employees work past 8 P.M. in New York, they get $10 toward dinner, and a free cab ride home—even to New Jersey.
- Employees get free copies of all Time Inc. magazines.
- Fathers and mothers get parental leave up to one year.
- Employees get free admission to the major museums in New York City.
- After five years of service, employees get free physical exams.

Close to a thousand firms in the New York metropolitan area pass out TransitChek MetroCard vouchers to their employees for buses, subways, ferries, and commuter railroads. Champion International Corporation in Stamford, CT, now a part of

International Paper, based in Memphis, offers $15 a month to van poolers and also buys TransitCheks. About 20 percent of employees who drove to work now use car pools, van pools, or mass transit.

———

Interstate Electronics in Anaheim, CA, gives $20 a month to each person in a car pool and the same amount to employees who take the train from San Diego. Xerox Corporation in Norwalk, CT, also gives workers discounts off monthly bus or train passes, subsidizes van pools, and provides preferential parking for car and van pools.

———

At *Reader's Digest*, employees can identify potential car or van pools in their areas through a computer access program that matches employees' transportation needs.

———

Medtronic Physio-Control Corporation subsidizes a bus service during off-hours on Fridays and weekends for employees who are working odd shifts.

———

At Nissan, office and factory employees are each provided with three work outfits at no expense. Wearing the work clothes is voluntary.

———

In its Dallas, TX, plant, Mary Kay, Inc., provides each production-line worker with three sets of work clothes a year. Women get a bright red jumpsuit as well as reddish outfits with printed blouses and slacks. Men get blue trousers and shirts and matching baseball caps.

———

Flight attendants choose from a variety of uniform styles at Delta Air Lines.

———

The City of Decatur, IL, gave each employee a "company jacket" with the city's logo on the front.

———

Shirley Kauppi, owner and manager of the King Copper Motel in Copper Harbor, MI, provides juice, pop, fruit, and snacks to the cleaning staff. Kauppi also allows spouses and children to use a designated motel room to watch TV or read until employees finish working.

> **"Here is a simple but powerful rule . . . always give people more than they expect to get."**
> —Nelson Boswell

———

Larry Hilcher of Larry Hilcher Ford in Arlington, TX, provided a catered lunch for employees at both Thanksgiving and Christmas and gave each person a box of steaks and a turkey.

———

Instill Corporation, a Pleasanton, CA, Internet commerce firm, has an open account for employees at a local Peet's. They can walk to the local coffeehouse on their break to get a cup of quality joe.

———

Leo Burnett Worldwide, Inc., the largest ad agency in Chicago, keeps a bowl of red apples in the reception rooms on every one of its 11 floors. Burnett gives away 1,000 apples daily.

———

All 6,000 employees at the main branch of JP Morgan Chase in New York City get a free lunch every day. The perk costs the company $8 million a year. Employees of Northwestern Mutual insurance and financial management, based in Milwaukee, also get lunch, which costs about $3 million a year.

———

A chef prepares a seven-course lunch daily for employees of Merle Norman Cosmetics, based in Los Angeles, at a minimal cost to the employee. There is no charge for snacks and beverages, which are spread out in the company dining room during morning and afternoon breaks. In the morning, employees can choose among muffins, pastries, and croissants, and in the afternoon they can pick from an assortment of pies or cakes, doughnuts, cookies, and ice cream.

———

Lunches are subsidized at Mary Kay, Inc. Each table also has a white cloth and a vase of flowers. At *Reader's Digest*, employees may choose from a variety of low-cost cold and hot lunches, including a complete "Lite Line" selection menu. The company also offers the convenience of a daily "take-out" dinner.

———

Every day at exactly 3:30 P.M., the Fox Chase Cancer Center in Philadelphia, PA, hosts high tea with cookies for all employees, patients, vendors, and guests who happen to be in the building. About 200 people a day enjoy this perk. Employee feedback on the daily tradition has been extremely positive. "It gives us the opportunity to get away from the routine, step outside, get fresh air, and recharge our batteries," says staff scientist Kathy Alpaugh. "It also gives you the chance to interact with your colleagues and try out your jokes," adds technical specialist Jack Zilfou. This tradition has endured through dramatic changes and challenges, and makes it a little easier for everyone to get through their day.

———

The International Mission Board of the Southern Baptist Convention, in Richmond, VA, gives all employees a card with candy at Thanksgiving. The gifts are delivered by managers carrying baskets. "People get so much at Christmastime," says Charlene Eshleman, staff development manager, "that this gift is more special."

———

Every Christmas, Remington Products gives out a turkey to each employee, and each year another item is added— cranberry sauce, stuffing mix, a coupon for a bottle of wine— all bagged by Remington executives.

A Case Study in Employee Benefits & Perks

When Valassis Communications, a marketing company headquartered in Livonia, MI, acquired NCR Marketing Services, headquartered in Lincolnshire, IL, with offices in the United Kingdom, Italy, Spain, Germany, France, and Mexico, the company's employee base went from about 1,600 to nearly 4,000 employees and its profile expanded from that of a U.S.–based company to one with a global presence. On the first anniversary of the successful acquisition, the CEO sent flowers to all the NCR locations, thanking them for a great year and looking forward to the future. Thank-you cards were also created by in-house graphic designers, translated into five languages, signed by Valassis Communications and NCR CEOs, and sent to all NCR employees in the United States and abroad.

During work hours, employees at Valassis are invited to sell handmade crafts and wares to other employees during their free time, at an event called Art Mart, held in November. It has been a well-received and highly anticipated annual event.

Employees are also encouraged to have their families join them for lunch in the cafeterias, which are equipped with booster seats and high chairs. The company has a family room that provides privacy for nursing mothers and is equipped with a breast pump, refrigerator, TV/VCR/DVD, toys, beanbags, and other kid-friendly items for parents who may need to bring children to work on snow days and during day care emergencies. Upon the birth or adoption of a child, the company offers new parents free car seats.

Additionally, Valassis provides graduation gifts to employees' children when they graduate from high school. The gift includes an all-purpose carry-on bag filled with an atlas, snacks, and other goodies for the "places they will go." Then, when they head off to college, care packages filled with necessities—detergent, a laundry bag, snacks, and phone cards so they can call home—are sent to their dorm rooms or apartments.

At their headquarters in Livonia, Valassis has an on-site hair and nail salon for employees. It also has an on-site doctor for office visits, who answers employee questions online. All employees get annual on-site, discounted flu shots.

Northwestern Mutual in Milwaukee has dozens of clubs, ranging from fishing and running groups to a company chorus. Retirees who continue to participate do not have to pay dues.

———

Hewlett-Packard employees anywhere in the world may make reservations to stay, at a modest cost for a limited number of days, at any of the company's recreation areas, which include Little Basin Park in the Santa Cruz Mountains, three facilities in Colorado, one resort in the Pocono Mountains of Pennsylvania, a beach villa in Malaysia, a lake resort in Scotland, and a ski-chalet complex in the German Alps.

———

Johnson Wax has nine resort facilities in different parts of the country for vacationing employees and their families, including the Lighthouse Resort in northern Wisconsin and resorts at Cape Cod and Lake Tahoe. Other companies that offer vacation spots include Springs Mill, a textile manufacturer in Fort Mill, SC, and Steelcase, the office furniture maker in Grand Rapids, MI.

———

IBM offers highly discounted memberships to recreational facilities, including country clubs at Poughkeepsie, Sands Point, and Endicott, NY.

———

At 3M, the Tartan Park Clubhouse—a country club in Lake Elmo, MN—is for the exclusive use of 3M-ers for a nominal membership cost.

———

Nearly 10,000 Wilmington, DE–area employees of E. I. du Pont de Nemours belong to the company's country clubs, which consist of four 18-hole golf courses—three in Wilmington and one in nearby Newark, DE—as well as tennis courts and facilities for dining and social gatherings.

Employee & Company Anniversaries

Celebrating anniversaries is an important way to acknowledge a long relationship between a company and its employees. Ninety-two percent of organizations have some type of reward for years of service, and about 50 percent of employees view such programs as very or extremely important to them. Although they recognize employee tenure rather than performance, employee longevity is itself crucial to the success and stability of most organizations.

Leslie Beck, director of Recognition and Rewards for Hilton Hotels, has a unique way that she celebrates her anniversaries with the company. On her anniversary date, she sends messages to people she has worked with over the years and thanks them for what they have done to help her.

———

ComDoc, a business document solution provider based in Uniontown, OH, hosted 50 Ways Comdoc Cares, a tribute to their 50th year in business, in 2005. Each branch location participated in projects and events throughout the year designed to honor customers, employee-partners, and outside communities. They surpassed their goal of 50 projects completed in their 50th-year celebration.

On their one-year anniversaries, employees of New Belgium Brewery, the Fort Collins, CO–based brewery famous for Fat Tire ale, receive a custom bicycle. Founder Jeff Lebesch is known for promoting a work culture for enthusiastic cyclists. Accompanying the one- or three-speed cruiser bike is a celebration, an initiation—all employees become part owners after a year's time. The brewery provides ample bike parking and on-site showers to encourage workers to commute with their new bikes.

Medtronics in Minneapolis, recently replaced their years of service awards with paid days off for employees on their anniversaries because that is what their employees most wanted.

> **"Brains, like hearts, go where they are appreciated."**
> —Robert McNamara, *Former U.S. Secretary of Defense*

The South Mountain Company, a design and construction firm in West Tisbury, MA, gives diamond bracelets to employees when they reach 20 years of service. At Elliott Co. in Jeannette, PA, which is owned by the Japan-based Ebara Corp., when workers reach a milestone anniversary, they are given $10 for each year of service.

Daxko, the Birmingham, AL, software firm, gives employees a four-week sabbatical after seven years of service. Washburn Communication, a marketing and communications strategy firm in Bellevue, WA, gives a one-month paid sabbatical to employees when they reach five years of company service. Semiconductor chip maker Intel, based in Santa Clara, CA, rewards employees with an eight-week, fully paid sabbatical following seven years of service.

———

ThoughtWorks, a Chicago-based information technology consulting firm, gives its employees a three-month paid sabbatical when their tenure reaches ten years.

———

Atria Senior Living Group, which operates three senior living complexes in Tucson, AZ, established new "career commitment anniversary gifts" to be awarded at intervals from a worker's ten-year anniversary on—and made the awards retroactive. A housekeeper at Atria Bell Court Gardens received a bonus check for $10,000 on her 25th anniversary. The company also set up "career commitment hourly rewards": an extra 20 cents to 75 cents an hour depending on the number of years with the company, in addition to regular pay and 3 percent to 5 percent merit-based raises.

———

Guard Insurance Group, of Wilkes-Barre, PA, pays for employee vacations, not just for the time off. To be eligible, an employee must work for the company for five years. "It was instituted at the inception of the company because a lot of people don't treat themselves to a vacation," says CAO Carl Witkowski. Guard gears its incentives toward recruitment and retention. The company gives the employee $2,000 to go on vacation. After ten years it increases to $2,500

EMPLOYEE ANNIVERSARY TIPS

➡ Fresh flowers on desk

➡ 1-, 5-, 10-, 15-year pins/jackets/robes/windbreakers

➡ Consumer electronics or grossed-up cash equivalents

➡ Paid day off for birthday/company anniversary

➡ Mini-vacations

➡ Sabbaticals

and then to $3,000 for 15 years. The industry retention rate is approximately 89 percent, and the company has exceeded that for the past nine years.

———

To mark the tenth anniversary of *O, The Oprah Magazine*, Oprah Winfrey gave every staffer—regardless of length of employment—an Apple iPad, a leather iPad case with the staffer's initials, and a check for $10,000.

———

Dr. Bob Shillman, CEO of Cognex, a Boston-based machine vision systems provider, established the Perseverance Awards at Cognex to reward individuals who have devoted significant time to the company's success. The awards increase in value, and when an employee reaches 25 years of service he or she is given the opportunity to become a philanthropist. The company sets up a $25,000 charitable giving account in the employee's name. The employee decides who and how much to donate to any IRS-approved charity.

———

At Country Kitchen International, headquartered in Madison, WI, restaurant employees are given an embroidered gold star to wear on their uniform after three months of employment, and other stars at six and nine months, respectively.

———

Every Westin Hotel holds an annual banquet honoring employees with more than five years' service.

———

On their 5th anniversary with Mary Kay, Inc., employees receive 20 shares of stock; on their 10th, 80 shares; on their 15th, 120 shares.

The H. B. Fuller Company, a St. Paul, MN, maker of glues, adhesives, and sealants, extends a special bonus vacation every 5 years, starting on an employee's 10th anniversary. That is, at the10th, 15th, and 20th year and every 5th year thereafter, a person gets an extra 2 weeks off with pay, as well as an $800 bonus.

- Give all employees one rose for each year of employment on the anniversary of their start date.
- Present awards at appreciation dinners.
- Ask employees how they'd like to be honored for a long-term service anniversary.

Griffin Hospital, in Derby, CT, wanted to do something special for employees who had worked there five years or more, resulting in its own version of *American Idol*: "Griffin Idol Fun Night." Eleven employees volunteered to be contestants, and their performances were taped at a local news studio.

Lands' End recognizes employees who have 10-, 20-, and 25-year anniversaries with the company. On the date of their anniversary, they receive their choice of merchandise and a framed and signed catalog cover from the year they began at Lands' End. In a recent year, all eligible candidates were asked how they wanted to celebrate their anniversary, with a choice among (1) a game show, (2) a Packers Party, and (3) a rock-and-roll celebration. The winning choice was the rock-and-roll celebration, so the company hired a band, served burgers and fries in baskets, decorated everything in pink and black and covered with 1950s icons. The party included icebreakers, trivia, and all kinds of '50s prizes and giveaways. To end the celebration, all honorees were sent off with old-fashioned root beer floats.

F or its employment anniversary program, media research firm Arbitron went beyond the usual watches, pens, and pearls. They offered employees the chance to shop online for a wide range of products and services—from furniture to food to travel. One employee remarked that after 20 years of standing on her feet in the mail room, the company owed her a foot massager— and she got one!

R obert W. Baird's Quarter Century Club recognizes those who have been with the company for 25 years or more. There are now over 74 associates in the club, which is about 20 percent of all associates. When Baird conducted an associate opinion survey that asked, "If you have your way, how likely are you to be working at Baird five years from now?" 82 percent responded that they were very likely or somewhat likely to be with Baird.

> **"Staff birthday bashes are more common than board meetings. When your big day comes, we round everyone up and sing 'Happy Birthday' to you. We do this for everyone."**
> —Harvey Mackay, *President, Mackay Envelope Corp.*

W hen an employee reached her 25th anniversary with the Office of Personnel Management in Washington, DC, she was asked what she would like to do to celebrate. She said she had always wanted to ride an elephant, so they asked the local zoo if it would be possible to arrange a ride. It was, and they did, taking pictures of the event and creating a day to remember for this loyal, long-term employee.

———

Mel Powell, manager of the training department for the Kellogg Company in Battle Creek, MI, converted a conference room into an office for one of his senior trainers to recognize the trainer's 25th anniversary with the company.

———

At Hallmark Cards in Kansas City, MO, employees can invite coworkers to share their 25th anniversary cake. Between 200 and 1,000 people show up for each celebration.

> **"Corporate management needs to recognize that the workforce has to have a partnership role in that process of rebuilding. And that pertains to matters not just of hiring and job opportunity, but to improving the quality and morale of the corporate workforce."**
> —Stephen Roach,
> *Chief Economist,*
> *Morgan Stanley*

Pitney Bowes, headquartered in Stamford, CT, gives employees with 25 years of service an extra month's vacation. The same benefit is then offered every fifth year.

———

The Employee Recognition Committee of the library at Wake Forest University needed to recognize each employee, but to do so in a cost-effective manner. Mary Lib Slate, government documents librarian, reports: "In our building, no food or drink is allowed, only water in a closed container. So we bought bottled water, and designed tags to tie around the necks with pretty ribbons. The tags had a picture of the building and said 'Drink to Your Good Health,' and could serve as bookmarks. The director or associate director presented the water to each employee on his or her birthday, which not only recognized their special days, but also gave them the opportunity to say a personal word to each employee. Total cost for 50-plus people was under $14."

Boardroom, Inc., the publisher of several of the country's leading newsletters, recently celebrated a company milestone in style. Chairman and CEO Martin Edelston says, "To make life more fun, we had a Dixieland marching band to celebrate the company's anniversary in a new space, a team member's coming back from maternity leave, and another coming back from a honeymoon."

> **COMPANY ANNIVERSARY TIPS**
> ➡ Hotel parties/dances
> ➡ Casino night
> ➡ Send all employees to industry's leading conference
> ➡ Send all employees to a vacation isle

At Leo Burnett Worldwide, Inc., an advertising agency headquartered in Chicago, every employee receives a gift on Anniversary Day. Gifts have included jams and jellies, a model train, statues, and customized bottles of wine. In addition, every employee receives one dollar for every year of the agency's life.

When Baxter International, Inc., had its 50th birthday, they celebrated by hosting 50 rank-and-file employee ambassadors from 50 facilities in 18 countries who traveled to the Deerfield, IL, headquarters to mark the occasion.

For Ryder System's 50th-anniversary celebration, employees shared a cake that was shaped like a truck and covered with yellow icing.

———

To mark the 70th anniversary of a British subsidiary, Johnson Wax closed its Racine, WI, plant for a week, chartered a Boeing 747 jet, and flew the entire British workforce—480 people—to the United States, where they were put up in hotels, toured the company's facilities, shopped, and enjoyed a banquet. One night, employees in Racine picked up the British guests and brought them to their homes for dinner. The visitors also spent two days sightseeing in New York City.

———

Alaska Airlines's 70th anniversary celebration consisted of a host of events:

- Trivia Contest: Employees who correctly answered questions about Alaska's history were entered into a drawing for a prize.
- Anniversary Luncheon: The company invited 70 of its senior employees to a luncheon at the Canadian Museum of Flight in Langley, British Columbia, to talk about the "good old days." Guest speakers included former and current CEOs of Alaska Airlines.
- Poem and Song Contest: Employees were invited to create a song or poem best depicting the airline's history. The winner received a vacation package to Alaska.

Company Stock & Ownership

One of the most powerful forms of recognition is to make employees owners of the company. This represents a long-term commitment to the individual, typically reserved for a select few. Employees who share a stake in an organization behave a lot differently from employees who don't.

According to one survey of American workers, 85 percent rank stock options as a positive incentive. On average, companies that have employee stock ownership plans and engage in participative management programs grow three to four times faster than those that do not. For example, after Avis became an employee-owned company, its complaint rate dropped 35 percent and its stock value rocketed 400 percent in two years.

If every employee can be made to feel that he or she is working for his or her own company, pride, effort, and performance will improve. The following exchange between Carl Buchan, founder of Lowe's Companies, and a store manager illustrates the importance of giving employees a sense of ownership.

"What is that?" asked Buchan.

"It's damaged merchandise, sir."

"Look at it more closely and tell me what you see."

"Well, that's a damaged water pump, and a dented refrigerator, and windows with broken glass," replied the manager.

"That's not what I see when I look over there. What I see is money—my money—because I paid for it. And before the year is out, we're going to have a plan whereby part of that will belong to you and the other employees. Then when you look you'll see money, too, and you'll take better care of your money than you're doing now, and consequently you'll take better care of my money."

*The Largest ESOPs**

COMPANY	BUSINESS	EMPLOYEES
Publix Super Markets	Supermarkets	60,000
Health Trust	Hospital management	23,000
Avis	Rental cars	20,000
Science Applications	Research and development	11,000
EPIC Healthcare	Hospital management	10,000
Charter Medical	Hospital management	9,000
Parsons Corporation	Engineering	8,600
Weirten Steel	Steel manufacturing	8,200
Avondale Shipyards	Shipbuilding	7,500
Dan River	Textiles	7,000

*ESOP: Employee Stock Ownership Plans
(at least 20 percent majority-owned)

Indianapolis, IN–based Mike's Carwash, with 37 locations in Indiana and Ohio, shares profits with all employees through a gain-sharing program. Locations that beat targeted labor costs each month split the difference among all nonmanagerial employees, based on how many hours they work. Recently, Mike's gave over $500,000 in gain-sharing.

———

Railroad Associates Corp., a Hershey, PA–based railroad engineering and contracting firm, offers employee stock-ownership, through which nonmanagement employees own about 40 percent of company stock.

———

Heavy Construction Systems Specialists (HCSS), a Houston-area software developer based in Sugar Land, TX, offers an employee stock-purchase plan—all employees own 30 percent of the company. It also shares profits, and recently gave employees a profit-sharing contribution of cash and stock valued at 22 percent of their salary.

———

Inn of the Governors, a Santa Fe, NM, hotel, offers profit sharing to its employees for achieving team goals. In November, the month the program started, the hotel made $1.8 million annually. By June, annual income climbed to $2.2 million. In the first year the hotel shared profits, each employee received a $3,000 bonus. A few years later it was $4,500. "It makes running a business very easy," hotel owner Jeff Vander Wolk says. Vander Wolk has since capped the amount of profit the hotel keeps, using any surplus for incentives. Employees share about 70 percent of the surplus profit in bonuses or gain shares. Managers set aside 30 percent in a growth fund for future investment opportunities in which the staff can participate. Turnover among its employees is minuscule, with the average worker spending 4.3 years at the Inn, compared with an industry average of 2 years. Although it differs in structure, the El Rey Inn, also in Santa Fe, NM, offers profit sharing, as well. Owner Terrell White launched the program in 1981 by investing a percentage of the payroll in a long-term growth fund. To date, the hotel has paid out $1.5 million to its employees when they retire or leave the company.

> **"We work under management but we are part owners. So everything doesn't come from the top down. A lot comes from the bottom up. I try to give my best. The better the company does, the more money that goes in my little kitty."**—Bill Harris, *Purchasing Agent, Lowe's Companies*

The South Mountain Company, a design and construction firm in West Tisbury, MA, offers employees a chance to buy a stake in the company after five years of service. Employee-owned Marco Inc., a technology firm based in St. Cloud, MN, shares all profits. It recently distributed $2.3 million to its employees on revenues of $62 million. Graham Group, a Calgary, Alberta–based construction and project management company, offers profit sharing. Coles Salon in Minneapolis–St. Paul, offers an employee stock ownership plan—unusual for a hair salon.

———

WestJet, a Calgary, Alberta–based airline, has profit sharing and share-ownership plans.

———

At Bovis Lend Lease's Atlanta, GA, office, interest on a stock fund set up for employees back in 1983 pays for various employee rewards. They can earn movie tickets, flowers, special classes such as skydiving or cooking, lawyer or accountant fees, a day off to help a charity of their choice, emergency elderly or child care, or permission to bring family members on business trips.

> **"Why do I work until two-thirty in the morning and then come back for a breakfast at eight o'clock almost every day? Because I own a piece of this. We've built this, and I feel a tremendous commitment to seeing it continue."**
> —A partner at Goldman Sachs

———

Approximately 9,500 American companies—about 10 percent of the workforce—have employee stock-ownership plans. Procter & Gamble, J. C. Penney, Lockheed Martin, Polaroid, and Time Warner all offer employee stock-ownership plans. Employees also own a large piece of the company at FedEx, Hallmark Cards, Lowe's, and Quad/Graphics.

———

Starbucks offers all employees "bean stock" each year, equivalent to 14 percent of their salaries. They are allowed to hold the stock for a minimum of five years. They can then keep the difference between the original price and the current price of the stock.

———

At Apple Computer, based in Cupertino, CA, the assembly-line workers received stock options for 200 shares (50 a year for 4 years), and middle managers received options ranging from 5,000 to 20,000 shares.

———

At Citibank's Diners Club, outstanding customer service can earn an employee $400 worth of stock.

———

> **"You get a sense that you own the business. What that means is that you're going to spend a lot less time worrying about whose toes you're going to tread on and much more time worrying about how you're going to move that business forward."**—James A. Meehan, *Manager, General Electric*

———

Companies that participate in the profit-sharing Scanlon Plan include Dana Corporation of Toledo, OH, which manufactures and distributes components for trucks and industrial vehicles; Magna Mirrors in Holland, MI; and Herman Miller, furniture manufacturers in Zeeland, MI. The plan has four principles: (1) Identity—everyone in the company must understand the business, its goals, and the need for profitability; (2) Participation—everyone in the company must have the opportunity to influence decisions; (3) Competence—each person must continually improve his or her abilities; and (4) Equity—returns should be shared with employees, investors, and customers, each receiving a fair share.

———

COMPANY STOCK TIPS

➡ Give shares of company stock.

➡ Give stock as part of a promotion.

➡ Give stock as reward for completing major project.

➡ Provide stock matching.

➡ Provide workshop on overall investment strategies.

At LifeUSA (now owned by AllianzLife Insurance Company), an insurance company located in Minneapolis, all employees are owners, receiving approximately 10 percent of their compensation in the form of stock options, and are more efficient and effective than employees of competing firms. According to founder Robert W. MacDonald, "We'll write more business than probably 98 percent of the companies out there. And we'll do it with fewer people. Because they're owners, they're involved, they run the company." Employees control options on more than 1.8 million shares of stock, or approximately 4,500 per employee. To help them learn how to improve the value of their stock, LifeUSA conducts quarterly financial briefings for employees, called "Share the Wealth" meetings, and classes in topics such as marketing, customer service, and "Working the Business" are regularly taught by senior staff.

———

At Lowe's Companies, employees own 25 percent of the company. Each store elects a representative to an advisory committee and holds monthly meetings for employees to discuss changes to operating procedures and merchandising. As a result, productivity at Lowe's is 200 to 300 percent above industry average and employee theft is less than one sixth of the average.

When Carl Buchan, founder of Lowe's Companies, died, his will specified that employees, through a profit-sharing plan and trust, had the option of buying all his stock.

———

Southwest Airlines developed the first profit-sharing program in the airline industry. It involves employees in company ownership by requiring that they invest at least one-fourth of their profit-sharing funds in company stock. They are provided with regular financial and performance data (such as profit-and-loss statements, revenue passenger miles, and so forth) to monitor the effectiveness of the operation. As a result, Southwest has won the industry's "triple crown" (fewest lost bags, fewest complaints, best on-time performance) a record eight times. In fact, Southwest is the *only* airline to have won the triple crown.

> **"Our philosophy is to share success with people who make it happen. It makes everybody think like an owner, which helps them build long-term relationships with customers and influences them to do things in an efficient way."** —Emily Ericsen, *Vice President of Human Resources, Starbucks Coffee Company*

———

At Missouri engine rebuilder Springfield ReManufacturing Corporation (SRC), employees own the company. One way that SRC involves them in decision making is through the use of what is known as the Great Game of Business—the company's form of open-book management. Introduced by CEO Jack Stack, the Great Game of Business trains all employees to understand everything about the company's financial data. They are then invited to play the game by monitoring weekly income statements and cash-flow reports, and to compare actual results against projected results. Then, on a quarterly basis, employees receive bonuses that are based on selected financial goals, such as return on assets. According to Stack, "What they learn is how to make money, how to make a profit. The more people understand, the more they want to see the result."

———

Science Applications International Corporation, based in McLean, VA, was founded on the principle of employee ownership. J. Robert Beyster knew that to own even a small stake in a business that is growing exponentially can be the most powerful incentive. Beyster has gone further than most companies, however, in relinquishing 98 percent of the company to employees.

———

APPENDIX I

Where to Get Specialty Reward Items

A. C. OEHMICH LEATHER COMPANY
3390 Lanam Rd.
Bloomington, IN 47408
(800) 903-0763
acoehmichleather.com

Manufacturer of high-quality, value-priced business and personal-use leather goods. Makes luggage, memo/notepads, business card cases, travel kits, etc.

ACTION IMAGES
7148 N. Ridgeway Ave.
Lincolnwood, IL 60712
(847) 763-9700
actionimagesinc.biz

Published a color poster depicting statistics and program-cover art from every Major League Baseball All-Star Game going back to the game's inception in 1933.

AMERICAN EXPRESS
Corporate Sales
4315 S. 2700 West
Rm. 3520
Salt Lake City, UT 84184
(800) 666-7317
americanexpress.com

The American Express Gift Cheque is an impressive award that offers the flexibility of cash.

BANG & OLUFSEN AMERICA, INC.
780 W. Dundee Rd.
Arlington Heights, IL 60004
(800) 840-4733
bang-olufsen.com

Offers high-end, visually appealing audio/video, speakers, and telephones.

BASS PRO SHOPS/ OUTDOOR WORLD INCENTIVES
2500 E. Kearney St.
Springfield, MO 65898
(800) 951-1000 x 2
owincentives.com

Offers customizable gift cards for Bass Pro Shops and Outdoor World.

BENNETT BROTHERS, INC.
30 E. Adams St.
Chicago, IL 60603
(800) 868-9132
bennettbrothers.com

Offers an annual catalog, Choose-Your-Gift, and Prize Book with 50+ gifts that can be customized in each of 14 price levels, from $16 to $1,000.

BULOVA CORPORATION
Special Markets Division
One Bulova Avenue
Woodside, NY 11377-7874
bulovaspecialmarkets.com

Offers solid brass miniature replicas of world-famous clocks and customized watches that you can add diamonds to as an award—one diamond at a time—by sending it back to Bulova.

CIBT
1451 Dolley Madison Blvd
Ste. 300
McLean, VA 22101
(800) 929-2428
us.cibt.com

Visa and passport services; provides legalization services.

COLEMAN COMPANY
3600 N. Hydraulic St.
Wichita, KS 67219
(800) 835-3278
coleman.com

Offers camping gear, gas grills, and backyard products.

CONCORD/ MOVADO GROUP

650 From Rd.
Paramus, NJ 07652
concord-watch.com

Makers of luxury watches.

THE COSTUME FACTORY

211 N. 5th St.
Columbus, OH 43215
(800) 596-9357 or
(614) 464-2115
costumefactory.com

Offers six-foot-tall inflatable costume characters for meetings, conventions, and trade shows.

CRAFTSMAN TOOLS

3333 Beverly Rd.
Hoffman Estates, IL 60179
craftsman.com

Designs custom tool sets conveniently packaged in a sturdy, versatile Craftsman tool box.

CRATE AND BARREL CORPORATE SALES

1250 Techny Rd.
Northbrook, IL 60062
(800) 967-6696
crateandbarrel.com

Home cookware, decorations, gift certificates, home furnishings, housewares.

CREATIVE CAKERY

6467 E. Pacific Coast
Highway
Long Beach, CA 90803
(800) 224-4261
creativecakery.com

Customizes baked goods— bundt cakes decorated with ribbons, bows, balloons, flowers. Ships nationwide.

EASTMAN KODAK

343 State St.
Rochester, NY 14650-0519
store.kodak.com

Presents its newest Fun Saver disposable camera, the Telefoto 35, which has a telephoto lens and high-speed film. Offers the basic Fun Saver 35, an upgraded version with flash, the water-resistant Fun Saver, and a panoramic model that produces wide-angle pictures.

FIGHTER PILOTS USA

505 N. Lakeshore Dr.
Ste. 5602
Chicago, IL 60611
(800) 56-TOP-GUN
fighterpilotsusa.com

Customers actually fly fighter jets and engage in aerial combat maneuvers. Mission includes one hour of ground school, one hour of combat flying, and a one-hour debriefing that includes photos and videos of the flight.

FONTAZZI (SUBSIDIARY OF GIFT BASKET SUPPLIES)

612 N. Eckhoff St.
Orange, CA 92868
(888) 224-7110
fontazzi.com

Will custom imprint gourmet popcorn tins and gift baskets.

FORTUNE COOKIE DIVISION, WONTON FOOD INC.

220–222 Moore St.
Brooklyn, NY 11206
(800) 776-8889
wontonfood.com

Offers fortune cookies, in several flavors, with personalized messages.

FRANKLIN ELECTRONIC PUBLISHERS

One Franklin Plz.
Burlington, NJ 08016
(800) 266-5626
franklin.com

New Big League Baseball Electronic Encyclopedia contains more than one million statistics on the sport. Also sells Crosswords, an electronic crossword-puzzle aid.

GARGOYLES, INC.

500 George Washington
Hwy.
Smithfield, RI 02917
(800) 426-6396
gargoyles-store.mwrc.net

Gargoyles eyewear and a full line of eyewear accessories and repair kits.

G. NEIL COMPANIES

720 International Pkwy
P.O. Box 450939
Sunrise, FL 33345-0930
(877) 968-7471
gneil.com

Personalized certificates, plaques, frames, and presentation folders.

GREENWORLD PROJECT, THE

P.O. Box 177
Cohasset, MN, 55721
(800) 825-5122
greenworldproject.net

Provides environmentally conscious gifts with customizable messages such as live tree seedlings wrapped in clear tubes and seed kits.

HAAS-JORDAN COMPANY

1447 Summit St.
Toledo, OH 43603
(419) 243-2189
haas-jordan.com

Sells a personal beach umbrella imprinted with your company logo.

HARRY AND DAVID

2500 S. Pacific Hwy.
Business Division
Medford, OR, 97501-2675
(877) 322-1200
harryanddavid.com

Offers rewards from fresh fruits and meats to savory seafood and gift baskets.

HILLERICH & BRADSBY COMPANY (LOUISVILLE SLUGGER)

800 W. Main St.
Louisville, KY 40202
(866) 785-BATS
sluggergifts.com

Offers sporting equipment that can be custom printed with your company name, logo, individual's name, or promotional message, including baseball bats, baseball gloves, and golf clubs.

HINDA INCENTIVES

2440 W. 34th St.
Chicago, IL 60608
(773) 890-5900
hinda.com

A full-service incentive company with in-house program administrators, creative and marketing professionals, merchandise recommendation and sourcing.

HISTORIC NEWSPAPER ARCHIVES

1582 Hart St.
Rahway, NJ 07065
(866) 219-0285
simplypersonalized.com

Original U.S. newspapers dating back to 1800. Encased in personalized

gold-embossed binder with certificate of authenticity.

HOUGHTON MIFFLIN HARCOURT

222 Berkeley St.
Boston, MA 02116
(617) 351-5000
hmhco.com

Offers books that can be customized with a personal message, company logo, or custom title.

IRWIN INDUSTRIAL TOOL COMPANY

8936 N. Pointe Executive Park Dr.
Huntersville, NC 28078
(704) 987-4555
irwin.com

Sells tools and tool sets that can be custom imprinted, including Vise-Grip locking hand tools.

IRWIN PRODUCTIONS

6340 Hinson St.
Las Vegas, NV 89118
(702) 616-4770
irwinproductions.com

Offers an Escapade show of singers and dancers who interact with the audience. The theme can be tailored to any corporate event.

J. C. PENNEY

6501 Legacy Dr.
Plano, TX 75024
(800) 832-4438
jcpgiftcard.com/corporate.htm

Gift certificates good at all retail stores and through all catalogs.

JET LAG WATCH COMPANY

4 Allston St.
West Newton, MA 02465
(617) 965-7010
jetlag.com

Offers a watch that lets the user adapt naturally to a new time zone by running more slowly or more quickly during a flight.

JOHN'S INC.

800 W. Johns Rd.
Apopka, FL 32703
(407) 886-8850

Growing gifts—live plants that can be customized with your name or company logo. Minimum order of 200 pieces.

KMART CORPORATION

Gift Certificate
Administration
3333 Beverly Rd.
Hoffman Estates, IL 60179
(866) 562-7848
kmart.com

Personalized "Cash Cards" in any denomination between $5 and $400.

LA CROSSE TECHNOLOGY

2817 Losey Blvd. S.
La Crosse, WI 54601
(608) 782-1610
lacrossetechnology.com

Offers a sunrise, sunset wireless weather control station. Displays a forecast for the next 12 to 15 hours.

LEGAL SEA FOODS

One Seafood Way
Boston, MA, 02210
(800) 343-5804
shop.legalseafoods.com

Offers lobsters, clams, steaks, other delicacies, and custom-imprinted lobster pots.

LOUISVILLE GOLF

2500 Grassland Dr.
Louisville, KY 40299
(800) 456-1631
louisvillegolf.com

Offers a wide range of premium wood golf equipment, replica clubs, and desk items. Each Louisville Golf wood mallet putter is handcrafted with over 100 hand operations and can be adorned with laser-etched logos and emblems.

MARKETING INNOVATORS

9701 W. Higgins Rd.
Rosemont, IL 60018
(800) 843-7373
marketinginnovators.com

Freedom to Choose retail gift certificates.

MCARTHUR TOWELS

700 Moore St.
Baraboo, WI 53913
(800) 356-9168
mcarthur-towels.com

Personalized towels and robes.

MEDIA SYSTEMS, INC.

727 Wainee St.
Ste. 201
Lahaina, HI, 96761
(800) 398-2271
mediasystemsmaui.com

Photography, video, and computer graphics.

MHP INTERNATIONAL

7520 N. St. Louis Ave.
Skokie, IL 60076
(888) 710-7206
mastermassagetables.com

Offers massage tables and massage chairs.

MULTI IMAGE PRODUCTIONS

8829 Complex Dr.
San Diego, CA 92123
(800) 736-0560
multiimage.com

Produces custom multimedia shows.

NORDICTRACK

1500 S. 1000 West
Logan, UT 84321
(888) 308-9616
nordictrack.com

Features the Back & Stomach Machine—a seat that rotates to exercise back, abdominals, and obliques.

OLYMPUS/MAR-SAN
6045 N. Keystone Ave.
Chicago, IL 60646
(800) 621-5582
mar-san.com

Offers a wide range of incentive technology products such as digital cameras, voice recorders, TVs, etc.

OMAHA STEAKS
10909 John Gait Blvd.
Omaha, NE 68103
(800) 228-2480
osincentives.com

Sample packages of steaks, all cuts.

ONEIDA SILVERSMITHS
P.O. Box 1
Oneida, NY 13421-2829
(888) 263-7195
oneida.com

Quality stainless-steel silverware/flatware gifts from $25 to $100.

ORREFORS KOSTA BODA
6185-K Huntley Rd.
Columbus, OH 43229
(800) 999-0655
kostaboda.us/
corporate.htm

Hand-crafted crystal awards that can be personalized.

PANASONIC
One Panasonic Way
Secaucus, NJ 07094
(800) 405-0652
panasonic.com

More than 400 electronic products from digital cameras to Blu-Ray players, from massagers to LED TVs.

PARKER PEN U.S.A. LTD.
Sanford Business to
Business Division
2200 Foster Ave.
Janesville, WI 53545
(800) 356-9466
sanfordb2b.com

Catalog of pens that can be personalized with your company's logo or an individual's name.

PC NAMETAG
124 Horizon Dr.
Verona, WI 53593
(877) 626-3824
pcnametag.com

Name tags.

PHYSICIANS SALES & SERVICE
4345 Southpoint Blvd.
Jacksonville, FL 32216
(904) 332-3000
Fax (904) 332-3213
pssd.com

Medical products distribution.

POLAROID CORPORATION
1265 Main St.,W2-2
Waltham, MA 02451
(800) 765-2764
polaroid.com

Offers customizable instant cameras.

PROMO DIRECT
931 American Pacific Dr.
Suite 100
Henderson, NV 89014
(800) 748-6150
promodirect.com

Offers huge selection of customizable items such as awards, plaques, pens, watches, golf balls, and portfolios.

PSP SPORTS MARKETING
519 Eighth Ave.
New York, NY 10018
(212) 697-1460
pspsports.com

Offers personalized desktop diary featuring profiles and color photos of America's Olympic heroes.

REI (RECREATIONAL EQUIPMENT INC.)
Sumner, WA
(800) 426-4840
rei.com

Outdoor gear and clothing products and gift certificates.

SANTA'S WORLD

Kurt S. Adler, Inc.
7 W. 34th St.
New York, NY 10001
kurtadler.com

Features more than 20,000 Christmas items including Disney and Sesame Street characters.

SEIKO CORPORATION OF AMERICA

The Premium Dept.
1111 MacArthur Blvd.
Mahwah, NJ 07430
(800) 545-2783
seikousa.com

Offers watches for color imprinting and embossed customization.

SENTRY

900 Linden Ave.
Rochester, NY 14625
(800) 828-1438
sentrysafe.com

Customized fire-safe products for protecting valuables.

SEVYLOR U.S.A. INC.

3600 North Hydraulic
Wichita, KS 67219
(800) 835-3278
sevylor.com

Full line of inflatable sports products like air mattresses, canoes, boats, and snow products.

THE SHARPER IMAGE

1370 Broadway
Ste. 1107
New York, NY 10018
(877) 312-7060
sharperimage.com

Offers a wide range of products such as air purifiers, foam neck pillows, travel products, etc.

SKIP BARBER RACING SCHOOL

P.O. Box 1629
Lakeville, CT 06039
(866) 932-1949
skipbarber.com

Offers classes in formula race-car driving at more than 20 different racetracks. They will arrange lodging, catering, and professional photography.

SMITH & HAWKEN

4 Hamilton Landing
Novato, CA, 94949
(800) 423-0117
smithandhawken.com

Garden catalog.

SONY CORPORATION

Sony Premium
Incentive Sales
1 Sony Dr.
Park Ridge, NJ 07656
(800) 833-6302
b2b.sony.com

Offers electronic equipment that can be used for incentives.

SPORTSOURCE, INC.

1300 Virginia Dr.
Ste. 401
Fort Washington, PA 19034
(800) 290-6120
sport-source.com

Offers customizable items such as basketballs, volleyballs, croquet sets, air hockey tables, tents.

STARBUCKS STORE

4086 Del Rey Ave.
Marina Del Rey, CA 90292
(800) 571-7289
starbucksstore.com

Coffee and related items.

STARLITE ORIGINALS

1601 N. Indiana St.
Los Angeles, CA 90063
(800) 726-9660
sollc.com

Supplies fine art sculptures in bronze, pewter, brass vermeil, and 24-karat gold vermeil.

STOCK YARDS

340 N. Oakley Blvd.
Chicago, IL 60612
(877) 785-9273
stockyards.com

Gifts, such as steaks, seafood, and gourmet treats.

SUGARDALE'S

Special Markets Division
1888 Southway St. S.E.
Massillon, OH 44646
(800) 860-5444
sugardale.com

Offers 130 gourmet food items, such as their signature "beauty ham."

They will include a personalized gift card.

SWISS ARMY BRANDS, INC.

7 Victoria Dr.
Monroe, CT 06468
(800) 243-4066
vsacorporate.com

Can custom-imprint the Swiss Army Brand Watch and Swiss Army Knife.

TELESCOPE CASUAL FURNITURE, INC.

82 Church St.
Granville, NY 12832
(518) 642-1100
telescopecasual.com/
preadspecial.php

Offers umbrellas, beach chairs, and a full line of director's chairs that can be customized with your company name and logo.

TIFFANY & CO.

727 Fifth Ave.
New York, NY 10022
(800) 770-0800
business.tiffany.com

Will custom-engrave crystal awards, plaques, clocks, or other specialty items.

TORRINGTON CHRISTINE PHOTOGRAPHY

210 Post St.
Ste. 902
San Francisco, CA 94108
(415) 921-6333
sfphotopro.com

Professional photographers.

TRAVEL GRAPHICS INTERNATIONAL

1199 Josephine Rd.
St. Paul, MN 55113
(612) 377-1080
tgimaps.com

Graphics of promotional material for destination, pocket maps, posters.

TUCKER-JONES HOUSE

P.O. Box 231
East Setauket, NY 11733
(800) 992-9883
tavernpuzzle.com

Metal puzzles offered. Packaging for puzzles can be personalized with company names and logos.

WATERFORD WEDGWOOD USA

41 Madison Ave.
New York, NY 10010
(866) 714-0592
waterford.com/cust/
business.asp

Features crystal and china at all price levels.

WELLS LAMONT

6640 W. Touhy Ave.
Niles, IL 60714
(800) 323-2830
wellslamont.com

Sells gloves that can be customized with your logo.

WILSON SPORTING GOODS CO.

8700 W. Bryn Mawr Ave.
Chicago, IL 60631
(800) 432-0321
wilson.com

Will imprint a golf ball with your four-color logo or name. Also offers laser-engraved putters and golf balls.

WORKMAN PUBLISHING CO.

Special Markets
Department
225 Varick St.
New York, NY 10014-4381
(212) 614-7509
workman.com
jenny@workman.com

Offers a full line of gift books, cookbooks, kids' books, and calendars. Will create customized books and calendars for corporate promotions and incentive programs.

WORLD HERITAGE RESEARCH & TRAVEL SERVICES

1311 Main St.
Angels Camp, CA 95222
(800) 336-0930
worldheritage.com

Travel and video production.

APPENDIX II

Companies That Arrange Unusual Reward Activities

ADAM PRODUCTIONS
1520 Daytonia Rd.
Miami Beach, FL 33141
(305) 865-0363
adamprod.com

Offers themed events such as Renaissance, pirate, or patriotic dinners complete with amazing decorations and staff dressed to the theme.

ADVENTURE CONNECTION
P.O. Box 475
Coloma, CA, 95613
(800) 556-6060 or
(530) 626-7385
raftcalifornia.com

River trips, whitewater rafting.

ATLANTIS SUBMARINES INTERNATIONAL, INC.
210 West 6th Ave.
Ste. 200
Vancouver, BC V5Y IK8
Canada
(604) 875-1367
atlantisadventures.com

Offers submarine tours off the shores of Hawaii's Waikiki, Maui, and Kona.

BLACK CANYON RIVER ADVENTURES
P.O. Box 60130
Boulder City, NV 89006
(800) 455-3490
blackcanyonadventures.com

Group raft trips down the Colorado River.

BOUNDARY COUNTRY TREKKING
11 Poplar Creek Dr.
Grand Marais, MN 55604
(800) 322-8327
boundarycountry.com

Offers cross-country ski trips, along with dog-sled trips, in winter, guided canoe trips in summer.

BRIER & DUNN DESTINATION MANAGEMENT
180 Harbor Dr.
Ste. 104
Sausalito, CA 94965
(415) 339-0539
brier-dunn.com

Travel incentive company that can, among other things, stage a jungle theme dinner at the San Francisco Zoo.

BURNSIDE MARINA
680 W. Lakeshore Dr.
Burnside, KY 42519
(606) 561-4223
burnsidemarina.com

Houseboat excursions.

CALIFORNIA LEISURE CONSULTANTS
77-530 Enfield Lane
Suite C-1
Palm Desert, CA 92211
(760) 200-0112
accessdmc.com

Offers unique theme events including Indian-Western barbecues with stuntmen who stage a gunfight, or baseball games with players wearing vintage uniforms.

CANADIAN PACIFIC HOTELS AND RESORTS
405 Spray Ave.
Banff, AB T1L 1J4
Canada
(866) 540-4406
fairmont.com/banffsprings

A legendary 850-room castle in Banff Springs in the Canadian Rockies.

CARLSON MARKETING GROUP
P.O. Box 59159
Carlson Pkwy.
Minneapolis, MN 55459
(763) 445-3000
carlsonmarketing.com

Houseboating and other excursions.

ECHO BAY RESORT
P.O. Box 16247
Irvine, CA 92623
(800) 752-9669
sevencrown.com

Houseboating excursions.

EGR INTERNATIONAL
30 Broad St.
New York, NY 10004
(800) 221-1072
egrinternational.com

Houseboating excursions.

FEATHER RIVER RAIL SOCIETY
P.O. Box 608
Portola, CA 96122
(530) 832-4131
wplives.org

Train fans and would-be engineers can go to the Western Pacific Railroad Museum, the only place in the world where you can rent and drive a real locomotive. The museum also offers rides on cabooses and flatcars.

INCENTIVES TO INTRIGUE
(707) 869-8205
incentivestointrigue.com

Organizes teams on a treasure hunt through San Francisco via streetcars.

INCREDIBLE ADVENTURES
6604 Midnight Pass Rd.
Sarasota, FL 34242
(800) 644-7382
incredible-adventures.com

Compete against friends or foes in a full-day aerial combat competition, Fighter Combat. The hangar facility at Fighter Combat International is tailor-made to provide group comfort.

LA COSTA RESORT AND SPA
2100 Costa Del Mar Rd.
Carlsbad, CA 92009
(800) 854-5000
lacosta.com

Offers a world-famous spa, golf courses, tennis courts, and 300-seat nightclub.

MANA, ALLISON & ASSOCIATES
1388 Sutter St.
Ste. 525
San Francisco, CA 94109
(415) 474-2266
mana-allison.com

Offers an array of leisure activities for conferences and conventions coming to San Francisco, including Renaissance fairs.

MARITZ TRAVEL
1400 S. Highway Dr.
Fenton, MO 63099
(877) 462-7489
maritztravel.com

Exclusively Yours Cheques, in denominations of $10 and $50, redeemed for unique travel experiences, including safaris, flying lessons, golf clinics, and baseball camps.

MARKETING INNOVATORS
9701 W. Higgins Rd.
Rosemont, IL 60018
(800) 843-7373
marketinginnovators.com

Freedom to Choose retail gift certificates.

MARRIOTT SURFERS PARADISE RESORT & SPA
158 Ferny Ave.
Surfers Paradise
Queensland 4217 Australia
61 (7) 5592-9800
marriott.com

Marriott Surfers Paradise Resort on Australia's Gold Coast features an aquatic playground with beaches, lagoon, simulated coral reef, and water sports.

MICATO SAFARIS
15 W. 26th St.
New York, NY 10010

(800) 642-2861
micato.com

Offers tented safari camps in Kenya and Tanzania.

THE MOORINGS
93 N. Park Place Blvd.
Clearwater, FL 33759
(888) 952-8420
moorings.com

Yacht-chartering company.

MOUNTAIN WINERY
14831 Pierce Rd.
Saratoga, CA 95070
(408) 741-2822
mountainwinery.com

Offers group events at this winery such as bridge building and casino parties.

MUSEUM OF SCIENCE AND INDUSTRY
57th St. & Lake Shore Dr.
Chicago, IL 60637
(800) 468-6674 or
(773) 684-1414
msichicago.org

Can rent the museum for private events.

MUSHING MAGAZINE
P.O. Box 1195
Willow, Alaska 99688
(907) 495-2468
mushing.com/resources/
tourlist.php

Website lists a number of companies offering dog-sledding trips.

NAPA CHAMBER OF COMMERCE
1556 First St.
Napa, CA 94559-0636
(707) 226-7455
napachamber.org/
dir_things.html

Website lists dozens of fun things to do in Napa Valley including ballooning, canoeing, and visiting wineries.

NAPA VALLEY ALOFT, INC.
6525 Washington St.
Yountville, CA 94599
(800) 627-2759
nvaloft.com

Hot-air balloon tours in the Napa Valley area.

NAPA VALLEY WINE TRAIN
1275 McKinstry St.
Napa, CA 94559
(800) 427-2124
winetrain.com

Scenic ride on 1915 Pullman train.

PACIFIC WHALE FOUNDATION
300 Maalaea Rd.
Ste. 2ll
Wailuku, HI 96793
(808) 249-8811
pacificwhale.org

Offers whale and dolphin watching in Hawaii.

PARAGON GUIDES
P.O. Box 130
Vail, CO 81658
(970) 926-5299
paragonguides.com

Weekend or six-day backcountry hiking trips.

PLAYTIME INC.
P.O. Box 25022
Seattle, WA 98165
(877) 652-0875
playtimeinc.com

Participants skillfully combine the use of GPS and cutting-edge office technologies—PDAs, cell phones, laptops, and digital cameras—to find a hidden cache of goods. Success will require both competition and collaboration. Teams must design a plan, execute it, and reach the final goal, all without a predesignated leader.

QUIZMASTER PRODUCTIONS
9845 Bankside Dr.
Ste. 1100
Roswell, GA, 30076
(770) 664-0648
quizmaster.com

Offers customized corporate contests.

SHERATON HOTELS & RESORTS
1111 Westchester Ave.
White Plains, NY 10604
(914) 640-8100
sheraton.com

Includes the Sheraton Parco de Medici, the first golf resort in Italy.

SOARING ADVENTURES OF AMERICA, INC.
P.O. Box 541
Wilton, CT 06897
(800) 762-7464
800soaring.com

Sailplane rides, glider rides, and skydiving all across the country.

SPACE CAMP
U.S. Space & Rocket Center
One Tranquility Base
Huntsville, AL 35805
(800) 637-7223
spacecamp.com

Experience astronaut training camp.

STAR CLIPPERS
7200 N.W. 19th St.
Ste. 206
Miami, FL 33126
(800) 442-0551
starclippers.com

Groups sail on the world's only modern-day clipper ship.

SUNRISE BALLOONS
P.O. Box 891360
Temecula, CA 92589
(800) 548-9912
sunriseballoons.com

Scenic balloon tours and charters in Southern California.

TEAM BUILDING USA
3925 Pebblebrook Lane
Bedford, TX 76021
(866) 351-8326
teambuildingusa.com

Offers fun events such as canoeing and wilderness adventures, scavenger hunts, and murder mystery games.

10TH MOUNTAIN DIVISION HUT ASSOCIATION
1280 Ute Ave.
Ste. 21
Aspen, CO 81611
(970) 925-5775
huts.org

Reserve huts deep within the Colorado Rockies.

VANCOUVER AQUARIUM
P.O. Box 3232
Vancouver, BC V6B 3X8
Canada
(604) 659-3474
vanaqua.org

Arranges activities such as breakfast with beluga whales, cocktails with killer whales, and dinner among octopuses, sea otters, and other aquatic creatures.

VENTURE-UP
(888) 305-1065
ventureup.com

A corporate training and wilderness adventure company offers team-building courses.

WATERFALL RESORT
Mike Dooley, Reservations
P.O. Box 6440
Ketchikan, AK 99901
(800) 544-5125
waterfallresort.com

Resort in Ketchikan, Alaska, offers mountain wildlife and salmon fishing. Also offers national wildlife trips and fly-fishing adventures.

WINDRIDGE YACHT CHARTERS
2950 N.E. 32nd Ave.
Fort Lauderdale, FL 33308
(800) 636-9910
windridgeyachts.com

Luxurious and elegant charter for corporate events or parties; 5-star-hotel dining quality.

WORLD YACHT
Pier 81
W. 41st St. & Hudson River
New York, NY 10036
(212) 630-8100
worldyacht.com

Yacht charters in the New York City area.

APPENDIX III

Incentive Travel Coordinators

ADI MEETINGS & INCENTIVES, INC.
1223 E. Broadway Rd.
Ste. 100
Tempe, AZ 85282
(480) 350-9090
adimi.com

ATLANTIS SUBMARINES INTERNATIONAL, INC.
210 West 6th Ave.
Ste. 200
Vancouver, BC V5Y 1K8
Canada
(604) 875-1367
atlantisadventures.com

ATS PACIFIC
Level 10
130 Elizabeth St.
Sydney, NSW 2000
Australia
61 (2) 9268-2111
atspacific.com

BATEAUX PARISIENS
Sodexo Loisirs
Port de la Bourdonnais,
75007 Paris, France
bateauxparisiens.com

BELL TOURS, INC.
12894 16th Ave.
White Rock, BC V4A IN7

Canada
(800) 665-9501
belltours.com

CANADIAN PACIFIC HOTELS AND RESORTS
155 Wellington St. West
Ste. 3300
Toronto, ON M5V 0C3
Canada
(800) 257-7544
cphotels.ca

CLASSIC CRUISE & TRAVEL CO.
5850 Canoga Ave.
Ste. 550
Woodland Hills, CA 91367
(800) 563-2238
classic-cruise.com

CREATIVE GROUP, INC.
619 N. Lynndale Dr.
Appleton, WI 54914
(920) 739-8550
www2.creativegroupinc.com

CREATIVE TRAVEL PLANNERS, INC.
5855 Topanga Canyon Blvd.
Ste. 220
Woodland Hills, CA 91367
(818) 704-7033
ctptravel.com

CRUZAN YACHT
18120 S.W. 88th Ct.
Miami, FL 33157
(800) 628-0785
cruzan.com

CURACAO CHAMBER OF COMMERCE AND INDUSTRY
Kaya Junior Salas #1
P.O. Box 10
Willemstad, Curacao
N.A. 611451
(599) 461-1451
curacao-chamber.an

DIETHELM TRAVEL
Diethelm & Co., Ltd.
Kian Gwan Bldg. 11
140-1 Wireless Rd.
Bangkok, Thailand 10330
(66) 2660 7000
diethelmtravel.com

DITTMAN INCENTIVE MARKETING CORP.
317 George St.
New Brunswick, NJ 08901
(732) 745-0600
dittmanincentives.com

EGR INTERNATIONAL MEETINGS & INCENTIVES
30 Broad St., 14th fl.

New York, NY 10004
(212) 949-7330
egrinternational.com

EMPIRE FORCE EVENTS
(212) 924-0320
empireforce.com

FOUR SEASONS HOTEL SYDNEY
199 George St.
Sydney, NSW 2000
Australia
61 (2) 9250-3100
fourseasons.com/sydney

FRASER & HOYT INCENTIVES
1505 Barrington St.
Ste. 107
Halifax, NS B3J 3K5
Canada
(902) 421-1113

HELEN MOSKOVITZ GROUP
95 White Bridge Rd.
Ste. 414
Nashville, TN 37205
(615) 352-6900
thekeyeventgroup.com

HOLT PARIS WELCOME SERVICE
12 Rue du Helder
75009 Paris, France
(33) 45 23 08 14
holtfrance.com

HOTELS OF SWITZERLAND
1214 West Elmdale Ave.
Chicago IL 60660

(312) 919-1500
hotelsofswitzerland.com

INCENTIVE HOLLAND GROUP
Pieter Braaijweg 101
1099 DK Amsterdam
Holland
(31) 20 5045750
incentive.nl

INCENTIVE SOLUTIONS
12505 N.E. 156th St.
Woodinville, WA 98028
(206) 283-7176
incentivesolutionscorp.com

INCENTIVE TRAVELERS CHEQUE INTERNATIONAL
505 N. Lakeshore Dr.
Ste. 6601
Chicago, IL 60611
(312) 527-1111
itcheque.com

INTERMEDIA CONVENTION & EVENT MANAGEMENT
547 Harris St.
Ultimo, NSW 2007
Australia
(61) 1300 365 976
eventplanners.com.au

ITA GROUP
4800 Westown Pkwy.
West Des Moines, IA 50266
(800) 257-1985
itagroup.com

JECKING TOURS & TRAVEL, LTD.
Unit 1703, 17/F
BEA Tower
Millennium City 5
418 Kwun Tong Rd.
Kwun Tong, Kowloon
Hong Kong
(352) 2731-3100
jeckingtours.com

JNR INC.
19900 MacArthur Blvd.
Ste. 700
Irvine, CA 92612
(800) 343-4546
jnrcorp.com

THE JOURNEYMASTERS, INC.
254 Essex St.
Salem, MA 01970
(800) 875-3422
Fax (978) 336-6535
journeymasters.com

KUONI TRAVEL LTD.
500 Seventh Ave.
New York, NY 10018
(212) 596-1000
Fax (212) 313-9800
kuoni.com

LANDRY & KLING CRUISE SPECIALISTS
1390 S. Dixie Hwy.
Ste. 1207
Coral Gables, FL 33146
(800) 448-9002
landrykling.com

LEADERS IN TRAVEL
200 Middleneck Rd.
Great Neck, NY 11021-1103
(516) 829-0880 Ext. 105
leadersintravel.com

LONGUE VUE HOUSE & GARDENS
7 Bamboo Rd.
New Orleans, LA 70124
(504) 488-5488
longuevue.com

MANDARIN ORIENTAL HOTEL GROUP
345 California St.
Ste. 1250
San Francisco, CA 94104
(415) 772-8800
mandarinoriental.com

MARITZ TRAVEL
1400 S. Highway Dr.
Fenton, MO 63099
(877) 462-7489
maritztravel.com

MARRIOTT HOTELS & RESORTS
10400 Fernwood Rd.
Bethesda, MD 20817
(301) 380-3000
marriott.com

MONARK TURISMO
Praca dom Jose Caspar
134, 11 andar
Sao Paulo, Brazil
(11) 3235-4322
monark.tur.br

MOTIVACTION
16355 36th Ave. N.
Ste. 100
Minneapolis, MN 55446
(800) 326-2226
motivaction.com

NEWTOURS
Via A. Righi
8 50019 Sesto Fiorentino
Florence, Italy
(39) 055 3611.1
newtours.it/english/
chi-siamo.html

NORWEGIAN CRUISE LINE
7665 Corporate Center Dr.
Miami, FL 33126
(866) 234-7350
ncl.com

OLSEN O'LEARY ASSOCIATES, INC.
565 Epsilon Dr.
Pittsburgh, PA 15238
(412) 963-7272
Fax (412) 963-9773
olsen-oleary.com/travel/htm

PARAGON GUIDES
P.O. Box 130
Vail, CO 81658
(970) 926-5299
paragonguides.com

THE RESORT AT PORT LUDLOW
1 Heron Rd.
Port Ludlow, WA 98365
(877) 805-0868
portludlowresort.com

SHERATON HOTELS & RESORTS
1111 Westchester Ave.
White Plains, NY 10604
(914) 640-8100
sheraton.com

SILKWAY TRAVEL LTD.
4012-4018 Cambie St.
Vancouver, BC V5Z 2X8
Canada
(604) 656-1000
silkway.com

SINO-AMERICAN TOURS
37 Bowery
New York, NY 10002
(800) 628-1168
sinoamericantour.com

SITA WORLD TRAVEL
16250 Ventura Blvd.
Ste. 300
Encino, CA 91436
(800) 421-5643
sitatours.com

SPACE CAMP
U.S. Space &
Rocket Center
One Tranquility Base
Huntsville, AL 35805
(800) 637-7223
spacecamp.com

STAR CLIPPERS
7200 N.W. 19th St.
Ste. 206
Miami, FL 33126
(800) 442-0551
starclippers.com

STATE OF TENNESSEE DEPARTMENT OF TOURIST DEVELOPMENT
312 Rosa L. Parks Ave.
25th Fl.
Nashville, TN 37243
(615) 741-2159
state.tn.us/tourdev/

SUNBELT MOTIVATION & TRAVEL, INC.
3010 LBJ Freeway
Ste. 500
Dallas, TX 75234
(214) 638-2400
sunbeltmotivation.com

SUNQUEST VACATIONS
75 Eglinton Ave. East
Toronto, ON M4P 3A4
Canada
(416) 485-1700
sunquestvacations.ca

10TH MOUNTAIN DIVISION HUT ASSOCIATION
1280 Ute Ave
Ste. 21
Aspen, CO 81611
(970) 925-5775
huts.org

TRANSEAIR TRAVEL
2813 McKinley Pl. N.W.
Washington, DC 20015
(202) 362-6100
transeairtravel.com

TRAVEL AND TRANSPORT, INC.
2120 S. 72nd St.
Omaha, NE 68124-6310
(800) 228-2545
tandt.com

TRAVEL NEW ORLEANS, INC.
P.O. Box 52406
New Orleans, LA 70152
(800) 535-8747
travelneworleans.com

TRAVEL LEADERS
212 W. Colfax Ave.
South Bend, IN 46601
(574) 232-3061
travelleaders.com

UNITED TRAVEL GROUP
International Tours,
African Tours
925 Harvest Drive
Ste. 270
Blue Bell, PA 19422
(800) 223-6486
unitedtravelgroup.com

USA HOSTS
3068 E. Sunset Road
Ste. 9
Las Vegas, NV 89120
(702) 798-1975 or
(800) 634-6133
hosts-global.com

VACATION CONNECTION
20224 State Rd.
Cerritos, CA 90703
(800) 300-1007
ta2000.com

VANTAGE WORLD TRAVEL
1324 E. North St.
Greenville, SC 29605
(864) 233-7703
travelvantage.com

VIRGINIA ESCAPE LTD.
215 McLaws Cir.
Williamsburg, VA 23185
(757) 229-1161
vaescape.com

VISTA TRAVEL, INC.
10 Rogers St.
Cambridge, MA 02142
(617) 588-4200
vistatravelinc.com

WALTHER'S TOURS PTY. LTD.
P.O. Box 689
Douglasdale, 2165
South Africa
27 11 467 8867
walthers.co.za

WATERFALL RESORT
Mike Dooley, Reservations
P.O. Box 6440
Ketchikan, AK 99901
(800) 544-5125
waterfallresort.com

WORLD HERITAGE RESEARCH & TRAVEL SERVICES
1311 Main St.
Angels Camp, CA 95222
(800) 336-0930
worldheritage.com

APPENDIX IV

Motivational & Incentive Companies & Associations

ABERCROMBIE & KENT
1520 Kensington Rd.
Ste. 212
Oak Brook, IL 60523
(800) 554-7016
abercrombiekent.com
Offers luxury travel all over the world.

ADCENTIVE GROUP, INC.
4801 Viewridge Ave.
San Diego, CA 92123
(858) 278-9200
adcentive.com
Unique employee recognition and motivational programs.

ALL STAR INCENTIVE MARKETING
P.O. Box 980
Fiskdale, MA 01518
(800) 526-8629
incentiveusa.com
Incentive marketing company.

AMERICAN RENTAL ASSOCIATION
1900 19th St.
Moline, IL 61265
(800) 334-2177
ararental.org
Trade association.

ASSOCIATION OF RETAIL MARKETING SERVICES, INC.
2417 Post Rd.
Stevens Point, WI 54481
(715) 342-0948
narms.com
Trade association.

BUSINESS IMPROVEMENT COMPANY
7630 Bush Lake Rd.
Edina, MN 55439
(952) 835-4800
biworldwide.com
Incentive consulting company.

EDWARD ENTERPRISES, INC.
240 Puuhale Rd.
Ste. 101
Honolulu, HI 96819
(808) 841-4231
ee3.com
Convention printing, newsletters, programs.

EXCELLENCE IN MOTIVATION, INC.
Six N. Main St.
Ste. 370
Dayton, OH 45402
(937) 222-2900
eim-inc.com
Offers wide range of motivating incentives such as travel, debit cards, and merchandise.

EXTRAORDINARY EVENTS
13425 Ventura Blvd.
Ste. 300
Sherman Oaks, CA 91423
(818) 783-6112
extraordinaryevents.net
Event planning.

THE GOLF CARD
164 Inverness Dr. East
Englewood, CO 80155
(800) 321-8269
golfcard.com
Golf discount card.

INCENTIVE MAGAZINE
355 Park Ave. S.
New York, NY 10010
(646) 654-5447
incentivemag.com

INTERMEDIA CONVENTION & EVENT MANAGEMENT
547 Harris St.
Ultimo, NSW 2007
Australia
(61) 1300 365 976
eventplanners.com.au
Conference organizers.

KOHALA COAST RESORT ASSOCIATION
69-275 Waikoloa Beach Dr.
Waikoloa, HI 96738
(800) 318-3637
kohalacoastresorts.com
Resort association.

KVL AUDIO VISUAL SERVICES, INC.
466 Saw Mill River Rd.
Ardsley, NY 10502
(800) 862-3210
kvlav.com
Event staging, video production.

MANA, ALLISON & ASSOCIATES
1388 Sutter St.
Ste. 525
San Francisco, CA 94109
(415) 474-2266
mana-allison.com
Motivational consultants.

MARDEN-KANE INC.
36 Maple Pl.
Manhasset, NY 11030-1962
(516) 365-3999
mardenkane.com
Promotional firm.

MARITZ, INC.
1375 N. Highway Dr.
Fenton, MO 63099
(877) 462-7489
maritz.com
Incentives and motivational consulting.

MARKETING INNOVATORS
9701 W. Higgins Rd.
Rosemont, IL 60018
(800) 843-7373
marketinginnovators.com
Freedom to Choose retail gift certificates.

MEDIA SYSTEMS, INC.
727 Wainee St.
Ste. 201
Lahaina, HI 96761
(800) 398-2271
mediasystemsmaui.com
Photography, video, and computer graphics.

NATIONAL 4-H CENTER
7100 Connecticut Ave.
Chevy Chase, MD
20815-4999
(301) 961-2801
4hcenter.org
Trade association.

ORANGE COUNTY CONVENTION CENTER
9800 International Dr.
Orlando, FL 32819
(800) 345-9845
occc.net
Convention facility.

PLAYFAIR
5883 Lucas Valley Rd.
Nicasio, CA 94946
(415) 662-9899
playfair.com
Humor and motivational consultants.

THE ROBBINS COMPANY
149 Crawford Rd.
Statesville, NC 28687
(704) 872-5231
tharperobbins.com
Recognition and reward programs.

SITE
401 N. Michigan Ave.
Chicago, IL 60611
(312) 321-5148
siteglobal.com
Travel incentive information, promotional and research society.

SITEWORK ASSOCIATES, INC.

P.O. Box 20068
Sarasota, FL 34276
(800) 323-1927
siteworkassociates.com

Conference site finding services.

STARR-SEIGLE COMMUNICATIONS

1001 Bishop St.
Pacific Tower, 19th Fl.
Honolulu, HI 96813
(808) 524-5080
starrseigle.com

Advertising for group conventions.

THE SWEEPSTAKES CENTER

P.O. Box 16350
Rochester, NY 14616
(585) 392-4322
thesweepstakescenter.com

Sweepstakes and contest consulting and administration.

USMOTIVATION

7840 Roswell Rd.
Bldg. 100, 3rd fl.
Atlanta, GA 30350
(866) 885-4702
usmotivation.com

Full-service incentive company.

APPENDIX V

Featured Companies

24 HOUR FITNESS
p. 112
San Ramon, CA.
Fitness center chain

AAA OF SOUTHERN CALIFORNIA
pp. 22, 268
Los Angeles, CA.
Motor club.

AAMCO TRANSMISSION & COMPLETE CAR CARE
pp. 177, 292
Horsham, PA.
Transmission-repair franchise.

ACAPULCO RESTAURANTS
pp. 411–412
Cypress, CA.
Restaurant chain

ACCENTURE
p. 486
Dublin, Ireland.
Management and technology consulting

ACCESS DESTINATION SERVICES
p. 383
Long Beach, CA.
Design management and event production

ACCO BRANDS, INC.
p. 425
Lincolnshire, IL.
Manufactures office products

ACCUDATA
p. 301
Ft. Myers, FL.
Mailing lists, data solutions

ADVANCED MICRO DEVICES
pp. 333, 421–422
Sunnyvale, CA.
Manufactures and markets complex monolithic circuits

ADVANCED TECHNOLOGY INSTITUTE
p. 446
North Charleston, SC.
Private R&D management

ADVANTA CORPORATION
pp. 286, 370
Spring House, PA.
Financial services

AFL-CIO
p. 265
Washington, DC.
Federation of labor orgnizations

AG EDWARDS
p. 117
St. Louis, MO. Financial services holding company

AIPSO
p. 203
Johnston, RI.
Auto insurance

AKRON CHILDREN'S HOSPITAL
pp. 446–447
Akron, OH. Hospital

ALASKA AIRLINES, INC.
pp. 379, 402–403, 516
Seattle, WA. Airline

ALBERTA HEALTH SERVICES
p. 230
Calgary, Alberta, Canada.
Health services

ALCOA, INC.
p. 134
Pittsburgh, PA.
Aluminum producer

ALLIED SIGNAL
p. 268
Moncure, NC.
Engineering company

**ALLIED STEEL
BULDINGS**
pp. 144–145
Fort Lauderdale, FL.
Supplier of pre-engineered
steel buildings

AMERICAN AIRLINES
pp. 441, 451
Fort Worth, TX. Airline

**AMERICAN
ASSOCIATION FOR
RETIRED PEOPLE
(AARP)**
p. 237
Washington, DC.
Retirement association

AMERICAN EXPRESS
*pp. 104, 182, 302, 395,
484–485*
New York, NY. Financial
services, magazines,
information services

**AMERICAN EXPRESS
FINANCIAL ADVISORS,
INC.,**
p. 320
Minneapolis, MN.
Financial planning
services

**AMERICAN EXPRESS
TRAVEL RELATED
SERVICES**
p. 263
New York, NY.
Travel agency

**AMERICAN
FOODSERVICE**
pp. 382–383
Dallas, TX.
Produce distribution

**AMERICAN HOSPITAL
ASSOCIATION**
p. 441
Chicago, IL.
Health care association

**AMERICAN
PRODUCTIVITY &
QUALITY CENTER
(APQC)**
p. 11
Houston, TX.
Best-practices consulting
and research

**AMERICAN SOCIETY
ON AGING**
p. 301
San Francisco, CA. Senior
services organization

AMERICAN STRAP
p. 157
Diamond City, AK.
Leather goods company

**AMES RESEARCH
CENTER**
pp. 252–253
Mountain View, CA.
NASA field center

**AMSCO STEEL
COMPANY**
p. 308
Fort Worth, TX.
Steel manufacturer

AMWAY CORPORATION
pp. 216–217
Ada, MI. Multimarketing;
distributors of house care,
health, personal products

ANALYSIS GROUP
p. 58
Boston, MA. Economic
consulting firm

**ANALYTICAL GRAPHICS
INC.**
p. 486
Exton, PA. Aerospace and
defense company

**ANCHOR
COMMUNICATIONS
LLC**
p. 301
Lancaster, VA.
Publishing company

THE ANDERSONS
p. 440
Maumee, OH. Retail stores

**ANGUS BARN
RESTAURANT**
pp. 318, 405
Raleigh, NC. Restaurant

**ANTHONY WILDER
DESIGN/BUILD**
p. 171
Cabin John, MD.
Home remodeling

APG ELECTRIC
p. 471
Clearwater, FL. Electrical
contractors and engineers

APPLE COMPUTER
pp. 255, 370, 498, 521
Cupertino, CA. Computer, software, communication products, peripheral products

APPLIED MATERIALS, INC.
p. 125
Santa Clara, CA. Capital equipment producer

AQUASCAPE
pp. 323, 346–347
St. Charles, IL. Landscaping

ARAMARK CORPORATION
p. 252
Philadelphia, PA. Food services, maintenance and housekeeping services, makers of industrial uniforms and business clothing.

ARBITRON, INC.
pp. 378, 513
Columbia, MD. Surveys radio ratings

ARKEMA, INC.
p. 252
Philadelphia, PA. Chemicals manufacturer

ASSURANCE AGENCY
p. 92
Chicago, IL. Insurance company

AT&T
p. 189
Dallas, TX. Communications

AT&T UNIVERSAL CARD SERVICES
p. 155
Sioux Falls, SD. Credit card

ATLANTA BUSINESS CHRONICLE
p. 419
Atlanta, GA. Regional business newspaper

ATLANTA CONSULTING GROUP
p. 224
Atlanta, GA. Consulting services

ATLANTIC ENVELOPE COMPANY
p. 467
Atlanta, GA. Business and specialty envelope manufacturer

ATLANTIC RICHFIELD COMPANY (ARCO)
p. 69
La Palma, CA. Oil and gas exploration and production.

ATRIA SENIOR LIVING GROUP
pp. 292, 324, 510
Tucson, AZ. Senior living complexes

AUGUSTA TECHNICAL COLLEGE
p. 348
Thomson, GA. Vocational technical school

AUSTIN MEDICAL CENTER
pp. 68–69
Austin, TX. Health services

AUSTIN TAYLOR
p. 413
Anaheim, CA. Men's clothier

AUTODESK
pp. 487, 489–490
San Rafael, CA. Software

AUTOMATIC ANSWER
p. 415
San Diego, CA. Automated phone systems

AVIS RENT A CAR
p. 403
Parsippany, NJ. Rental cars

AVONDALE SHIPYARDS
p. 518
New Orleans, LA. Ship building

AWARDS.COM
p. 285
Lyndhurst, NJ. Recognition and rewards product company

BAILARD, INC
p. 200
Foster City, CA. Private investment firm

Littlehampton, England.
Cosmetic franchise chain

BOEING
p. 51
Chicago, IL.
Aircraft manufacturer

BORREGO SOLAR SYSTEMS
p. 293
Boston, MA. Commercial solar power systems

BOVIS LEND LEASE USA
p. 520
New York, NY. Real estate services and real estate investments

BRAINSTORM MARKETING
pp. 56, 177, 277
Des Moines, IA. Marketing

BRASSELER USA, INC.
p. 423
Savannah, GA. Dental instrumentation provider

BRENTMOOR RETIREMENT COMMUNITY
pp. 267–268
St. Louis, MO.
Retirement community

BRIER & DUNN
p. 387
Sausalito, CA. Destination management company

BRIGATE TRADING
p. 177

New York, NY.
Trading firm

BRONSON HEALTHCARE GROUP, INC.
pp. 234–235, 312
Kalamazoo, MI.
Health care services

BROWARD COUNTY GOVERNMENT
p. 436
Ft. Lauderdale, FL.
Local government agency

BRUCE POWER
pp. 62, 445
Tiverton, Ontario, Canada.
Private nuclear generator

BRUNSWICK MINING AND SMELTING CORP.
p. 291
Toronto, Ontario, Canada,
Mining company

BUCKINGHAM, DOOLITTLE & BURROUGHS LLP
p. 119
Canton, OH. Law firm

BURGER KING
p. 298
Miami, FL.
Fast-food restaurant chain

BUSCH GARDENS-TAMPA
pp. 23, 273, 432
Tampa, FL. Entertainment

BUSCH STADIUM
pp. 441–442

St. Louis, MO.
Sports stadium

BUSINESS FIRST OF COLUMBUS
pp. 338, 408
Columbus, OH. Regional business newspaper

BUSINESS FIRST OF LOUISVILLE
p. 246
Louisville, KY. Regional business newspaper

CAFE NATURA
p. 156
Sault Ste. Marie, Ontario,
Canada. Restaurant

CALIFORNIA PUBLIC EMPLOYEES' RETIREMENT SYSTEM (CALPERS)
p. 236
Sacramento, CA.
Pension system

CAMDEN PROPERTY TRUST
pp. 365–366
Houston, TX. Apartment management firm

CAMELBACK HYUNDAI-KIA
pp. 248–249
Phoenix, AZ. Auto dealer

CANON USA,
pp. 186, 309
Lake Success, NY.
Marketing and distribution of printers and copiers

CAPITAL ONE FINANCIAL CORPORATION
pp. 104, 269, 349, 488
McLean, VA.
Credit card services

CARGILL, INC.
p. 151
Winnipeg, Manitoba, Canada. Pharmaceutical company

CARLSON MARKETING GROUP
pp. 263, 314–315
Minneapolis, MN.
Trading stamp, coupon redemption; manufactures and distributes telescopes and binoculars

CARMEL CLAY PUBLIC LIBRARY
pp. 341–343
Carmel, IN.
Local public library

CARMICHAEL LYNCH
p. 177
Minneapolis, MN.
Advertising agency

CAROLINA SAFETY ASSOCIATES
p. 172
Gastonia, NC.
Fire protection equipment company

CASCADES DIAMOND, INC.
pp. 478–479
Thorndike, MA.

Manufactures egg cartons

CATHAY PACIFIC
p. 318
Hong Kong, China. Airline

CDW
p. 413
Vernon Hills, IL.
Technology vendor

CEDRA CORPORATION
p. 402
Austin, TX. Bioanalytical chemical services

CELESTIAL SEASONINGS, INC.
p. 300
Boulder, CO.
Herbal tea company

CELLULAR ONE
p. 443
Bellevue, WA. Cellular phone service provider

CENDANT CORPORATION
p. 483
Orlando, FL. Vacation ownership company

CENSEO CONSULTING GROUP
p. 61
Washington, DC.
Strategy and operations firm

CENTRAL TELEPHONE COMPANY
p. 325
Chicago, IL.
Telephone company

CERAC
p. 181
Milwaukee, WI. Specialty chemical company

CERAMICS PROCESS SYSTEMS CORPORATION
pp. 406–407
Chartley, MA. Technical ceramics manufacturer

CHAMPAIGN PARK DISTRICT
p. 226
Champaign, IL.
Local city-park services

CHAMPION INTERNATIONAL CORPORATION
pp. 501–502
Stamford, CT.
Paper and wood products

CHAPARRAL STEEL COMPANY
p. 466
Midlothian, TX.
Manufactures steel

CHARLES SCHWAB
pp. 187, 242
San Francisco, CA.
Financial services

CHARLESTON MEMORIAL HOSPITAL
pp. 348–349
Fall River, MA.
Medical services

CHARLOTTE OBSERVER
p. 398
Charlotte, NC. Newspaper

THE CONTAINER STORE
pp. 183, 337, 367–368, 389
Copell. TX.
Storage and organizational solutions retail store

CONVIRGENT TECHNOLOGIES
p. 489
Schaumburg, IL. Building safety and security systems

CORE CREATIVE
pp. 209-210
Milwaukee, WI.
Marketing solutions

CORONET/MTI FILM AND VIDEO
p. 420
Deerfield, IL Production and distribution of educational films

CORPORATE RESOURCE DEVELOPMENT
p. 278
Atlanta, GA. Sales and marketing company

COUNTRY KITCHEN INTERNATIONAL
p. 511
Madison, WI.
Restaurant chain

COURIER SERVICE
p. 490
London, England.
Delivery company

COX ENTERPRISES
pp. 64, 204
Atlanta, GA.
Diversified media company

CRITTER CLEANERS
p. 490
San Diego, CA.
Pet grooming company

CUNA MUTUAL GROUP
p. 404
Madison, WI. Offers life insurance, investment advisory and information technology to credit unions

CUNO
pp. 361–362
Meriden, CT. Manufactures water filtration and purification systems

CVS DRUG STORES
p. 224
Lowell, MA.
Pharmacy chain

CYANAMID CANADA
p. 452
Mississauga, Ontario, Canada. Manufactures pharmaceuticals

CYGNA GROUP
p. 176
Oakland, CA.
Engineering and consulting

D'AGOSTINO SUPERMARKETS, INC.
pp. 307, 409
Larchmont, NY.
Supermarket chain

DAIRY MART (CIRCLE K)
p. 374
Tempe, AZ.
Convenience stores

DALLAS BUSINESS JOURNAL
p. 299
Dallas, TX. Regional business newspaper

DALLAS, TX, CITY OF
p. 494
Local government

DANA CORPORATION
p. 521
Toledo, OH. Manufactures and distributes components for truck and industrial vehicles

DANIELS COMPANY
p. 456
Springfield, MO.
Trucking firm

DAXKO
pp. 344, 487, 509
Birmingham, AL.
Software firm

DDB WORLDWIDE COMMUNICATIONS GROUP, INC.
pp. 67, 318, 380
New York, NY.
Advertising agency

DEAN COLLEGE
p. 365
Franklin, MA.
Private college

DECATUR, IL
pp. 325, 503
Local government

DECISION ANALYST, INC.
p. 66
Arlington, TX.
Market research and consulting services

DEERE & COMPANY
p. 449
Moline, IL.
Farm equipment

DELL COMPUTERS
p. 484
Round Rock, TX.
Information technology company

DELOITTE TOUCHE TOHMATSU
pp. 97, 105
New York, NY.
Accounting services

DEL TACO
pp. 432–433
Lake Forest, CA.
Fast-food chain

DELTA AIR LINES
pp. 335, 440, 500, 503
Atlanta, GA. Airline

DENNY'S RESTAURANT
p. 466
Spartanburg, SC.
Restaurant chain

DESIGNER CHECKS
pp. 350–351
Colorado Springs, CO.
Manufactures designer checks

DEVELOPMENTAL DISABILITIES RESOURCE CENTER
p. 449
Lakewood, CO.
Disability services

DIGITAL EQUIPMENT CORPORATION
p. 369
Maynard, MA. Computer systems company

DIMENSION DATA CANADA INC.
pp. 55–56
Mississauga, Ontario, Canada. Network technology

DISNEY SPORTS ATTRACTION
p. 267
Lake Buena Vista, FL.
Division of Walt Disney Company

DOLE FOOD COMPANY, INC.
p. 353
Westlake Village, CA.
Produce producer

DOMINO'S PIZZA, INC.
pp. 223, 360, 370
Ann Arbor, MI.
Fast-food chain

DOMINY & ASSOCIATES
pp. 56–57
San Diego, CA.
Architectural firm

DOW CHEMICAL COMPANY
pp. 64–65, 382, 369
Midland, Ml. Chemical products, plastic products, consumer products

DOWNTOWN HONDA
p. 60
Spokane, WA.
Automobile dealer

DR PEPPER SNAPPLE GROUP, INC.
p. 389
Plano, TX.
Soft drink manufacturer

DUKE POWER
p. 190
Charlotte, NC.
Energy company

DUNKIN' BRANDS
p. 486
Canton, MA.
Fast-food restaurant chain

DURKEE-MOWER
p. 487
Lynn, MA.
Foodstuff purveyor

EASTMAN KODAK COMPANY
pp. 162, 353 , 448
Rochester, NY.
Photographic products and services, chemicals, imaging, information services

EAT MY WORDS
p. 271
San Francisco, CA.
Branding firm

EDDIE BAUER, INC.
p. 59
Bellevue, WA.
Retail clothing stores

E. I. DU PONT DE NEMOURS AND COMPANY
pp. 307, 508
Wilmington, DE. Energy, consumer products, insecticides, firearms, pharmaceuticals, industrial chemicals, medical products

EDWARDS JONES
pp. 112–113, 491
St. Louis, MO.
Financial investment firm

ELECTRONIC DATA SYSTEMS (EDS)
p. 321
Piano, TX. Computer outsourcing services

ELETTER
p. 416
Portland, OR. Direct mail marketing services

ELI LILLY & COMPANY
p. 498
Indianapolis, IN.
Pharmaceuticals

ELIZABETH ARDEN, INC.
p. 429
Miramar, FL.
Personal care products

EL REY INN
p. 519
Santa Fe, NM. Hotel

EL TORITO RESTAURANTS (REAL MEX RESTAURANTS)
pp. 405–406
Cypress, CA. Food service

ELLIS WELL DRILLING
p. 483
Clermont, FL.
Well-drilling company

EMC MORTGAGE CORPORATION
p. 236
Lewisville, TX. Mortgage financial services

EMERSON PROCESS MANAGEMENT POWER & WATER SOLUTIONS, INC.
p. 402
Pittsburgh, PA.
Power generation and water/wastewater treatment services

EMPIRE OF AMERICA FEDERAL SAVINGS BANK
p. 288
Buffalo, NY. Bank

EMPLOYCO
p. 175

Westmont, IL.
Human resources company

EMPLOYERS RESOURCE COUNCIL
p. 276
Mayfield Village, OH.
Human resources and consulting organization

EPCOR UTILITIES
p. 492
Edmonton, Alberta, Canada. Utility company

ERNST & YOUNG
pp. 197–198
London, England.
Financial services firm

THE ESTEE LAUDER COMPANIES, INC.
pp. 227–228
New York, NY.
Personal care products

EURO RSCG
p. 95
Chicago, IL. Marketing and advertising

EXCELON
p. 140–141
Chicago, IL.
Energy services provider

EXXON MOBIL CORPORATION
p. 500
Irving, TX. Petroleum products, exploration and refining, coal mining, chemical products

Charlotte, NC.
Industrial chemicals,
machinery, precious
metals, defense systems

FMC LITHIUM
p. 440
Charlotte, NC.
Battery company

**FORDHAM
UNIVERSITY, CAREER
PLANNING AND
PLACEMENT OFFICE**
p. 359
New York, NY.
Educational services

**FORD MOTOR
COMPANY**
pp. 66, 255, 353
Dearborn, Ml.
Manufacture and sale of
cars, financial services

FORTIS ADVISORS
p. 271
Scottsdale, AZ.
Life insurance company

**FORTRESS SAFE
AND LOCK**
p. 375
Cincinnati, OH.
Manufactures locks,
safes, and access control
systems

**FOUNDERS TITLE
COMPANY**
p. 289
Salt Lake City, UT.
Title company

**FOUR PI SYSTEMS
(HEWLETT-PACKARD)**
pp. 376, 460
San Diego, CA.
Developer of
manufacturing test
equipment

**FOUR SEASONS
FLOWER SHOP**
p. 68
Poway, CA. Florist

**FOX CHASE CANCER
CENTER**
pp. 504–505
Philadelphia, PA.
Biological research on
cancer prevention and
treatment

**FRANK IMPLEMENT
COMPANY**
p. 400
Scottsbluff, NE.
Farm equipment company

**FRED PRYOR
SEMINARS & CAREER
TRACK**
p. 66
Mission, KS.
Public seminar company

FTEN
pp. 58–59
New York, NY.
Financial technology firm

**FURST-MCNESS
COMPANY**
p. 471
Freeport, IL. Manufactures
premixed animal food

GAP, INC.
pp. 165–166, 303
San Francisco, CA.
Retail clothing stores

GARTNER, INC.
p. 373
Stamford, CT.
IT Industry market
research and consulting

GENENTECH
pp. 172, 491
San Francisco, CA.
Biotechnology

GENERAL CINEMA
p. 499
Newton, MA.
Theater chain

**GENERAL ELECTRIC
COMPANY**
pp. 274, 445, 467
Fairfield, CT. Electrical
and electronic equipment

GENERAL MILLS
pp. 245–246, 275
Minneapolis, MN.
Produces breakfast
cereals and other foods

**GIRL SCOUTS
OF NORTHERN
CALIFORNIA**
p. 172
Oakland, CA.
Youth service organization

GLASS DOCTOR
p. 188
Ocala, FL.
Glass company

HARDEE'S FOOD SYSTEMS, INC.
pp. 358–359
St. Louis, MO.
Fast-food restaurants

HARTFORD STEAM BOILER INSPECTION AND INSURANCE COMPANY
pp. 313–314
Hartford, CT. Boiler and machinery insurance

HASTINGS BOOKS, MUSIC, AND ENTERTAINMENT, INC.
pp. 403–404
Amarillo, TX.
Retail media entertainment stores

HATFIELD QUALITY MEATS
pp. 301–302
Hatfield, PA.
Food processing

HEALTH ALLIANCE
pp. 200–201
Cincinnati, OH.
Hospital consortium

HEARTLAND DENTAL CARE
p. 294
Effingham, IL.
Dental care center

HEAVY CONSTRUCTION SYSTEMS SPECIALISTS (HCSS)
pp. 487–488, 519
Sugar Land, TX.
Software developer

HERBALIFE, INC.
pp. 240–241
Los Angeles, CA.
Manufactures and sells natural wellness products

HERMAN MILLER
p. 521
Zeeland, MI. Manufactures office furniture

THE HERSHEY COMPANY
p. 26
Hershey, PA.
Makers of candy

HEWITT ASSOCIATES
p. 440
Lake Forest, IL.
Human resources and consulting firm

HEWLETT-PACKARD COMPANY
pp. 146, 250–251, 281–282, 369, 377, 414, 507
Palo Alto, CA.
Manufactures computers, servers, storage products, printers, networking equipment, and software

HILTON WORLDWIDE
p. 508
McLean, VA.
Hotels and casinos

HITACHI
p. 173
Tokyo, Japan.
International conglomerate

HI-TECH DURAVENT, INC.
p. 493
Plymouth, IN.
Manufactures flexible hoses

HI-TECH HOSE
p. 176
Newburyport, MA. Hose and ducting product maker

HOK
p. 206
St. Louis, MO.
Architectural design firm

HOME DEPOT, INC.
pp. 117, 183–184, 244, 254, 408–409, 435
Atlanta, GA.
Home improvement supply center

HOME SHOPPING NETWORK (HSN)
pp. 178–179
St. Petersburg, FL.
Home shopping television network

HOMESCOUT REALTY
pp. 95–96
Chicago, IL. Real estate

HONDA OF AMERICA MANUFACTURING
pp. 240, 267, 454
Maysville, OH.
Manufactures and sells cars

HONEYWELL INTERNATIONAL, INC.
pp. 25, 249, 255–258

Morristown, NJ. Produces industrial controls systems, avionics equipment, environmental controls for homes and buildings, and navigational equipment

HOSPIRA INC.
pp. 157–158
Lake Forest, IL. Pharmaceutical company

HOTEL ASSOCIATION OF NEW YORK CITY
pp. 360–361
New York, NY. Hospitality

HOUGHTON MIFFLIN HARCOURT PUBLISHING COMPANY
p. 326
Boston, MA. Publishing company

HOUSEHOLD AUTOMOTIVE FINANCE
p. 333
San Diego, CA. Financial services

HR NETWORKS
p. 60
Garden Grove, CA. Human resources company

HUGHES NETWORK SYSTEMS, INC.
pp. 117, 245
Germantown, MD. Provider of broadband satellite services, networks and products for businesses and consumers

HURON CONSULTING GROUP
p. 141
Chicago, IL. Health care consulting

HYATT HOTELS CORPORATION
pp. 24, 264
Chicago, IL. Hotels and industrial companies

ICI PHARMACEUTICALS GROUP
p. 409
Wilmington, DE. Pharmaceuticals

ID MEDIA
p. 200
New York, NY. Advertising agency

IKEA
p. 493
Delft, Netherlands. Home furnishings

I LOVE REWARDS (ILR)
pp. 456–457
Toronto, Ontario, Canada. Employee recognition company

IMRE COMMUNICATIONS
p. 413
Baltimore, MD. Branding company

INCENTIVES TO INTRIGUE
p. 387
San Francisco, CA.

Customized games, programs, and events

INDIANAPOLIS POWER & LIGHT COMPANY
p. 288
Indianapolis, IN. Electric utility

INFOSURV
p. 293
Atlanta, GA. Market research firm

INN OF THE GOVERNORS
p. 519
Santa Fe, NM. Hotel

INSTILL CORPORATION
p. 503
Pleasanton, CA. Manufactures supply chain information software for restaurants and foodservice manufacturers

INTEL CORPORATION
pp. 116, 401, 509–510
Santa Clara, CA. Manufactures semiconductors, memories, computer systems, software

INTERNAL REVENUE SERVICES (IRS)
pp. 266, 304
Washington, DC. Government agency

INTERNATIONAL BUSINESS MACHINES CORPORATION (IBM)
pp. 165, 288, 353, 424, 453–454, 493, 507

Armonk, NY.
Computer and business
machine manufacturer

**INTERNATIONAL
DATA GROUP**
p. 278
Boston, MA.
Technology media firm

**INTERNATIONAL
PAPER COMPANY**
p. 319
Memphis, TN.
Manufactures plywood,
paper, pulp, and packaging

**INTERSTATE
ELECTRONICS**
p. 502
Anaheim, CA.
Electronics manufacturer

INTUIT, INC.
*pp. 70, 84–85, 96,
295–297*
Mountain View, CA.
Tax and financial
software provider

**IOWA STATE
UNIVERSITY**
p. 341
Ames, IA.
Educational services

ISLAND ONE RESORTS
p. 104
Orlando, FL. Hospitality

ITERIS, INC.
pp. 353–354, 377
Santa Ana, CA.
Manufactures equipment
for the security systems

and transportation
industries

**IVANHOE CAMBRIDGE
INC.**
p. 151
Quebec, Canada.
Shopping centers

JAYCRAFT
p. 308
Spring Valley, CA.
Manufactures precision
components for the
aerospace and industrial
industries

**J. C. PENNEY
CORPORATION, INC.**
p. 263
Plano, TX.
Clothing retailer

JOHNSON & JOHNSON
pp. 7, 41–42
New Brunswick, NJ.
Consumer products and
pharmaceuticals

JOHNSON INC.
p. 151
St. John's, Newfoundland,
Canada. Insurance broker

**JOIE DE VIVRE
HOSPITALITY**
pp. 170–171
San Francisco, CA.
Hotel and restaurant
company

**JOSSEY-BASS, INC.
(JOHN WILEY &
SONS, INC.)**
p. 254

Hoboken, NJ.
Publishing company

**JPMORGAN
CHASE & CO.**
*pp. 264, 304, 469, 497,
504*
New York, NY.
Holding company for
financial services

JS COMMUNICATIONS
pp. 176–177
Fort Lauderdale, FL.
Telecommunication
services

**KACEY'S FINE
FURNITURE**
p. 164
Denver, CO.
Furniture retailer

KAISER PERMANENTE
*pp. 67, 239, 333, 380,
387*
Oakland, CA. Health
insurance company

**KANSAS CITY
SYMPHONY**
p. 331
Kansas City, MO.
Symphonic organization

**KATZINGER'S
DELICATESEN**
pp.456, 465
Columbus, OH. Deli shop

KB HOMES
p. 148
Houston, TX.
Homebuilders

Mason, OH. Optical stores

LEO BURNETT WORLDWIDE, INC.
pp. 392, 497, 504, 515
Chicago, IL.
Advertising agency

LEOMINSTER CREDIT UNION
p. 134
Leominster, MA.
Financial cooperative

LEVI STRAUSS & COMPANY
pp. 162, 423
San Francisco, CA.
Apparel manufacturer

LEWIS-GOETZ AND COMPANY, INC.
p. 292
Pittsburgh, PA. Industrial products manufacturer

LIEBERT CORPORATION
p. 371
Columbus, OH.
Manufactures air conditioning and power supply systems for computer rooms

LIFEUSA (ALLIANZ LIFE INSURANCE COMPANY)
p. 522
Minneapolis, MN.
Life insurance company

LIZ CLAIBORNE, INC.
p. 320

New York, NY. Apparel manufacturer

LOCKHEED MARTIN CORPORATION
pp. 93–94
Bethesda, MD.
Defense contractor

LONE STAR PARK
p. 378
Grand Prairie, TX.
Horse-racing park

LONGS DRUGS
p. 319
Walnut Creek, CA.
Drugstore chain

L'OREAL
p. 97
Clichy, France. Cosmetics and beauty company

LOS ANGELES DODGERS
p. 324
Los Angeles, CA.
Major- and minor-league baseball clubs

LOS BANOS ENTERPRISE
pp. 436–437
Los Banos, CA.
Newspaper

LOWE'S COMPANIES, INC.
pp. 181, 375, 517, 522–523
Mooresville, NC.
Lumber and hardware supply retailer

LUXURY RETREATS
p. 192
Montreal, Quebec, Canada.
Travel broker

MAGNA MIRRORS
p. 521
Holland, Ml.
Mirrors, windows, and other glass products

MANA, ALLISON & ASSOCIATES
p. 383
San Francisco, CA.
Management and event-planning company

MANAGEMENT 21
pp. 285–286
Nashville, TN.
Management training and consulting

MANAGING PERSONAL GROWTH
pp. 206–207
Princeton, NJ. Employee development program

THE MARCUS CORPORATION
pp. 443, 470
Milwaukee, WI.
Food service

MARION LABORATORIES, INC.
pp. 372–373
Kansas City, MO.
Pharmaceutical company

MARITZ, INC.
pp. 255, 313

METLIFE
p. 199
New York, NY.
Insurance, annuities, and employee benefit provider

METRO HONDA
p. 273
Montclair, CA.
Auto dealership

MIAMI VALLEY HOSPITAL
p. 223
Dayton, OH. Hospital

MICROAGE COMPUTER
p. 332
Tempe, AZ. Franchise and wholesale computers and business machines

MICROSOFT CORPORATION
pp.172, 337, 344, 350, 356
Redmond, WA.
Computer software firm

MICROSOFT DYNAMICS GP
p. 403
Redmond, WA.
Software company

MIDLAND MEMORIAL HOSPITAL
p. 104
Midland, TX. Hospital

MIDMICHIGAN REGIONAL MEDICAL CENTER
pp. 479–482
Midland, MI.
Medical services

MID-STATES TECHNICAL STAFFING SERVICES
p. 355
Davenport, IA.
Employment services

MIKE'S CARWASH
pp. 431, 489, 518
Indianapolis, IN.
Carwash chain

MILES & ASSOCIATES
p. 351
Gig Harbor, WA.
Seminar-planning firm

MILLER NISSAN
p. 415
Van Nuys, CA.
Automobile dealership

MILWAUKEE BUSINESS JOURNAL
p. 418
Milwaukee, WI.
Newspaper

MINI MAID SERVICE COMPANY
p. 466
Marietta, GA.
Cleaning services

MINNESOTA MINING AND MANUFACTURING COMPANY (3M)
pp. 200, 461, 507
St. Paul, MN. Industrial consumer and electronic products, life sciences products, information and imaging technologies, and commercial and consumer products

MIRAGE RESORT & CASINO
p. 499
Las Vegas, NV. Casino and entertainment services

MITRE
pp. 195–196
Bedford, MA.
Not-for-profit national technology resource

MOLSON COORS BREWING COMPANY
pp. 389–390
Denver, CO.
Beer brewer and distributor

MONA'S LANDSCAPING & DESIGN
p. 248
Chanhassen, MN.
Landscaper

MONSANTO COMPANY
p. 353
St. Louis, MO.
Chemical manufacturer

MONTANA'S COOKHOUSE
pp. 48–49
Mississauga, Ontario, Canada. Restaurant chain

MONTEFIORE NURSING HOME
pp. 333–334
Beachwood, OH.
Medical services

Northfield, IL.
Food services

AN OUNCE OF PREVENTION (OOP!)
p. 346
Providence, RI. Store that sells collections of crafts, jewelry, furniture, and toys by artisans

OVERFLOW
pp. 294, 366, 395
Queensland, Australia. Discount store chain

PACIFIC GAS & ELECTRIC COMPANY
p. 252
San Francisco, CA. Utility company

PACIFIC JAYCRAFT
p. 308
Spring Valley, CA. Aerospace equipment manufacturer

PACIFIC POWER
p. 349
Portland, OR. Utility company

PANACHE DESTINATION MANAGEMENT
p. 386
San Francisco, CA. Event planning services

PARKER HANNIFIN CORPORATION
pp. 449–450
Cleveland, OH. Manufactures motion control devices, tubing, valves, aerospace components

PARK LANE HOTELS INTERNATIONAL
p. 442
Hong Kong, China. Hotel services

PARKVIEW HEALTH SYSTEM, INC.
pp. 434–435
Fort Wayne, IN. Medical services

PARSONS CORPORATION
p. 518
Pasadena, CA. Engineering firm

PATAGONIA
p. 58
Ventura, CA. Outdoor-clothing maker

PATHWISE
pp. 312–313
American Fork, UT. Training and consulting firm

PAYCHEX
pp. 224, 237, 347–348, 417, 423, 492
Rochester, NY. Automated payroll services

PCL CONSTRUCTION
p. 193
Edmonton, Alberta, Canada. General contracting organization

PEACE CORPS
p. 94
Washington, DC. Volunteer program

PEAVEY ELECTRONICS CORPORATION
p. 448
Meridian, MS. Manufactures amplifiers and speakers

PELICAN PRODUCTS
p. 155
Los Angeles, CA. Lighting system designer and manufacturer

PELLA CORPORATION
p. 467
Pella, IA. Markets windows

PENTEL OF AMERICA, LTD.
p. 427
Torrance, CA. Manufactures and sells pens

PEOPLE POTENTIAL GROUP, INC.
p. 222
Woodbury, MN. Executive and leadership coaching firm

PEOPLES NATIONAL BANK OF KEWANEE
pp. 362–363
Kewanee, IL. Financial services

PEPSICO, INC.
p. 70
Purchase, NY.
Soft drink and snack
food manufacturer

**PERFORMANCE
LEADERSHIP
CONSULTING**
pp. 231–232
Brevard, NC. Management
and leadership consulting

PERISCOPE
p. 490
Minneapolis, MN.
Advertising agency

**PERSISTENCE
SOFTWARE, INC.**
p. 319
San Mateo, CA.
Manufactures data
management software

**PETCO ANIMAL
SUPPLIES**
p. 490
San Diego, CA.
Pet supply chain

PETRO-CANADA
p. 250
Calgary, Alberta, Canada.
Petroleum products

**PFEIFFER & COMPANY
(JOHN WILEY &
SONS, INC.)**
p. 302
Hoboken, NJ.
Publishing company

PHELPS COUNTY BANK
p. 171
Rolla, MO.
Financial services

THE PHELPS GROUP
p. 398
Santa Monica, CA.
Marketing and
communications firm

PHILIPS ELECTRONICS
p. 186
Amsterdam, Netherlands.
Electronics company

**PHOENIX BUSINESS
JOURNAL**
pp. 355, 418
Phoenix, AZ. Regional
business newspaper

PHYSIO-CONTROL
p. 285
Redmond, WA.
Defibrillator maker

PIONEER/ECLIPSE
p. 151
Sparta, NC.
Floor care systems

PITNEY BOWES, INC.
pp. 299, 422, 514
Stamford, CT.
Office equipment

PLAYFAIR
pp. 351–352
Nicasio, CA.
Humor seminars

**POLAROID
CORPORATION**
p. 520
Waltham, MA.
Photographic equipment

POOL COVERS, INC.
pp. 275–276
Fairfield, CA.
Manufactures and sells
pool covers

**PORTERVILLE
DEVELOPMENTAL
CENTER**
p. 375
Porterville, CA.
State hospital

**PORTLAND BUSINESS
JOURNAL**
p. 461
Portland, OR. Regional
business newspaper

PREMIER TRAVEL INN
p. 229
Luton, England. Hotel chain

**PRESBYTERIAN
HOSPITAL**
p. 271
Greenville, TX. Hospital

**PRICEWATERHOUSE
COOPERS
INTERNATIONAL, LTD.**
pp. 389, 495
New York, NY. Accounting
and auditing, management
consulting, mergers and
acquisitions, international
trade

**PRO STAFF
PERSONNEL SERVICES**
p. 270
Minneapolis, MN. Interim
staffing and executive
search company

RAYTHEON AIRCRAFT COMPANY (HAWKER BEECHCRAFT)
p. 233
Wichita, KS. Manufacturers aircraft products

READER'S DIGEST ASSOCIATION, INC.
pp. 105, 494, 502
Pleasantville, NY. Publishing company

RECREATIONAL EQUIPMENT, INC. (REI)
pp. 106, 298, 375, 382, 401, 500
Kent, WA. Camping and hiking equipment

REMINGTON PRODUCTS, INC. (SPECTRUM BRANDS)
pp. 303, 358, 505
Atlanta, GA. Personal care products

RESTAURANT EQUIPMENT WORLD (REW)
pp. 57–58, 414
Orlando, FL. Restaurant supplies

REXAIR
pp. 424–425
Troy, MI. Sells cleaning systems

RHC (RESIDENT HOME CORPORATION)
pp. 260–261

Cincinnati, OH. Provides opportunities to people with disabilities

RIGHT AT HOME
p. 365
Bloomington, MN. In-home care provider

THE ROBERT MONDAVI WINERY
p. 499
Oakville, CA. Wine company

ROBERT W. BAIRD, INC.
pp. 66, 105, 356–357, 374, 379–380, 400–401, 434, 513
Milwaukee, WI. Offers wealth management, asset management, and middle-market investment banking services

ROCK AND ROLL HALL OF FAME
p. 320
Cleveland, OH. Entertainment

ROOT LEARNING, INC.
p. 134
Sylvania, OH. Management consulting

ROSENBLUTH INTERNATIONAL
pp. 27, 447
Philadelphia, PA. Travel agency

ROSS PRODUCTS
pp. 474–477

Abbott Park, IL. Manufactures pediatric, pharmaceutical, and nutritional products

ROYAL APPLIANCE MANUFACTURING COMPANY
p. 318
Glenwillow, OH. Appliance manufacturer

ROYAL VICTORIA HOSPITAL
pp. 50–51
Barrie, Ontario, Canada. Hospital

RTC RELATIONSHIP MARKETING
p. 276
Washington, DC. Marketing firm

RUDI'S ORGANIC BAKERY
p. 385
Boulder, CO. Bakery

RUSH-COPLEY MEDICAL CENTER
p. 467
Aurora, IL. Medical services

RYDER SYSTEM, INC.
pp. 460, 495–496, 516
Miami, FL. Rents and leases trucks

SACRAMENTO, CITY OF, DEPARTMENT OF PUBLIC WORKS
p. 432
Sacramento, CA. Local government agency

SAFETY VISION
p. 418
Houston, TX.
Sells mobile cameras

SAN DIEGO CONVENTION AND VISITORS BUREAU
p. 443
San Diego, CA. Tourism

SAN DIEGO COUNTY
pp. 272, 459–451
San Diego, CA.
Local government agency

SAN DIEGO DEPARTMENT OF SOCIAL SERVICES
pp. 278–280
San Diego, CA.
Local government agency

SAN DIEGO HOUSING COMMISSION
p. 251
San Diego, CA.
Local government agency

SAN DIEGO STATE UNIVERSITY
p. 64
San Diego, CA.
State university

SAN FRANCISCO BUSINESS TIMES
p. 239
San Francisco, CA.
Regional business newspaper

SAS
pp. 65, 91, 354, 491

Cary, NC.
Business intelligence and software provider

SBT CORPORATION
p. 347
Sausalito, CA.
Manufactures accounting software

SCAN HEALTH PLAN
p. 108
Long Beach, CA.
Not-for-profit health plan

SCHMIDT PRINTING COMPANY
pp. 304–306
Byron, MN.
Printing company

SCHOOL ON WHEELS
p. 239
Ventura, CA.
Tutoring organization

SCHWARTZ COMMUNICATIONS, INC.
p. 347
Waltham, MA.
Public relations firm

SCIENCE APPLICATIONS INTERNATIONAL CORPORATION (SAIC)
p. 524
McLean, VA. Research and development

S. C. JOHNSON & SON (JOHNSON WAX)
pp. 49, 193, 493, 507, 516

Racine, WI. Manufacturer of household and personal care products

THE SCOOTER STORE, INC.
pp. 158, 376, 417, 448
New Braunfels, TX.
Sells motorized scooters and wheelchairs

SCOTIABANK
p. 52
Toronto, Ontario, Canada.
Bank

SCOTTRADE
p. 96
St. Louis, MO. Discount retail brokerage firm

SCRIPPS MEMORIAL HOSPITAL
pp. 369–370
Encinitas, CA. Hospital

SEARS, ROEBUCK AND CO.
p. 498
Hoffman Estates, IL.
Department store

SEAWORLD SAN DIEGO
pp. 232–233, 499
San Diego, CA.
Theme park

SENTINEL PRINTING CO., INC.
p. 248
St. Cloud, MN.
Printing company

SGI
p. 263

Mountain View, CA.
Technology company

SHELL OIL COMPANY
pp. 156–157
Houston, TX.
Manufactures and sells
automobile gasoline and
lubricant

SHERPA CORPORATION
pp. 282–283
San Jose, CA.
Software company

SIERRA CHEESE
p. 484
Compton, CA.
Cheese-making company

**SIERRA VIEW
DISTRICT HOSPITAL**
p. 268
Porterville, CA. Hospital

SIMPLY SWANK
p. 365
Hudson, OH. Hair salon

SKF USA, INC.
pp. 433–434
Kulpsville, PA.
Manufactures rolling
bearings

SME VISTA OPTICS
p. 365
Cheshire, England.
Contact lens product
manufacturer

SMITH & HAWKEN
p. 441
Novato, CA. Garden catalog

**SMURFIT-STONE
CONTAINER
CORPORATION**
pp. 315–316
Chicago, IL. Manufactures
corrugated containers,
paper bags, and other
packaging

**SOCIETY FOR
FOODSERVICE
MANAGEMENT (SFM)**
p. 354
Mount Laurel, NJ.
Food services
management

**SOIL CONSERVATION
SERVICE**
p. 324
Champaign, IL.
Natural resource
conservation service

**SOLAR
COMMUNICATIONS,
INC.**
pp. 304–306
Naperville, IL.
Direct-mail and packaging

**SOUTH CAROLINA
FEDERAL**
p. 288
Columbia, SC. Bank

**SOUTH MOUNTAIN
COMPANY**
pp. 491, 509, 520
West Tisbury, MA. Design
and construction firm

**SOUTHERN BAPTIST
CONVENTION**
p. 505

Augusta, GA.
Christian denomination

**SOUTHERN CALIFORNIA
EDISON COMPANY**
p. 495
Rosemead, CA.
Electric utility

**SOUTHERN NEW
ENGLAND TELEPHONE
COMPANY**
p. 470
New Haven, CT.
Telephone utility

**SOUTHERN
WINE & SPIRITS
OF AMERICA, INC.**
p. 471
Miami, FL. Distributor of
wine and spirits

SOUTHWEST AIRLINES
*pp. 185, 255, 269, 358,
408, 431, 499, 523*
Dallas, TX. Airline

SPACE CAMP
p. 373
Cannes, France.
Experience astronaut
training camp

**SPECTRUM CHEMICALS
& LABORATORY**
pp. 50, 188–189, 331
Gardena, CA.
Chemical manufacturer
and distributor

**SPRINGFIELD
REMANUFACTURING
CORPORATION (SRC)**
pp. 523–524

Springfield, MO.
Remanufactures jet
engines

SPRINT
pp. 60, 266
Overland Park, KS.
Telecommunications firm

**SSM HEALTHCARE
SYSTEM, INC.**
p. 241
St. Louis, MO.
Health care services

ST. ANN-MACY'S
p. 226
St. Louis, MO.
Department store

**STANDARD AUTO
PARTS**
p. 331
Baltimore, MD.
Auto parts store chain

**STARBUCKS
CORPORATION**
pp. 165, 521
Seattle, WA. Coffee retailer

**STARWOOD HOTELS &
RESORTS**
p. 431
White Plains, NY.
Hospitality management
and ownership
organization

**STATE FARM
INSURANCE
COMPANIES**
p. 350
Bloomington, IL.
Insurance services

STEELCASE, INC.
p. 495
Grand Rapids, Ml.
Manufactures office
furniture

STERLING GROUP
p. 53
Mishawaka, IN. Property
management group

STERLING OPTICAL
p. 327
Garden City, NY.
Retail optical chain

STEW LEONARD'S
*pp. 258, 281, 287, 322,
385, 407–408, 437, 450*
Norwalk, CT.
Retail dairy and food store

**STONES CROSSING
SENIOR LIVING
COMMUNITY**
pp. 266–267
Greenwood, IN.
Senior living community

SUBARU
p. 148
Ota, Japan.
Automobile manufacturer

**SUN
MICROSYSTEMS**
p. 178
Santa Clara, CA.
Computer and technology
company

SUPERCUTS, INC.
p. 419
Edina, MN. Haircut chain

**SYMANTEC
CORPORATION**
p. 50
Cupertino, CA.
Software maker

**SYNCRUDE
CANADA, LTD.**
pp. 398–399
Fort McMurray, Alberta,
Canada. Oil mining and
refining company

SYNOVATE
p. 396
Chicago, IL. Market
research organization

**SYNOVUS FINANCIAL
CORP.**
p. 399
Columbus, GA.
Financial services

**SYSTEM
IMPROVEMENTS**
pp. 276–277
Knoxville, TN.
System analysis firm

TALKING BOOK WORLD
p. 419
Royal Oak, MI.
Audio book store

TANDY CORPORATION
p. 323
Fort Worth, TX.
Leather goods company

TD BANK
pp. 205–206
Toronto, Ontario, Canada.
Bank

TD:CANADA TRUST (THE TORONTO-DOMINION BANK)
pp. 316–317
Toronto, Ontario, Canada.
Financial services

TEGRANT CORPORATION
p. 388
DeKalb, IL.
Packaging materials and solutions provider

TEKTRONIX, INC.
p. 231
Beaverton, OR.
Manufactures oscilloscopes and other electronic instruments

THE TENNANT COMPANY
pp. 223, 462–464
Minneapolis, MN.
Manufactures floor-cleaning equipment

TEXAS A&M UNIVERSITY
p. 360
College Station, TX.
Educational services

TEXAS COMMERCE BANK
p. 157
Houston, TX. Bank

TEXAS RANGERS BASEBALL CLUB
p. 382
Arlington, TX. Club for professional baseball team

TEXAS ROADHOUSE
pp. 57, 69
Louisville, KY.
Restaurant chain

TEXAS UTILITIES COMPANY (TXUENERGY)
p. 67
Dallas, TX.
Utility company

THOMAS J. LIPTON COMPANY (UNILEVER)
p. 461
Englewood Cliffs, NJ.
Food distributor and manufacturer

THE THOMSON CORPORATION
p. 67
Stamford, CT.
Information company

THOUGHTWORKS
p. 510
Chicago, IL.
Information technology consulting firm

THYMES
p. 70
Minneapolis, MN.
Bath and body products

TIMBERLAND COMPANY
pp. 400, 498
Stratham, NH.
Manufacturer of outdoor wear

TIME WARNER, INC.
pp. 251–252, 371, 501
New York, NY. Media Conglomerate

TODAYS OFFICE PROFESSIONALS
p. 467
Dallas, TX.
Employment services

TOM THUMB (RANDALL'S FOOD & DRUGS)
p. 67
Houston, TX.
Convenience store chain

TOPPS COMPANY, INC.
pp. 390–391
New York, NY. Baseball card and bubblegum manufacturer

TOTAL ATTORNEYS
p. 94
Chicago, IL. Attorneys

TOYOTA MOTOR COMPANY OF AMERICA
pp. 188, 469
New York, NY.
Automobile manufacturer

TRAVEL RELATED SERVICES (TRS)
pp. 464–465
New York, NY. Division of American Express

TRAVELERS CORPORATION (ST. PAUL TRAVELERS COMPANIES)
p. 391
St. Paul, MN.
Travel agency

Holden, MA.
Custom builders

WORKMAN PUBLISHING
p. 252
New York, NY.
Publishing company

THE WORKS BAKERY CAFE
p. 307
Keene, NH. Bagel shop

WORZALLA BOOK MANUFACTURING
pp. 459–460
Stevens Point, WI.
Publishing company

W. R. GRACE & COMPANY
pp. 293, 447, 469–470
Columbia, MD.
Manufactures silica-based
products and chemical
catalysts

WRIGHT BUSINESS GRAPHICS
pp. 338–339
Chino, CA.
Printing company

WS PACKAGING GROUP, INC.
p. 306
Green Bay, WI.
Manufactures packaging
and printing supplies

WYOMING VALLEY HEALTH CARE SYSTEMS
p. 294
Wilkes-Barre, PA.
Health and medical
facilities

XEROX CORPORATION
pp. 249–250, 252, 427
Norwalk, CT.
Manufacturer of copiers,
business products and
systems, offers financial
services

YELL UK
pp. 222–223, 248, 277
Reading, England.
Directories company

YOUDECIDE
p. 483
Atlanta, GA. Voluntary
benefits outsourcing firm

ZAPPOS.COM
pp. 37, 138–140
Henderson, NV. Online
shoe and apparel shop

ZIFF DAVIS MEDIA
p. 404
New York, NY.
Media company

ZUBI ADVERTISING
p. 92
Miami. FL. Advertising

ACKNOWLEDGMENTS

I'd like to thank Mario Tamayo, who helped find, edit, and endlessly rework research and examples obtained for this revision; Nick Swisher, who personally contacted everyone and every place referenced in the previous version of this book to update, correct, delete, or add information as necessary; and Jeanie Casison, who did much of the primary research on new examples and quotes that were used in this edition in addition to my own field work with clients.

I'd also like to thank the 1,000 or so organizations I've worked with on this topic since the original publication of *1001 Ways to Reward Employees* and those Nelson Motivation, Inc., clients from the 150,000 in our client database who submitted examples of their recognition practices, techniques, and programs for potential inclusion in this revision.

Dr. Joe Maciariello of The Peter F. Drucker Graduate Management School of The Claremont Graduate University in Los Angeles for giving me the initial inspiration for this book; my doctoral committee: Drs. Don Griesinger, Harvey Wichman, and David Drew for their help in shaping my research and thinking on why managers do and do not use recognition with their employees; and my professor Dr. Peter Drucker for his advice to first learn the insights of the topic through field research and client interviews and then prove those insights through my doctoral research.

At Workman Publishing: CEO Peter Workman and Editor in Chief Susan Bolotin for their vision and support of this book; my editor, Bruce Tracy, and his team for their editorial assistance and layout; and the incredible marketing and promotions group who have helped make the book so successful, including Jenny Mandel, Emily Krasner, James Wehrle, and Page Edmunds. I can truly say working with you all has been, and continues to be, a joy.

And my best friend, confidante, and spouse, Jennifer, and our wonderful children, Daniel and Michelle, for their ongoing love, support, and encouragement.

ABOUT BOB NELSON

Dr. Bob Nelson is considered one of the leading authorities on employee recognition, motivation, and engagement. He is president of Nelson Motivation Inc., a management training and consulting company based in San Diego that specializes in helping organizations improve their management practices, programs, and systems. He has worked with 80 percent of the Fortune 500 and has presented on six continents. Dr. Bob worked closely with Dr. Ken Blanchard (coauthor of *The One Minute Manager*) for ten years and currently serves as a personal coach for Dr. Marshall Goldsmith (author of *What Got You Here Won't Get You There*, *Mojo*, and *Triggers*) who is the Number One ranked executive coach in the world today.

Dr. Nelson has sold 3.5 million books on management and employee motivation, including *1001 Ways to Reward Employees, The 1001 Rewards & Recognition Fieldbook, 1001 Ways to Energize Employees, 1001 Ways to Take Initiative at Work, The Management Bible, Ubuntu!: Inspiring Teamwork and Collaboration at Work, Companies Don't Succeed, People Do!, 50 Ways to Motivate Your Team*, and *Recognizing & Engaging Employees for Dummies*.

He has appeared extensively in the national media, including CBS's *60 Minutes*, CNN, MSNBC, PBS, NPR, and has been featured in *The New York Times, The Wall Street Journal, The Washington Post, The Chicago Tribune, Fortune, BusinessWeek*, and *Inc.* magazines to discuss how best to motivate today's employees. He has written regular columns for American City Business Journals ("Return on People") and *Corporate Meetings & Incentives* magazine ("Motivation Matters"), *Bank Marketing*, and has been featured in *Costco Connection, Workforce Management, Human Resource Executive,* and numerous other trade publications.

He received an MBA in organizational behavior from UC Berkeley and earned his PhD in management with Dr. Peter Drucker ("The Father of Modern Management") at The Peter F. Drucker Graduate Management School of the Claremont Graduate University in Los Angeles, where his doctoral dissertation was on "Factors that Encourage or Inhibit the Use of Non-Monetary Recognition by Managers." He has taught organizational behavior for the Rady School of Management at the University of California in San Diego. Visit his website at drbobnelson.com.

Dr. Bob Nelson is available to help your organization through Speaking & Consulting Services:

Speaking: Dr. Bob is available to present to companies, conferences, and associations of all types in all formats: keynotes, concurrent sessions, pre-conference workshops, executive briefings, master series, and webinars. His presentations parallel many of his book topics and include:

1. Recognizing & Engaging Employees Today
2. Five Trends Shaping the Future of Work
3. Strategies for a More Engaged Workforce
4. Beyond the Paycheck: The Rewards of Recognition
5. Creating a Culture of Recognition
6. Managing & Motivating the Millennials
7. Engaging & Retaining High Potential Employees
8. Inspiring Exceptional Performance: Taking Initiative
9. Ubuntu: Inspiring Teamwork & Collaboration at Work
10. Hiring & Retaining the Different Generations

Consulting: Dr. Bob and his associates are also available to work in-house with companies to help assess needs, make recommendations, and align services and service providers to help clients better develop their recognition and engagement practices.

For more information about Dr. Bob's speaking and consulting services, books, and related products, please visit his website at drbobnelson.com or contact him directly at bob@drbobnelson.com or call him at (858) 673-0690. Many thanks!

OTHER BESTSELLERS BY BOB NELSON

1001 WAYS TO ENERGIZE EMPLOYEES • *Foreword by Ken Blanchard* • Bob Nelson reveals what real companies across America are doing to get the very best out of their employees—and why it's the key to their success. Weaving together case studies, examples, techniques, research highlights, and quotes from business leaders, it's a practical handbook chock-full of suggestions for increasing employee involvement and enthusiasm. Over half a million copies in print. ISBN 978-0-7611-0160-4, $10.95 paperback.

1001 WAYS TO TAKE INITIATIVE AT WORK • Take charge of your job and your career. This management guide for employees weaves together case studies, quotes, research highlights, and the author's own "Tool Box" of techniques and exercises to show every reader how to develop self-leadership, set goals, and learn firsthand that the "biggest mistake you can make in life is to think you work for somebody else." ISBN 978-0-7611-1405-5, $10.95 paperback.

THE 1001 REWARDS & RECOGNITION FIELDBOOK • *Cowritten with Dean Spitzer, Ph.D.* • *Foreword by Dr. Aubrey Daniels* • Packed with creative ideas, practical tools, and successful examples from the field, this book is the complete nuts-and-bolts fieldbook. It shows how to develop, implement, and manage an effective rewards and recognition program on the individual, team, or organizational level. The perfect companion to the original bestseller with over 1.6 million copies in print. ISBN 978-0-7611-2139-8, $17.95 paperback.

Available wherever business book are sold.